Taming the Elephant

California History Sesquicentennial Series
Edited by Richard J. Orsi

1. *Contested Eden: California before the Gold Rush,* edited by Ramón A. Gutiérrez and Richard J. Orsi
2. *A Golden State: Mining and Economic Development in Gold Rush California,* edited by James J. Rawls and Richard J. Orsi
3. *Rooted in Barbarous Soil: People, Culture, and Community in Gold Rush California,* edited by Kevin Starr and Richard J. Orsi
4. *Taming the Elephant: Politics, Government, and Law in Pioneer California,* edited by John F. Burns and Richard J. Orsi

Taming the Elephant

POLITICS, GOVERNMENT, AND
LAW IN PIONEER CALIFORNIA

Editors
JOHN F. BURNS and RICHARD J. ORSI

Illustrations Editors
JOSHUA PADDISON
and TEENA STERN

Associate Editor
MARLENE SMITH-BARANZINI

Published in association with the California Historical Society

UNIVERSITY OF CALIFORNIA PRESS
Berkeley · Los Angeles · London

University of California Press
Berkeley and Los Angeles, California

University of California Press, Ltd.
London, England

© 2003 by the Regents of the University of California

Library of Congress Cataloging-in-Publication Data

Burns, John F.
    Taming the elephant : politics, government, and law in pioneer California / John F. Burns, Richard J. Orsi ; illustrations editors Joshua Paddison and Teena Stern ; associate editor Marlene Smith-Baranzini.
        p.   cm—(California history sesquicentennial series ; vol. 4)
    "Published in association with the California Historical Society."
    Includes bibliographical references and index.
       ISBN 0-520-23411-1 (alk. paper)— ISBN 0-520-23413-8 (pbk. : alk. paper)
       1. California—Politics and government—1846–1850. 2. California—Politics and government—1850–1950. 3. Frontier and pioneer life—California. 4. Law—California—History—19th century.
5. Legislation—California—History—19th century. 6. California—Social conditions—19th century. I. Orsi, Richard J. II. Title.
III. Series.

F864 .B955   2003
979.4'04—dc21   2002032225

Manufactured in the United States of America
10 09 08 07 06 05 04 03
10 9 8 7 6 5 4 3 2 1

The paper used in this publication meets the minimum requirements of ANSI/NISO Z39.48-1992 (R 1997) (*Permanence of Paper*).♾

Contents

PREFACE · Stephen Becker and Richard J. Orsi · vii

1. *Taming the Elephant: An Introduction to California's Statehood and Constitutional Era* · John F. Burns · 1

2. *A Violent Birth: Disorder, Crime, and Law Enforcement, 1849–1890* · Roger D. McGrath · 27

3. *The Courts, the Legal Profession, and the Development of Law in Early California* · Gordon Morris Bakken · 74

4. *"We Feel the Want of Protection": The Politics of Law and Race in California, 1848–1878* · Shirley Ann Wilson Moore · 96

5. *Capturing California* · Joshua Paddison · 126

6. *"Officialdom": California State Government, 1849–1879* · Judson A. Grenier · 137

7. *"None Could Deny the Eloquence of This Lady": Women, Law, and Government in California, 1850–1890* · Donna C. Schuele · 169

8. *The Beginnings of Anglo-American Local Government in California* · Edward Leo Lyman · 199

9. *An Uncertain Influence: The Role of the Federal Government in California, 1846–1880* · Robert J. Chandler · 224

LIST OF CONTRIBUTORS · 273

INDEX · 277

Preface

As much as today's state legislators, officials, and bureaucrats are criticized in California—sometimes with just cause—the first generation of political and governmental leaders was even more vilified in its own day. Many of them, it turned out, were—like their fellow Argonauts—short-termers, more passionate about "making their pile" and heading back to where they had hailed from than they were about building a new community and polity. Addicted to party and factional infighting, giving and receiving patronage, and even on occasion fighting or dueling to redress petty slights or to get their way, California's "founding fathers" were roundly condemned for their corruption, low moral standards, and general lack of accomplishments. Meeting in the winter of 1849–50, the first body of representatives, for example, was widely ridiculed as the "Legislature of a Thousand Drinks." Nor did governors escape the representatives' ill repute. Contemporary historian Hubert Howe Bancroft criticized the first governor, Peter Burnett, as "too slow in action, too wordy in speech, too conservative for the period, and too prejudiced for the rapid changes taking place"; even Burnett described himself as having "feeble - abilities ... [that] allowed me to accomplish so little for the state." Another early governor—John McDougal—the public labeled "that gentlemanly drunkard."

With a few exceptions, later historians have followed the lead of the state's first citizens. In historical accounts, the first politicians, to the extent that they are even discussed, are portrayed as self-interested, disengaged, racially prejudiced, and venal, or at best incompetent. As a result, historians treat pioneer California's government as generally ineffective in coping with the great challenges of rapid population growth and economic change. Most often, however, in the historical literature, the establishment of early government in the state is simply ignored.

The first major dissenter from this evaluation, the first to take the subject seriously and to examine the creative origins of state government, was Gerald D. Nash, the recently deceased major historian of the American West. Nash's pioneering work, *State Government and Economic Development: A History of Administrative Policies in California, 1849–1933* (Institute of Governmental Studies, University of California, Berkeley, 1964), demonstrated that many Californians, like pioneers on all previous frontiers, demanded effective government to facilitate and regulate economic development. In response to pressures from groups in the state, early officials, often drawing on their political and administrative experiences from before they arrived in the new Golden State, met challenges creatively, if not without error. As a result, reasonably effective laws guiding economic development were passed and state agencies were founded and took on the great challenges of encouraging and regulating transportation systems, business, mining, agriculture, and the administration of the state's public lands. Implicit in the book was a revolutionary reinterpretation of early state government, but, although subsequent historians read and cited Nash's book, few of them took up his themes for further study and elaboration.

That is precisely what the scholars in the current volume, *Taming the Elephant*, propose to do. Discarding common preconceptions in analyzing politics, government, and law in California from 1846 through the adoption of the second state constitution in 1879, the authors examine patterns of interest and politics, the inception of constitution, law, jurisprudence, government-agency formation, and public policy. In studying the building of what has come to be called "the public sector," the authors chart out the roles played by diverse groups—from criminals to peace officers, judges, and attorneys, from entrepreneurs to miners and farmers, from voters to elected and appointed officials, from defenders of traditional racial and gender oppression to emerging articulate women and African Americans. Along the way, some of these essays investigate subjects largely overlooked in the past, including the origin and significance in pioneer California of local and federal government, as well as civil rights for women and racial minorities.

All of this volume's authors discover ambiguity and contradiction: a body of civil rights achieved by oppressed groups, but evolving within a society that remained fundamentally racist and sexist; strengthening traditions of law, order, and social responsibility emerging in a population prone to self-aggrandizement, violence, and disregard of community values; enlightened laws passed by a legislature that refused to provide sufficient funds to enforce them; dedicated officials attempting to work for the general welfare while self-seeking, factionalism, and corruption still tainted public affairs; effective government coexisting with favoritism, inefficiency, and inequity. Nevertheless, workable forms of government took shape; nagging problems of settlement and economic development were addressed, even while some were ignored and worsened; and legacies were created for future Californians that have lasted to the present day.

Taming the Elephant: Politics, Government, and Law in Pioneer California is the fourth volume in the California History Sesquicentennial Series, presented by the California Historical Society—the state's officially designated historical society—and the University of California Press, with the support of California State University, Hayward, and many other partners. Four topical, but interrelated, volumes, published beginning in 1998, reexamine the meaning, particularly from today's perspective, of the founding of modern California in the pre-1848 and gold-rush-era experiences. Each of the volumes collects essays by authors, drawn from the ranks of leading humanists, social scientists, and scientists, reviewing the best, most up-to-date thinking on major topics associated with the state's pioneer period through the 1870s. The authors have been asked to consider, within their area of expertise, the general themes that run through all four volumes: the interplay of traditional cultures and frontier innovation in the creation of a distinctive California society; the dynamic interaction of people and nature and the beginnings of massive environmental change; the impact of the California experience on the nation and the wider world; the shaping influence of pioneer patterns on modern California; and the importance and legacy of ethnic and cultural diversity as a major dimension of the state's history.

The California History Sesquicentennial volumes have been published simultaneously as expanded issues of *California History,* the quarterly of the Historical Society, and as books for general distribution. Each volume has been co-edited by Richard J. Orsi, Professor of History (now emeritus), California State University, Hayward, and editor (now emeritus) of the quarterly, who has worked with a consulting editor who is a leading scholar in the specific field. Volume 1 in the series, *Contested Eden: California before the Gold Rush,* co-edited by Ramón A. Gutiérrez, Professor of Ethnic Studies and History, University of California, San Diego, and issued in 1997/98, dealt with the social, economic, cultural, political, and environmental patterns of Native American, Spanish, and Mexican California through 1848. Volume 2 in the series, *A Golden State: Mining and Economic Development in Gold Rush California,* co-edited by James J. Rawls, member of the history faculty at Diablo Valley College, and issued in 1998/99, examined the pioneer industry of gold mining, its inception and development, and its impact on the state, the West, and the national and world economies. Volume 3 in the series, *Rooted in Barbarous Soil: People, Culture, and Community in Gold Rush California,* co-edited by Kevin Starr, State Librarian of California, and issued in 2000, focused on the Gold Rush and the migration and settlement of peoples, cultures, organizations, and institutions. Volume 4, the present work, co-edited by John F. Burns, former California State Archivist and State Historian and currently history and social science consultant with the California Department of Education, investigates the inception of government and politics—statehood, early constitution-building, law, bureaucracy, and civil rights.

The California Historical Society's issuing of these major sesquicentennial publications is made possible through the contributions of all the Society's members, as well as a host of direct and indirect supporters. Chief among the helping agencies are the University of California Press, the California State Archives, California State University, Hayward (which until 2001 furnished support for editing the quarterly and these special issues), Loyola Marymount University (Los Angeles), the California Supreme Court Historical Society, the Foundation of the State Bar of California, and the Mericos Foundation of South Pasadena, which has provided a generous grant specifically for the Sesquicentennial Series.

Many individuals have also shared their time, knowledge, energy, and resources. The Historical Society's particular appreciation goes to Executive Directors emeriti Michael McCone and Michael Duty, whose dedication to the Society, faith in its quarterly, and executive ability made this series possible; Lynne Withey, Director of the University of California Press, who has been an indispensable part of the Sesquicentennial History project from inception to completion; Mrs. Johan Blokker of the Mericos Foundation, whose belief in the project has been critical to its success; John F. Burns, co-editor of this volume, who from the beginning of the series was an important contributor to the conceptualization of this volume and whose unique perspective as the major historian of California's state government has added immeasurably to the quality of its contents; Dr. Janet Fireman, Editor of *California History*, who picked up the torch on the Sesquicentennial Series and graciously shepherded this volume through to completion; Dr. Norma Rees, President, and Dr. Frank Martino, Vice President and Provost, California State University, Hayward, who have provided generous assistance for the Sesquicentennial Series and the general editing office of *California History*; Dr. Henry Reichman, Chair, Department of History at California State University, Hayward, as well as other history colleagues, who during the publication of each of the sesquicentennial volumes, as in all the issues of the quarterly, made available the magnificent resources and staff of the department to encourage and assist the quarterly; Dr. Kevin Starr, State Librarian of California and preeminent scholar of California culture, whose enthusiastic support of the California History Sesquicentennial Series project when he was a Trustee of the California Historical Society and chair of its Publications Committee was indispensable to the development of the series, as well as of volume 3 specifically; Joshua Paddison and Teena Stern, insightful historians and illustrations editors of this volume, who discovered, edited, and captioned a magnificent set of images, in many cases never before published; Marlene Smith-Baranzini, historian, author, associate editor of *California History*, and true partner in every facet of this volume, this series, and all other undertakings of the quarterly; and Anthony Kirk, cultural historian and expert on California iconography, who has for a decade served as an invaluable consultant and friend of the quarterly on the history of art and photography and many other subjects of which he is a master. Other important contributors included our sharp-eyed assistant editors Joshua Paddison, Peter Orsi, and Zac Baranzini; Liz Ginno, historian and member of the library faculty at California State University, Hayward; and Larry Campbell, Patricia Keats, Jennifer Liss, Scott Shields, Emily Wolff, Bo Mompho, Judith Deaton, Tanya Hollis, and other members of the loyal, dedicated, and professional staff of the California Historical Society, San Francisco.

Our thanks also go to all the individuals and institutions who made it possible to use images from their collections in this work or who provided other assistance. Many of the following not only participated in important ways in the preparation of this volume, but have served as friends and invaluable resource persons over years of *California History*'s publications. Although space precludes listing all their names, special mention should be made of Dace Taube, Curator, Regional History Collections, Doheny Library, University of Southern California, who served, as always, as a knowledgeable and generous adviser on illustrations for the quarterly; Peter Blodgett and Jennifer Watts, the Huntington Library; Jeff Crawford, Placer County Department of Museums; Jack von Euw and Susan Snyder, the Bancroft Library; Ellen Harding and Gary Kurutz, the California State Library; Genevieve Troka, California State Archives; Diane Curry, the Oakland Museum of California; Pat Johnson, Sacramento Archives and Museum Collection Center; Mary Haas, Fine Arts Museums of San Francisco; Vito Sgromo, California State Capitol Museum; and Peter E. Palmquist of Arcata, California, photographer, photography collector, and, of course, the leading historian of photography of the American West.

One final debt needs acknowledgment: there can be no more talented, exacting, resourceful, dedicated, and collegial an editor than Kathleen MacDougall, our project editor at the University of California Press, who has now guided and speeded the production of the last three volumes of the Sesquicentennial Series.

Stephen Becker
Executive Director,
California Historical Society

Richard J. Orsi
Professor of History (Emeritus),
California State University, Hayward,
and Editor (Emeritus), *California History*

1

Taming the Elephant

An Introduction to California's Statehood and Constitutional Era

John F. Burns

The phrase "seeing the elephant" was frequently used during the California Gold Rush by western sojourners to describe their encounters with strange and alien situations or exotic and enlivening experiences—something as unique as actually seeing an elephant was at that time. The reality of seeing the elephant sometimes did not match the anticipation of the event. Thus, "seeing the elephant" became an apt metaphor for the Gold Rush, in which most people found more disappointments than riches. Although the phrase was generally applied to a gold-seeking adventure, the task of bringing discipline and order to the new state's politics and government in its chaotic infancy was a mammoth undertaking in its own right. California's extraordinary gold-rush-induced growth during a period of difficult transition from Mexican to American sovereignty was a challenge of elephant-like dimensions, as the essays in this book demonstrate. Those people involved in early California governance not only "saw the elephant," but they also had to attempt to corral it.

The extraordinary and rapid development of California's public sector after 1848 is a fascinating but largely obscure story. Driven by the rare occasion of immediate statehood and the subsequent necessity to quickly institute a broad range of civic activities, governmental development played a key role in the transformation of California from conquered place and unbridled frontier into a viable entity that could take its place alongside the other states of the Union. But how instrumental was that role in the making of California as we know it? Although the social, cultural, and economic ramifications of California's first thirty years as a state have been treated extensively in historical literature, no comparable body of work has yet emerged that thoroughly delves into the public arena. The state sesquicentennial anniversary prompted the preparation of several excellent new works on the Gold Rush and its

Constitution Wall, entitled "Rights," part of the Golden State Museum in the California State Archives in Sacramento, invites today's Californians to consider what ideas and values state government should represent. The six-story wall is covered with words and phrases from the California constitution that shift in prominence as the angle of sunlight changes throughout the day and year. *Courtesy California State Archives and Golden State Museum.*

aftermath, but the emergence of the state and its public institutions has been ignored or, at best, slighted.

A prevalent notion is that California's early efforts at government were unimportant, incompetent, and principally devoted to fleecing whatever unfortunate souls could be victimized. Historian J. S. Holliday recently contended that "certainly no other state endured an adolescence so orphaned from the steadying hand of enlightened leadership as California . . . narrow ambition and greed ruled the time. . . . California did not inspire political idealism [and] statecraft seemed a pestering distraction." Earlier authors were no more complimentary. Andrew Rolle, for instance, echoed Hubert Howe Bancroft's characterization of the state's politics as permeated by "corruption, mediocrity, and bossism," and Rolle labeled the constitutional era "one of the dullest periods in California's political life."[1]

Yet that may not be the whole story. In his interpretive history of the state, Edward Staniford, for example, maintained that "party and public affairs rumbled with political turbulence. In such precarious times, mixed concentrations of people produced unstable and unrestrained communities. The California cauldron was boiling with the elements of both lowly and heroic achievement." Even more affirmative, Judson A. Grenier called California's initial political period "almost as important as gold in shaping the state." Indisputably, government agencies and public policy were formed and civic activities undertaken in the frontier period, and it is reasonable to assume that, to some degree, they affected subsequent California politics and government. Staniford asserted that the leadership impulses, political bargaining, and interest-group pressure that characterized California's early governmental efforts continue "to be the basic manner of operation of California's party and governmental system."[2]

The essays in this volume begin an overdue examination of some of these issues and test and modify long-standing perceptions. It is hoped that these brief treatises will tantalize others to initiate more thorough study of the seminal elements and individuals, both the base and the noble, that shaped the founding of California's public affairs. Historian William Leuchtenburg asserted in 1986 that "there is mounting evidence of a renascent interest in political history" and that such study would be "the historian's next frontier." In California, at least, the opportunity exists to realize Leuchtenburg's prediction, and with greater knowledge of California's political and governmental legacy, society might gain a needed, more comprehensive understanding of contemporary California's public environment.[3]

What to do about governing California was an urgent matter confronting the nation in 1849. Congress, typically not the speediest of bodies and hamstrung by the very tenuous balance between free and slave states, could not immediately decide, presenting those living or arriving in California with a serious situation as to governance.

General Bennet Riley, the appointed military governor, presided by treaty over an area of the United States that was no longer simply a conquered province but one that was transiting from one type of civil administration based on Spanish and Mexican codes to another, very different type rooted in common law derived from English and American precedent. And this was occurring in an incredibly tumultuous socioeconomic environment caused in large measure by the Gold Rush, leading Riley to describe with considerable restraint the governmental situation as "the embarrassments of our present position."[4]

There were certainly pressing concerns. The signing of the Treaty of Guadalupe Hidalgo in 1848 concluded the armed conflict between the United States and Mexico and transferred what is now the southwest United States to American jurisdiction. It was a lightly occupied, vast area that gained worldwide attention with unprecedented speed. The discovery of gold in early 1848, even before the treaty had been ratified by the U.S. Senate, fueled extensive journalistic coverage and hype and launched a rush of mostly young men (and a few women) from all regions of the globe, but especially from the eastern United States, into the ports and then the foothills of northern California. While Riley was confronted with congressional inaction in the middle of 1849, California's population was increasing dramatically. Within a year the nonnative population would double to around a hundred thousand, ten times that of 1846. Of the migrants, about 80 percent were young males—in the 1850 census, fifty-eight thousand of these said they were miners.

What they discovered when they arrived in California was exceptional. The former Spanish-Mexican economy had been mostly based on subsistence for relatively few people. Then, in the instant boom of the Gold Rush, scarcity became the rule. Everything, including much food, had to be imported. Many new arrivals to mushrooming cities such as Sacramento lived in tents. Most early buildings were prefabricated and shipped to California. Prices were bizarre; items could cost twenty or more times what they did in the East, such as a dollar for a mere egg. There were few roads, and transportation was mostly limited to navigable waterways. Living conditions could be harsh. When Frank Marryat arrived in Sacramento he found it "terribly dusty . . . the dirtiest dust I ever saw, never visited by a shower until the rainy season sets in and suddenly converts it into a thick mud," overrun by "rats distinguished for their size and audacity" that "come out after dark in street gangs, as if the town belongs to them, and attack anything."[5] Diseases such as cholera became epidemic. Public and governmental operations were virtually nonexistent.

It is difficult to imagine how overwhelming this situation was to the Mexican Californians (Californios), who soon constituted less than 5 percent of the population, or the disastrous consequences to the Native American peoples and their way of life. Even the migrants themselves were often caught bewildered. Gold seekers who left San Francisco for a mere three months found upon their return that the

Benicia, a major supply stop for prospectors on their way to the Sierra foothills, briefly served as the state capital during the legislature's fourth session, in 1853. This building, originally intended to be Benicia's city hall, is the only pre-Sacramento state capitol still standing today. *Courtesy City of Sacramento, History and Science Division, Sacramento Archives and Museum Collection Center.*

town had quadrupled in size. The existing governmental institutions of a formerly pastoral, now conquered, California did not have a chance of coping with such a demographic onslaught. Moreover, most gold seekers did not view California as a permanent destination and had little interest in civic affairs. The majority of the young men heading for the gold-saturated foothills were passing through; they talked about "making their pile" and going home. When the California constitution was put up for ratification in late 1849, with virtually all white men able to vote, "interest could not have been intense," and only about 15 percent exercised the franchise.[6]

But there were also growing numbers of merchants, lawyers, city builders, and tradesmen who needed reliable governmental order. To these people, many of them intending to stay, Riley's "holding pattern" of governing through existing formerly Mexican institutions, with a small military presence backing it up, was very unsettling. Where was the guarantee that, if you bought property, it would be recorded properly? Who would maintain these government records? Could your person and belongings be made secure? As David Alan Johnson observed: "Mexican law was alien and could not provide the desired framework to order the complexities of an instantly created market economy."[7] Not even a rudimentary legal system existed in the mining regions, which lacked any significant earlier Spanish-Mexican presence. It was up to the new arrivals to determine what to do, and the response was *ad hoc* mining camp "law." More than five hundred camps adopted local mining codes. There were influences on those codes from Spanish-Mexican, English, and other customs, but underlying them was pragmatic American frontier self-government, coupled with "vigilance" promptly laid upon alleged lawbreakers. Today, such justice administered by miners is often considered arbitrary and unjust, but one scholar's reexamination of the evidence submits that "in cases of severe antisocial behavior, such as theft, homicides or attempted rape, and in cases involving mining claims or possessory rights, they had a clear understanding of legal customs and tried to abide by them."[8]

In the mining camps, apart from the establishment of necessary local codes to regulate mining claims and assure a modicum of order, state-making and politics generally were not a matter for much attention. The movement for a more regularized system of government was one urged by a few city dwellers and property holders. To these individuals, "public order and commercial opportunity demanded the certainty of American law."[9] By the middle of 1849 this element of the population was already largely American, entrepreneurs who had come west in search of opportunity, full of the ebullience of a victorious people, confident in the values that underpinned and promoted western expansion. They were the young, impatient, eager children of Manifest Destiny, who created "a new state based on their collective experience. The new society was a California version of the American system—so unlike its Mexican predecessor and its American successor, yet a genuine blend of both. That society was democratic with a note of racial discrimination. It favored individual enterprise over corporate enterprise, and professed liberal sentiments while including conservative restraints."[10]

On June 3, 1849, Riley issued the proclamation that would move California to a more stable government and eventual statehood. He was influenced to make this decision by virtue of an expanding population that had overwhelmed the existing structure and that was relentlessly and restlessly moving toward self-government in any event. As in the mining camps, communities were taking action on their own. In Sacramento, for example, "activists in the local area moved to create a municipal government . . . without mandate or direction from higher authority."[11] Using Congress's failure to act on the question of California's status as a rationale, but with no legal authority, Riley proclaimed that "it becomes our imperative duty to take some active measures to provide for the existing wants of the country . . . by putting in full vigor the administration of the laws as they now exist. . . . While at the same time a convention . . . shall meet and frame a State constitution or a Territorial organization, to be submitted to the people for their ratification, and then proposed to Congress for its approval."[12]

Early in September 1849 a total of forty-eight delegates elected from districts around the state assembled in Monterey to begin drafting a state constitution. The majority quickly decided to opt for statehood, despite reservations by the minority of landowning delegates from southern California, who rightly feared that they would be beleaguered by excessive property taxation to support the government, and who therefore favored territorial status. The delegates were not a representative body of those who were in California at the time. In keeping with the practices of the era, there were no women, Native Americans, African Americans, or anyone of Asian descent. Only eight were Hispanic. Southern California had eleven delegates, well outnumbered by those from the far more populous north. They were young; half were under thirty-five. They were not Forty-niners, as most of them had been in California for three years or more. They were not primarily miners. Several delegates from the mining districts did not attend, because they were busy working their claims and, for them, the pursuit of gold took precedence over constitution-making. Fourteen, or 30 percent, were lawyers. Eleven were farmers, and seven were businessmen. One described himself as a man of "elegant leisure," though what that pursuit entailed remains a matter of speculation.

Robert Semple, the convention president, in his opening address said, "I am confident . . . that we can prove to the world that California has not been settled entirely by unintelligent and unlettered men."[13] The principal model that delegates followed in crafting the California constitution was that of Iowa, although elements of other state constitutions were also included. Nonetheless, as they framed the various provisions and debated their construction, the delegates encountered situations that demanded a novel, California solution. One of these was the question of what to do about married women's property, and it was proposed that the existing Mexican practice be followed. Under Spanish and Mexican civil law a woman retained legal right to property she acquired as an individual before and during marriage. English common law, however, to which many of the convention delegates were predisposed, ordained that all property of a woman became legally owned by her husband upon marriage. Heated arguments ensued. Charles T. Botts, a married proponent of the common law, pleaded that "the God of nature made women, frail, lovely and dependent . . . the only despotism on earth that I would advocate is the despotism of the husband." But bachelor Henry Halleck, backed by the Hispanic delegates and those who were younger, rejoined, "I am not wedded to the common law, or the civil law, or yet to a woman . . . but I do not think we can offer a greater inducement for women of fortune to come to California," arguing that it was the best way to get wives. Halleck's practical argument was more persuasive, and the proposal passed.[14] A suggestion by the southern California delegates to publish all laws in both English and Spanish was also accepted.

One of the most engaging questions to face the convention was the issue of

PEOPLE'S TICKET.

Judge of the Superior Court.
PETER H. BURNETT.

Prefect.
HORACE HAWES.

Sub Prefects.
FRANCISCO GUERRERO,
JOSEPH R. CURTIS.

First Alcalde.
J. W. GEARY.

Second Alcaldes.
FRANK TURK,
JOHN VIOGET.

Town Council, or Ayuntamiento.
TALBOT H. GREEN,
THOMAS B. WINSTON,
JOHN TOWNSEND,
H. A. HARRISON,
A. J. ELLIS,
STEPHEN HARRIS,
WM. H. DAVIS,
~~J. H. MERRILL~~,
WM. M. STEWART,
B. SIMMONS,
S. BRANNAN,
R. M. PRICE.

Delegates for Convention.
Dr. WM. M. GWIN,
JOSEPH HOBSON,
~~MYRON NORTON~~,
EDWARD GILBERT,
WM. M. STEUART.

Supernumeraries.
FRANCISCO SANCHEZ,
R. M. PRICE,
FRANCIS J. LIPPITT,
W. D. M. HOWARD,
A. J. ELLIS.

REPUBLICAN TICKET.
REGULAR NOMINATIONS.

For Judge of the Superior Court.
PETER H. BURNETT.

For Prefect.
W. A. BUFFUM.

For Sub Prefects.
J. R. CURTIS,
FRANCISCO GUERRERO.

For First Alcalde.
J. W. GEARY.

For Second Alcaldes.
J. M. HUXLEY,
W. LANDERS.

For Ayuntamiento.
STEPHEN HARRIS,
T. J. AGNEW,
~~A. J. ELLIS~~,
W. C. PARKER,
F. D. KOHLER,
T. H. GREEN,
J. P. HAVEN,
M. L. MOTT,
M. G. LEONARD,
H. A. HARRISON,
E. G. POST,
T. W. PERKINS.

For the Convention.
E. GILBERT,
J. D. STEVENSON,
MYRON NORTON,
J. A. PATTERSON,
E. GOULD BUFFUM.

Supernumeraries.
W. M. SMITH,
J. B. BIDLEMAN,
W. HAIGHT.

People's Party *(left)* and Republican *(right)* tickets distributed in San Francisco in 1849. During the nineteenth century, workers outside polling places gave voters tickets featuring only the names of their party's candidates (although in several cases candidates were endorsed by both parties), forcing voters who wished to "split" their ticket to write in candidates from other parties (as shown here on the Republican ticket). Voting was conducted openly, in full view of campaign activists and other voters. Only in the 1890s did county and state governments begin providing secret voting booths and printing official ballots listing all candidates' names, reducing the power of political parties. *Courtesy Huntington Library.*

California's boundary. How much territory could California undertake to control? Some delegates wanted to include most of the unorganized former Mexican territory, namely parts of what now is Nevada, Arizona, and Utah. The convention was badly split on this issue, the irrepressible Mr. Botts sardonically commenting, "why not indirectly settle it by extending your limits to the Mississippi. Why not include the Island of Cuba." The winning reasoning in the end was that there was nothing on the other side of the Sierra Nevada of any value, and thus acquiring "interminable plains of artemesia, vast bodies of salt water a great part of the year, and immense deserts," as delegate J. R. Snyder put it, would only be a burden. The boundary question was interwoven with the consequential issue of whether slavery should be allowed in the state. A ban on slavery was quickly accepted, as some delegates were abolitionists and others simply did not want the unfair competition that owners with slaves might offer. There was more extensive debate about permitting "free Negroes" to enter and reside in the state, resolved in favor of such admission, and settling on a reasonable boundary for the state virtually eliminated any possibility that sections of the state might eventually be carved into slave territory.[15]

The constitutional outcome was an amalgamation of influences. It was the last time until the late twentieth century that a sizable number of Latino Californians had a significant role to play in state political events. Most Californios had experience, not always pleasant, in dealing with Americans. Employing skillful negotiation and argument, the Californios helped to guide the convention to adopt provisions on such matters as voter qualifications, taxation, lands, state boundaries, and civil liberties, in addition to property and language, that protected certain practices that existed under the former regime, although in later years the Californios found that constitutional intent was not easy to maintain. In a referendum predictably characterized by low turnout, the constitution was overwhelmingly ratified 12,061 to 811 on November 13, 1849. The final document was largely "in the main stream of American constitutional history in the several states. . . . [It] may not have been the best of its time, but neither was it the worst. It was representative of, neither in advance of nor behind, the thinking and political climate of its time."[16] The 1849 constitution began with an extensive declaration of rights, emblematic of California's "adamant resistance to government restrictions on private personal conduct."[17] This litany of rights is one that has expanded over the years, but from the outset it included "pursuing and obtaining safety and happiness." As one group of authors observed: "How characteristically Californian to guarantee not only the pursuit but the achievement of happiness!"[18] Although superseded by the adoption of the 1879 constitution and by many amendments subsequent to that time, elements of the 1849 constitution, including the right to happiness, remain today.

One of the more peculiar and notable legacies of the original constitution relates to the state legislature. In 1849 the number of Assembly members was constitution-

The national Whig Party, powerful from the mid-1830s to the mid-1850s but united only in its opposition to Democrats, elected two presidents—William Henry Harrison in 1840 and Zachary Taylor in 1848. Though active in California politics, the state Whig Party never managed to elect a governor or senator, despite the exhortations of the party newspaper, *The Whig*. In the September 1, 1855 issue (masthead shown here), the editor of *The Whig* urged readers to "Vote the Whig ticket! Vote early! See that your tickets are correctly printed! Urge your friends to vote the true Whig ticket!" Shortly thereafter, the national Whig Party divided into northern and southern factions and then dissolved. *Courtesy City of Sacramento, History and Science Division, Sacramento Archives and Museum Collection Center, Eleanor McClatchy Collection.*

ally fixed in a range of thirty to eighty, with the number of senators being no more than half that number, and with the exact numbers to be determined by the legislature itself. At that time, one Assembly member represented fewer than four thousand people and, given that less than half of the adult population could vote, needed to reach only several hundred voters to be elected. The later 1879 constitution fixed the number permanently at the upper levels of 1849, namely, eighty assembly persons and forty senators, with each Assembly district representing about ten thousand people. Unchanged in maximum numbers since 1849, today each of California's assembly persons now represents four hundred thousand people. And each state senator, serving double the number of constituents present in an Assembly district, represents substantially more people than does a U.S. member of Congress. In New York, the next closest state in population size, each assembly delegate represents 120,000 constituents, or about a quarter of a California district. (In the "mentor" state, Iowa, there is one representative for every twenty-seven thousand people.) The result is remoteness for the average voter from his or her representatives in Sacramento, contributing to the media orientation of California campaigns, the enormous amounts of money involved in winning political office, the excessive influence of political consultants, and the vast pressure of special interests. All of these consequences spring in part from the initial constitutional provisions fixing the size of the legislature.

After the constitution was ratified, it was immediately put into effect, with state officials and legislators being elected, although there was still no legal recognition from Congress. Vilified as the "Legislature of a Thousand Drinks," California's initial statecrafters have often received little respect for their work. Historian John Caughey labeled them "gold-mad westerners" characterized by "inexperience" and "inattention induced by the absorbing and highly profitable nature of private enterprise. In the conduct of state government the result of this crass neglect was a record of the grossest abuses." However, such a low opinion of the early legislators is not universal. William Henry Ellison claimed that "it is doubtful whether . . . any legislature has ever done more work . . . or more important or better work, than that done by the [first]. . . . The adaptation of the governmental structure of the state to changing conditions is a perennial tribute to the devotion and political wisdom of the builders in California's first legislative session." Studies such as that by Judson A. Grenier in his biography of the first state controller and in his essay in this volume can help to more judiciously evaluate the impact and character of these individuals.[19]

Whatever the quantity of alcohol consumed by the early statecrafters, it is important to recall that they were attacking governance in the midst of a wild and fluid situation, a political entity growing in population at breakneck speed with no infrastructure to support such growth and without financial resources, given the uncertainty of the government's legal status. In the middle of this maelstrom, the first legislature did organize some of the machinery of government and adopted the Anglo-American common law as the basis of law in California. The effects of its actions continue to be felt in the present. It provided for a local government structure, creating the majority of counties in the more populous north and thereby leaving contemporary California with many small county governments in the north, the tiniest being twelve-hundred-person Alpine County, and a few large counties in the south, such as nine-million-person Los Angeles County. It appointed pilots for ports and harbors, assembled the state archives and library, created a state printing operation, set up elections, provided for limited partnerships, organized the state militia, and tried to regulate steamboats, in part to stop the often fatal practice of racing them. It also failed to launch a public school system and could not settle on the location of a capital; Sacramento was finally chosen in 1854. The first legislature also imposed an odious and discriminatory tax on foreign miners in a blatant attempt to drive nonwhite miners from the gold fields. The first legislature had a mixed record. It operated to a degree within the norms of American state legislative activity, but it was also driven by other factors and elements as outlined by the essays in this volume.

Despite the positive or negative mythology that sometimes surrounds stories of the state's founding fathers of 1849–50 and the actions they took, by and large they rather predictably were a product of their era, values, prejudices, and economic circumstances. California's political reputation from its earliest days has been often that of "a land of loony schemes and political extremes, an image which has stuck and refuses to come unglued."[20] As debate raged in Congress over California statehood, the legendary South Carolina senator John C. Calhoun fumed about California's impatient actions to govern itself, prophetically charging California with being "revolutionary" and "anarchistic." Later, the feud between David Broderick and William Gwin and the impact of the Civil War overshadowed other elements of the state's political life, including the irregular development of the state's political parties, unsuccessful movements for state division, and the expanding application of state governmental procedures. As there is evidence that California's politics bore significant resemblance to that of other states, a reexamination of the negative political image that California has garnered since its early governmental period is in order. The essays in this volume also address that goal.

After the question of statehood was resolved and the initial state organizational efforts were completed, it was time to get on with business. California was finally admitted to the Union on September 9, 1850, thanks to a compromise between the free and slave states crafted by Henry Clay. Not surprisingly, economic affairs were predominant in much of the work of the next several legislatures. Gerald Nash, the only scholar to examine in depth the economic impact of the early state government, wrote that the practices that the founders brought with them served as the "institutional heritage with which California's first constitution makers and legislators were acquainted. On the foundations of English local legislation and mercantilist administrative practices Americans had fashioned an intricate institutional framework to which they adhered with remarkable consistency. The functions of government were to promote and regulate private enterprise, to engage in research where needed, and to undertake public ownership and operation under certain conditions. Techniques to carry out these functions had been developed over the course of two centuries, ranging from noncoercive methods to formal sanctions."[21] However, up to this point little work has been done to examine the manner in which governmental functions were initially carried out in California. Adequate histories of governmental functions and agencies have been few in number, and much scholarship remains to be accomplished.

Thirty years later, the constitution of 1849 came under considerable attack, and an effort to replace it with a new one gained momentum, as the original constitution was held responsible for some of the adverse economic circumstances the state then confronted. In three decades the face of California had changed substantially. The population had grown eightfold, and its demographic characteristics had changed as well. The formerly Mexican population had declined substantially in proportion to people of European American origin, and Californio political impact had essentially disappeared. African Americans remained small in number and excluded from most political participation, and Native Americans, their populations much reduced by disease, violence, and dislocation, were struggling for sheer survival. The most substantial numerical minority was Asian, predominately Chinese, but they were politically prostrate and made scapegoats for many of the woes afflicting the state that had escalated as the state's economy moved beyond the Gold Rush. Historian Kevin Starr summarized California's unhappy situation, observing, "from start to finish, north and south, the 1870s had been an unmitigated disaster of drought, crop failure, urban rioting, squatter wars, harassment and murder of the Chinese, cynical manipulation of politics by the railroad, depression, price fixing, bank failure, and stock swindles."[22]

The constitution of 1849 had been considered for overhaul as early as the middle of the 1850s. Numerous attempts were made at calling a new constitutional convention, but they were unsuccessful until the election of September 5, 1877, by which time economic circumstances had deteriorated to the point that many in the Workingmen's Party and those sympathetic to it especially felt that substantial reform was in order. Primary issues included regulation of the railroads, changes in taxation to reduce the burden on farmers, more accountability on the part of corporations and banks, protection for labor, and anti-Chinese provisions. The duration of the convention that gathered in Sacramento beginning in September 1878 extended to six months, or four times as long as the first convention. Three times the number of delegates were in attendance, 152 compared to the forty-eight in Monterey. Of the delegates, fifty-seven were lawyers and thirty-nine were farmers, with the rest distributed among a wide range of occupations. All were Caucasian males, most born outside the state; as such they were representative only of those allowed to participate politically. One proposal that they turned down would have extended suffrage to women. An idea that they accepted eliminated the 1849 requirement to publish laws in both English and Spanish.

The results of the overall efforts of the 1878–79 delegates have not often been applauded. The unwieldy product that emerged was vastly different from the constitution of 1849. The new constitution was an extremely detailed document full of minor provisions on such topics as nut trees and wrestling that in many other states would have been deemed of statutory, not of constitutional, import. The document was many times longer than the Constitution of the United States or the original California constitution; at one point only the constitutions of the state of Louisiana and the nation of India were wordier. Moreover, the principal aims of the new constitution were not realized. The railroads continued to escape strong regulation until the Progressive era reforms of the early twentieth century. The degree of tax relief for farmers was disappointing, and the operations of neither banks nor other corporations were significantly altered. Workers found that the new constitution did little to protect their interests. The racist efforts to restrict and exclude the Chinese were not truly accomplished, as most of the specific provisions offered would have violated elements of the U.S. Constitution. Severe limitations on Chinese immigration were eventually instituted by the federal government, not the state, when Congress passed the Chinese Exclusion Act in 1882.

When the new constitution was submitted to the people for adoption, there was little enthusiasm for the convention's product, although the vote ultimately came down in favor of ratification largely because the farmers hoped that it would result

The product of a heterogeneous committee, the state constitution of 1879 managed to disappoint almost every California group. Conservatives condemned it as radical and socialistic; workers insisted it did too little for labor. This 1879 lithograph, titled *I Am the New Constitution!!!!* shows farmers and Chinese Americans fleeing from the constitutional behemoth. *Courtesy Bancroft Library.*

The Workingmen's Party of California, led by San Francisco drayman Denis Kearney, emerged as a major force in California politics in 1877 by decrying political corruption, the exploitation of workers, and Chinese immigration. In the pages of *The Wasp*, cartoonist Edward Keller offered his interpretation of a Workingmen Thanksgiving parade in 1877. *Courtesy California State Library.*

in much lower freight rates and taxes. The new constitution won acceptance on May 7, 1879, by a vote of 77,959 to 67,134, with more than 80 percent of the eligible electorate participating. The large northern California cities, where Workingmen's Party influence was strongest, turned the document down, while most rural counties and southern California voted for it. The greatest percentage of votes against it were in Alameda County. It received the largest favorable majority in Los Angeles County. Amended more than 350 times and substantially revised and shortened through the efforts of a constitutional revision commission one hundred years later, the 1879 constitution remains the fundamental law of California. The most significant reform subsequent to the adoption of the 1879 document was "people's lawmaking" in the form of the initiative and referendum, enacted in the Progressive period. Widely used in the twentieth century, people's lawmaking may reflect the desire displayed in 1878–79 to constitutionally embed most elements of public policy and to circumvent what was seen as an ineffective legislative process.

Although the constitution has been amended more than three hundred times since the 1879 version was ratified, many facets of the 1879 document continue to directly affect contemporary California. For example, the University of California remains a separate constitutional agency as set up in 1879, exempt from most of the laws that apply to the rest of the government. The basic judicial system was reconstructed into its present form. Almost the same number and type of constitutional officers continue to be elected as specified in 1879, even though today several of the functions supervised by these constitutional officers could be handled by other constitutional officers or appointed officials, as is often seen in other states. Moreover, the policy discretion of these independently elected constitutional officers is severely limited by the wishes of the governor, who controls the budget process, personnel regulations, and decisions of executive agencies with overlapping authority. Accountability for a variety of constitutional functions is thereby blurred, but change in the system is difficult because substantive alterations require a constitutional amendment. As previously noted, the numerical composition of the legislature remains the same as in 1879, even though the state's population is now more than thirty times larger. Former Speaker of the Assembly Bob Monagan's assessment of badly needed change in California's system of representative government places expansion in the numbers of legislative representatives as one of the foremost reforms to repair major defects in the 1879-based governmental structure. Others he recommends include a new method for reapportionment, shorter legislative sessions, enforceable campaign finance reform, and a revised initiative process.[23]

All of this strongly infers that greater study of the long-term impact of California's constitution-making endeavors would likely be quite fruitful, though such a comprehensive effort is beyond the scope of this volume. Particularly scant historical analysis has been undertaken in respect to the constitution of 1879 and its effects. Most general histories mention its development only in passing, or dismiss its impact. Rolle and Gaines, for instance, merely offered that "in spite of the constitution's many technical defects, California has developed a workable and efficient governmental system." A more elaborate analysis appears in *The Elusive Eden*, whose authors suggest that "whatever its shortcomings, the new constitution established important principles of state economic regulation, . . . distributed the tax burden more widely, . . . and created the machinery for increasing state revenues. The state now

Approximately sixteen thousand Californians served in the U.S. military during the Civil War, including a "California Battalion" that fought with the Second Massachusetts Cavalry in Virginia. Because of prohibitive transportation costs, most enlisted Californians were stationed in their home state, such as the men of Sacramento Company I, Second Regiment, who in 1863 posed for this photograph alongside "Union Boy," an artillery cannon they fired after each Union victory. *Courtesy City of Sacramento, History and Science Division, Sacramento Archives and Museum Collection Center, Eleanor McClatchy Collection.*

possessed a stronger legal and fiscal framework for dealing more actively with the economic, scientific, and environmental problems of modernization." David Alan Johnson's perceptive evaluation takes an even longer view: "The 1879 constitution of California was thus an effort to make sense of a modernizing corporate order.... the delegates, Workingmen and nonpartisan alike, were anticipating the regulatory state that would be established by Progressive reformers a generation hence. They intended to widen government's role as the guarantor of individual liberty, giving it the responsibility to limit and control, but also assist, the pursuit of private advantage."[24]

President Robert Semple, concluding his opening remarks to the first constitutional convention, predicted: "The knowledge, enterprise and genius of the old world will reappear in the new, to guide it to its destined position among the nations of the earth. Let us, then, go onward and upward, and let our motto be, 'Justice, Industry, and Economy.'"25 If movement indeed was "onward and upward," it was to unfold in erratic fashion, as the articles in this volume indicate. But no matter how erratic, what happened in California public life during the state's first thirty years was vital to the state's future, and it certainly invites greater study and comprehension to help understand public life in the present. The essays in this volume provide an initial step in that direction. Each discusses an important element of California's early affairs, with an emphasis on looking anew at government's role.

Roger D. McGrath challenges several prevailing conceptions about crime, violence, and law enforcement in California's early governmental period. Novels and motion pictures have contributed to a heavily romanticized and often fictional picture of law and order on the frontier and about the characters who played a part in it. But McGrath shows, for instance, that Joaquín Murieta was just a brutal bandit from Mexico, not a Hispanic Robin Hood, and that he was prone to assault easy victims, including other Mexicans. Vigilantes, according to McGrath, "operated coolly and deliberately" and "left the community in a better state" as they focused their remedial attention on those who preyed on the innocent. McGrath found few damsels in distress on the California frontier. In fact, women were a "protected class" rarely the subject of criminal activity. He judges pioneer defense attorneys "highly competent," and also asserts that "it is difficult to cite an instance of an innocent man being hanged" by vigilantes. On numerous matters, including the first state prison system, early lawmen, and the effects of an armed citizenry "too dangerous to rob," McGrath reevaluates popular notions and explores new ground.

The essay by Gordon Morris Bakken logically succeeds that of McGrath, as it treats the development of the California courts and the legal system. Bakken examines the constitutional underpinnings of California's initial judicial efforts and finds that they reflected "the popular sovereignty and Jacksonian democratic rhetoric of the times." His history of the early bar and judicial action sheds considerable light on the practice of justice in the state's tumultuous early days, including its "dismal" record on matters related to racial equity. Especially useful is his elaboration on real estate law, tort law, mortgages, and mechanics liens, important subjects that rarely gain even a modicum of attention. While Bakken found that judges "clearly favored entrepreneurs and insulated them" from liability, he also found that the state Supreme Court "exhibited an independence that produced extraordinary decisions." His overall research concludes that there was substantial judicial activity in the constitutional era that was far from amateurish and that this activity contributed materially to California's maturation as a state.

Shirley Ann Wilson Moore's essay provides insight in respect to some of the important and troubling issues on racial prejudice and discrimination raised by Bakken.

Frederick Law Olmsted (photographed here ca. 1865), the father of landscape architecture, came to California in 1863 to manage John C. Frémont's Mariposa estate south of Yosemite Valley. Entranced by Yosemite, Olmsted helped convince President Lincoln to turn the valley over to the state of California in 1864, the first time the federal government set aside an area of land as a public park. Lacking any precedents or any other national parks, Congress, following custom at the time, entrusted administration of the preserve to California. Olmsted became the first chairman of the state's Yosemite Valley Commission and during his brief tenure labored to create a park that was protected while still "laid open to the use of the body of the people," a philosophy that would later guide the National Park Service. *California Historical Society, FN-26251.*

Unsympathetic to the popular premises of Manifest Destiny and focusing on the theme of law and race, she synthesizes the thirty-year period of California's early state experience, beginning with the state constitution that gave "legal sanction to discrimination" and the first legislative enactments against miners of color "erecting a bulwark of laws that deprived them of civil rights." She demonstrates that such laws were no accident of ignorance, nor did they have only casual impact. Moore traces the web of statutes that purposefully, blatantly served to keep nonwhite people in a subservient and disfranchised economic, educational, and political status, and reveals the reality of slavery in the sometimes not-so-free Golden State. Prominent among early laws were those that barred any judicial redress for Native Americans, Chinese, and African Americans, who were all prevented from even testifying in any action involving whites. Moore concludes by pointing out that, far from remaining silent, active responses were undertaken by some individuals and groups, especially African Americans, as they often successfully contested frontier California's legal strictures and began to challenge second-class citizenship.

A fascinating interlude is provided by Joshua Paddison in the essay that follows Moore's, as Paddison discusses some of the visual archival materials that vividly illustrate political and governmental activity and people associated with it. The color plates remind the reader of certain realities and conflicts associated with the emergence of Americanized government in California, and Paddison's text relates these and other images of early California to the eventual mythology of the state. Representations of such figures as Joaquín Murieta, Andrés Pico, and the Peralta family recall actual people displaced by and adapting to or taking advantage of forces of conquest, and a painting of Chinatown unveils a more benign portrayal of the Chinese than that prevailing throughout most of the nineteenth century. Elements of American-style governments, such as the post office, state capitol, and fire department, symbolize and cement the newcomers' presence, while views of the majesty of Yosemite, effects of hydraulic mining, and the island of Alcatraz in San Francisco Bay hint at contrasting approaches to governmental handling of the state's remarkable natural resources.

Topical treatments of California's governmental legacy resume with Judson A. Grenier's unique essay on early California officials. Grenier's research upends the conventional wisdom that denigrates early California officialdom with charges of ineptitude and graft. To the contrary, he argues that California was "fortunate that most of its officials were responsible men," whose service "often meant relinquishing a more lucrative career," and that their governmental conduct was "creative and generally responsible." The first legislature was the "most creative and probably the most competent," was noticeably less racist than subsequent legislatures, and proved so capable that some of their acts "endure to the present." Grenier asserts that the 1879 constitution in fact did little to alter the fundamental structure of officialdom

The members of the California State Geological Survey team posed for this photograph, titled *The Immortal Few,* in December 1863. From left to right are Chester Averill, William Gabb, William Ashburner, State Geologist Josiah D. Whitney, Charles F. Hoffman, Clarence King, and William H. Brewer. The state legislature created the team in April 1860 to "make an accurate and complete Geological Survey of the State, and to furnish . . . proper maps and diagrams thereof, with a full and scientific description of its rocks, fossils, soils, and minerals, and of its botanical and zoological productions." Though overwhelmed by California's immense size and hindered by a lack of funds, Whitney's survey furnished valuable maps and geological data and inspired similar civilian surveys in other states. *Courtesy California State Library.*

imposed by the first constitution-builders and legislators. Especially valuable are his detailed descriptions of the offices, departments, and functions of the early government, and his capsule histories of the various gubernatorial administrations during the first thirty years of the state.

The preceding essays focus primarily on men in the creation of California as a state. Although prevented by law and custom from exercising overt political participation, women also played a role in the evolution of state law as they fought for

Map of California counties, from Mildred Brooke Hoover, Hero Eugene Rensch, and Ethel Grace Rensch, *Historic Spots in California* (Stanford: Stanford University Press, 1990). *California Historical Society, FN-32395.*

equal rights in an arena dominated by men. Donna C. Schuele's essay treats these developments in considerable depth and draws some surprising conclusions that impel a fresh look at female experiences in pioneer California. For example, one of the most celebrated provisions of the 1849 constitution was the one that provided defined marital property rights to women. Schuele demonstrates, however, that the reality of application of this provision was far different from what the mythology holds, and that it "actually rendered California wives worse off than their eastern sisters." She also connects California's "subsistence frontier environment" with an increase in employment for white women, and that in turn spurred the development of women's literature, the suffrage movement, and the development of female leaders. She shows that early lawmakers were somewhat receptive in the end to demands for equal occupational treatment, and that a more positive response to job discrimination against women arrived in the 1879 constitution.

While these first six essays all emphasize developments in state law, government, and politics, the final two essays turn to the development of local government and the continuing presence of the federal government, respectively. Edward Leo Lyman discusses how local government was initiated "in an amazingly short time." He uncovers details about local government actions undertaken for a variety of functions, such as the improvement of roads and bridges so that rudimentary transportation arteries might be initialized and the establishment of county care for the "indigent ill" as a "precursor of the later welfare system." Lyman illustrates the difficulties confronting county officials in the north (El Dorado County) and the south (San Bernardino County), as well as in San Francisco and Sacramento, as samples of the struggles counties faced to provide schools, law enforcement, fire and flood protection, and other basic services. He finds that despite manifest problems, they "rather quickly laid the institutional and infrastructural foundation for local government," citing the work of both newcomers and Mexican Americans to provide local order.

The concluding essay, by Robert J. Chandler, examines the continuing and important federal role in the state's development, determining that while routine matters such as providing harbor defenses and building lighthouses were often handled successfully, the national government "failed in any actions that required speed," as in the timely resolution of land, mineral, and water issues. Chandler shows that federal involvement was vital in certain arenas; chief among them was the creation of California's transportation system, including the railroads. His investigation of the federal patronage system in California, especially in the Post Office and Treasury Department, is also revealing, as is his extensive discussion of military affairs during the Civil War and federal political effects on the state. As a fascinating bonus, interesting tidbits jump out of Chandler's broad research, such as the continuing efforts of the California legislature to receive recompense as promised by the federal government for the Civil War military services provided by the state, or the "ingenious" drug smuggling methods employed 140 years ago that are not unlike those the federal and state governments fight against today.

This exploration of the political and governmental side of the gold-rush years and California's constitutional era collectively gives the reader an intensive new look at the formation and growth of the early state and suggests that there may be a great deal more depth to California's initial civic experiences than has been heretofore assumed. Moreover, much of the information offered implies that the mythology that has grown up around the politics and government of the state's first thirty years may be faulty or, at best, imprecise.

The essays in this volume range across numerous seldom-treated topics, with substantial, if sometimes merely tantalizing, results. Nineteenth-century constitution-building efforts and the statutes that soon followed were deliberative and complex, and they left strong residual effects. Frontier law and order, and the government's role in it, was evidently more measured and "orderly" than previously understood. The initial courts and justice system laid some important and thoughtful groundwork for the future, as did the struggles and successes of state, local, and federal jurisdictions and their unheralded officials, who brought considerable prior experience and organizational skill to bear in a unique frontier environment. At the same time, economic and governmental interplay favored certain groups, and flagrant racial discrimination flourished, materially aided and abetted by political actions. Both minorities and women fought to secure and maintain basic rights in the face of significant, intended institutional and legal barriers.

The story of political and governmental California in the state's constitutional and statehood period is connected to national issues, and to the ideals and misdeeds that accompanied them, with adaptation to the unparalleled and unprecedented governance situation that California presented. A recently conquered province with a diverse population, expanding exponentially in the midst of the phenomenal Gold Rush, had to quickly find a way to govern itself, and then almost as rapidly to modify its governing practices to reflect ever-changing economic and demographic imperatives. From the ambiguous mists of early state realities—adventure, profit, failure, boldness, tradition, creativity, compassion, and prejudice—the shape and substance of modern California emerged and remains today.

NOTES

1. J. S. Holliday, *Rush for Riches* (Berkeley: Oakland Museum of California and University of California Press, 1999), 201; Andrew F. Rolle, *California: A History* (New York: Thomas Y. Crowell, 1969), 330.

2. Edward Staniford, *The Pattern of California History* (San Francisco: Canfield Press, 1975), 161; Judson A. Grenier, *Golden Odyssey: John Stroud Houston, California's First Controller and the Origins of State Government* (Los Angeles: Historical Society of Southern California, 1999), 14.

3. William E. Leuchtenburg, "The Pertinence of Political History: Reflections on the Significance of the State in America," *Journal of American History* 73 (December 1986): 588–89. The existing literature on California's early political and governmental history is

sparse and, for the most part, dated. The best work on California's first constitutional convention, for example, remains Woodrow James Hansen, *The Search for Authority in California* (Oakland: Biobooks, 1960). Textbooks typically point to sources such as the following for further reading: Cardinal Goodwin, *The Establishment of State Government in California, 1846–1850* (New York, 1914); Joseph Ellison, *California and the Nation, 1850–1969* (Berkeley: University of California Press, 1927); James A. B. Scherer, *Thirty-First Star* (New York: G. P. Putnam's Sons, 1942); William Henry Ellison, *A Self-Governing Dominion: California, 1849–1860* (Berkeley: University of California Press, 1950); and Theodore Grivas, *Military Governments in California, 1846–1850* (Glendale, Calif.: The Arthur H. Clark Company, 1963). Little scholarship has appeared since the 1960s. Notable exceptions include Grenier, *Golden Odyssey;* David Alan Johnson, *Founding the Far West: California, Oregon, and Nevada, 1840–1890* (Berkeley: University of California Press, 1992); Shelley Bookspan, *A Germ of Goodness: The California State Prison System, 1851–1944* (Lincoln: University of Nebraska Press, 1991); and the material in this volume.

4. J. Ross Browne, *Report of the Debates in the Convention of California, on the Formation of the State Constitution, in September and October, 1849* (Washington, D.C.: J. T. Towers, 1850), 3.

5. Frank Marryat, *Mountains and Molehills* (New York: Harper and Brothers, 1855), 203–205.

6. David Lavender, *California: Land of New Beginnings* (Lincoln: University of Nebraska Press, 1972), 199.

7. Johnson, *Founding the Far West*, 27–28.

8. Martin Ridge, "Disorder, Crime, and Punishment in the California Gold Rush," *Montana: The Magazine of Western History* 49 (Autumn 1999): 27.

9. Johnson, *Founding the Far West*, 27.

10. Staniford, *Pattern of California History*, 155.

11. Edward H. Howes, "The World's Gateway to the Gold, 1848–1860s," in *Sacramento: Gold Rush Legacy, Metropolitan Destiny*, ed. John F. Burns (Carlsbad, Calif.: Heritage Media, 1999), 30.

12. Browne, *Debates*, 3.

13. Ibid., 18.

14. Ibid., 258–59.

15. Ibid., 137–200 (the quotations are on pp. 178 and 182).

16. William J. Palmer and Paul P. Selvin, *The Development of Law in California* (St. Paul, Minn.: West Publishing Co., 1983), 24.

17. Charles P. Sohner and Mona Field, *California Government and Practices Today* (New York: HarperCollins, 1993), 13.

18. Bernard L. Hyink, Seyom Brown, and Ernest W. Thacker, *Politics and Government in California* (New York: Thomas Y. Crowell, 1967), 21.

19. John W. Caughey, *California: A Remarkable State's Life History* (Englewood Cliffs, N.J.: Prentice-Hall, 1970), 216; Ellison, *A Self-Governing Dominion*, 77; Grenier, *Golden Odyssey*.

20. Neal R. Peirce, *The Pacific States of America* (New York: W.W. Norton, 1972), 26.

21. Gerald D. Nash, *State Government and Economic Development: A History of Administrative Policies in California, 1849–1933* (Berkeley: University of California Press, 1964), 26.

22. Kevin Starr, *Americans and the California Dream, 1850–1915* (New York and Oxford: Oxford University Press, 1973), 132.

23. Robert T. Monagan, *The Disappearance of Representative Government* (Grass Valley, Calif.: Comstock Bonanza Press, 1990).

24. The most useful monograph on the 1879 constitutional convention remains Carl Brent Swisher, *Motivation and Political Technique in the California Constitutional Convention, 1878–79* (New York: Da Capo Press, 1969). Quoted here are Andrew F. Rolle and John S. Gaines, *The Golden State: A History of California* (Arlington Heights, Ill.: Harlan Davidson, 1979), 150; Richard B. Rice, William A. Bullough, and Richard J. Orsi, *The Elusive Eden: A New History of California* (New York: Alfred A. Knopf, 1988), 280; Johnson, *Founding the Far West*, 255.

25. Browne, *Debates*, 18.

2

A Violent Birth

Disorder, Crime, and Law Enforcement, 1849–1890

Roger D. McGrath

On the winter morning of February 20, 1853, more than a hundred Chinese miners were working their claims near Rich Gulch. Without warning, five mounted and gun-brandishing bandidos swept down upon them. Taken by surprise and without arms themselves, the Chinese could do little but comply when ordered to hand over their gold. An American who happened to be in the Chinese camp refused and made a rush for the bandidos. He was joined by two Chinese. The bandidos opened fire, killing the three men instantly. Stray bullets wounded five others. The bandidos collected some $10,000 worth of gold dust and nuggets and left as suddenly as they had come. Two days later the same gang of bandidos hit another Chinese camp with equally bloody, if less profitable, results. The robbers killed three Chinese, wounded five more, and got away with $3,000 worth of gold.

Charlie Clarke, the leader of a small posse on the trail of the killers, described them as "five well dressed Mexicans, well armed and mounted on beautiful animals." Their leader was Joaquín Murieta. Probably the most mythologized figure in California history, Murieta has been portrayed as a social bandit who waged war against the hated gringos by robbing and killing them. In truth there was nothing social about his banditry. He robbed and killed those who had money, be they American, Chinese, or Mexican. He killed nearly as many Chinese as whites and robbed and murdered several of his fellow Mexicans. His cause was his own.

California's unsettled early years were certainly violent, with no one group having a monopoly on mayhem. Gangs of bandidos, using horses to great advantage, were especially conspicuous. The Murieta gang was only one of many, which is one reason Murieta's reputation grew to legendary proportions. Nearly every robbery committed by bandidos was attributed to Murieta. If robbed by a gang of Mexicans, was there anyone who did not want to attribute the crime to the notorious Joaquín

Murieta? A similar phenomenon occurred a generation later in Missouri and adjacent states. No bank teller would admit that the leader of the gang of robbers who cleaned out the vault was not Jesse James.

Violence was not confined to bandidos. Caucasian newcomers used both the legal system and individual and group violence to suppress the nonwhite population. Conflict between Indians and other groups was also a feature of the early years of California but was of such significance and different character that it requires a separate treatment.[1] However, violence did not have to cross racial and cultural lines. Fighting among young American white men was a common occurrence in the saloon. The watering hole could be in the booming city of San Francisco, at a way station, or in a mining camp. It hardly mattered. Tradition and the code of the frontier required that the American male stand and fight if challenged or insulted. If both men were armed, the fight often resulted in death. Stagecoach holdups became commonplace by the 1870s, but train robberies can be counted on the fingers of one hand. Women, so often the target of the criminal today, only rarely suffered from any kind of violence or lawlessness. In many ways they were a protected class. Prostitutes were an exception to this rule. Their victimization, though, most often took the form of an assault by another prostitute or by a drunken customer. Even for them, murder or rape was rare. When they died prematurely, it was usually the result of suicide or habitual use of alcohol and drugs.

Certain kinds of violence were looked upon with equanimity by gold-rush Californians. If two healthy young men chose to fight—with fists, knives, or guns—and the results proved deadly, few people became terribly upset. When stage robbers were courteous, left the passengers unmolested, and took only the contents of the treasure box, the general public hardly uttered a peep. However, if an innocent person were killed or robbed, the citizenry would be outraged and the response to the dastardly deed frequently came in the form of vigilantism. More often than not, vigilantes, unlike members of a lynch mob, operated coolly and deliberately, exercised good judgment, prosecuted and punished the guilty, and left the community in a better state for their operations. San Francisco experienced two episodes of vigilantism. One episode was enough for most mining camps.

During the gold-rush years a significant amount of the violence in the Mother Lode country, and in rural California in general, was the product of bandidos. Legend has it that the bandidos were old Californians displaced by the arrival of thousands of Yankees. Actually, many of the bandidos were recent arrivals from Mexico. They raced into California in the rush of '49 just like the Yankees and other Argonauts. The most notorious of the bandidos, Joaquín Murieta, was born in Mexico and did not arrive in California until 1849. Unfortunately, most of what people think they know about Murieta comes from a wildly fictional tale created by John Rollin Ridge. In 1854 the part-Cherokee Ridge published *The Life and Adventures*

This portrait of Joaquín Murieta by Charles Christian Nahl appeared in the original edition of John Rollin Ridge's *The Life and Adventures of Joaquin Murieta, the Celebrated California Bandit*, published in San Francisco in 1854. Ridge, a part-Cherokee journalist who wrote under the name Yellow Bird, drew on local legends to create a martyred Mexican swashbuckler who struck back against American injustices in gold-rush California. Later writers, including Joaquin Miller, Pablo Neruda, and Isabel Allende, have likewise used Murieta for their own purposes. *California Historical Society, FN-244-A.*

of Joaquin Murieta, the Celebrated California Bandit. Ridge says that Americans drove Murieta from his claim, flogged him and raped his wife, and hanged his brother. Murieta then set out on a course of revenge, killing all those gringos responsible. The tale seems inspired more by the removal of the Cherokee and the conflict that occurred both within the Cherokee tribe and with the whites than by anything that Murieta experienced. (Ridge's paternal grandfather, Cherokee leader Major Ridge, and his father, John Ridge, were both killed during the conflict over removal.) Nonetheless, Ridge's fictional version of Murieta's life was accepted as fact and became a template for nearly all the bandidos.[2]

Stories about Murieta multiplied, and articles mixing fact and fiction appeared in newspapers and magazines for years. The romantic myth was more powerful than the awful truth. Walter Noble Burns took the myth to new heights with the publication of *The Robin Hood of El Dorado* in 1932. Although as long ago as 1949, Joseph Henry Jackson, in *Bad Company*, revealed the fictional nature of most of the literature on Murieta and demonstrated clearly that most authors relied heavily upon Ridge, the early 1970s saw a revival, especially by activist Chicano authors, of the myth of the wronged Californio becoming a social bandit.[3]

In reality, the man who inspired the fictional Joaquín Murieta of popular culture was not a Californio but a Mexican from Sonora. Most important, his wife was not raped by American miners, nor was his brother hanged. Moreover, it was Murieta's brother-in-law, Claudio Feliz, who first turned to crime when he stole a large nugget of gold. The theft had nothing to do with racial antagonism. He was panning with a party of American miners at the time and was said to be well liked by the Yankees. Feliz was put in jail for the theft but escaped almost immediately. Within a year he was leading a gang of bandidos, intent on enriching themselves, not on avenging wrongs. Some of those who rode with Feliz were Americans. Feliz led attacks on ranchos owned by Americans and those owned by Mexicans, killing and looting without compunction. The first rancho he raided was that owned by the famous "Dr." John Marsh, an American ranchero who had been in California since 1836. The third rancho Feliz attacked was that of an old Californio, Anastacio Chabolla. Feliz returned to the southern Mother Lode country for his next crime. With the help of his younger brother, Reyes, he robbed and murdered a fellow Mexican near Chinese Camp.[4]

Other crimes followed, and by the fall of 1851 Murieta had joined Feliz and his band. On November 10 they lassoed a man named Gallagher and his black servant, dragged them off their horses, and slit their throats. For the gang's bloody efforts they were rewarded with only two ounces of gold. They then robbed and killed an American teamster and two American travelers, and they shot Yuba County sheriff Robert "Buck" Buchanan in the back. The sheriff managed to recover, but a Mexican whom Feliz later shot did not. Feliz was actually jailed for the latter crime but soon

Vol. III. Complete In One Number.   *Beadle & Adams, Publishers,* No. 98 WILLIAM STREET, NEW YORK.   Price, Ten Cents.   No. 38.

The Velvet Hand;
OR,
The Iron Grip of Injun Dick.

BY ALBERT W. AIKEN,
AUTHOR OF "OVERLAND KIT," "ROCKY MOUNTAIN ROB," "KENTUCK, THE SPORT," "INJUN DICK," ETC.

PROLOGUE.
NOT DEAD BUT SLEEPING.

DARK and gloomy were the clouds that lowered around great Shasta's snow-covered peak. The hour of midnight was near at hand, and the slow-rising moon, struggling in the embrace of the thick and envious clouds, barely lighted up the night.

On the north-western side of the peak, where one of the edges of the old crater had broken away, thus forming a small circular plateau about a hundred yards in diameter, a huge fire was brightly burning.

By the fire, and feeding the flames, stood a tall, dark form.

The copper-colored face, the massive features, as well as the forest-prairie garb of deerskin which he wore plainly told that the man was native to the soil.

Far below in the valley twinkled the lights of the mining town of Cinnabar, and in the main street of that young metropolis of the Shasta valley, a group of miners were gathered, eagerly trying, with the aid of a powerful glass, to discover the meaning of the unusual beacon blazing so brightly on the side of giant Shasta's peak.

"Some of the buck's heathen ceremonies!" the word went around, as, by the aid of the glass, the miners made out that the tall form standing by the burning pile was a savage chief.

Little did the men of Cinnabar dream that the blazing beacon was to serve as a funeral pyre for the mortal remains of the long-bearded Cherokee, the Injun Dick of "Overland Kit," the untiring pursuer of "Rocky Mountain Rob," the Richard Talbot, superintendent of the Cinnabar Mine, of "Kentuck," and the dreaded White Rider, the Death-Shot of Shasta, who made such fearful fight for the Cinnabar lode, as detailed in the pages of "Injun Dick."

"Give my body to the flames on Shasta's side," the hero had muttered, after receiving the chance shot, his death-wound, seemingly.

And O-wa-te (Mud-turtle), the Blackfoot chief, who had traveled far from the home of his tribe, seeking the friend of his early days in the golden California land, promised to respect the injunction.

Then the stricken man had swooned away, and the Indian, bending anxiously over the still form, believed that death's dark angel had set his fatal signet upon the brow of lion-hearted Talbot.

Motionless by the side of the body, with his head muffled in his blanket after the fashion of his people when mourning for the loved and lost, the chief had remained until the midnight hour was at hand; then, to the top of Shasta's peak he bore the senseless form of the man who had been to him like a brother.

The funeral pyre was kindled, and as the flames roared and sparkled high in the air, the Indian knelt by the side of the form, now so cold and still, a last farewell to take.

A NICKEL-PLATED REVOLVER GLISTENED IN VELVET HAND'S WHITE FINGERS, AND NOT A MAN CARED TO TEST HIS MARKSMANSHIP.

Frontier California's reputation for violence and vigilantism persisted for decades after the Gold Rush, encouraged by writers who served up romantic stories to eager East Coast readers. This illustration adorned a cover of the New York periodical *Beadle's Dime Library* in 1878, accompanied by a breathless tale of violent retribution set in California called "The Velvet Hand; or, The Iron Grip of Injun Dick." *Courtesy City of Sacramento, History and Science Division, Sacramento Archives and Museum Collection Center, Eleanor McClatchy Collection.*

escaped. He and his compadres next made news at the mining camp of Humbug. There, the town constable, John Leary, saw Reyes Feliz wearing two stolen revolvers and took him into custody.

With Caleb Dorsey, a Harvard-educated lawyer, and two other Americans, Leary headed to Columbia to lodge his prisoner in jail. Lurking along the route, however, was the Feliz band. The bandidos opened fire from ambush, but Leary and his boys were equal to the occasion. They returned the fire with effect, killing one of the bandidos and badly wounding Claudio Feliz. In the confusion Reyes Feliz managed to escape. Claudio tried to do the same, but his wound slowed his progress up a hillside, and as Leary closed in, Claudio turned and emptied his revolver at the constable. Leary, his Irish temper getting the better of him, charged madly at Feliz. Somehow he managed to reach Feliz without one of the bandido's bullets striking him. He then put his own revolver to Feliz's head and cocked the hammer. Whether Leary would have fired is not known. Dorsey arrived on the scene and pushed Leary's gun barrel to the side.

Claudio Feliz was soon standing trial, not for all his murders and robberies, which were as yet unknown to Columbia authorities, but for attempting to "rescue a prisoner from a public officer, and shooting at said officer." Feliz retained none other than Caleb Dorsey to represent him, and the Harvard graduate convinced a jury, composed solely of non-Hispanic whites, to find Feliz not guilty. Contrary to the popular impression, justice was often neither swift nor certain on the frontier. Frequently, if a defendant, be he American, Mexican, or Chinese, retained a good attorney, that defendant was acquitted. The case of Claudio Feliz, the bandido from the Mexican state of Sonora, is but one of hundreds of examples.

While Feliz was being tried, leadership of the gang fell to Murieta. Through the early 1850s the new leader led the bandidos in outbursts of robbery and murder down the San Joaquin Valley, into southern California, and back to the Mother Lode. Murieta and his bandidos robbed and killed without compunction and without discrimination. Their killing of an otherwise common American farmer, Allen Ruddle, proved to be both their undoing and a catalyst for the creation of the California Rangers. Ruddle's family offered a large reward for the capture of the murderers. One of those attracted to the case by the reward was Harry Love. Love was a rough-hewn, six-foot-two veteran of the Mexican War. A native of Vermont, he had lived on the frontier for two decades by the time he arrived in California, at the age of forty-two, in December 1850. He was ornery, fearless, deadly, and always well armed. His personal sidearm was a .44 Colt Dragoon.

Early in June 1852 Murieta and his gang arrived in Los Angeles with Love and his partner hot on their trail. Love chased two gang members to Ventura, where, after a brief shoot-out, he had one of them, Pedro Gonzales, in custody. When they stopped at a creek near present-day Thousand Oaks, Gonzales broke for the brush. Love calmly drew his .44 and put a bullet through Gonzales's head.

Joaquín Murieta proved to be a wily foe, however, and his depredations continued. In January 1853, he began a two-month reign of terror. He and his gang members robbed Chinese miners at Yaqui Camp and murdered one of them. Only a few days later they robbed and killed two Chinese and two American miners not far from Yaqui Camp. A posse caught up with the bandidos, but after a running gun battle they escaped. Riding through Yaqui Camp they let bullets fly in all directions, killing an American. That night they killed two Americans at a quartz mill. This was more than enough for the local miners, and a vigilance committee was organized at San Andreas. A vigilante posse followed a trail of blood from the quartz mill and found a wounded Mexican hiding in a tent. Before he was hanged he admitted that Murieta was the leader of the group. At Cherokee Flat the vigilantes found another wounded bandido and shot to death his fleeing compadre. The wounded man was soon stretching hemp.

Murieta's bandidos next robbed and murdered two Chinese four miles outside of Angels Camp, then three Americans near French Camp. The vigilante posse managed to capture a scout for Murieta near Angels Camp. He was hanged. With Calaveras County up in arms, Murieta fled north to Amador County. During early February he and his bandidos robbed Chinese at four different camps, leaving one dead and two wounded. Then on February 13 the bandidos hit a Chinese camp on Jackson Creek. They murdered a Chinese miner and an American butcher. The Chinese raced into nearby Jackson and reported the attack. A hastily raised posse was quickly on Murieta's trail. The posse tracked the bandidos to a ravine, where they found Murieta and the others dismounted, readjusting their saddles and dividing their ill-gotten gains. The posse members let out a whoop and, firing their revolvers, swept down into the ravine. The bandidos mounted their horses and scattered, leaving behind stolen horses and sacks of gold.

Two days later the posse caught one of Murieta's bandidos and brought him into Jackson. The Chinese identified him as one of the gang. He admitted that he had participated in the raid but claimed that he had not committed the murders. The miners' court was unmoved and sentenced him to death. Escorted to a large oak tree in front of the Astor House, he was soon dangling from a prominent limb. He was the fifth victim of Jackson's "hanging tree."

Murieta now made his bloodiest raids to date, his aforementioned attacks on the two Chinese camps on February 20 and 22, 1853, leaving six dead and at least ten wounded. He then fled into Mariposa County and holed up near the Mexican camp of Hornitos. Two months of raiding, robbing, and murdering had made him notorious. Although several of his bandidos had been shot and killed or captured and hanged, he remained on the loose. Following him was difficult at best. Local posses did not like to stray far from home, and they did not have the resources to stay in the field for long. Moreover, few miners had horses to donate to the cause and even fewer had blooded stock that could run with the mounts stolen by the bandidos from ranchos. As a result, in May, the state legislature created the California Rangers, a small force authorized to exist for three months and to hunt down evildoers statewide. Harry Love was appointed captain and put in command. He made Patrick Edward Connor, an Irish immigrant and captain of volunteers in the Mexican War (and later a brigadier general in the Civil War), first lieutenant and second in command. Some twenty men were enlisted as rangers, most of them war veterans and frontiersmen who had years of experience in tracking and fighting. Murieta's days were now numbered.

Love led his men through the Mother Lode country, then across the San Joaquin Valley to Mission San Jose. They were on the right trail. Murieta had a hideout nearby, in Niles Canyon. It was a member of his band, Jesus Feliz, though, who was first captured. Feliz, Murieta's brother-in-law, agreed to cooperate with Love. Feliz identified Murieta's favorite haunts in the Coast Range, in particular Cantua Creek. Packing three weeks' provisions, Love let leak misinformation about the destination of his rangers. On the hot afternoon of July 12 they set off in their stated direction. They made camp in the evening, but when darkness fell, they quietly broke camp and rode hard toward Cantua Creek. Often riding at night, switching directions, and breaking into smaller parties, they closed in on their prey. Finally, at 2 A.M. on the morning of July 25, they began to follow fresh tracks down Cantua Creek into the San Joaquin Valley. By the time they reached the valley, dawn was breaking. Three miles distant, smoke rose from a campfire.

The rangers approached within four hundred yards of the camp before being seen. The bandidos raced to gather their horses, but it was too late. With guns drawn, the rangers galloped up to the camp and froze the bandidos in their tracks. One of the bandidos, described as handsome with long hair and a fair complexion, stepped forward. Evidently thinking that he could convince the Americans that he and his compadres were simply innocent vaqueros hunting wild mustangs, the fair one said, "Talk to me. I am the leader of this band." A ranger who had known Murieta back in Sonora in 1850 shouted, "This is Joaquín, boys! We have got him at last!"

From under their serapes Murieta and his bandidos pulled revolvers and blazed away. The rangers followed suit. A bullet grazed Harry Love's head, neatly parting his hair. One of the bandidos was not so lucky. A bullet struck him in the head, and he fell dead. After firing a shot or two, Murieta raced for his horse, leaped onto the saddleless animal, and galloped down an embankment and into a creek. A ranger followed in hot pursuit. As Murieta tried to race his horse up the opposite bank, the ranger opened fire. The round broke the animal's leg and sent horse and rider crashing to the earth. Murieta took off running, but the ranger's accurate fire brought him down. The notorious bandido pleaded that the ranger shoot no more and then, in Spanish, said, "I'm dead." Within seconds he expired.

During the Gold Rush, massive immigration and competition over scarce resources exacerbated xenophobic violence against nonwhite groups. In July 1849, a band of American vigilantes descended on a tent community near San Francisco called Chiletown, murdering its Chilean residents and pillaging their makeshift homes. Chilean Argonaut Vicente Pérez Rosales later wrote that the vigilantes—disparagingly known as the Hounds—consisted of "vagrants, gamblers, or drunks, drawn together in a fellowship of crime; and they had as their motto, 'We can get away with it.' Fear and hatred spread in advance of their appearance. . . . Everywhere they went they established their control by quarrelsomeness and violence." The *Annals of San Francisco*, published in 1855, included this depiction of the Hounds' attack on Chiletown. *California Historical Society, FN-31984.*

Meanwhile, back at the camp, two more bandidos were killed in the gunfight and two others were captured. Several more, although wounded, managed to escape. Carrying the bodies of the dead bandidos back to Sacramento would have required a wagon. Instead, Love decided to decapitate Murieta's corpse and return with the head to prove that he had gotten the right man. The grisly trophy brought Love a

$1,000 reward, a princely sum in the 1850s. Bottled in alcohol, the head was made a touring exhibit in the Mother Lode country. The head was then put on display in a San Francisco gun shop, and later in a museum, before it was destroyed in the 1906 earthquake and fire.

The gang led first by Claudio Feliz and then by Joaquín Murieta was unusual only for its success. There were other Mexican gangs of a similar nature in the early years of American California, but none robbed and stole as frequently or killed as often.[5] Murieta and the others fought for no cause but their own. They attacked targets of opportunity. If the victim was a ranchero from an old Californio family, a Mexican teamster, or a Sonoran miner, so be it. Those with gold and without firearms were especially vulnerable, as was often the case with the Chinese. For Mexican bandidos Chinese mining camps were rich environments. The Feliz-Murieta gang alone murdered more than a dozen Chinese, several whites, one black, and at least three Mexicans. The gang members simply preyed upon the weak, the outnumbered, or the unsuspecting.

If the bandidos were the scourge of rural California, then the Hounds were the scourge of the city.[6] The Hounds were organized by San Francisco's merchants to provide a body of men who could capture and return runaway sailors. During the summer and fall of 1848, gold fever struck the sailors of nearly every ship that docked in San Francisco. Sailors, and occasionally their officers, jumped ship by the dozen and headed for the Mother Lode. By the end of 1848 the problem had grown so large that merchants had difficulty moving their goods. At first, the Hounds' income came solely from the merchants, but the group soon developed a protection racket. They were a tough bunch. Many of them had been members of the New York Volunteers, a regiment sent to California during the Mexican War. Others were beached sailors or Sydney Ducks from Britain's penal colony of Australia. Vicente Pérez Rosales, a gold seeker from Chile, recorded in his diary, "There is a gang of ruffians in this city called the Hounds. They are young, vicious, and shameless, and seem to have sworn a mutual pact to protect one another's lives and interests. They start fights in the cafes all the time, and if anyone rises to the provocations of these united ruffians he is beaten up."[7]

That Rosales was a Chilean and not a Mexican should not come as a surprise. The Chileans were the first Latin Americans to arrive in California in large numbers. Word of the gold strike reached Valparaiso during August 1848 and thousands of Chileans, many of them experienced miners, boarded ships for a relatively easy voyage to California. Although most of the Chileans headed for the diggings, a tent city called Chiletown developed on Telegraph Hill. For a while the Hounds victimized with impunity the Chileans who lived there. Any Chilean who refused to pay the

Hounds was pummeled and his tent destroyed. In June 1849 one of the Hounds got in a row with a Chilean merchant. The merchant pulled out a revolver and fired. The round struck and killed not the Hound, but another man, who happened to be in the Hound's company.

A month passed before the Hounds retaliated. When they did, they provoked the larger citizenry to act against them. After a day of drinking and revelry, twenty of them stumbled into Chiletown and wreaked havoc, destroying tents, beating men, and looting goods. When one Chilean resisted, Sam Roberts, the leader of the rampaging Hounds, fired a couple of rounds at the man as he fled into his tent. The bullets tore through the canvas and struck two boys huddled inside, leaving one dead and the other wounded. The drunken rampage was finally too much for the merchants of San Francisco, who realized too late that their sailor-catchers had become a gang of thugs. Sam Brannan, the town's leading merchant, held a general meeting the morning after the ransacking of Chiletown. Hundreds attended. Money was collected for the Chilean victims of the Hounds, and a militia of 230 men was organized. By the end of the day the citizen force had the twenty offending Hounds in custody. Nine of them were found guilty of various charges, including murder. Now that they were convicted, nobody seemed to know what to do with them. There was talk of hanging, but that seemed too severe for most of the miscreants, especially because the Hounds had been organized and supported by the town's leading citizens. Exacerbating the problem was a lack of any facilities for long-term incarceration. Finally, it was decided that the territorial governor should determine the punishment. The governor sentenced Sam Roberts to ten years "in some penitentiary." The others received lesser sentences. Eventually, the sentences of the Hounds were changed to banishment from California under the pain of death should they return. A few of them ultimately escaped even banishment.

As in San Francisco, conflict between Americans and Chileans also occurred in the Mother Lode, with similar citizen reaction. Americans generally felt that foreigners had no right to American gold. Chileans, Mexicans, and Chinese were often driven from claims. Responding to the prevailing American sentiment, the state legislature enacted a foreign miners' tax in 1850.[8] By then much blood had already been spilled. The worst episode occurred near Mokelumne Hill in 1849.[9] A hundred Chilean peons, indentured to wealthy Chilean masters and under the supervision of ten Chilean overseers, were mining an area that came to be called Chili Gulch. At the southern end of the gulch, two miles distant, was a camp of American miners called Iowa Cabins. The Americans resented the Chileans not only as foreigners, but also as an organized party of indentured workers. It was difficult for an individual and independent American to compete with a large company of men. The Americans could stake only one claim, while the Chilean group could stake more than a hundred, even though any particular peon was not about to operate independently. Hostilities by the Americans grew into the "Chilean War."

In December 1849, the Americans of the mining district that included Chili Gulch held a general meeting at Double Springs and issued an order expelling all foreigners from the area. When the Chileans failed to comply, the alcalde from Double Springs, Lewis Collier, led a body of Americans into the gulch and took the Chilean camp by surprise. They bound the Chilean overseers with rope and then looted the camp of food, gear, and gold. Collier evidently thought that this action would send the Chileans packing. However, the leaders of the Chileans made a forty-mile trek to Stockton and got the alcalde there to issue an arrest warrant for Collier and his men. The Chileans hiked back into the hills and handed the arrest warrant to John Scollan, another alcalde and the proprietor of a trading post on the South Fork of the Calaveras River. Scollan reluctantly agreed to ride over to Double Springs and present the warrant to Collier. Once there, Scollan read the warrant to Collier and a group of assembled men. They nearly killed him on the spot. Collier declared that Scollan should be hanged for a traitorous alliance with the Chileans and said, "The people are sovereign in the United States, and we are the people; and as such we have elected our own government or judge, and we recognize only his authority."

Scollan returned to his trading post and announced to the Chileans that he had done all he could do. Some of the Chileans lost heart and left the diggings for San Francisco. Armed with guns, knives, and clubs, about sixty others descended on Iowa Cabins during the night and took several of the Americans there by surprise. When the Chileans charged into one of the cabins, however, they found a half-dozen Americans awake and playing cards. A brief exchange of gunfire erupted when two of the Americans drew their revolvers and fired a few rounds before they were overwhelmed. The shoot-out left one American dead and another dying of his wounds. The Chileans had one man killed and one wounded.

The next morning the Chileans took the Americans they had captured in the raid—thirteen in all—to Alcalde Scollan. Having taken Collier's threat of hanging to heart, Scollan wanted nothing to do with them. He told the Chileans they had committed a criminal act and that they must release their prisoners at once. Disregarding Scollan, the Chileans headed for Stockton, hoping that the alcalde there would look more favorably upon their actions. Meanwhile, as word of the killings at Iowa Cabins had spread through the local mining district, several groups of armed Americans set out in search of the Chileans. Joining forces and forming one body of men as they picked up the trail, the Americans numbered nearly a hundred by the time they caught up with the Chileans a dozen miles short of Stockton. Already having suffered some desertions, the Chileans decided it would be suicidal to resist and surrendered without firing a shot.

Now the tables were turned once again. The captive Americans were freed and the Chileans were marched, as prisoners, to Mokelumne Hill for a mining-camp trial. The trial lasted several days before verdicts were announced. Three of the Chileans were found guilty of murder and were sentenced to death; five were sentenced to fifty lashes and head shavings; and three were sentenced to thirty lashes and ear croppings.[10] Thus ended the "Chilean War."

Dueling also reflected the violent character of many Californians and eventually brought action from the state. The Argonauts came to California to strike it rich—a purely materialistic goal. Yet they often sacrificed their lives or at least their well-being for a highly developed sense of honor. Honor could not be bought; it had to be earned. An insult or a challenge meant a fight. There was no duty to retreat. A man stood his ground and fought—with fists, knives, or guns. The polished gentlemen preferred a formal duel. During the 1850s more duels were fought in California than in any other place in America, including the South. By 1854 the practice had become so common that the state legislature made dueling a criminal offense. The new law, however, was ignored by much of the honor-bound public. The legislator himself who drafted the bill later shot a man to death in an affair of honor. If a man killed his adversary in a duel, he was generally arrested and tried. However, practicing nullification, juries invariably found the accused not guilty.[11]

Newspaper editors, lawyers, judges, politicians, and other men of position, power, and wealth dueled. William Walker, a San Francisco newspaper editor, who later became famous for his filibustering in Nicaragua, fought two duels in a year's time and was badly wounded in both affairs. The two men who wounded Walker both fought several more duels. Newspaper editors, an outspoken bunch in frontier California, often accepted challenges from politicians and other newspaper editors. John Nugent, the editor of the *San Francisco Herald*, engaged in three duels—the first when he challenged Edward Gilbert, the editor of the *Alta California* who was also California's first U.S. representative, and the second and third when San Francisco aldermen John Cotter and Thomas Hayes, on separate occasions, challenged Nugent over comments in his editorials. In the first duel, Gilbert, on the field of honor, offered to retract his offending statement. Cotter and Hayes, however, were more determined foes. The aldermen, in their separate duels with Nugent, each left the newspaper editor badly wounded. Dueling pistols were not always used. The Colt Navy was the weapon of choice in the Cotter duel, the rifle in the Hayes affair.[12]

Dueling with revolvers, rifles, and even shotguns was not unusual in California. Dueling pistols of very small caliber were common in Europe; they satisfied honor but rarely killed. In California, men evidently felt that honor was best satisfied by killing one's adversary. In several duels, the weapons were shotguns loaded with buckshot. Under such conditions men were almost always killed or horribly wounded. Occasionally, European practices did prevail in California. There is an instance of two Frenchmen meeting on the field of honor and dueling with swords. After one was badly wounded, their seconds tried in vain to convince them to stop. The fight continued until the wounded man suddenly found an opening and drove his sword deep into his opponent's chest, dramatically ending the duel. By the next morning the man who had suffered the chest wound was dead.[13]

Dueling enhanced one's reputation in the West. *Alta California* editor Edward Gilbert, who had faced *Herald* editor John Nugent, got himself into another duel only a few months later.[14] This one had disastrous results for Gilbert. He took a bullet in the stomach and died within minutes. The man who shot him, James W. Denver, a lawyer and Mexican War veteran, went on to an illustrious political career, first as California's secretary of state, then as one of the state's U.S. representatives, and later as the governor of Kansas Territory. The city of Denver, then a part of Kansas Territory, was named in his honor. During the Civil War he served the Union as a general. When following the war he was proposed as a Democratic candidate for president, his 1852 duel with Gilbert became an issue. Out West his affair of honor was simply a part of the frontier culture, but back East the Democratic establishment considered his killing of Gilbert a dangerous liability.[15]

Of California's many duels, the affair of honor between David Broderick and David Terry is the most celebrated. Broderick was a Democrat and a U.S. senator. Terry was a Democrat and the chief justice of the state Supreme Court. Their similarity ended, however, with party affiliation and high political office. Broderick, the son of Irish immigrants to New York, was strongly antislavery. Terry, a southerner from Texas, was strongly proslavery. They got into a political squabble in 1859 that led to Terry's challenging Broderick to a duel. Broderick had already fought one duel and was known to be a crack shot. With a redoubtable reputation himself, Terry had been a Texas Ranger and had fought with distinction in the Mexican War. He also had used a bowie knife to nearly stab to death a member of the San Francisco Committee of Vigilance in 1856.[16]

When Broderick and Terry met at the appointed time and place, San Francisco police chief Martin J. Burke was there to arrest them. However, a judge ruled that since they had not yet commenced dueling when arrested, there were no grounds for prosecution and they were released. By the next morning they had arrived at a new dueling site. Terry won the coin toss—his dueling pistols would be the ones used. They were set with hair triggers. Terry had practiced with them, Broderick had not. The call to fire was given. Broderick's gun went off prematurely, and the ball dug harmlessly into the ground between the two men. A split second later Terry's well-aimed shot drilled Broderick in the chest. He struggled on for three days and died.

The duel was big news, and authorities could not ignore the affair. San Francisco police duly arrested Terry, and prosecutors filed charges. However, Terry got a change of venue to Marin County, and a friendly judge dismissed the case. Terry practiced

This sensationalistic depiction of David S. Terry's stabbing of Sterling A. Hopkins in San Francisco captures the violence that often lurked behind politics in frontier California. Terry, a justice of the state Supreme Court, opposed the Committee of Vigilance that attempted to control San Francisco in 1856; during a scuffle on June 21, he stabbed committee policeman Hopkins with a bowie knife. Three years later, Terry shot and killed political rival David C. Broderick in a famous duel. *California Historical Society, FN-05655.*

law in California for another thirty years, his southern sympathies, hot temper, and high-profile cases keeping him in the public eye. His end came in 1889 when U.S. Supreme Court justice Stephen J. Field, acting as chief justice of the federal Tenth Circuit Court, rendered a decision that left Terry furious. Terry swore vengeance. On a train en route from Los Angeles to San Francisco, Terry happened to stumble upon Field, who was eating breakfast in a dining car. Evidently oblivious to Field's U.S.-appointed bodyguard, Terry struck the chief justice in the face. Reacting immediately, the bodyguard drew a concealed gun and shot Terry twice. The onetime chief justice dropped to the floor of the car, dead.

Many California men did not bother with *code duello;* they just fought. "I'll die before I'll run" was a common sentiment. And die they did. Since most men were armed with a revolver and a knife, disputes could quickly turn deadly. The most popular sidearm during the first years of the Gold Rush was the .44 caliber Colt Dragoon. Then in 1851, the .36 caliber Colt Navy was introduced. Much lighter, better balanced, and more accurate than the Dragoon, it quickly became the favorite of those interested in serious gunfighting. Sam Clemens, who arrived in the mining country a decade later, carried a Colt Navy. He later remarked that he had had no intention of killing anybody with the Navy but had "worn the thing in deference to popular sentiment, and in order that I might not, by its absence, be offensively conspicuous, and a subject of remark."[17]

Some might suspect that Clemens, later famous as Mark Twain, was perhaps engaging in a little western hyperbole. Not so. Hundreds of miners in letters, diaries, and articles described the well-armed state of the citizenry. Stephen J. Field, the chief justice later attacked by David Terry, was elected to the state legislature in 1851. "It was the common practice of those days to go armed," said Field. "Of the thirty-six members of which the Assembly then consisted, over two-thirds never made their appearance without having knives or pistols upon their persons, and frequently both. It was a thing of every-day occurrence for a member, when he entered the House, before taking his seat, to take his pistols and lay them in the drawer of his desk. He did it with as little concern and as much a matter of course, as he took off his hat and hung it up. Nor did such a thing excite surprise or comment."[18]

Several California gunfighters became legendary figures during the 1850s. Sam Brown was one. Standing more than six feet tall, weighing a muscular two hundred pounds, and wearing shoulder-length red hair, the Alabama-born Brown was a sight to behold. He had already killed a man in Texas before joining the Gold Rush. In the Mother Lode country he spent most of his time gambling. In a card game at the mining camp of Agua Fria in 1850 he got into a quarrel with a Texan over a hand. The two went for their guns, and "Longhair Sam" drilled the man in the head for his first kill in California. He got his second in 1853 and his third in 1854. According to legend it was Sam Brown who coined the phrase "I want a man for supper." He did not get in trouble with the law until 1855, when he and a friend got into a fight with a group of Chileans. The two Americans stabbed two of the Chileans to death and wounded a third. With more Chileans joining the fray, the Americans took to their horses. Several of the Chileans pursued, but Brown put a stop to that when he killed one of them with a well-placed shot.[19]

It would seem to have been another case of self-defense—the Chileans had started the fight, and they outnumbered the Americans. Nonetheless, Brown was arrested and tried. The jury evidently thought that the fearsome Brown needed to be reined in, and they convicted him of manslaughter. He subsequently served two years in San Quentin. His release from prison coincided with Peter O'Riley and Patrick McLaughlin's great strike, the Comstock Lode. Brown hurried across the Sierra and renewed his gambling and gun-and-bowie-knife fighting. He killed three more men there before he himself was blown to eternity by a load of buckshot.

Equaling Brown in kills was John Daly. Born in New York to Irish immigrants, Daly came to California as a teenager in the 1850s. The *Aurora Times* later described him as "rather fine looking" and commented that "nature had done enough for him to have entitled him a position of respectability." Daly found his respectability among the gambling and gunfighting set. He enjoyed cards, fine whiskey, and fast women. He rarely spent a night without all three. Unlike many others of the era, he never let himself become inebriated and was always in a condition to engage in the deadliest of all contests, the gunfight. He wielded a Colt Navy with astonishing speed and accuracy. He killed his first man in Sacramento and then added others during trips to the mining camps of the Fraser River country, in British Columbia, and Virginia City, Nevada.[20]

Operating out of Sacramento, Daly became one of California's first "hired guns." Often one mining company's claim would conflict with another's. Instead of an immediate gun battle, which occasionally occurred when the claims were being contested by individuals, the companies would go to court. Large mining companies had the lawyers, the time, and the money for such legal battles. A threat of violence was often employed as well. Gunfighters with fearsome reputations were hired, and paid handsomely, to intimidate witnesses and mining company executives.

The beginning of the end for John Daly came when he was hired by the Pond mining company in Aurora, a mining town of more than five thousand people situated high in the Wassuk Range on the California-Nevada border. The Pond was waging a legal battle with the Real Del Monte mining company over conflicting claims on Last Chance Hill. Daly was well paid because he was effective. Threatened by Daly, a witness for the Real Del Monte sold his interests in mines on Last Chance Hill and departed for the East Coast. The president of Real Del Monte hired a bodyguard and carefully calculated his every move about town, as did the chief company attorney.

In January 1864, when a second trial ended in a hung jury after both companies had spent the equivalent of millions in today's dollars, the Pond and Del Monte settled their differences out of court. Although Daly's services were now no longer needed, he decided to settle one last personal grudge before returning to Sacramento. William Johnson, the operator of a way station near Aurora, had been indirectly responsible for the killing of one of Daly's gang members. Daly decided to square things. He shot and killed an inebriated Johnson as the station operator emerged from a saloon. Aurorans were outraged. Gunfighters killing gunfighters was one thing, but this time an innocent man had been shot down. A vigilance committee was organized almost immediately, and within days the vigilantes had most of the Daly gang in custody. After waiting for a coroner's jury to determine responsibility for Johnson's demise, the vigilantes erected a special gallows and, with great pomp and circumstance, hanged Daly and three of his gang members.

Like John Daly, the Irish-born Billy Mulligan was an enforcer. It would seem that he took on an unlikely role. He stood only five feet, seven inches, and never weighed much more than 140 pounds. However, he had learned to box in New York City and became a noted prizefighter. He was quick, had a powerful punch, and was seemingly indestructible. Tammany Hall made him a ward heeler. He spent much of his time in saloons and gambling dens and occasionally ran afoul of the law. When finally thrown in jail, he escaped, fled to New Orleans, and promptly joined the Louisiana Mounted Volunteers. He fought in several battles and skirmishes during the Mexican War and then headed for California.[21]

Mulligan killed his first man in California in a saloon fight at the mining camp of Sonora during February 1851. During the next year Mulligan fought not only another saloon brawl but also a formal duel. He suffered bullet wounds in each of the fights but rapidly recovered. In San Francisco, Mulligan found many of his old Tammany Hall friends intent on building a political machine similar to the one they had left behind in New York City. Foremost among them was David Broderick, a rising political star. Mulligan was one of the precinct officers who made certain that Democrats turned out and that they voted for Broderick. Broderick rewarded Mulligan by making him tax collector for San Francisco County. Mulligan served faithfully and honestly in that position for two years, but it did not stop him from brawling, once even decking James "Yankee" Sullivan, the former bare-knuckle champion. Mulligan was still an enforcer.

In 1855 Mulligan was made a deputy sheriff and put in charge of the county jail. He discharged his duties at the jail faithfully but was arrested by the San Francisco Committee of Vigilance in May 1856 after helping rig an election in San Mateo County. Mulligan was held in custody for a month and then put on a ship bound for New York. Once back in New York he rejoined Tammany Hall, but a shooting scrape with police in 1860 landed him in prison. By 1863 he was out of prison and back in San Francisco. The next year he fought a duel in Austin, Nevada. Mulligan's end was characteristically violent. Evidently suffering from delirium tremens, he imagined vigilantes were pursuing him and got into a wild gun battle. He killed two men before he himself was shot to death by police.

Be they newspaper editors such as William Walker, John Nugent, and Edward Gilbert, or politicians such as David Broderick and David Terry, or gunmen and enforcers such as Sam Brown, John Daly, and Billy Mulligan, many Californians were fighters. They fought when drunk and when sober. They fought in the middle of the day and in the wee hours of the morning. They fought in formal duels and in wild brawls. They fought unarmed and they fought with knives and guns. Because they were honor-bound and brave to a fault, they fought.

The fighting men of California were willing combatants, but they rarely attacked the innocent. When they did, the citizenry reacted with outrage. Committees of vigilance were often immediately organized following an egregious transgression. They were organized even though institutions of law enforcement and justice had been established in frontier California, because many people believed that those institutions could not be relied upon to arrest, convict, and punish the guilty. For many reasons, arrest was not assured in the wide-open West. Local authorities rarely pursued anyone far from town or beyond the county line. The expense of a long-range pursuit was prohibitive. Once someone had eluded the town marshal or the county sheriff, he was usually gone for good. If captured, all was not lost for the alleged evildoer. Then, as now, a criminal defendant enjoyed the presumption of innocence. It was the job of the prosecutor to prove not only that the defendant was guilty, but guilty beyond a reasonable doubt. Moreover, the prosecutor had to convince all twelve jurors; one dissenter and a mistrial was declared. Because people moved about regularly in frontier California, and the West in general, witnesses to a crime were often long gone by the time a trial was held. Defense attorneys were usually highly competent and, seemingly, they regularly outperformed prosecutors. For all of these reasons, convictions were not easy to obtain. It appeared not to disturb most citizens if a gunman were found not guilty in the shooting death of another gunman, but the citizenry became outraged if the killer of an innocent victim walked free.

To preclude such an outcome, vigilance committees were organized. In California this occurred on more than forty occasions, from such mining camps as Columbia, Grass Valley, Jackson, and Bodie, to such cities as San Francisco, Sacramento, Los Angeles, and Monterey. The committees stated unequivocally, in a phrase that was used repeatedly, that "self-preservation is the first law of nature."[22] The vigilance committees were commonly led by the most prominent residents of a town or a region and enjoyed widespread support. A grand jury report on the vigilance committee of Aurora, notable for hanging John Daly and his accomplices, said that the committee was "composed of over six hundred of our best, most substantial and law-abiding citizens."[23] The names of individual vigilantes who participated in various movements in the West suggested that Aurora's committee of vigilance was typical. William T. Coleman, a wealthy merchant and importer, was president of San Francisco's 1856 vigilance committee. Another member of the committee was Leland Stanford, a successful merchant who would become one of the "Big Four" of railroad fame as well as a governor of California and a U.S. senator.

Typically, vigilantes formed an executive committee and adopted a constitution. They had a chain of command and were often organized into companies and squads. Although impassioned and violent, vigilantes were usually highly disciplined, orderly, and deliberate. This was not accidental. Many of them had military experience, and some were combat veterans, having served in the Mexican War, the Civil War, or one or more of the Indian wars. Officially constituted authorities, realizing that they would have to oppose hundreds of well-organized and well-armed vigilantes, rarely attempted to interfere with such extralegal activities. Moreover, vigilantes generally represented the will of the majority of citizens in any particular community.

Following the murders of U.S. marshal William H. Richardson and journalist James King of William in 1856, San Francisco civic leaders formed a Committee of Vigilance to punish the killers and reform the city government. During its three-month reign, the committee hanged four accused murderers and exiled thirty accused criminals. After a grand parade, captured in this daguerreotype, the committee disbanded, only to regain its power—democratically this time—in elections a few months later as the fiscally conservative People's Party. *Courtesy Collection of The New-York Historical Society.*

The actions of vigilantes should not be confused with those of a lynch mob. Vigilance committees usually gave those suspected of wrongdoing a form of hearing or trial, and not all tried were found guilty and executed. Of the ninety men taken into custody by the San Francisco vigilance committee of 1851, forty-one were exonerated and released, fifteen were remanded to the custody of the regular authorities, one was whipped, and twenty-eight were banished. Only four were executed. Likewise for the San Francisco vigilance committee of 1856, which arrested dozens of men but executed only four. Although a popular theme in motion pictures and novels, it is difficult to cite an instance of an innocent man being hanged at the direction of a vigilance committee.

Although innocent men do not seem to have been hanged by committees of vigilance, vigilantes may occasionally have had ulterior motives for their actions. While most historians have accepted the Committee of Vigilance of 1851 in San Francisco as having been formed solely as a response to rampant crime, Kevin J. Mullen has argued that the vigilantes wanted, first and foremost, an overhaul of the criminal justice system.[24] He demonstrates that while crime did increase prior to the formation of the committee, the vigilantes inflated the number of offenses to further their own ends. Their ends were not nefarious, however, but much needed reforms for a city that had grown from a tiny hamlet in 1848 to a booming metropolis in 1850. The city's established institutions were no longer able to deal effectively with either the numbers of people or the new social fabric. The Committee of Vigilance of 1856 in San Francisco has come under much greater criticism, both by contemporaries and by historians, and has been a topic of debate since its formation. Dominated by Protestants and Masons who supported the American or "Know Nothing" Party, the committee may have been at least partly motivated by a fear of growing Irish Catholic political and economic power in the city. Several historians of San Francisco vigilantism, including Richard Maxwell Brown and Robert M. Senkewicz, think so. On the other hand, nineteenth-century historians John S. Hittell and Hubert Howe Bancroft were effusive in their praise of the vigilantes, arguing that the committee was solely a response to crime and corruption in San Francisco.[25]

The Committee of Vigilance of 1856 was organized following two sensational fatal shootings, that of General William Richardson by gambler Charles Cora and that of James King of William, crusading editor of the *Daily Evening Bulletin*, by politician James P. Casey. The chain of events that led to the shootings began in November 1855 at the opening of the American Theater. General Richardson, serving as a U.S. marshal at the time, and his wife were among those in the audience. Sitting in a box directly behind the general were Cora and his mistress, Arabella Ryan, better known as Belle Cora, the wealthy madam of a notorious brothel. Richardson's wife and several other women complained to the management about the presence of the harlot at the theater. For a time it looked as if something more serious might erupt, but the theater management was able to pacify the various parties and the evening's performance went off as planned.

Two nights later, Richardson, with several drinks in him and still upset about the affair at the theater, found Cora at the Blue Wing, a saloon regularly patronized by San Francisco's politicians. Richardson asked Cora to step outside to discuss matters. After some preliminary banter the discussion turned heated. Suddenly, Cora drew a derringer and shot Richardson. The general collapsed, mortally wounded. Cora claimed that Richardson was about to draw his own derringer, that the general had had his hand in his pocket resting on his own gun. Police were on the scene immediately and arrested Cora. At the *Bulletin*, James King of William practiced a sort of journalistic vigilantism. "If the jury which tries Cora is packed," editorialized King,

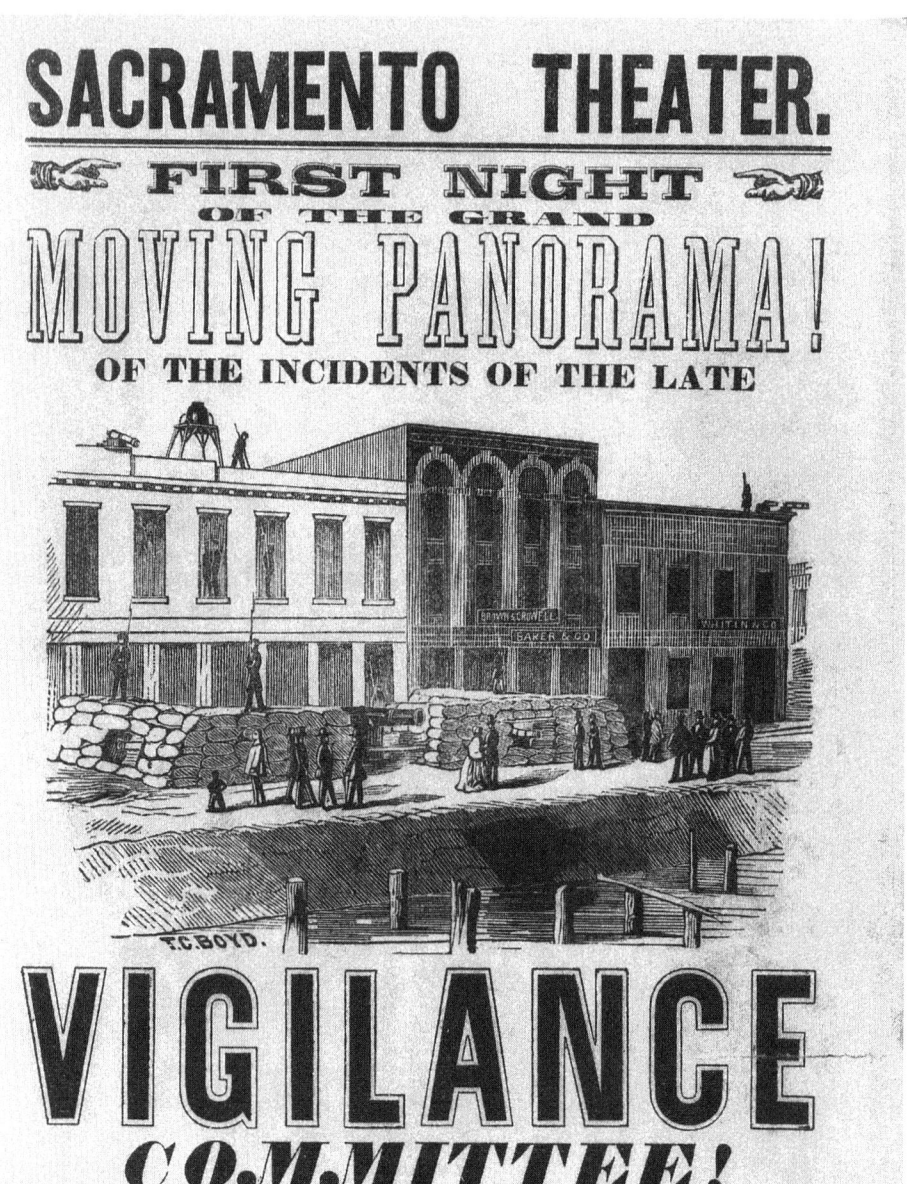

The Committee of Vigilance that controlled San Francisco for three months in 1856 inspired the moving panorama *Vigilance Committee!* shown in Sacramento in November of that year. Eighteen tableaux painted on ten thousand square feet of canvas were unrolled and passed before viewers' eyes, probably accompanied by music and narration. Scenes in *Vigilance Committee!* included "The Shooting of James King of William," "The Execution of Casey and Cora," and "The Stabbing of Hopkins by Judge Terry." A precursor to films, moving panoramas traveled from community to community in the mid-nineteenth century; unfortunately, fewer than twenty survive today. *Courtesy City of Sacramento, History and Science Division, Sacramento Archives and Museum Collection Center, Eleanor McClatchy Collection.*

"either *hang the sheriff* or drive him out of town and make him resign. If Billy Mulligan lets his friend Cora escape, *hang Billy Mulligan* or drive him into banishment." When Cora's trial ended in a hung jury in January 1856, King exclaimed: "Rejoice ye gamblers and harlots! rejoice with exceeding gladness! Assemble in your dens of infamy tonight and let the costly wine flow freely, and let the welkin ring with your shouts of joy!"

While Cora was in jail awaiting a second trial, another controversy arose. King fired a broadside at James Casey, who had won a seat on the county board of supervisors in an election widely denounced as corrupt. It may have been. Casey was a part of David Broderick's political machine, and he had a background in ballot-box stuffing for Tammany Hall. He was a rough character who could fight with his fists or with guns. At one point he had served time in New York's Sing Sing prison. In San Francisco he was involved in a bloody brawl at a political meeting in 1854. In California an attack on a man's current activities was one thing, and it might bring a challenge to duel, but dredging up a man's past was considered unseemly and might bring a violent response. On the afternoon of May 14 the *Bulletin* containing King's attack appeared on the streets of San Francisco. Minutes later Casey stormed into the newspaper's office and confronted King. Somehow King and others managed to convince Casey to leave the premises. However, an hour later, Casey found King on the street and shot him to death. Casey was quickly arrested and lodged in jail.

That evening, former members of the 1851 vigilance committee revived the organization and elected William Tell Coleman president. Most downtown merchants immediately joined the committee, which hastily set about collecting arms and forming a military unit. Unlike 1851, there was important opposition this time. The *Herald*, San Francisco's largest newspaper in 1856, opposed the formation of the new committee, as did San Francisco mayor James Van Ness, San Francisco county sheriff David Scannell, General William Tecumseh Sherman, who commanded the San Francisco district of the California militia, and future senator David Broderick, who led the formation of the "Law and Order" group of citizens. Their opposition had little effect. On May 16, some twenty-five hundred vigilantes descended on the lockup and took control of the killers. Legally constituted authorities, facing a virtual army, made no effort to resist. Cora and Casey were each afforded a trial before a vigilante tribunal. They were both found guilty and sentenced to death. On May 22, amid great public ceremony, the two men were hanged.

The Law and Order group now hoped that the vigilance committee, having hanged the killers, would disband. Instead the committee took more men into custody and fortified its headquarters building, nicknamed Fort Gunnybags. The committee even arrested Supreme Court justice David Terry after Terry had fought with and stabbed a vigilante. Terry was tried and convicted for the assault by the vigilante

Sarah Althea Hill, photographed here ca. 1880, stood at the center of two of the most sensational legal cases in late-nineteenth-century California. In 1883 she sued the estate of her lover, former U.S. senator William Sharon, for financial support, claiming that the two had been legally wed. During the trial, Hill married her attorney, David S. Terry, famous for killing U.S. senator David Broderick in a duel in 1859. Hill lost her case. A few years later she and Terry accidentally met the trial judge during a train stop near Stockton. History repeated itself when David Terry threatened the judge, whose bodyguard shot and killed Terry. The subsequent trial of the bodyguard, a U.S. marshal named David Neagle, eventually reached the U.S. Supreme Court, which exonerated him in a groundbreaking decision that expanded the powers of the federal government. Hill spent the last forty-five years of her life in a state asylum. *Courtesy Bancroft Library.*

tribunal but was released after a bitter debate among the vigilante leaders. The vigilantes went on to hang two other killers and to banish thirty miscreants for various crimes. They finally disbanded on August 18 following a great parade of six thousand armed men.

The editor of the *San Francisco Herald*, John Nugent, and later California historian Josiah Royce, called the work of the vigilantes in 1856 a "Business Man's Revolution." In the elections of November 1856 the leaders of the vigilantes, organized as the People's Party, drew up a slate of candidates that swept every city office. Under the new party, the cost of city and county government in San Francisco was dramatically reduced for a time. The People's Party remained in power for more than a decade.

While murder sometimes brought a death penalty at the hands of vigilantes, lesser crimes usually got the culprit sentenced to jail. Incarceration was costly, however, and fell to county officials, who soon began pressuring the state to build a prison for those sentenced to terms of more than six months. In 1851 the state legislature created a private system of incarceration. Prisoners would be leased to a private contractor who agreed to feed, clothe, and house them in return for using them as convict labor. The first lease, for a ten-year period, was awarded to James Madison Estell, a Democratic politician who would shortly become a state senator, and his partner, Mariano Guadalupe Vallejo, the wealthy ranchero of Sonoma Valley. Late in 1851 Vallejo left the partnership, and Estell became the sole lessee.[26]

Estell quartered his first prisoners, some three dozen, on the brig *Waban*, moored off Angel Island in San Francisco Bay. He put them to work during the day in a rock quarry on the island. Within a year he had more than a hundred prisoners crammed aboard the *Waban*. Living conditions for the prisoners had been poor; now they were miserable. Escapes were frequent. Residents of surrounding areas complained; Estell himself complained. He reminded state legislators that when he had signed the lease, they had promised him they would build a prison. Responding to both citizen complaints and Estell's pleas, the state legislature appointed three commissioners to search for an appropriate prison site. The commissioners thought that any of the islands in San Francisco Bay would be ideal but found that the titles to the islands were clouded. As a result, they settled on Point San Quentin, on the Marin County mainland, and purchased twenty acres there.

Two attempts were necessary before the prison could actually be built. The original plans for a costly, capacious prison with separate quarters for women were scrapped after it was revealed that the contractor who had won the bid had done so by bribing state legislators. A much smaller, less elaborate, and less costly structure, nicknamed "the Stones," was erected by none other than James Estell, the lessee. The two-story structure had forty-eight cells on the upper floor in two rows back-to-

Prisoners enter the gate of San Quentin State Prison sometime in the late nineteenth century. Founded in Marin County in 1852, San Quentin was a privately operated penal institution until joining the state prison system in 1860. California's oldest and largest prison, San Quentin houses all of the state's death row inmates. *Courtesy Bancroft Library.*

back. The cells were designed to hold two men each, but within a year they were crammed with four.

Overcrowding again led to problems, including escapes. Particularly upset by the escapes were Marin County residents. The Marin County grand jury demanded an annulment of Estell's contract. Escaping was not that difficult, especially for trustee prisoners. Estell granted a number of privileges to trustees, many of whom were housed outside the prison walls. With little or no supervision, trustees ran errands and performed special jobs for Estell. A few even worked as servants in Estell's San Francisco home. Several were allowed to work as laborers in San Rafael. Some simply walked away from the prison and never returned. Thomas McFarland Foley was one of them. Estell thought that Foley should never have been imprisoned for killing John H. Dunn, the editor of the *Pacific Police Gazette*. Estell considered Foley an upstanding and respectable gentleman who would soon receive a pardon from the governor. Two weeks after Foley arrived at the prison, Estell issued him a gun and allowed him to serve as a guard. He performed admirably in the role until he grew tired of waiting for his pardon and left for parts unknown. Ever the gentleman, Foley left behind a note thanking Estell for a $500 loan and promising that he would repay it in full. Sure enough, $500 was found missing from the prison safe.

As a result of the escapes and other problems at the prison, including drinking and guards having sex with female inmates, the state decided to buy out Estell's lease and take control. Estell was not averse to the idea. He was troubled by the many escapes and was not making the profit he had expected. When the state met his price, he relinquished control gladly. The state legislature then created a three-man board of prison directors. One of the directors would serve as president of the board, one as warden of the prison, and one as clerk. The director with the most ironic name became the first warden—John Love. Tough love it was. A large wall was erected around the Stones, and guards were issued orders to shoot to kill any prisoner attempting to escape or incite a riot.

The directors succeeded in reducing the number of prison escapes by two-thirds but found costs escalating dramatically. A year later, the operation of the prison was returned to Estell. However, Estell was soon accused of involvement in the killing of James King of William, the editor of San Francisco's *Daily Evening Bulletin* who had been shot to death by James Casey. The *Bulletin* subsequently launched other attacks against Estell for his poor operation of the prison. The board of prison directors tried to find a lessee to replace him, but there were no takers. Finally, in 1857, the directors agreed to allow Estell to sublease the last four years of his contract to two businessmen, Lloyd Tevis and John F. McCauley.

Under the new management, conditions at the prison worsened. A report to the state legislature in 1858 said that an inspecting committee found the prisoners ill fed and poorly clothed and living in filthy, overcrowded conditions. Moreover, the report said that first-time teenage offenders were quartered with hardened middle-aged convicts, making reformation of the youths impossible. The state took action quickly, claiming that by failing to provide properly for the prisoners, Tevis and McCauley had violated their contract. In March 1858 the state took control of the prison for a second time. Several reforms were instituted, including the segregation of prisoners according to their age and crimes. Sanitation was greatly improved and construction of new facilities was begun. By the end of May, journalists from Bay Area newspapers were reporting that conditions at the prison were much better.

Meanwhile, Tevis and McCauley sued the state for the unilateral and unlawful revocation of their lease and temporarily regained control of the prison during 1859. In July 1860 the state Supreme Court ruled in the plaintiffs' favor and awarded them $275,000, although operation of the prison was returned to the state. The state continued a policy of reform: limiting convict labor outside prison walls; clothing all prisoners in uniforms; housing women in newly constructed quarters instead of in guards' houses; and building additional cell blocks, a hospital, a church, and a library.

Despite the improvements, San Quentin, as the prison came to be called, was not a model of humane incarceration. Punishments for unruly prisoners included floggings with leather straps, beatings with rubber truncheons, hosings of naked prisoners with high-pressure jets of water, and stretchings by tying a prisoner's arms behind his back and lifting him onto a hook, where he would remain suspended until he passed out. Moreover, teenage offenders were still sent to San Quentin, where they faced homosexual rape. Not until 1877 were the boys and men strictly segregated. In 1880 floggings and beatings were prohibited; the water torture and stretchings ended in 1882. Punishment from then on usually consisted of a diet restricted to bread and water and solitary confinement in a dark cell. One prison physician believed such confinement to be worse than the beatings.

During the 1850s and 1860s very few men were confined in San Quentin for murder. Convicted murderers, as a rule, were executed, either by vigilantes or legally constituted authorities, and never reached the state prison. Most of those incarcerated at San Quentin had been convicted of grand larceny. Assault with intent to kill, burglary, and manslaughter were a very far distant second-, third-, and fourth-ranked causes of imprisonment.

Frontier California was certainly wild and woolly, and men fought and killed each other at extraordinarily high rates. For example, Nevada County, in the Mother Lode country, and the mining town of Bodie, on the eastern side of the Sierra, had homicide rates many times higher than the rates for contemporary eastern counties or cities. On the other hand, rates of robbery, theft, and burglary in frontier California were not greatly, if at all, higher than those found in the East and were substantially lower than those found in the United States today.[27]

Bodie might be considered representative of California's mining camps. In its heyday in the late 1870s and early 1880s it boasted a population of more than five thousand. It was alive twenty-four hours a day, sported dozens of saloons, brothels, and gambling dens, and produced gold and silver bullion worth hundreds of millions in today's dollars. Its economy was boom and bust, as new veins were discovered and old ones pinched out. Its population was transient, half were foreign-born, and men outnumbered women ten to one. The people were adventurous, enterprising, brave, young, unmarried, intemperate, and armed. A few had struck it rich, but most had not. The ingredients were there, it would seem, for a crime epidemic. Nothing of the sort occurred.

Only rarely was a resident of Bodie robbed. During its boom years, a five-year stretch from 1878 through 1882, only ten individuals were robbed, an average of only two people falling victim to a robbery per year. The stagecoach was robbed more often, suffering eleven holdups. When highwaymen stopped the stage, they nearly always took only the express box and left the passengers untouched. Passengers frequently remarked that they had been treated with the utmost courtesy by the road agents. Only twice were passengers robbed. In the first instance the highwaymen later apologized for their conduct, and in the second the holdup artists were drunk. Highwaymen understood that they could take the express box without arousing the citizenry, but if they insulted or robbed passengers they would precipitate a vigilante reaction.

In Bodie, if passengers were not the targets of highwaymen, neither were stagecoaches carrying large bullion shipments. With shipments worth millions in today's dollars, they would seem inviting targets. Yet not one stage with such a shipment was ever attacked. Unlike the regular stages, the bullion coaches were guarded by two, and occasionally three or four, rifle- and shotgun-wielding marksmen. Road agents preferred to prey on the unguarded coaches, taking whatever was in the express box, and escaping with their health intact. Only once did highwaymen and guards exchange gunfire, and on that occasion the road agents had not expected to encounter any guards. The miscalculation cost one of the highwaymen his life. For similar reasons neither of the two banks that operated in Bodie ever experienced a robbery. Bankers went about armed, as did their employees, and robbers evidently had no desire to tangle with armed men.

Robberies of individual citizens followed a clear pattern: the victim had spent the evening in a gambling den, saloon, or brothel; he had revealed in some manner that he had a goodly sum of money on his person; and he was drunk, staggering home late at night when the attack occurred. More robberies might have occurred had not Bodieites gone about armed and ready to defend themselves. Unless thoroughly inebriated, they were simply too dangerous to rob. The attempted robbery of miner C. F. Reid is but one example. When a robber told Reid to throw up his hands, Reid said "All right" and began raising them. As he did so, he suddenly drew a foot-long bowie knife and drove the steel blade into the robber's shoulder. The robber recoiled in pain and took off running "like a deer." Reid gave chase but soon lost sight of the inspired runner. Reid felt satisfied, though, commenting later that he "cut the man to the bone."

Such actions were applauded by the populace and the local newspapers. Unlike a stage holdup, the robbery of an individual citizen was considered dastardly and provoked talk of vigilantism. "This business of garroting," as the *Bodie Standard* termed mugging and robbery, "is getting a little too common. The parties engaged in it may wake up one of these fine mornings and find themselves hanging to the top of a liberty pole." The *Daily Free Press* later called for the formation of a committee of vigilance, saying that one or two examples of vigilante justice were usually "sufficient to purify" a mining camp.

Despite such talk, Bodie actually suffered rarely from robbery. A statistical comparison of the rowdy mining camp with modern American cities demonstrates that today's cities, such as Detroit, New York, and Miami, have twenty times as much robbery per capita. The United States as a whole averages three times as much robbery per capita as did Bodie. A comparison of robbery in Bodie directly with robbery in eastern towns during the nineteenth century suggests that Bodie had rates below those in major cities such as New York and Philadelphia and comparable to those found in Boston. Burglary and theft were also infrequent in Bodie. Most American cities today average thirty or forty times as much burglary and theft per capita as Bodie. The national rate today is ten times higher. Eastern cities in the nineteenth century had rates several times higher. Again, an obvious factor in discouraging burglary and theft was the armed homeowner and armed merchant.

Women, often the target of criminals today, suffered only rarely from violence in Bodie. Prostitutes bore the brunt of the little violence that did occur. Most incidents involved a drunken brothel patron slapping or punching one of the women. Even in such assaults, women often evened the odds by grabbing a gun. One prostitute frightened off an attacker with a shot from her revolver, which sent the man running for his life. Another prostitute chased a customer out of a brothel and emptied her revolver at him. His "hair stood on end," reported the *Bodie Standard*, "as he expected any second to be reduced to a state of perfect inutility." Prostitutes were not the only women in Bodie to use guns in the defense of person or property. When a dispute arose between a man and a woman over the ownership of a city lot, the woman, believing herself the rightful owner, ordered the man off the property. However, as the *Bodie Standard* noted, since "he was a large man and she was a small lady, he concluded to tarry yet a while." It proved to be a very short while. The small lady pulled out a six-shooter, took dead aim at the man, and again ordered him to leave. Now, with an inspired sense of urgency, he did just that.

This letter sheet from the early 1850s satirized the lawlessness of gold-rush California as well as the relentlessness of its entrepreneurs, who in this case hawked "every description of flagellator at reasonable cost." *Courtesy California State Library.*

There were no reported cases of rape in Bodie. Nonetheless, rape might have occurred but gone unreported, as even today victims are sometimes reluctant to report an attack. However, Bodie reported two cases of attempted rape, a possible indication that had rape occurred it would have been reported. Moreover, there is no evidence of any sort that rape occurred that escaped the attention of the authorities. Absolutely no suggestion of it surfaces in any letters, diaries, newspapers, or public records from the period. A large body of evidence indicates that Bodie women—excluding prostitutes—experienced almost no crime of any sort and were treated with the utmost respect. Women enjoyed an elevated status in frontier California, and the Old West in general, partly because of nineteenth-century Victorian morality and partly because they were a rarity on the frontier, especially in mining camps. In Bodie, men were fined and jailed merely for swearing in the presence of women.

Anyone insulting a woman—again, excluding prostitutes—risked being shot. As a former resident of Bodie recalled, "One of the remarkable things about Bodie, in fact, one of the striking features of all mining camps in the West, was the respect shown even by the worst characters to the decent women.... I do not recall ever hearing of a respectable woman or girl in any manner insulted or even accosted by the hundreds of dissolute characters that were everywhere. In part, this was due to the respect that depravity pays to decency; in part, to the knowledge that sudden death would follow any other course." Woman after woman described the respect she was shown on the frontier. One of the most famous was Nellie Cashman, an Irish immigrant who came to California following the Civil War and spent time in nearly every mining camp from Mexico to Alaska in a career that spanned sixty years. Shortly before she died, a reporter asked her if she had ever feared for her virtue while trekking from one strike to another and living in nearly all-male mining camps. "Bless your soul, no!" replied Nellie. "I never have had a word said to me out of the way. The 'boys' would sure see to it that anyone who ever offered to insult me could never be able to repeat the offense."

With armed citizens populating the mining camps, when men did fight, their confrontations, because they were armed, were often more deadly. During Bodie's five-year heyday there were thirty-one homicides. That gave Bodie a homicide rate dramatically higher than rates found in the East during the same years and double or triple the rates for most U.S. cities today. Nonetheless, from the late 1980s through the mid-1990s certain sections of some cities and a few cities themselves approached Bodie's high homicide rate, such as Los Angeles, Compton (directly south of L.A.), Detroit, Washington, D.C., New Orleans, and East St. Louis.

There are substantial differences in the homicides between then and now, however. In Bodie nearly all of those killed were willing combatants. Some were professional gunmen, but most were miners, teamsters, bartenders, carpenters, gamblers, and the like. They were usually young and single, and always brave. They scrupulously observed a code of conduct that put honor above physical well-being. These ingredients, often laced with alcohol, led to fights over who was the better man, real or imagined insults, and challenges to the pecking order in the saloon. When a willing combatant was killed in a gunfight, Bodieites considered it justifiable homicide—two men had chosen to fight, and if one died, so be it.

Minorities were not a particular target of violence in Bodie. There were very few of them to begin with, and the violence they suffered was mostly from others in their own racial group. Chinese were the only substantial nonwhite portion of the population. This was true throughout California during the second half of the nineteenth century. Census data reveals that Bodie was about 92 percent white. Chinese accounted for about 6.5 percent of the population. Blacks constituted only 0.3 percent—only eighteen souls in Bodie's population of some fifty-four hundred. Census data for California is similar—blacks accounted for 1 percent or less of the population in the 1860, 1870, and 1880 census reports, while Chinese averaged about 9 percent. Persons with Spanish surnames constituted about 1.9 percent of the population in Bodie. Some of them had been born in California, but most had come from Mexico. Categorizing them as white or nonwhite is difficult, because many of them were both, designated in Mexico as mestizo—a combination white and Indian.

In Bodie, no organized violence was ever reported as having been directed at either the Chinese or Mexicans, the only two minority groups with any significant numbers. They certainly would not have been hapless victims. Many of them were armed with guns and knives too, and were not averse to using them. Almost all their fights were with members of their own groups. With the Chinese this occasionally meant clashes between rival tongs for control of Chinatown's gambling halls, brothels, and opium dens. One such battle erupted in gunfire on a warm summer evening in Bodie's Chinatown and continued for more than an hour before police could separate the warring factions. Hundreds of rounds were fired during the battle, and at least one Chinese was killed, several others seriously wounded. Witnesses said that another three or four Chinese had been killed, but their bodies had been carried away before police arrived. Some thirty Chinese were arrested, and eight were charged with murder. However, one by one the charges were dropped for lack of evidence. It proved impossible to get any Chinese to testify. They preferred to take care of things among themselves.

An atypical Chinese who became notorious outside of Bodie's Chinatown was Sam Chung. A member of the Yung Wah tong, he spoke fluent English and had forsaken the traditional Chinese queue and dress for an American haircut and western clothes. Because of his bilingual fluency, he often acted as an interpreter for justice and superior courts in cases involving Chinese. Chung was also Chinatown's leading businessman, owning a two-story building that contained a lodging house, restaurant, and laundry. It was this building that first brought Chung notoriety. Late one night a fire erupted in the building, which within minutes was engulfed in flames. Volunteer firemen rushed to the scene, but they could do nothing more than save neighboring buildings. It was thought that a defective stovepipe in the roof of the kitchen had caused the conflagration.

All was not lost for Chung. He had insured the building for fire and collected the handsome sum of $5,000. Meanwhile, the insurance company quietly began an investigation. Within a few months Chung and two accomplices were arrested for setting the fire. The county district attorney, relying on information provided by the Board of Underwriters of San Francisco, told Bodie newspapers that he had "evidence which will undoubtedly convict all of them." Chung, however, retained one of Bodie's most respected and successful attorneys, John McQuaid, and within weeks the arson charges were dropped.

Chung made news again when he shot and badly wounded Ah Goon and Sam Wang, an opium den proprietor. Chung disappeared before police arrived but was later identified as the shooter and arrested. He was charged with assault with intent to commit murder, remanded by the justice court to the custody of the sheriff, and unable or unwilling to post a bond of $3,000, was taken to the county jail at Bridgeport. A month later he was indicted by the Mono County grand jury. John McQuaid, again serving as Chung's lawyer, again got the charges dismissed, and Chung was released.

Chung was soon back at work, which now included vegetable farming a tract behind his cabin on Rough Creek. Early one morning Prudencia Encinos, "a well known and much respected Mexican," in the words of the *Bodie Chronicle*, was driving his wood-laden mules past Chung's cabin when the mules strayed into Chung's vegetable fields. Angrily, Chung grabbed a double-barreled shotgun and sent a load of buckshot into Encinos. The Mexican was rushed to a doctor, but he died that night. Chung was arrested and lodged in the Bodie jail. When rumor spread that a group of Encinos's friends were planning to take him, town marshal John Kirgan shackled Chung to a deputy and, under the cover of darkness, sent the pair to the county jail at Bridgeport. And none too soon. A party of a dozen masked Mexicans arrived at the jail. Brandishing six-shooters, four of them rushed into the jail's office and demanded that Marshal Kirgan hand over Sam Chung. Kirgan told them that Chung had been taken to a secret location in the mountains and was heavily guarded. The Mexicans ordered the doors to the cells opened and did not leave until they had identified each prisoner.

Safe in the jail at Bridgeport, Sam Chung this time retained Patrick Reddy as his lawyer. The tall, handsome Reddy had never lost a case in Bodie and would soon become one of San Francisco's most famous and distinguished attorneys. Before he turned to law he had been a wild, hard-drinking miner who never backed down and fought equally well with fists or guns. He turned that natural aggression, passion, and courage to law after he was bushwhacked and lost an arm. He prepared his briefs carefully and thoroughly, had near-total recall, and captivated judge and jury with a commanding voice and beautiful diction. If one were facing the death penalty, it was wise to retain Reddy.

Indicted for murder by the grand jury, Chung was brought to trial in superior court. His chances for acquittal appeared hopeless. "There is no doubt in the mind of any person at all familiar with the circumstances of the killing," said the *Bodie Standard*, "that Sam Chung committed an unprovoked, cold-blooded and barbarous murder." Yet, in a brilliant forensic display Patrick Reddy put doubt in the minds of at least a few of the jurors. The trial ended in a hung jury.

The prosecution moved to have Chung retried, but through deft maneuvers Reddy was able to have the new trial delayed nearly a year. The delay, a particularly useful tactic in the Old West, proved beneficial as usual. In the intervening time one key prosecution witness died and another left California. In the second trial the jury deadlocked, six to six. The prosecution, now thinking that it would be impossible to win a conviction, asked the court to dismiss the murder charge against Chung. The motion was denied, and two months later Chung went to trial for a third time. Patrick Reddy was his usual brilliant self, and the jury returned a unanimous verdict of not guilty. "It is hardly necessary to state," said the *Bodie Standard*, "that in this Chinaman's case justice has not been done, neither has public sentiment been satisfied. But this is nothing new in Mono County, and now it only remains for Chung to settle down, behave himself and become a good American."

If Sam Chung was Bodie Chinatown's most notorious badman, then Black Bart was California's most notorious and most romantic outlaw. Born on a farm in upstate New York in 1830 to immigrant English parents, Charles Boles, as he was known then, grew up quietly with his older brother, David. The Boles boys joined the rush to California in '49 but did not reach the gold fields until 1850. David died in 1852, but Charles continued prospecting until 1854, when he left for New York. He got as far as Decatur, Illinois, where he married and settled down to raise a family. Life was uneventful until the Civil War erupted and Charles Boles found a real calling. He enlisted in the Union Army and served with distinction, fighting at Vicksburg, Chattanooga, Kennesaw Mountain, and Atlanta. He was severely wounded in one battle but recovered and returned to his unit. He rose from private to first sergeant and then, just before the war ended, was commissioned a second lieutenant. His unit was deactivated immediately, and he never had the opportunity to actually serve as an officer.[28]

Boles returned to his wife and daughters in Illinois, but a quiet life would never again satisfy him. He was soon off for the mining camps of Montana and Idaho, writing his wife every few months saying he would be home presently. His wife, Mary, was overjoyed when a letter arrived, always fearing for her husband's safety in the Wild West. She received what proved to be her last letter from him in 1871. He was in Silver Bow, Montana, and again said that he would be on his way home soon. For unknown reasons he stopped writing but did not stop moving about, first to Utah and then, in 1874, to California. Meanwhile, his wife was frantic. She sold the family home to raise money to search for her missing husband and moved in with relatives. She and her daughters eked out a living by sewing.

Instead of prospecting in California, Boles taught school. Then on a hot July day in 1875, he committed his first robbery, of a stagecoach with a Wells Fargo express box aboard, which was working its way up a steep grade between Sonora and Copperopolis in the Sierra foothills. Twenty-eight more stagecoach holdups would follow, making Boles the most prolific highwayman in U.S. history. His holdups all followed a similar pattern. Always working alone, he was well disguised by a hood and long duster and impossible to identify, although his deep and resonant voice was distinctive. He kept a polite demeanor. He wielded a double-barreled shotgun. He took only the contents of the Wells Fargo express box and left the passengers unmolested. He disappeared into the brush and escaped on foot. Also, beginning with his second stagecoach robbery, he left behind scraps of paper with rhyme. The first one said:

> I've labored long and hard for bred
> For honor and for riches
> But on my corns too long you've tred
> You fine haired Sons of Bitches
> —Black Bart, the Po8

"Black Bart," the gentlemanly poet bandit, immediately caught the public's fancy. Wells Fargo was not nearly so enamored with him. Following his first robbery, the express company put James B. Hume on the case. Jim Hume was California's first famous detective, and deservedly so. However, this Black Bart character had him stumped. First of all, he had no idea of Black Bart's real identity. Slowly and methodically Hume began to assemble evidence until he had a good understanding of Black Bart's modus operandi. He also developed a profile for Black Bart. Although Black Bart usually wore socks over his boots to confuse trackers, Hume determined from footprints that the highwayman wore a size eight boot. From that he assumed that Black Bart was of medium height. Because Black Bart could cover thirty miles or more a day on foot through rugged country, Hume knew he must be lean and extraordinarily fit. From the road agent's conversations with various drivers and passengers, it was also clear that he spoke with authority and was articulate, well mannered, and educated. The poetry also suggested some education. Finally, there was the voice—deep, resonant, and well modulated. Hume concluded that the voice was not that of a young man but of someone at least in his thirties or forties. Witnesses eventually began to confirm Hume's deductions. Over months and years, Hume painstakingly put together the descriptions until a clear picture emerged: the stranger was middle aged but taut and muscular with a military bearing. He was of medium height. He was handsome, with blue-gray eyes and gray hair. He had a very deep, resonant voice.

Jim Hume surmised that Black Bart was not the type to hole up in a mountain cabin for long periods between holdups. He thought that the highwayman probably sought refuge in the city. Hume was right again. Black Bart loved San Francisco, its culture and amenities. When in the city, which was most of the time, he dressed elegantly, wearing a derby hat, a silk cravat with diamond stickpin, a tailored tweed suit, and a velvet-collared overcoat. He looked and sounded like a prosperous businessman. He said that he had investments in several mines and speculated in mining stock. No one doubted him.

As Black Bart's stage robberies continued, the price on his head increased. Wells Fargo offered a $300 reward, the state of California another $300, the U.S. government $200. His luck nearly ran out on his twenty-third holdup when a guard's bullet creased his scalp. Finally Lady Luck did desert him, on his twenty-ninth robbery. On a Sunday morning in early November 1883, Black Bart robbed his last stagecoach. The holdup took place just outside Copperopolis at almost the same spot where he had begun his career as a highwayman eight years earlier. After stopping the stage and taking gold coins and gold dust from the express box, Black Bart was surprised when a teenage boy, who was some distance away, opened fire with a rifle. Black Bart leaped for the brush on the side of the road and quickly disappeared. But he left several articles behind in his hasty departure, including a handkerchief with a badly faded laundry mark on it that read "F.X.O.7."

Hume gave the handkerchief to a detective he had hired six months earlier to do nothing but work on the Black Bart case. The detective was Harry Morse, a former sheriff of Alameda County, who was beginning to develop his own private detective agency. Since Hume reckoned that Black Bart lived in San Francisco between stagecoach robberies, he told Morse to start there. All Morse had to do was identify the laundry with the mark on the handkerchief. This was not a simple task—there were more than ninety laundries in the city. Morse hit the streets, visiting laundry after laundry, hour by hour, day by day. On the eighth day, he walked into Ferguson & Bigg's California Laundry. The proprietor recognized the mark and said that such laundry must have gone through one of their outlets, a tobacco shop on Post Street.

Morse hurried to the tobacco shop and had the owner check his records for the mark. The owner identified it as that of Charles Bolton, a wealthy mining man. Under the guise of a business proposition, Morse got himself introduced to Bolton. Bolton looked every inch the wealthy mining man he purported to be. He was dressed in an expensive wool suit and bowler hat. He carried a walking stick, wore a diamond ring, and had a heavy gold watch suspended from a gold chain in a vest pocket. He stood five feet, eight inches, and was ramrod straight. He was solidly built, with gray hair and mustache and deep-set blue eyes. "One would have taken him for a gentleman who had made a fortune and was enjoying it," said Morse. "He looked anything but a robber."

For some time after he was apprehended, Bolton denied that he was Black Bart, even after the driver of the last stage that he had robbed identified him, not by sight but by sound—his distinctive deep voice. More and more evidence was presented to Bolton. He finally accepted his fate and confessed, not only to his last robbery but to all of them. His life as Black Bart poured out of him—stage holdup by stage holdup, getaway by getaway, life in San Francisco. A deal was struck, and he pled guilty to his last holdup. He was sentenced to six years in San Quentin and served four before he was released in 1888. When a reporter then asked him if he intended to resume his career as a highwayman, he answered with a vehement, "No!" Another reporter asked if he might write more poetry, and he replied, "Young man, didn't you hear me say I would commit no more crimes?"

Black Bart, or Charles Boles, returned to San Francisco. He refused an offer to appear on stage in a theatrical production and seemed interested only in living as quietly as possible. Jim Hume had his men tail Boles daily, but suddenly he disappeared. A few days later Hume received a report that Boles was in Modesto, then Merced, then Visalia. In Visalia Boles left a pair of shirt cuffs behind in his hotel room after checking out. On the shirt cuffs was the laundry mark F.X.O.7. He was never seen again.

His long pursuit of Black Bart had helped make Jim Hume a household name. He was arguably the greatest of the many lawmen who served as county sheriffs, town marshals, or policemen in the decades after 1850. He had arrived in the Golden State from an Indiana farm in 1850 and prospected throughout the Mother Lode country for a dozen years before he was appointed city marshal of Placerville, the El Dorado County seat. In 1864 he became the undersheriff of El Dorado County and fought his first gun battle when he and his deputies attempted to capture the Ike McCollum gang. He solved several important criminal cases and helped to make criminal investigation a science, while earning a reputation for honesty, intelligence, and perseverance. In 1873 Wells Fargo made him chief of their detectives. Although he was forty-six years old at the time, he would serve the company for thirty years. He was known as a square shooter by both lawmen and outlaws. Several outlaws looked upon Hume not as an enemy but as an adversary. Hume often humorously noted that nowhere was his personal standing higher than among the residents of San Quentin.

Second only to Jim Hume among early California lawmen was another man

In this 1890 photograph, members of the Los Angeles Police Department drill team display their department's first uniforms, which their predecessors had adopted in the late 1860s. Informally organized during the Gold Rush, California police officers and firefighters became increasingly professionalized in the 1860s. *California Historical Society Collection at the University of Southern California: Title Insurance and Trust Photo Collection.*

whom the pursuit of Black Bart helped make famous, Harry Morse. Morse was reared in New York City and went to sea as a cabin boy in 1845, when he was only ten years old. He arrived in California in '49 and prospected for a time before turning his energies to various business ventures. He found his true calling in 1864, when he became sheriff of Alameda County. He tamed numerous gangs of bandidos who operated in the East Bay and in the coastal ranges and shot to death in gun battles the notorious bandidos Narato Ponce and Juan Soto. He retired from office in 1878 and formed his own detective agency. By 1888 he had sixty men in his employ, both plainclothes detectives and uniformed private police.

Operating out of San Francisco, the Morse Detective Agency could not help but develop a rivalry with the San Francisco Police Department. Morse's counterpart in the SFPD was Isaiah Lees, who served as captain of detectives from 1856 until 1897, when he became chief of police. Lees was one of the seminal figures in urban policing, not only in California but also in the United States. Although there was no love lost between Morse and Lees, they nevertheless cooperated on a number of cases. Morse remained actively involved in his detective agency until the early 1900s, when rheumatism slowed him down and eventually forced him to retire.

Thomas Cunningham, another county sheriff involved in the pursuit of Black Bart, became one of California's legendary lawmen. Born in Ireland in 1838, Cunningham immigrated to New York as a boy of ten in 1848 and then to California in 1855. By 1860 he had his own harness-making shop in Stockton and was serving as a volunteer fireman. In 1865 he was made chief of the fire department and, in the same year, was elected to the city council. Six years later he was elected, for the first of many times, sheriff of San Joaquin County. For the next three decades he was a terror to the outlaws who roamed the San Joaquin Valley and the foothills of the Sierra Nevada. He led manhunts for several of California's most notorious outlaws, including Tiburcio Vasquez, Black Bart, and Bill Miner, the "Grey Fox."[29]

Unlike many lawmen of the era, Cunningham did everything he could to avoid bloodshed. It often meant taking great personal risks and required nerves of steel. He made numerous arrests of desperate men but never had to take a life. On one occasion he shot a horse from underneath an outlaw and then handcuffed the man before he was able to recover from the fall and go for his gun. On another occasion he rode alone into the midst of a hundred armed and angry men to peacefully settle a land dispute between the men and the railroad. When nearly sixty years old, he and three of his deputies trailed two train robbers for twelve days on horseback and then chased them on foot through a marsh alongside a river. At that point Cunningham could have opened fire. Instead he and his deputies closed in on the fugitives, and a deputy yelled to the men to throw up their hands. One of the men dropped his shotgun and raised his hands, but the other aimed his rifle at Cunningham. The sheriff, with his sawed-off shotgun trained on the man, coolly told the robber to drop his gun. The two stared at each other for a moment, and then the robber threw his rifle to the ground.

The first police department in California was organized in San Francisco in 1849.[30] Irish-born Malachi Fallon was appointed chief of the thirty-officer force.[31] He looked the part. An old photo reveals a strong face with a Celtic chin marked by a prominent cleft. He had served with the New York Police Department after it was established in 1845 but left for California late in December 1848, when news of the gold strike finally began sweeping the East Coast. Not long after his appointment, he personally effected the arrest of a man who had murdered his business partner on a hunting trip and then made an arrest of an intoxicated Texan that left witnesses in awe. Fallon found the Texan standing on the sidewalk, waving a Colt revolver, and challenging one and all to fight. When Fallon ordered the man to surrender, he

Los Angeles's first jail and city hall, ca. 1878. Los Angeles grew much more slowly than San Francisco and retained a reputation for lawlessness well into the 1880s. According to local lore, crime was so rampant in 1870 that the U.S. census office wrote back in disbelief after it received the town's statistics. *California Historical Society Collection at the University of Southern California: Title Insurance and Trust Photo Collection.*

leveled his gun at the police chief and fired. The bullet whistled by Fallon's head. Seemingly unfazed, Fallon walked toward the Texan and repeated the demand to surrender. The Texan fired again, and again, the rounds narrowly missing the chief. By now Fallon was within a few feet of the man and, as a witness described, "leaped for the scoundrel, and overpowered him by his herculean strength, and led him gently but firmly to the station house."[32]

San Francisco city government was reorganized during 1850, and Fallon was elected city marshal in August of that year. Although his title was different, he still ran the police department. The number of officers under his charge was growing, but not quickly enough to keep pace with San Francisco's rapidly increasing population. Crime became more of a problem, and frustrated citizens, on several occasions, tried to take prisoners from the police and administer summary justice. Each time, Fallon managed to take control of the situation, demonstrating the same kind of steely nerve he had when confronting the gun-wielding Texan. He was not around to confront the Committee of Vigilance in 1851, however. Two months before the organization of the committee, he and his fellow Democrats were swept out of office in a Whig victory. Fallon never returned to law enforcement. He remained in the Bay Area, operating several businesses before dying at the age of eighty-five in 1899. He recalled his days as chief with fondness, saying:

> San Francisco's population was then made up of rough young men with adventurous spirits, excited by the discovery of gold. They needed a strong and experienced hand to keep them in control. Many of them were of the cowboy class, while the worst were deserting whalemen coming from all parts of the world. They were not men of evil principles but they felt the excitement of the time and enjoyed the lack of restraint in a town where there was no social organization or adequate legal control. Outside of this looseness of moral forces at the time, they were good fellows.[33]

Lawmen such as Malachi Fallon, Tom Cunningham, Harry Morse, and Jim Hume helped to tame the California frontier and control the "good fellows." It was not an easy task. California, in its early years of statehood, was disproportionately armed, young, and male, and full of Sam Browns, John Dalys, and Billy Mulligans. Much of the state was wild and unsettled. Gangs of bandidos, Indian wars, and aggression among and within the state's many ethnic groups added to the mix. Dozens of saloons in every mining camp kept the boys well oiled and ready for action. The mores of frontier society put honor and courage above physical safety and well-being. In ways, though, those same mores protected the old, the weak, the innocent, and the female and tempered the highwaymen who took the express box from the stagecoach but left the passengers unmolested. When the moral code was violated, however, vigilantism often resulted. At the heart of the code was the belief that violent behavior, if within the bounds of honorable conduct, was not only perfectly acceptable, but highly respected and admired.

Again and again the code of the West made the mining camps of California stages for deadly tests of will, skill, and honor. In a Bodie saloon, Tom McDonald had just been knocked down by a vicious blow from the larger and more powerfully built Alex Nixon. McDonald climbed to his feet and said, "Will you give me even chances?" "Yes, by God!" exclaimed Nixon, and the two men drew their guns . . .

NOTES

1. A full and fair discussion of Indian-white conflict, which stands apart from the other kinds of violence discussed in this chapter, would require a chapter-length treatment all its own. Moreover, aspects of the conflict have been described elsewhere in this Sesquicentennial Series. See, for example, James A. Sandos, "'Because he is a liar and a thief': Conquering the Residents of 'Old' California, 1850–1880," in *Rooted in Barbarous Soil: People, Culture,*

and Community in Gold Rush California, ed. Kevin Starr and Richard J. Orsi (Berkeley: University of California Press, 2000), 86–112, and Sandos, "Between Crucifix and Lance: Indian-White Relations in California, 1769–1848," in *Contested Eden: California before the Gold Rush*, ed. Ramón A. Gutiérrez and Richard J. Orsi (Berkeley: University of California Press, 1998), 216–20. Much has been written on the subject, varying from careful and judicious appraisals of the conflict to those flawed by the use of hyperbolic rhetoric. Standard works include: Sherburne F. Cook, *The Population of the California Indians, 1769–1970* (Berkeley: University of California Press, 1976); Cook, *The Conflict between the California Indian and White Civilization* (Berkeley: University of California Press, 1943); Cook, "The American Invasion, 1848–1870," *Ibero-Americana* no. 23 (Berkeley: University of California Press, 1943); George Harwood Phillips, *Chiefs and Challengers* (Berkeley: University of California Press, 1975); Phillips, *Indians and Intruders in Central California, 1769–1849* (Norman: University of Oklahoma Press, 1993); Phillips, *Indians and Indian Agents: The Origins of the Reservation System in California, 1849–1852* (Norman: University of Oklahoma Press, 1997); George E. Anderson, W. H. Ellison, and Robert F. Heizer, *Treaty Making and Treaty Rejection by the Federal Government in California, 1850–1852* (Socorro, N.M.: Ballena Press, 1978); James J. Rawls, *Indians of California: The Changing Image* (Norman: University of Oklahoma Press, 1984).

The two most important conflicts that the U.S. Army participated in were the Owens Valley Indian War and the Modoc War. The former is treated by Roger D. McGrath in *Gunfighters, Highwaymen, & Vigilantes: Violence on the Frontier* (Berkeley: University of California Press, 1984) and the latter by Richard Dillon in *Burnt-Out Fires* (Englewood Cliffs, N.J.: Prentice-Hall, 1973). Massacres of parties of whites and individual white deaths at the hands of Indians, as well as slaughter of Indians at the hands of whites, were regularly reported in the *Alta California* and the *Sacramento Union*. Such killing is also recorded in numerous gold-rush diaries, letters, and memoirs. Useful personal accounts include: William Jackson Barry, *Up and Down; or, Fifty Years' Colonial Experience in Australia, California, New Zealand, India, China, and the South Pacific* (London: S. Low, Marston, Searle, and Rivington, 1879); E. Gould Buffum, *The Gold Rush: An Account of Six Months in the California Diggings* ([London?] 1850); Lucius Fairchild, *California Letters of Lucius Fairchild*, ed. Joseph Schafer (Madison: State Historical Society of Wisconsin, 1931); Jasper S. Hill, *The Letters of a Young Miner: Covering the Adventures of Jasper S. Hill during the California Goldrush, 1849–1852*, ed. Doyce B. Nunis, Jr. (San Francisco: John Howell, 1964); William Perkins, *Three Years in California: William Perkins' Journal of Life at Sonora, 1849–1852*, ed. Dale L. Morgan and James R. Scobie (Berkeley: University of California Press, 1964); Daniel B. Woods, *Sixteen Months at the Gold Diggings* (New York: Harper and Brothers, 1851).

2. John Rollin Ridge, *The Life and Adventures of Joaquin Murieta, the Celebrated California Bandit* (1854; reprint, with an introduction by Joseph Henry Jackson, Norman: University of Oklahoma Press, 1955).

3. Walter Noble Burns, *The Robin Hood of El Dorado* (New York: Coward McCann, 1932); Joseph Henry Jackson, *Bad Company* (New York: Harcourt, Brace, 1949). For Chicano authors arguing the social bandit thesis, see Pedro Castillo and Albert Camarillo, eds., *Furia y Muerta: Los Bandidos Chicanos* (Los Angeles: UCLA Chicano Studies Center, 1973).

4. While much has been written on Murieta, the best scholarly works are William B. Secrest, *Joaquin: Bloody Bandit of the Mother Lode* (Fresno, Calif.: Saga West Pub. Co., 1967); James F. Varley, *The Legend of Joaquin Murrieta, California's Gold Rush Bandit* (Twin Falls,

Idaho: Big Lost River Press, 1995); and Remi Nadeau, *The Real Joaquin Murieta* (Corona del Mar, Calif.: Trans-Anglo Books, 1974). An excellent summary and historiographical discussion is found in John Boessenecker, *Gold Dust and Gunsmoke* (New York: John Wiley & Sons, 1999), 73–99. Flawed but useful in part is Frank Latta, *Joaquin Murrieta and His Horse Gangs* (Santa Cruz, Calif.: Bear State Books, 1980). The account that follows is taken from these sources.

    5. Not widely known today, Pio Linares led a band of highwaymen on California's central coast that was, for a time during the mid-1850s, nearly as murderous as Murieta's gang. Linares had been born in California, but he robbed and murdered other native Californians, Sonoran Mexicans, Americans, or anyone else who traveled El Camino Real. Moreover, his gang included Jack Powers (or Power), an Irish immigrant and U.S. Army veteran of the Mexican War, who came to share the leadership role with Linares. One of the gang's most dastardly deeds was committed without the leadership of Linares or Powers, but demonstrated the willingness of the bandidos to prey on their own. Six gang members led by Joaquin Valenzuela and Juan Salazar swept down upon Rancho Las Cruces on the evening of June 7, 1856, and shot Tomas Romero, leaving him severely wounded. They then tied up a sixty-year-old widow and raped her before fleeing with two hundred stolen dollars. After another year of robbery and murder, a vigilance committee was organized in San Luis Obispo to deal with the Linares bandidos. Of the 148 men who signed the committee's muster roll, 62 had Spanish surnames. Linares was eventually killed in a gun battle with vigilantes, and several members of his gang were captured and later hanged. Powers escaped by steamer to Mexico but was killed in Arizona a few years later.

    For Linares and other bandidos of the central coast and southern California, see Myron Angel, *History of San Luis Obispo County, California* (Oakland: Thompson & West, 1883), esp. 131, 133, 167–68, 294–96, 299–306, 356; Hubert Howe Bancroft, *History of California*, vol. 4 (San Francisco: The History Company, 1888), esp. 655–56; Bancroft, *Popular Tribunals*, vol. 1 (San Francisco: The History Co., 1887), esp. 487; Boessenecker, *Gold Dust and Gunsmoke*, 100–133; Robert Glass Cleland, *The Cattle on a Thousand Hills: Southern California, 1850–1880* (San Marino, Calif.: The Huntington Library, 1951), esp. 92–93, 96, 250–63; Leonard Pitt, *The Decline of the Californios* (Berkeley: University of California Press, 1966), esp. 149, 169–71; Jesse D. Mason, *History of Santa Barbara County, California* (Oakland: Thompson & West, 1883), esp. 104; W. W. Robinson, *The Story of San Luis Obispo County* (San Luis Obispo, Calif.: Title Insurance and Trust Co., 1957), esp. 20; Dudley T. Ross, *Devil on Horseback* (Fresno, Calif.: Valley Publishers, 1975), esp. 108–28, 165–68.

    Newspapers carried dozens of stories on Linares and other bandidos. Especially useful are the *Los Angeles Star; Sacramento Union; Alta California* (San Francisco); *San Francisco Bulletin; Santa Barbara Gazette;* and *Santa Cruz Pacific Sentinel*. An excellent biographical sketch of John Powers is found in William B. Secrest, *Lawmen & Desperadoes: A Compendium of Noted Early California Peace Officers, Badmen, and Outlaws, 1850–1900* (Spokane: The Arthur H. Clark Company, 1994), 268–73.

    6. Kevin J. Mullen, *Let Justice Be Done: Crime and Politics in Early San Francisco* (Reno: University of Nevada Press, 1989), 55–71.

    7. Edwin A. Beilharz and Carlos U. Lopez, eds., *We Were 49ers! Chilean Accounts of the California Gold Rush* (Pasadena, Calif.: Ward Ritchie Press, 1976), 31.

    8. The law required foreigners to pay a fee of $20 a month. The fee was substantial, even in the cost-inflated diggings. It caused a particular problem for Mexicans (mostly Sonorans)

who had rushed into the southern end of the Mother Lode. They held a mass protest meeting in the mining camp of Sonora (there were good numbers of Frenchmen among the protestors as well) and announced that they would refuse to pay the fee. Hundreds of American miners, many of them wearing their uniforms from the Mexican War, rushed to the aid of the tax collectors. Reeling from the tax and the threat of violence, the great majority of Mexicans—some ten thousand—left the Mother Lode during the summer of 1850 and returned to Mexico. Although American miners were happy with the exodus, American merchants were not. The merchants had lost thousands of customers, and they immediately began lobbying the state legislature for a repeal of the tax, which was effected the very next year, in 1851. See Secrest, *Lawmen & Desperadoes,* 318; Pitt, *Decline of the Californios,* 60–62; M. Colette Standart, "The Sonora Migration to California, 1848–1856: A Study in Prejudice," *Southern California Quarterly* (Fall 1976): 335–38, 342; Carol M. DeFerrari, ed., *Annals of Tuolumne County* (Sonora, Calif.: The Mother Lode Press, 1963), 133, 138.

9. Beilharz and Lopez, *We Were 49ers!* 104, 123, 127, 139–49; Boessenecker, *Gold Dust and Gunsmoke,* 47–51; James J. Ayers, *Gold and Sunshine: Reminiscences of Early California* (Boston: The Gorham Press, 1922), 46–58.

10. The three convicted murderers were executed by firing squad. John Boessenecker, in *Gold Dust and Gunsmoke,* 51, argues that the ear croppings were excessively harsh punishments and were intended to intimidate other Chileans into leaving the diggings. This very well may have been the case, but it is worth noting that ear cropping was not an uncommon punishment for American thieves in frontier California, and that punishments for thieves included hanging.

11. For dueling, see Benjamin C. Truman, *The Field of Honor* (New York: Fords, Howard & Hulbert, 1883); William B. Secrest, *Blood and Honor* (Fresno, Calif.: Saga West Publishing Co., 1970); Robert Baldick, *The Duel: A History* (New York: Barnes & Noble Books, 1996). An excellent summary of dueling in California during the 1850s is found in Boessenecker, *Gold Dust and Gunsmoke,* 204–24.

12. *San Francisco Post,* September 7, 1878; Truman, *Field of Honor,* 315; Hubert Howe Bancroft, *California Inter Pocula* (San Francisco: The History Company, 1888), 754–55; Boessenecker, *Gold Dust and Gunsmoke,* 209–13.

13. *Alta California,* June 7 and 8, 1854; Bancroft, *California Inter Pocula,* 760; Boessenecker, *Gold Dust and Gunsmoke,* 215–16.

14. For Edward Gilbert's career in San Francisco, see Mullen, *Let Justice Be Done,* 17, 40, 42, 49, 66, 70.

15. *San Francisco Examiner,* February 13 and 20, 1881; Truman, *Field of Honor,* 308–13; George C. Barns, *Denver the Man* (Wilmington, Ohio: The Author, 1949); Boessenecker, *Gold Dust and Gunsmoke,* 213–14.

16. The Broderick-Terry duel is the most famous and most written about in California history. Excellent scholarly works on the parties involved are David A. Williams, *David C. Broderick: A Political Portrait* (San Marino, Calif.: The Huntington Library, 1969), and A. Russell Buchanan, *David S. Terry of California: Dueling Judge* (San Marino, Calif.: The Huntington Library, 1956). See also Truman, *Field of Honor,* 81–82, 392–410; Bancroft, *California Inter Pocula,* 763–73; Boessenecker, *Gold Dust and Gunsmoke,* 219–23.

17. Samuel L. Clemens, *Roughing It* (New York: Harper & Row, 1913), 197.

18. Stephen J. Field, *Personal Reminiscences of Early Days in California* (privately published, 1893), 79–80, as quoted in Boessenecker, *Gold Dust and Gunsmoke,* 302.

19. *Mariposa Chronicle,* April 21, 1854; *San Francisco Chronicle,* May 1, 1892; Myron Angel, *History of Nevada* (Oakland: Thompson & West, 1881), 344; San Quentin Prison Register, convict no. 762; Sally S. Zanjani, "Sam Brown: The Evolution of a Frontier Villain," *Pacific Historian* (Winter 1985): 6–10; John Boessenecker, *Badge and Buckshot* (Norman: University of Oklahoma Press, 1988), 61–65.

20. McGrath, *Gunfighters, Highwaymen, & Vigilantes,* 86–101.

21. Secrest, *Lawmen & Desperadoes,* 241–45; William B. Secrest, "There Once Was a Badman Named Mulligan," *Real West* (August 1984): 14–15, 161.

22. See Hubert Howe Bancroft, *Popular Tribunals* (San Francisco: History Publishing Co., 1887), and Richard Maxwell Brown, *Strain of Violence: Historical Studies of American Violence and Vigilantism* (New York: Oxford University Press, 1975).

23. *Esmeralda Union,* March 31, 1864.

24. Mullen, *Let Justice Be Done.* Mullen argues that the 1851 committee has escaped close scrutiny and criticism because of the work of Mary Floyd Williams, which makes a persuasive case for the vigilantes. See Mary Floyd Williams, *History of the San Francisco Committee of Vigilance of 1851* (Berkeley: University of California Press, 1921), and Williams, ed., *Papers of the San Francisco Vigilance Committee of 1851* (Berkeley: University of California Press, 1919). Mullen, a former deputy chief of the San Francisco Police Department, has painstakingly compiled the first accurate data for criminal offenses in San Francisco during the early 1850s. His pioneering work makes it clear that claims of twelve hundred murders in the city during those years are wild exaggerations. See, for example, *Let Justice Be Done,* 110, 144, 203, 216, 230.

25. Interpretations of the Committee of Vigilance of 1856 in San Francisco vary greatly. Besides Bancroft and Brown, mentioned in note 22, see John Hittell, *The History of San Francisco and Incidentally of California* (San Francisco: A. L. Bancroft and Co., 1878); Roger W. Lotchin, *San Francisco, 1846–1856: From Hamlet to City* (New York: Oxford University Press, 1974); and Robert M. Senkewicz, *Vigilantes in Gold Rush San Francisco* (Stanford: Stanford University Press, 1985), especially his historiographical analysis on pages 203–31. Also excellent for historiography is Doyce B. Nunis, Jr., ed., *The San Francisco Vigilance Committee of 1856: Three Views* (Los Angeles: Westerners, 1971).

26. Kenneth Lamott, *Chronicles of San Quentin: The Biography of a Prison* (New York: David McKay Co., 1961); Shelley Bookspan, *A Germ of Goodness: The California State Prison System 1851–1944* (Lincoln: University of Nebraska Press, 1991).

27. McGrath, *Gunfighters, Highwaymen, & Vigilantes,* esp. 247–60; Ben Nickoll, "Violence on the American Frontier: Nevada County, California, 1851–56" (history honors thesis, UCLA, 1986); McGrath, "Violence and Lawlessness on the Western Frontier," in *Violence in America: The History of Crime,* vol. 1 (Newbury Park, Calif.: Sage Publications, 1989), 122–45.

28. Richard Dillon, *Wells, Fargo Detective: A Biography of James B. Hume* (Reno: University of Nevada Press, 1986); Jackson, *Bad Company;* William Collins and Bruce Levene, *Black Bart: The True Story of the West's Most Famous Stagecoach Robber* (Mendocino, Calif.: Pacific Transcriptions, 1992); John Boessenecker, *Lawman: The Life and Times of Harry Morse, 1835–1912* (Norman: University of Oklahoma Press, 1998).

29. Boessenecker, *Badge and Buckshot,* 101–29; *An Illustrated History of San Joaquin County* (Chicago: Lewis Publishing Co., 1890), 95–100, 617; Secrest, *Lawmen & Desperadoes,* 101–105; George Henry Tinkham, *History of San Joaquin County, California* (Los Angeles: Historic Record Co., 1923), 218, 289–90.

30. Mullen, *Let Justice Be Done*, 77. The establishment of the SFPD in 1849 came only five years after the organization of the nation's first police force in Philadelphia. New York City founded its force in 1845. See David R. Johnson, *Policing the Urban Underworld* (Philadelphia: Temple University Press, 1979).

31. Kevin J. Mullen, "Malachi Fallon," *California History* (Summer 1983), 100–105; Mullen, *Let Justice Be Done*, 77, 81, 105, 126, 133, 145, 165, 205, 250.

32. "Further Reminiscences of Pioneer Days: Malachi Fallon as Chief," *Alta California*, October 26, 1884.

33. Mullen, "Malachi Fallon," 100; *Oakland Tribune*, April 2, 1961.

3

The Courts, the Legal Profession, and the Development of Law in Early California

Gordon Morris Bakken

The Gold Rush flooded California with people seeking riches and expecting the institutions of the law to protect their interests. To create those institutions, delegates went to Monterey in 1849 for the first state constitutional convention. The delegates assembling in Monterey in 1849 had a variety of concerns in writing a constitution for the new state. When considering the judiciary, delegates were anxious about the need for a fair and speedy trial, the costs of litigation, and the role of judges in making law. In discussing these issues, the delegates acknowledged both our national constitutional traditions and California's uniqueness in its Spanish and Mexican heritage. They also debated the nature of a constitution and the need to keep legislation out of fundamental law. The concepts of justice, industry, and economy in government were in contest in these debates. Justice was what courts dispensed, but the extent to which courts should have the authority to "legislate" for the state was at issue. Industry was what the delegates wanted to bring prosperity to the state, and the issue was how the lawgiving branches of government could facilitate that goal. Economy in government was what delegates thought taxpayers wanted. Good government at absolute minimum expense was a Jacksonian goal that obviously found voice in 1849 in California. But a broader political philosophy of popular sovereignty also clearly resonated at the 1849 convention. As historian Christian G. Fritz has so ably pointed out, the delegates knew that they had a charge as constitution-makers to organize civil government and establish social institutions through fundamental law. Although the people were sovereign and the legislature was to do the will of the people in passing statutes, a constitution, when ratified by the people, became higher, fundamental law.[1] In the American mind, the judiciary was the institution that would have to interpret and apply that fundamental law.

The structure of the judiciary was not a serious question for the delegates, but the function of a system of justice was. The structure of the California judiciary set out in the 1849 constitution was a traditional hierarchical one based on local trial courts run by a justice of the peace. The second-level trial court was the county court. The district court was the next level of trial court. It had civil jurisdiction over controversies involving more than $200. Each county had one judge, who, sitting with two justices of the peace, constituted a court of sessions. Finally, the California Supreme Court sat as the highest court of the state to hear appeals from the district courts. Other inferior trial courts quickly emerged to fit local circumstances. Justices of the peace for cities and counties, municipal courts, and police courts became part of the judicial landscape of California.

During the 1849 debates, many delegates wanted certain provisions of law set in constitutional concrete so that neither the legislature nor the judiciary could tamper with their handiwork. L. W. Hastings, a Sutter County attorney from Ohio, proposed that "as the true design of all punishment is to reform and not to exterminate mankind, death shall never be inflicted as a punishment for crime in this state." M. M. McCarver, a Sacramento farmer, retorted that "as California is situated at present, it [reformatory institutionalization] is impracticable. The construction of penitentiaries would be enormously burdensome." He also cited history, noting that as the death penalty "has been a practice ever since the world was created, perhaps it would be as well to let it rest awhile longer."[2] The convention voted down the Hastings proposal to abolish the death penalty.[3]

In the California of 1849, the death penalty and the costs of incarceration in prison were related issues. The practice of the mining camps was to give the criminally accused a trial by jury, and if the accused were found guilty, to sentence the criminal ("enemy deviant," in modern parlance) to whipping, banishment, or death. The sentence was carried out immediately.[4] This procedure and punishment scheme was one learned from the American experience and driven by the absence of jails in the diggings. With the creation of towns and jails, the question became whether local taxpayers and later state taxpayers wanted to build prisons or to save the costs of incarceration by imposing the penalties of whipping or death.

In 1851 the California legislature would decide that juries, the sovereign people, should impose the appropriate penalties for crimes against property. The statute gave the jury discretion in robbery cases of setting prison sentences of one to ten years or death. Grand larceny had the same provisions and petit larceny, then defined as stealing property worth less than $50, had the penalty of "imprisonment in the County jail not more than six months, or . . . fine not exceeding five hundred dollars, or . . . any number of lashes not exceeding fifty upon the bare back, or . . . such fine or imprisonment and lashes in the discretion of the jury."[5] The first appellate case to test this statute found it constitutional. The defendant, George Tanner, stole $400 worth of food on April 3, 1852, went to trial before a court of sessions on

In his lively memoir *Mountains and Molehills* (1855), British adventurer Frank Marryat included this woodcut of a "Carpenter Judge" who dispensed informal justice in the tiny mining camp of Tuttle-Town. "A Sonorian was found one day in possession of a mule not his own," Marryat recalled. "While the culprit quakes in the grip of our constable, our judge exhorts the villain to be more honest in his dealings." *California Historical Society, FN-31985*.

April 14, lost an appeal in the district court on April 24, lost his petition before the Supreme Court on July 16, and lost his life on July 23. Justice was swift, sure, and carried out the will of the people as expressed by a jury. For the delegates of 1849 or the jury of 1852, the incarceration of enemy deviants was an unwelcome expense for local taxpayers, created the possibility of having the convict back on the streets in the future, and did not present the same type of lesson as the more severe penalties to others in the society who would prey on law-abiding citizens.

Other 1849 delegates saw equally great evils on California's horizon. Henry Wager Halleck, a San Francisco attorney and later President Abraham Lincoln's chief of staff, thought that a provision prohibiting lotteries had to be in the constitution because they were "immoral." The "evils of the lottery system" had to be crushed regardless of arguments that such a prohibition was legislation, not fundamental law. Kimball Dimmick, a San Jose lawyer, agreed. "Whatever might have been usual in other Constitutions," he argued, "it was time for this Convention to present to the people of California a Constitution which would prohibit any injurious or immoral practice."[6] William Gwin, perhaps the best-informed and politically seasoned delegate, saw another monster, the banks. He moved an amendment to prohibit banking in California.[7] J. M. Jones, a San Joaquin attorney, similarly announced that he was "prepared to go to any extent against banks in this country. The inhabitants are against them; public opinion everywhere is against them."[8] Gwin went further. "Public opinion throughout the United States is against the banking system," he contended.[9] For California, it was a time to be tested. "Let us guard against infringing on the rights of the people, by legalizing the association of capital to war upon labor," Gwin remonstrated.[10] Charles T. Botts, a Monterey attorney, also wanted "to crush this bank monster." He warned, "if you leave a loop-hole, this insinuating serpent, a circulating bank, will find its way through, because of the absolute necessity of the community for a paper currency."[11] In the Jacksonian rhetoric and mind of the time, the evil was banking and the remedy was constitutional prohibition.

When the delegates debated the judicial article, they expressed the problems of their times in their rhetoric. Kimball Dimmick wanted a permanent judicial system, not subject to the legislative and popular winds of time. The system of courts "should not be established with any view to a change at some future period; that when practitioners in these courts bring in their cases they may know where they are to end." Dimmick wanted to "prevent endless litigation" stemming from rapid judicial personnel changes.[12] McCarver was concerned about swift and sure justice. He favored "a fair trial before a jury, and whenever they have decided the case, if they say hang him, then hang him in thirty days." He did not want to give the convict "an opportunity to escape." The Sacramento farmer did not want a convict "to get free . . . by any quibble of the law."[13] But Winfield Sherwood, a Mormon Island lawyer, supported the right of appeal, noting that "if he is guilty, he will be punished notwithstanding the appeal."[14] One delegate retorted that the problem was not appeal, but the lawyers representing men of money who could afford the process. To him, lawyers were "like vultures upon dead bodies . . . although the lawyers know they cannot succeed in their suits, they urge them to go on."[15] Thomas L. Vermeule, a Stockton lawyer, controverted the argument, stating his belief "in abstract principles. I believe in their justice. If a principle be good in the abstract, it must be good in practice; and I believe in the right of appeal as a righteous abstract principle."[16]

Attorney Henry Wager Halleck came to California as an Army officer during the Mexican War and soon established the state's largest legal firm by specializing in land-grant disputes. San Francisco–based Halleck, Peachy & Billings represented more than 120 Californios in their struggles to establish legal claim to their lands. Halleck himself grew fabulously wealthy and in 1853 built the Montgomery Block in San Francisco. He posed for this photograph during the Civil War while serving as Abraham Lincoln's chief of staff. *Courtesy Huntington Library.*

Additionally, Vermeule castigated the anti-lawyer sentiment in the convention. "Lawyers are a very useful body of men, and when this Constitution goes forth to the world it well [sic] be greatly indebted to them for the part they took in its formation," he declared.[17]

The convention also considered the role of trial judges and juries. Pacificus Ord, a Monterey attorney, proposed that judges could not charge juries on fact, but could "state testimony and declare the law."[18] Delegate Botts thought that judges given too much latitude "could become a party to a suit . . . [and] great injustice may proceed from it."[19] Swayed by the arguments, Ord changed his position on stating testimony and favored limiting the judge to stating or expounding the law.[20] Winfield Sherwood regarded the judge as "an impartial umpire" who needed to sort out the testimony and the law for the jury.[21] Hastings agreed with Botts, based on abuses from the bench in his experience.[22] As the debate wore down, Kimball Dimmick attacked the proposal as legislation. "I am opposed to introducing [into] our Constitution sections which are more properly matters for legislative action," he maintained. Rather, "our object is to establish in this article a fundamental judiciary system, and it is not necessary that we incorporate these trivial incidents which belong to the statute books of the State, or the books of the common law," Dimmick submitted.[23] With the trivial aside, the delegates passed a hierarchical system of courts. A California Supreme Court and state trial courts were established.[24]

The discussion of law, lawyers, judges, and juries again highlights the popular sovereignty and Jacksonian democratic rhetoric of the times. Those who feared the caprice of the people, the democratic rabble, wanted juries harnessed and elite judges in control of trials and appeals. Lawyers were not to be trusted, regardless of the fact that Andrew Jackson was a lawyer, because they used procedure, technicalities, and the like to thwart the will of the people. Whigs saw this thinking as destructive of American society and anti-bank actions as economically naive at best. In the judiciary, at least, there was some protection for the future: elite lawyers on the bench could preserve the republican government that Whigs thought necessary for the future of California.

California's constitutional convention was not unique in its time. Utah held a constitutional convention in 1849 in a failed effort to escape territorial status. New Mexico's first constitutional convention movement started in November 1849 and ended in Congress in 1850.[25] California's unauthorized constitutional convention, its 1849 constitution, and the Compromise of 1850 brought statehood. For Utah and New Mexico, decades would pass before statehood.

The first legislature meeting in San Jose in December 1849 put judges on the bench in 1850. Serranus C. Hastings became California's first chief justice, and nine men became district judges. James A. McDougall became the first attorney general, as the legal system moved into a period of constitutional legitimacy.[26] Hastings was

A "PILE,"

OR,

A GLANCE AT THE WEALTH

OF THE

MONIED MEN

OF

SAN FRANCISCO AND SACRAMENTO CITY.

ALSO,

AN ACCURATE LIST OF THE LAWYERS,

THEIR FORMER PLACES OF RESIDENCE,

AND

DATE OF THEIR ARRIVAL IN SAN FRANCISCO.

SAN FRANCISCO,
COOKE & LECOUNT, BOOKSELLERS,
1851.

This 1851 pamphlet listing the "monied men" of San Francisco and Sacramento includes more than 150 lawyers. The author compiled the pamphlet in the hopes of convincing easterners that California did not lack "permanency." He also hoped that future historians would point to these men as "evidences of the boundless resources of our state, the enterprise of her early settlers, and of the breadth and solidity of that government, whose liberal principles encouraged them in founding a mighty empire on the shores of the Pacific." *Courtesy City of Sacramento, History and Science Division, Sacramento Archives and Museum Collection Center, Eleanor McClatchy Collection.*

born in New York, had practiced law in Iowa, served Iowa in the U.S. House of Representatives and as state chief justice, and came to California in 1849. He was thirty-six at the time of appointment and left the chief justiceship in 1852 to become attorney general. The legislature also elected Nathaniel Bennett and H. A. Lyons as associate justices, but both would leave the court by 1852. There simply was not enough money in the position and so much more to be made in private practice.[27]

The legislature, in addition to electing justices to the Supreme Court, was passing laws designed to institutionalize civic racism. California was at its birth an equal-opportunity racist state based on the civic racism dating back to Thomas Jefferson and Andrew Jackson.[28] Most notably, the legislature on April 22, 1850, passed an "Act for the Government and Protection of Indians" to guarantee their continued slavery and peonage as part of a labor system.[29] The genocide practiced by California's pioneers on American Indians largely went unpunished—another odious aspect of the state's early history.[30] The legislature also assured blacks and Chinese, along with Indians, that they were basically without the protection of the law by excluding their testimony in court.[31]

The California Supreme Court was no better. In *People v. Hall* (1854) Justice Hugh C. Murray, speaking for the court, upheld Section 14 of the Criminal Proceedings Act excluding African American and American Indian testimony against white persons and extended the ban to Chinese witnesses. Murray wrote that "American Indians and the Mongolian, or Asiatic, were regarded as the same type of human species." Even more certainly, because the legislature had used the word *black* in the statute, all nonwhite races were excluded from testifying against whites. In the land of liberty and opportunity, the California legislature made a clear statement that justice was not for African Americans, American Indians, or Chinese.[32]

Murray's racist opinion propelled him as a candidate for the Supreme Court on to the Know Nothing Party ticket in the 1855 election. The Know Nothing candidates accomplished a clean sweep of the California election, including governor, attorney general, two of three Supreme Court justices, and a majority of both houses of the legislature. Racism, bigotry, and California-for-whites-only prevailed.[33] But this brief hold of the Supreme Court did not prevail in all trial courts. In *Brown v. Omnibus Railroad Company* (1866) San Francisco's streetcars were desegregated by court order.[34] Black activism in the Bay Area challenged the de jure racism and won.

In Los Angeles, people in the streets challenged Justice Murray's transparent racism. In September 1854 David Brown murdered Pinckney Clifford in a Los Angeles livery stable over a trivial matter. Brown was a well-known lawbreaker.[35] The community wanted assurances that this murderer would receive his just desserts; so, too, for Felipe Alvitre, who arrived for trial in October, accused of multiple homicides. Brown's attorney asked for and was refused a change of venue. The press called for equal and swift justice. The juries did their job, and the trial judge sentenced both Brown and Alvitre to death. Justice Murray stepped in on January 11, 1855, and issued a stay of execution for Brown. The *Los Angeles Star*, in its edition that day, reported that Californios—Mexican residents of the province before the American conquest—were agitating for equal treatment for Alvitre. The *Southern Californian* joined that day's chorus, declaring that Brown's stay of execution was "another evidence of injustice" and asking "whether money, friends, color, or race is to be henceforth, as heretofore the sole arbitrators in our Criminal courts." The district court had done its job, the paper said, objecting to the "interfering hand" of Murray. The next day, Alvitre died at the end of Sheriff James Barton's rope, and a mob "yelling like incarnate devils" seized Brown and dispatched him by hemp. The *Los Angeles Star* reported these events on January 18, 1855, and also that Brown had requested "to be hung by white men, but none came forward to perform his last and only request." This mob violence was a popular response to the rule of law, but also an expression of demands for racial justice and equality. For the rule of law to prevail in frontier California, both the institutions of law and the officers of the law would have to demonstrate that justice—that is, due process and equal protection—was for all.

To many in the legal profession, vigilante justice was supportive of the formal legal system.[36] The nineteenth-century lawyer was a vigorous exponent of law and order who supported the system's goals of crime repression but tolerated due process violations to increase the effectiveness of the vigilante system. At the same time, these supporters within the legal community worked to modify the formal system to provide what vigilante justice offered: simplicity, certainty, and severity of punishment.

In the 1850s a transition took place from punishment by whipping and banishment, common in the gold fields, to hanging. California's gold-rush pioneers had started to face enemy deviants by the summer of 1849. Local miners used the forms of criminal procedure, and if the accused was found guilty, the sentence of whipping, banishment, or hanging was carried out immediately. Jails were seldom available, and these other punishments were considered practical and culturally acceptable. Further, the whip could have important benefits, as Alcalde Stephen J. Field, later a United States Supreme Court justice, found when he sentenced a man to a sequence of whippings that ultimately produced the missing bags of gold dust.[37] In San Francisco, the vigilante committees of 1851 and 1856 used hanging and the threat of hanging to enforce their versions of order. The problem was that by supporting vigilantism, the public was bypassing the formal institutions of the law and their procedural protections for the criminally accused.

In Calaveras County, William Higby worked another transition, from popular justice to the institutions of justice. Higby was in San Francisco to witness the 1851 vigilance committee's work. In June he wrote to his father that "the people have become dissatisfied with the public authorities of the city because criminals are not

Firsthand accounts of the Gold Rush are rife with descriptions of speedy and brutal vigilante action. A miner working the Yuba River in 1849 recorded that "if a man steals, they flog him for the first offense; second offense they crop his ears, and third, they hang him." Perhaps California's most infamous vigilante groups were two Committees of Vigilance that rose to power in San Francisco in 1851 and 1856. These forbidding committee "sharpshooters" were photographed in May 1856. *Courtesy Oakland Museum of California.*

brought to justice and punished as their deeds merit." Some criminals did get what they deserved, such as a burglar caught red-handed at nine o'clock one evening. He got his due process in a trial that same day and execution at 2:30 A.M. the next morning. Higby characterized it as "a fearful retribution inflicted by an indignant and outraged people." Actually, the legislature on April 22, 1851, had prescribed the death penalty for burglary. But in the Mother Lode country, Higby found that the people would not let the institutions of justice operate, because they had "lost all confidence [in the legal system] and charge[d] the authorities with letting murderers escape." This complaint of pervious jails and corruptible jail keepers was a familiar one. It was the administration of the law, rather than law itself, that the Argonauts did not trust.

Higby, as county district attorney, settled into his office in Mokelumne Hill to do something about this attitude. He vigorously prosecuted criminals and worked hard to obtain guilty verdicts, while a midsize vigilance committee operated concurrently in the county from 1852 until 1856. In December 1853, he reported that the "people are becoming more civilized or stand in greater fear of the law, for crimes are not so frequent as they were, although 12 persons are now in jail." Civilization, fear of the law, and a diminished crime rate were all related. Higby was the instrument of civilization and law to suppress those who would threaten community stability. For the main, the citizenry held that the value of speedy justice was great, and the regularly constituted authorities were best. Popular sentiment and institutional process seemed to be converging in the county by 1854. Yet the Jackson vigilance committee dispatched a horse thief that year, to Higby's dismay. He rode over and "talked plainly" to the residents. He "was possessed with mixed emotions to find such a total disregard of law, of right, of justice, of humanity, of public decency and morality, in the village where I had resided so long and when too I had done so much to punish crime as was admitted generally."

Despite this setback, Higby redoubled his efforts. He acted with celerity to prosecute the accused, try defendants, and secure convictions. In March, he obtained thirteen convictions in Jackson and reported that the town was "quiet and peaceful." By 1856, the vigilance committees of Jackson and Mokelumne Hill had retired. Law, with order dependent upon the institutions of the law, had prevailed. In many ways, William Higby had established the rule of law in his county for all time. So it was throughout the state. Popular justice gave way to institutional forms. Lawyers, as officers of the court, worked to establish the rule of law across California. They also turned to doing the business of the law.

The California bar of the period from 1850 to 1865 was small relative to that of the remainder of the century, and its lawyers were less well educated than those after 1880. The lawyers in the first decade and a half of the state's history were schooled in letters and honed by apprenticeship, and they were primarily occupied with the business of litigation and real estate transactions. The *Roll of Attorneys* for the state contains 619 names for the bar in the 1850s. By contrast, 2,412 persons would be admitted to practice in the state in the 1890s.[38] Men who were not college educated and who had served three to five years as law clerks to an attorney characterized the gold-rush-era bar. Law-school-educated attorneys became prevalent after 1880. The earlier generalists had used oratory and general historical and philosophical principles to persuade audiences, whether political or legal, but with the rise of industrialization, particularly the building of the railroad, this classical tradition gave way to specialization.[39]

These pioneer attorneys commonly formed partnerships, but rarely did their firms persist into the twentieth century. Henry Wager Halleck, Archibald C. Peachy, and Frederick Billings formed their partnership in 1849 and constituted one of San Francisco's leading firms until the Civil War called the men to other pursuits. Halleck, a West Point graduate, returned to the army to serve as President Lincoln's chief of staff (1862–64). Billings returned to Vermont and later became president of the Northern Pacific Railroad. Similarly, Richard Tobin arrived in California via Ireland and Chile as secretary to the Most Reverend Joseph Sadoc Alemany, the first Catholic archbishop of San Francisco. After the Gold Rush he turned to law, founding Tobin and Tobin in 1852, and in 1859, with his brother Robert Tobin, the Hibernia Savings and Loan Association. The law firm and the Tobins who would follow were part of that financial institution.[40] So too was the firm of Athearn, Chandler, Hoffman, and Angell of San Francisco, one of whose founding partners, Giles H. Gray, was admitted to practice in 1856, served on the 1856 San Francisco Committee of Vigilance, and helped found the Savings Union and Trust Company of San Francisco. That firm's early linkage to financial institutions gave way to mining litigation and corporate representation in the 1860s.[41] In Santa Barbara, Charles Huse and Charles Fernald formed a partnership that controlled most of the litigation in the court system there, but such partnerships were temporary.[42] Partnerships were common, but those that persisted into the twentieth century were rare.

A legal topic that has persisted from the Gold Rush until today has been the legal rights of women. In Spanish and Mexican California, civil law included community property, which recognized marriage as a partnership that shared benefits and burden equally. Common property was that acquired during marriage, and each spouse held equal ownership rights in that property. Essentially, the law recognized the wife's economic contribution to the marriage and valued it equally with the husband's.[43] Separate property was that brought to the marriage, as well as that acquired outside the efforts of the couple, such as gifts, legacies, and inheritances.[44] The delegates to the 1849 Monterey convention wrote a community property section into the state constitution. Although the delegates did not do so to further women's rights, later women's rights activists used the constitutional categories of common and separate property to their advantage.[45]

The constitutional provision was clearly background for legislative and judicial actions that followed. In 1863 the legislature provided that married women could designate someone with the powers of attorney. In 1866 the California Supreme Court upheld the statute despite a constitutional challenge. Chief Justice Silas Sanderson considered a good deal of treatise material and found the statute remedial, subjecting it to a liberal construction. He noted that "statutes which operate to divest vested rights, or in other words, which take the property of one citizen and, without compensation or his consent, bestow it upon another, are opposed to natural right and subversive of any government founded upon fixed laws." Sanderson construed the statute to be remedial and confirming of contracts rather than violating substantive due process of law. Hence, he found the statute was constitutional, and thereby the court lifted another disability of married women in the marketplace.[46]

In the realm of real estate mortgages, however, the California Supreme Court

California daguerreotype artist Robert H. Vance took this wedding portrait sometime in the 1850s. The California Supreme Court ruled in 1855 that a married woman had "no power to make a contract"—all financial and legal documents had to be signed by her husband. Widows were allowed to own property only through their connection to their dead husbands. *Courtesy Peter E. Palmquist.*

retained the English common-law doctrine that a married woman's signature on a note and mortgage without her husband's did not form a contract. In 1855, Justice Solomon Heydenfeldt stated that a married woman "has no power to make a contract" and that this constituted a doctrine of law "which this Court has no power to disturb."[47] In *Ramsdell v. Fuller and Summers* (1865) the court warned that the fact of a woman's name on a deed "afforded to all persons seeking to acquire title under it a clue to the title, which they were bound to pursue, or suffer the consequences." The presumption of the law was that she was not married and could pass title, "but she may be married, and her deed may not pass title."[48] These cases were protective of husbands' interests in lands and were clear warnings to financial institutions.

Beyond the fact that women were involved in these transactions, the work of the Supreme Court was significant for the marketplace. The court warned the lender-plaintiffs to be more careful in drafting documents, securing a wife's signature, searching title, or prosecuting foreclosure in a timely manner. The court was making an overt effort to protect creditor expectations, preserve statutory procedures, and maintain the debtor's statutory recourse of redemption. The justices attempted to rationalize the legal system to these ends while according the legislature's statutory pronouncements appropriate deference. This laid the foundation for the extensive litigation that would follow in the period from 1866 to 1890.[49]

Another area of English common law that the Supreme Court gave a great deal of attention to was real estate transactions. California case law involved the problems of getting land, developing land, and selling land. Land—particularly urban land—became a commodity to be traded. San Francisco real estate was a hot commodity in the 1850s. Los Angeles saw a similar period in the 1880s. The rapid completion of transactions often resulted in the legal formalities being overlooked or delayed, to the disappointment of one of the parties. Such cases ended up in court.

The cases of 1850 to 1865 reflected the hectic nature of the real estate market. In *Hoen v. Simmons* (1850), the buyer made an oral agreement to buy a lot in San Francisco for $5,000 and paid $1,000 down. The parties agreed to have a written contract drafted, but before the seller signed he went to Oregon, and the buyer proceeded to erect a building on the lot. When the seller returned, he refused to perform—that is, to carry out—the terms of sale, and the court refused specific performance (mandating that the seller convey in accordance with the contract) on a verbal agreement because the buyer had not "fully complied with the substance of all the provisions."[50] In *Tewksbury v. Laffan* (1850) the court told the buyer that absent a covenant to have the seller evict the squatters swarming over his San Francisco lot, he had the sole responsibility to do so.[51] Another buyer, in *Salmon v. Hoffman* (1852), found that the court required complete performance regardless of title or other considerations. The facts told the tale. Henry Fisher was attorney-in-fact for the heirs of James Scott to sell 1,250-vara lots in San Francisco. (A vara is a Mexican land-grant measure equal

Stephen J. Field, nineteenth-century California's most distinguished judge, served in the state legislature before joining the state Supreme Court in 1857. In 1863, President Lincoln appointed him to the U.S. Supreme Court, where Field served an unprecedented thirty-four years. (He served concurrently as the chief justice of the Tenth Circuit Court of the United States, in Los Angeles.) Field (far left) sits with other U.S. Supreme Court jurists in this portrait, ca. 1870. *California Historical Society, FN-31541.*

to 32.9927 inches.) Francis Salmon, acting as attorney-in-fact for his sister Mary Catherine Salmon, went angling for the property and landed it for $34,000, with $1,000 paid to bind the deal as earnest money. Three weeks later, another $9,000 changed hands, and Francis executed notes and mortgages. Five months later and one month before the next payment of $12,000 was due, Francis asked Henry to obtain conveyances of the lots to a third party. The heirs, suspecting something fishy, tendered the conveyances on demand for the $24,000 balance. Francis refused and sued. The court firmly stated that the heirs had acted properly and noted that "it is but a just precaution on his part, that he should withhold the title until the purchase-money is fully paid; and the law will not deprive him of the only security which he has."[52] Simply put, the court stated that buyers had to fulfill the terms of their contracts before they could trawl for subsequent buyers.

A collateral problem for the financing of transactions was a money supply problem. Today the Federal Reserve System guarantees money supply and liquidity, banks transfer millions on computers, and people buy on plastic. In much of nineteenth-

This photograph by J. A. Todd from the early 1880s depicts the scoured walls of the Malakoff Diggins in Nevada County, a seven-thousand-foot-long pit formed by water shot from hydraulic miners' cannons. Todd's photographs were used as evidence in the important federal case *Woodruff v. North Bloomfield Gravel Mining Co.*, which outlawed hydraulic mining in 1884, one of the government's first legal protections of the environment. *California Historical Society, FN-29935.*

century California and the West, the supply of money was scarce, and the exchange of promissory notes and other financial instruments was more a part of frontier trade. Cash flow, accounts receivable, and time lag on receipts and payments were daily problems for mercantile concerns. Promissory notes circulated as currency, and letters of credit and drafts on accounts were common throughout the period. When these credit or finance relations went sour, some disputes made their way to the California Supreme Court. The court promoted the negotiability of the promissory note and its utility in support of the marketplace.[53] The chronically specie-and-currency-starved West needed such instrumental jurisprudence.

The California Supreme Court in its first decade also disposed of a variety of tort claims. A tort is an injury outside of contract and today is characterized by personal injury cases. The early court was evenhanded in its treatment of corporations and persons under negligence doctrine and visited strict liability only on those in custody of animals known to be dangerous. The fault standard for negligence was part of the molding of law and societal behavior. Despite this approach to the developing law of tort, the court exhibited an independence that produced extraordinary decisions.[54]

Moody v. McDonald (1854) was one such decision. The facts were simple. Blasting in a rock quarry had injured a woman. The law, too, seemed simple. People using extraordinarily dangerous instrumentalities were held to the standard of strict liability. Once cause in fact was established, the question was how much the tortfeasor was to pay. But that was not the court's analysis. It held that the plaintiff must establish the blaster's negligence. Further, the court allowed only actual damages, not punitive damages. Punitive damages, the court ruled, could be allowed only after the plaintiff had established actual malice.[55] The holding was significant. The court established a policy position recognizing that in a frontier context, dangerous enterprises, involving a high degree of risk to others, were clearly indispensable to the development of the new land. The court would not make enterprise the insurer of developmental activities.

Even more certainly, the Supreme Court favored enterprise where nuisance law was at issue. In *Middleton v. Franklin* (1853) the plaintiff sought an injunction to halt the operation of a steam boiler that the defendant had erected to run a gristmill in the basement of a building the plaintiff occupied. The noise and smoke alone seemed a nuisance, but the fact that steam boilers had exploded in the past gave the complaint some weight. The court, however, found that the boiler did not constitute a sufficiently probable threat to warrant an injunction. Even if it did, damages were the appropriate remedy, not the termination of the enterprise.[56] The court clearly favored entrepreneurs and insulated them via enterprise-liability jurisprudence.

The court also confronted tort cases generated by transportation enterprises. In cases of stagecoaches overturning, the court developed a presumption that the cause was the negligence of the coachman. But the presumption was rebuttable. Further, damages were limited to actual damages, thus providing a measure of enterprise protection. The court was willing to impute the negligence of an employee to the employer, setting the stage for fellow-servant developments in the latter part of the century. In a case involving the burning of a grain field caused by steamboat sparks, the court retained for its discretion the determination of the proper standard of care. In that particular case, the absence of catches on the steamboat's chimney constituted negligence. Although the cases were not extensive, the court did display a general attitude favoring enterprise.[57] The record here was mixed with some lost opportunities for judicial craftsmanship.[58]

Two other legal ingredients of enterprise found in statutes in the period were chattel mortgages and mechanics' liens. In both areas of law, the court worked with flawed statutes. The chattel mortgage was a legal invention of the nineteenth century and a financing device for personal property. The legislature rejected such a law in 1850, but passed another in 1853. The legislature's Chattel Mortgage Act of 1857 listed the personal property that could be mortgaged, stated the required contents of the instrument, and provided for the document's recording. The list was long, but

Despite the uproar over gold, California's most contested natural resource has been its water supply. In the late nineteenth century, aggressive developers who attempted to divert water to industrial mines angered local residents, who responded with lawsuits and violence. This ditch-tender guards a section of the twenty-nine-mile-long, above-ground La Grande Ditch near Weaverville. *Photo by C. E. Goodyear, Courtesy Trinity County Historical Society.*

limited. For example, hotel furniture and upholstery could be mortgaged "when for purchase money," but billiard tables were not listed and hence not covered. A merchant who wrote a chattel mortgage on a billiard table as it went off the showroom floor did so without the protection of the statute. Much like in the mortgage cases, the court told creditors to heed the statute and write contracts accordingly.[59]

Mechanics' liens differed from other credit devices. They were nonetheless important for the expansion of the economy. The mechanic's lien provided that persons covered thereunder could foreclose on properties they had worked on or provided materials to if not paid for their labor or goods. This was crucial to wage security and thereby gave entrepreneurs a line of credit for the building of California. In extensive case law, the court construed the statute strictly and provided plenty of advice to the legislature on how to accomplish its public policy goals. By the 1870s the court would view the statutes as remedial and pursuant to a workable policy.[60]

In the period from 1850 to 1865, the institutions of justice and its officers worked diligently to provide for social and economic stability in California. Although the legislature and Supreme Court records on race were dismal, the development of law and the interaction of the bar and the courts, the legislators, and the people worked to establish a foundation that would enable California to emerge as a leader in private law and public policy.

NOTES

The section of this essay on the 1849 constitutional convention is taken in whole, or in part, from Gordon Morris Bakken, "California's Constitutional Conventions Create Our Courts," *California Supreme Court Historical Society Yearbook* (1994), 33–54.

1. Christian G. Fritz, "Popular Sovereignty, Vigilantism, and the Constitutional Right of Revolution," *Pacific Historical Review* 58 (February 1994): 39–66. Also see J. Ross Browne, *Report of the Debates in the Convention of California of the Formation of the State Constitution in September and October, 1849* (Washington, D.C., 1850), 50–51.

2. Fritz, "Popular Sovereignty," 45–46.

3. Ibid., 46.

4. Gordon Morris Bakken, *Practicing Law in Frontier California* (Lincoln: University of Nebraska Press, 1991), 101.

5. Gordon Morris Bakken, "Death for Grand Larceny," in *Historic U.S. Court Cases, 1690–1990: An Encyclopedia*, ed. John W. Johnson (New York, 1992), 34–35.

6. Ibid., 92–93.

7. Ibid., 108.

8. Ibid., 115.

9. Ibid.

10. Ibid., 117.

11. Ibid., 125.

12. Ibid., 215.

13. Ibid., 226.
14. Ibid., 227.
15. Ibid., 228 (Noriego).
16. Ibid., 229.
17. Ibid., 231.
18. Ibid., 234.
19. Ibid.
20. Ibid., 235.
21. Ibid.
22. Ibid., 237.
23. Ibid., 239.
24. See Cardinal Goodwin, *The Establishment of State Government in California, 1846–1850* (New York: Macmillan, 1914); Lately Thomas, *Between Two Empires: The Life Story of California's First Senator, William McKendree Gwin* (Boston: Houghton Mifflin & Co., 1969); Walter Colton, *Land of Gold; or, Three Years in California* (New York: Cleaves, MacDonald & Co., 1850), 410–11; and Rockwell Dennis Hunt, *The Genesis of California's First Constitution* (Baltimore: Johns Hopkins Press, 1895). For the best comparative analysis of the politics of the 1849 convention, see David Alan Johnson, *Founding the Far West: California, Oregon, and Nevada, 1840–1890* (Berkeley: University of California Press, 1992), 15–40, 101–38, 233–68.
25. Gordon Morris Bakken, *Rocky Mountain Constitution Making, 1850–1912* (Westport, Conn.: Greenwood Press, 1987), 8–9.
26. See a short description of these events in Nathaniel Bennett, *Reports of Cases Determined in the Supreme Court of the State of California* (San Francisco: Bancroft-Whitney Co., 1906), vi–vii.
27. Orrin Kip McMurray, *Historical and Contemporary Review of the Bench and Bar of California* (San Francisco: The Recorder Printing and Publishing Co., 1926), 24.
28. Gordon M. Bakken, "Constitutional Convention Debates in the West: Racism, Religion, and Gender," *Western Legal History* 3 (Summer–Fall 1990): 228–39. On Jefferson and Jackson, see Rogers M. Smith, *Civic Ideals* (New Haven: Yale University Press, 1997), 138, 198–99, 206, 210–15.
29. Clifford E. Trafzer and Joel R. Hyer, *"Exterminate Them": Written Accounts of the Murder, Rape, and Slavery of Native Americans during the California Gold Rush, 1848–1868* (East Lansing: Michigan State University Press, 1999), 19–20.
30. Ibid., 81–133. It is indeed surprising that law-abiding pioneers on the Overland Trail would become willing instruments of holocaust. For the lawful pioneer behavior, see John Phillip Reid, *Policing the Elephant: Crime, Punishment, and Social Behavior on the Overland Trail* (San Marino, Calif.: The Huntington Library Press, 1997). I believe that Rogers M. Smith's version of American civic life is most informative. Some Jacksonian Americans were hard-core racists who, when given the opportunity, killed, brutalized, or marginalized racial minorities and women. On the gender issue, see Linda K. Kerber, *No Constitutional Right to be Ladies: Women and the Obligations of Citizenship* (New York: Hill and Wang, 1998), 47–67.
31. Albert S. Broussard, *Black San Francisco: The Struggle for Racial Equality in the West, 1900–1954* (Lawrence: University Press of Kansas, 1993), 17. The Criminal Proceedings Act of 1851 explicitly excluded Indian and "black" testimony. The California Supreme Court

would interpret the language of the statute to include Chinese testimony. Charles J. McClain, *In Search of Equality: The Chinese Struggle against Discrimination in Nineteenth-Century California* (Berkeley: University of California Press, 1994), 20–23. To make clear the depth of the racism of the California legislature, they codified the Supreme Court decision in 1863 and extended the ban for Chinese testimony to civil cases. *Act of March 18, 1863*, chapter 70, 1863 Cal. Stat. 69. The same statute repealed the ban on black testimony due to the Emancipation Proclamation. Also see Tomas Almaguer, *Racial Fault Lines: The Historical Origins of White Supremacy in California* (Berkeley: University of California Press, 1994).

32. McClain, *In Search of Equality*, 20–21.

33. Gerald F. Uelmen, "The Know Nothing Justices on the California Supreme Court" *Western Legal History* 2 (Winter–Spring 1989): 89–106.

34. Delores Nason McBroome, *Parallel Communities: African Americans in California's East Bay, 1850–1963* (New York: Garland Publishing, 1993), 20. Frank Ball, the publisher of *The Sluice Box*, a handwritten newspaper of Orleans, California, wrote on October 6, 1856, that "all three of the Presidential candidates are the greatest scoundrels that ever went unhung, and each sure to be elected." He was critical of the Democrats as "bullies and ballot-box stuffers, so long the tools with which the leaders of the Democracy worked to secure office.... [They] have rendered that party so obnoxious, that good citizens have withdrawn from it in disgust although still faithful to its principles." He castigated the Know Nothings as grafters and thieves of $125,000 in a prison contract. Regarding Republicans, he thought them supportive of African American aspirations for office and in the pocket of the Pacific Railroad. *The Sluice Box*, MSS, Huntington Library.

35. Brown was a conspirator in the planned robbery of prominent citizen Jonathan Temple. See Horace Bell, *Reminiscences of a Ranger; or, Early Times in Southern California*, 2d ed. (Santa Barbara, Calif.: Wallace Hebberd, 1927), 236–37. He also had been charged with previous crimes. See *People v. Dave Brown and Charles Saville*, Court of Sessions, January 18, 1851, and *People v. Dave Brown*, January 24, 1852, Records in Los Angeles County Courts collection, Seaver Center for Western History Research, Natural History Museum of Los Angeles County. Paul R. Spitzzeri, "Trembling on the Brink: Criminal Justice Administration in Los Angeles County, 1850–1865" (unpublished paper, California State University, Fullerton 1999), 34–38. Also see Robert W. Blew, "Vigilantism in Los Angeles, 1835–1874," *Historical Society of Southern California Quarterly* 54 (Spring 1972): 11–30; Ronald C. Woolsey, *Migrants West: Toward the Southern California Frontier* (Sebastopol, Calif.: Grizzly Bear Publishing Co., 1996). For a unique inquiry into crime in San Francisco, see John Joseph Stanley, "Burning Baghdad by the Bay: Fire and Arson in Early California," in *Law in the Western United States*, ed. Gordon Morris Bakken (Norman: University of Oklahoma Press, 2000), 104–13.

36. Bakken, *Practicing Law in Frontier California*, 100. Hereinafter, unless otherwise noted, the text duplicates my prior work on pages 100–113.

37. The best work on Field is Paul Kens, *Justice Stephen Field: Shaping Liberty from the Gold Rush to the Gilded Age* (Lawrence: University Press of Kansas, 1997).

38. Bakken, *Practicing Law in Frontier California*, 2.

39. Ibid., 19.

40. Ibid., 34–36.

41. Ibid., 37.

42. Ibid., 4–5.

43. Donna C. Schuele, "Community Property Law and the Politics of Married Women's Rights in Nineteenth-Century California," *Western Legal History* 7 (Summer–Fall 1994): 249.

44. Ibid., 249–50.

45. Ibid., 259–60. Also see David J. Langum, *Law and Community on the Mexican California Frontier* (Norman: University of Oklahoma Press, 1987).

46. *Dentzel v. Waldie*, 30 Cal. 138, 144 (1866).

47. *Simpers and Craumer v. Sloan and Sloan*, 5 Cal. 457 (1855). Also see *Pfeiffer and Wife v. Riehn and Scannell*, 13 Cal. 643 (1859).

48. *Ramsdell v. Fuller and Summers*, 28 Cal. 37, 43 (1865).

49. See Gordon Morris Bakken, *The Development of Law in Frontier California: Civil Law and Society, 1850–1890* (Westport, Conn.: Greenwood Press, 1985), 41–72.

50. *Hoen v. Simmons*, 1 Cal. 119 (1850).

51. *Tewksbury v. Laffan*, 1 Cal. 129 (1850).

52. *Salmon v. Hoffman*, 2 Cal. 138, 143 (1852).

53. Gordon Morris Bakken, "Law and Legal Tender in California and the West," *Southern California Quarterly* 62 (Fall 1980): 239–59.

54. See Gordon Morris Bakken, "The Development of the Law of Tort in Frontier California, 1850–1890," *Southern California Quarterly* 60 (Winter 1978): 405–19.

55. Ibid., 75.

56. Ibid.

57. Ibid., 75–76.

58. The California Supreme Court gained national stature in the 1850s and 1860s due, in part, to its pioneering decisions in tort law. From the law of product liability to sovereign immunity, the court's decisional law led the nation. For example, in the 1854 blasting case, the court could have noted the special relationship of a woman and her home. Glenda Riley makes such a connection in *A Place to Grow: Women in the American West* (Arlington Heights, Ill.: Harlan Davidson, 1992), 65, 151. Also see Arien Mack, *A Place in the World* (New York: New York University Press, 1993), and Beatriz Colomina, *Sexuality and Space* (New York: Princeton Architectural Press, 1992). The final paper by Mark Wigley, "Untitled: The Housing of Gender," in the 1990 symposium reproduced in this book is particularly on point. Even if courts did not notice gendered space, it certainly is an important topic for historical inquiry.

59. Bakken, *Development of Law in Frontier California*, 92–93.

60. Ibid., 93–101.

4

"We Feel the Want of Protection"
The Politics of Law and Race in California, 1848–1878

Shirley Ann Wilson Moore

California's history has been entangled in romanticized accounts of the daring Spanish conquest of savage but pliant Indians, of tradition-bound Californio stewards, and of hard-driving, entrepreneurial Yankee Argonauts.[1] These fictions were promulgated and abetted by influential early historians such as Hubert Howe Bancroft, who contended that California's passage from Spanish and Mexican rule to Anglo-American hegemony represented the triumph of superior racial, political, and cultural forces over the "descendants of the people of Montezuma."[2] This school also held that conquest and admission of California to the Union was the "Manifest Destiny" of white, Christian Americans.[3] Bancroft, acknowledging that crimes and brutalities abounded in the European settlement of California, nevertheless concluded:

> The idea of conquest in the American mind has never been associated with tyranny. On the contrary, such is the national trust in its own superiority and beneficence, that either as a government or as individuals we have believed ourselves bestowing a precious boon upon whomsoever we could confer in a brotherly spirit our institutions. And down to the present time the other nations of the earth have not been able to prove us far in the wrong in indulging this patriotic self-esteem.[4]

However, in the past two decades historians have begun to reassess California's history, probing the notions of inevitability, progress, race, gender, and politics to reveal a context far more complex, dynamic, and nuanced than was once believed.[5] From the beginning, racial and ethnic conflict have been embedded in the matrix of California's development. The pre-statehood invasion of an army of Anglo-American and European immigrant entrepreneurs and gold seekers overwhelmed, supplanted, and eventually delegitimated Indians, Californios, African Americans, Asians, and other people of color. The influx of white Americans gave rise to "Anglo" domination and established a society that severely marginalized California's other populations. The politics of race and law in California has been contextualized recently in what historian Quintard Taylor has called "multiracial [and] multiethnic" communities in which "Anglos" not only interacted with people of color, but people of color interacted with one another and with "Anglos in varied ways over the centuries and throughout the region." Moreover, Anglo sociopolitical domination displaced the earlier culturally and racially based hegemony of Spanish and Mexican political rule. In 1850, when California entered the Union as a free state, the nature and scope of freedom and equality continued to be hotly contested.[6]

"WHAT ARE YOU LOOKING FOR? LEAVE OUR COUNTRY!"

Decades before California became a state, race and ethnicity shaped the development of the region. The Spanish and Mexican colonists who inhabited California enjoyed vast landholdings, economic success, and autonomy that made the region prosperous. This prosperity would make the territory ripe for American exploitation and conquest, but even before the full-scale Yankee invasion, Spanish and Mexican settlers pursued a policy of exploitation, conversion, and subordination of Indian populations that eventually led to the decimation of indigenous peoples and the suppression of their traditional ways of life. Spanish missionaries, aided by military force, embarked on a campaign of religious conversion and colonization. Recalling the alarm that the presence of missionaries often inspired among indigenous peoples, mission-born, Franciscan-educated Pablo Tac noted that his people, the Quechnajuichom, initially attempted to bar the Franciscans from their southern California lands. When the foreigners approached, "the chief stood up . . . and met them," demanding, "what are you looking for? Leave our country!"[7]

The establishment of the mission system resulted in the foreigners' claiming native lands in the name of the church and compelling Indian "neophytes" to live and work in conditions that often were tantamount to slavery. Priests could and did administer floggings, maimings, imprisonment, and other tortures to recalcitrant Indians who resisted by fleeing, fighting back, or occasionally mounting open rebellions.[8] As partial justification for this treatment, missionaries and other Spanish settlers differentiated themselves from the native population by identifying themselves as *gente de razon,* or "people who possessed reason." By contrast, they labeled Indians *gente sin razon,* or "people without reason." Such racial distinctions served to legitimize the settlers' sociopolitical system and to undermine indigenous structures.[9]

By the time of the gold discovery, Indians had paid a high price for missionization and interaction with whites. European diseases, from which they had little immunity,

Disease, starvation, and violence reduced California's Indian population, more than 300,000 at the time of first Spanish contact, to about 30,000 by 1870. Furthermore, American laws stripped California Indians of their lands, encouraged exploitative labor practices, and denied them equal rights. A group of white citizens sent this petition to the San Diego County Board of Supervisors in 1877 to protest the county's inquest into the death of a local Indian named Olegario. Noting that "the Indian died in a perfectly natural way for an Indian" and that "he was not a citizen or taxpayer of this state or county," the petitioners asked that "officious white people who want to dig up Indians should do it at their own expense." *Courtesy San Diego Historical Society Research Archives, Photograph Collection.*

had ravaged native populations. The policy of concentrating missionized Indians within the missions' adobe walls also contributed to the rising death rate by disrupting traditional sanitation practices, diets, and work habits. While mission Indians had varying experiences depending on the mission, their death rate after conversion was notable. For example, records from Mission Santa Cruz indicate that on average, converts survived eight and one-half years after conversion; at San Luis Obispo they survived seventeen. Infant mortality numbers were similarly dismal. More than half of mission-born Indians did not live beyond five years of age.[10]

At the beginning of Spanish settlement, the native population numbered approximately 300,000. By the end of the Spanish reign in 1821 the number had fallen to 200,000. At the time of gold discovery, nearly 150,000 native people resided in California. By the 1870s California's Indian population stood at approximately 30,000, an 80-percent decrease.[11] When the Mexican-American War erupted in 1846, both the Californios and the Indians would be overpowered by American and European foreigners.

"YANKEE DOMINATION IN ONE FORM OR ANOTHER"

The Mexican revolution that began in 1810 and eventually toppled Spanish colonial rule in 1822 thrust California into the economic and political mainstream of the Mexican colonial empire. In an effort to reduce the power of the church and free up land for loyal sons of the revolution, the Mexican government secularized the missions in 1834. In theory, secularization gave former Indian neophytes the right to claim a share of mission land (but not precolonial church landholdings) and emancipated them. In actuality, Indians were reduced to a system of land peonage, working on ranchos for food and shelter, voluntarily or through coercion. Franciscan missionary Narciso Duran noted that "all in reality are slaves." While the *gente de razon* continued to make invidious distinctions between themselves and Indians, the increasing presence of Americans and other white immigrants, merchants, traders, and entrepreneurs in California aroused new political tensions that manifested themselves racially and targeted not only the Indians, but also the Californios and their lifestyle.[12]

The American and European interlopers who flooded into California defined themselves in relationship to and against the Californios. Many of the newcomers evaluated Indians and Californios as undisciplined, profligate, and inferior. For example, in his widely read book of 1840, *Two Years before the Mast,* Richard Henry Dana, Jr., asserted that "In their domestic relations these people [Californios] are not better than in their public. The men are thriftless, proud, extravagant, and very much given to gaming." Alfred Robinson (a Yankee married to a Californiana) published in 1846 the influential *Life in California,* in which he declared that

The history of Indians in California has been marked by resistance, accommodation, and survival. The Yuma Indians, who had lived along the banks of the Colorado River for millennia, struck back at encroaching Spanish settlers in July 1781 by destroying two missions and killing thirty-four Spaniards and Mexicans, effectively closing the Anza Trail from Sonora to California for forty years. During the Gold Rush, travelers hired the Yuma to ferry them across the Colorado, angering local white entrepreneurs also in the ferry business, and violence broke out between the two groups. Finally, the U.S. Army, aware of the crossing's strategic location, established Fort Yuma (drawn here by lithographer George Baker) in 1850 to distribute supplies to military posts in Nevada, Arizona, Utah, New Mexico, and Texas. After the arrival of the Southern Pacific Railroad in 1877, the fort was fittingly turned over to the Yuma Indians. *California Historical Society, Templeton Crocker Collection, FN-02548.*

Californio men were "generally indolent, and addicted to many vices, caring little for the welfare of their children, who like themselves, grow up unworthy members of society." Such racial and cultural vilifications seemed to justify American annexationist ambitions toward Mexican California. Indeed, political tension, exacerbated by cultural conflict, erupted into the Mexican-American War in 1846. This conflict would topple the Californios and elevate the American invaders to authority in California.[13]

The United States declaration of war against Mexico threw American designs for California into stark relief. In his memoirs, José Maria Amadór, the owner of a vast land grant in what is now Santa Clara and Alameda counties, expressed deep misgivings about the Bear Flag Revolt and the fate of his compatriots: "The bear flag and the presumptuous revolt it symbolized showed the Californios that independence would likely translate into Yankee domination in one form or another." Amadór's

Mariano Guadalupe Vallejo, military governor of Alta California during Mexican rule, was a longtime supporter of U.S. annexation of the region. However, later in life he expressed regret that the change in government had brought "damage to the morale of the people, whose patriarchal customs have broken down little by little through contact with so many immoral persons who came to this, my country, from every nook and corner of the known world." *Courtesy California State Library.*

forebodings were perceptive. During the course of the Mexican-American War, the American military occupied California, American squatters flooded into the area, and American military forces eventually defeated the disorganized Mexican army. The signing of the Treaty of Guadalupe Hidalgo brought an end to the war in 1848, transferring one-third of Mexico's territory, including long-coveted Texas and California, to the United States.[14]

The provisions of the treaty guaranteed that any Mexican citizen in California who did not choose to retain allegiance to the Mexican government would, within a year, be automatically granted the "title and rights of citizens of the United States." It also guaranteed that Mexicans in California "shall be maintained and protected in the free enjoyment of their liberty and property." Articles 8 and 9 of the treaty proclaimed that "property of every kind . . . shall be inviolably respected." However, Congress, with an eye to American westward expansion, rejected the provision in Article 10 that stated, "all grants of land made by the Mexican government . . . shall be respected as valid." The deletion of this provision threw Californio land titles into chaos, paving the way for the federal Land Act of 1851, which opened Californio lands to litigation in American courts. As a result of fraud, manipulation, and indebtedness, nearly 40 percent of the land held by Californios before 1846 was transferred to American ownership. Thus, the legal system economically marginalized Mexicans, forcing them into dependency and wage labor, making the development of California's wealth exclusively an "Americano affair." Douglas Monroy has argued that the deterritorialization of Mexicans and their attempts to resist resulted in the "criminalization" of the Mexican population in California.

Similarly, Indians, lacking civil and property rights, suffered when the treaty was abrogated. Article 11 stated, "A great part of the territories which, by the present treaty, are to be comprehended for the future within the limits of the United States, is now occupied by savage tribes" for whom the United States government was responsible. The government, in moving and resettling their Indian "wards," denied their right to claim title to ancestral lands or land to which they had held title in the Mexican era. The protections outlined in the Treaty of Guadalupe Hildalgo proved hollow. The Gold Rush would accelerate these ethnocentric trends with the construction of a state constitution that gave legal sanction to discrimination.[15]

"THE ONE WILL RULE AND THE OTHER MUST SERVE"

Even with the ratification of the Treaty of Guadalupe Hildalgo, California remained under military rule, in what historian Malcolm J. Rohrbough has called a "political vacuum," with no permanent form of government forthcoming from a U.S. Congress that was locked in bitter debate over the fate of slavery in the new territories. In June

1849, after Congress adjourned with still no agreement on the organization of California, "civil governor" General Bennet Riley called for a state constitutional convention. Forty-eight delegates (eight of whom were Californio), elected from various districts, convened in Monterey to forge a constitution to be submitted for congressional approval as a prerequisite for statehood. The convention delegates made it clear that the issue of race, compounded by notions of Manifest Destiny (or what Monroy has called "bonanza capitalism"), would restructure California's political system and redefine citizenship despite the Treaty of Guadalupe Hidalgo.[16] Whiteness became the new criterion upon which citizenship in California now rested. The constitution being hammered out at the convention favored extending the franchise only to white males. Mexican Californians, guaranteed American citizenship under the treaty, however, had Indian ancestry, and many were dark skinned. Thus, the primary task for the delegates was to determine just who was "white." Arriving at an awkward compromise on the issues of suffrage and citizenship, the delegates adopted an amendment that bestowed "whiteness" on Mexican Californians, giving the franchise to "every white male citizen of the United States, and every white male citizen of Mexico." A unanimously adopted proviso to this amendment left it to the discretion of the state legislature to extend the vote to Indians or their descendants—an unlikely possibility. Indeed, at the first meeting of the California legislature, the body quickly moved to restrict suffrage to white citizens exclusively.[17]

The convention was equally clear that African Americans were unwelcome in California. Sharing the traditional frontier aversion to competition from slave labor, the delegates quickly moved to bar slavery unanimously, but they had no desire for African Americans to reside in the territory regardless of status. The constitution's Declaration of Rights stated that "Neither slavery, nor involuntary servitude, unless for the punishment of crimes, shall ever be tolerated in the state." This section passed not on humanitarian grounds, but because the delegates feared that slavery would "degrade labor" and give slave owners an unfair advantage in the gold fields and other areas of the labor market. Like most of the convention delegates, former Louisiana resident and physician O. M. Wozencraft, a delegate from the San Joaquin district, virulently opposed any proposal to allow blacks to reside in California. Wozencraft argued that

> there was just reason why slavery should not exist in this land, there is just reason why part of the family of man, who are so well adapted for servitude, should be excluded from amongst us.... We see the instinctive feeling of the negro [sic] is obedience to the white man.... If you wish that all mankind should be free, do not bring the two extremes in the scale of organization together; do not bring the lowest in contact with the highest, for be assured the one will rule and the other must serve.

Colton Hall in Monterey, photographed here in the late nineteenth century, housed the state constitutional convention in 1849. The forty-eight delegates included eight native-born Californios. *California Historical Society Collection at the University of Southern California: Title Insurance and Trust Photo Collection.*

The convention proposed a provision excluding all African Americans, regardless of status, from the state, but rejected it out of concern that Congress would find that it violated the federal constitution and thus jeopardized California's bid for statehood.[18]

SORDID CRIES OF "GOLD, GOLD, GOLD!"

With the Compromise of 1850, California entered the Union as a free state. However, the state's constitution and subsequent legislation so restricted the lives of African Americans and other people of color that freedom in the Golden State became a precarious proposition. Within the first decade of statehood, California had established what one historian described as an "appallingly extensive body of discriminatory laws" that marked people of color as inferior outsiders.[19]

The native populations in California experienced particularly harsh treatment under American rule, targeted by notions of Manifest Destiny, nativism, racism, and gold fever. Immigrants who streamed into California searching for gold encroached on traditional Indian communities, breached treaties, and exploited Indian labor, resources, and goodwill. Indians were overwhelmed by sheer numbers and brutal policies.[20] Roger Daniels has argued that California Indians "fared even worse than did most native Americans." An examination of the "Act for the Government and Protection of Indians," passed by California lawmakers in April 1850, reveals that from the beginning, white Americans and other newcomers wanted to strip California native populations of all claims to land, citizenship, and autonomy. The act completed the process, begun in the Spanish and Mexican eras, of divesting Indians of sovereignty. Under the new law, white justices of the peace could adjudicate in "all cases by, for, or against Indians." The act permitted Indians to reside in traditional "homes and villages," but, at the request of a "white person or proprietor," they could be removed to other land where they would remain until "otherwise provided for." Foreshadowing the restrictive work contracts, vagrancy laws, and black codes that would subjugate the freedmen and freedwomen in the post–Civil War South a decade and a half later, the new California law controlled Indian labor, permitting the indenture of Indian children and mandating that all Indians work. On the word of any white person, any Indian deemed to be "loitering or strolling about" could be arrested and sold to the highest bidder to labor for a period of four months. These drastic policies, the consistent abrogation of peace and land treaties by whites, and an ongoing "war of extermination" against many Indian tribes, led to the decline of the Indian population in the state. Indian resistance to white encroachment was not uncommon but was usually quashed by stronger white military force.[21]

Nativism and racism also converged in California's gold fields, as white Argonauts competed with people of color and foreigners of all nationalities for riches from the Mother Lode. As news of the discovery of gold (which had occurred nine days before the ratification of the Treaty of Guadalupe Hidalgo) flashed across the continent and around the world, a frenzied rush to the gold fields depleted the populations in almost every town in California. On May 29, 1848, the *San Francisco Californian* newspaper reported that "The whole country, from San Francisco to Los Angeles, from the sea shore to the base of the Sierra Nevadas, resounds with the sordid cry of gold, GOLD, GOLD! while the field is left half-planted, the house half-built, and everything neglected but the manufacture of shovels and pickaxes."[22]

The world may have rushed in to California when gold was discovered, but racial and cultural egalitarianism, like most other amenities, were in short supply in the gold fields. In 1849 an estimated 85,000 miners lived and worked in the gold regions. Of this number some 23,000 were foreign-born, including immigrants from Europe, Australia, Asia, and Latin America. The census of 1850 shows 962 people of color residing in California, with African Americans making up most of this number, or about 1 percent (1,000) of the state's total population. Along with African American miners, Indians, Mexicans, and Chinese also worked the gold fields. About 15,000

Maria Paula Rosalia Vallejo Leese, ca. 1854, sister of statesman Mariano Guadalupe Vallejo and wife of American merchant Jacob P. Leese. During the Gold Rush, most Americans lumped together Californios like the Vallejos with Spanish-speaking immigrants from Mexico, Chile, and Peru and at one point required all to pay an oppressive foreign miners' tax. *California Historical Society, FN-25807.*

Painter and daguerreotype artist Solomon Nuñes Carvalho, who posed for this self-portrait in the late 1840s, was one of several thousand Jews from the United States and Europe who had emigrated to California by 1860. Born in South Carolina, Carvalho accompanied John C. Frémont on his fifth and final western expedition in 1853. After reaching Los Angeles, Carvalho established a photography studio and joined the local Jewish community in forming a Hebrew Benevolent Society. *Courtesy Library of Congress.*

Mexican miners, classed in the census as "white," concentrated in the southern mining region (Calaveras, Tuolumne, and Mariposa counties) of the state. Although the census of 1850 did not list Chinese as a separate group, and few Chinese arrived before 1852, immigration records indicate that the Chinese population in California increased rapidly after 1852 (from 10,000 in 1852 to almost 35,000 by 1860). A substantial number of Chinese miners, like gold-rushers of all backgrounds, were sojourners who intended to return to their homeland after striking it rich. All of the Argonauts came for economic opportunity and advancement.[23]

Hostility from white, American-born miners toward foreign miners of all types was rampant, but people of color bore the brunt of xenophobia. Discrimination was codified into law when the California legislature of 1850 enacted a $20 foreign miners' tax in response to complaints from white native-born American miners. The monthly tax was levied against all miners who were not U.S. citizens. Ostensibly the law, published only in English and Spanish, affected all foreign miners, but it especially targeted Mexican immigrants, and later also the Chinese, of whom 24,000, or two-thirds of the entire Chinese population in the United States, worked in the mines by the mid-1850s. In several mining regions, Chinese accounted for one-third of the foreign population there. The tax, and tax-related violence, drove thousands of people of color out of the gold fields. Many Chinese and Indians were forced to quit independent mining altogether. Mexican miners in Sonora, California, who refused to pay the tax were attacked by hundreds of armed whites. Nearly ten thousand of the fifteen thousand Mexican miners in the southern fields were forced to leave the region and return to Mexico in 1850. Ironically, some of the ousted Mexican miners were American citizens under the terms of the Treaty of Guadalupe Hidalgo. In 1850 the state Supreme Court upheld the law, ruling in *People v. Naglee* that the tax did not conflict with the California constitution, the Bill of Rights, or the Treaty of Guadalupe Hidalgo. Under pressure from local merchants, who saw their revenues sharply decline when their foreign clientele departed, the legislature repealed the tax in 1851, but then reinstated it as a $3 monthly fee targeted especially at the Chinese.[24]

"OUTRAGES, INJUSTICES, AND UNMITIGATED WRONGS"

Racist legislation and nativism were not restricted to the gold fields, however. African Americans and other people of color in California had to contend with discriminatory laws and policies in virtually every aspect of life. Although lawmakers had failed in their attempts to ban black entry to the state, California's legislators attempted to deter people of color by erecting a bulwark of laws that deprived them of civil rights and left them vulnerable to exploitation. Denied citizenship, they could not legally homestead public land; they were forbidden from voting, holding public office, giving court testimony against whites, serving on juries, sending their children to public schools, and using public transportation.[25]

Despite this barrage of discriminatory laws, for African Americans, slavery remained the most critical issue confronting them in the Golden State. Despite the state's constitutional prohibition against the institution, slavery was in fact practiced. Slaves were transported by citizens of other states to California before and after the discovery of gold. Some slaves accompanied their white masters as part of the household. Others were brought by gold-hungry slave owners to toil in the gold fields for their masters' benefit, with promises of manumission for faithful service. Between five hundred and six hundred slaves were actually used to work the gold sites, while others were hired out as laborers in non-mining-related work. Some were employed as personal servants and assistants to whites.[26]

California's fugitive slave law dealt the most crushing blow to African Americans' aspirations for freedom and galvanized the black community, inspiring a vigorous abolitionist movement in the state. The Fugitive Slave Act of 1852 mandated the return of runaway slaves to their masters. That same year, the Perkins case became the first test of the law. The case involved three Mississippi slaves (Carter Perkins, Robert Perkins, and Sandy Jones) who were brought to California by their master, C. S. Perkins, in 1849 and left there ostensibly as free men when he returned to Mississippi that year. Upon the passage of the Fugitive Slave Act in 1852, C. S. Perkins issued an order for the arrest of his former slaves, seeing an opportunity to reclaim his human property under the provisions of the new law. When the former slaves took their case to court, the state Supreme Court dismissed their appeal and ordered that they be remanded to their owner in Mississippi. The court ruled that the residency of the former slaves in a free territory had no legal bearing on their condition of servitude under California's Fugitive Slave Act.[27]

In another celebrated case, Georgia-born Bridget "Biddy" Mason, the slave of Mississippian Robert Smith, was part of a contingent of Mormon emigrants known as the "Mississippi Saints," who were initially bound for Utah in 1848. The Smith entourage eventually moved to San Bernardino in 1851 and later Los Angeles, where Mason and thirteen of her family members would be rescued in a daring raid by abolitionists. In 1856 Mason, aided by members of the free black community and antislavery whites in Los Angeles, successfully sued for her freedom and that of her family. Los Angeles District Court Judge Benjamin Hayes, an abolitionist sympathizer, ruled that "all of the said persons of color are entitled to their freedom and are free forever." Mason died in Los Angeles in 1891, respected in the community as an influential businesswoman, generous philanthropist, and prosperous property owner.[28]

The Biddy Mason case involved the largest number of African Americans to successfully challenge California's Fugitive Slave Law. A year after the Mason decision, however, the United States Supreme Court's 1857 *Dred Scott* ruling cemented the

Although nominally a free state, California in the 1850s had only about 2,500 African American residents, who were denied the right to vote and to provide legal testimony against whites. The California Fugitive Slave Act, passed in 1852, meant that all blacks in the state lived under a perpetual threat of capture and enslavement. In 1851, abolitionist Mifflin Wistar Gibbs and other black leaders published California's first public call for equal rights for African Americans in the *Alta California*. "The announcement caused much comment and discussion among the dominant class," Gibbs noted. In fact, because of limited economic opportunities, many African Americans in California found themselves reliant upon that dominant class for employment, such as this governess, photographed by William Shew in the 1850s. *Courtesy The Society of California Pioneers.*

rights of slave owners to retrieve their property regardless of their residency in a free state. That same year, the Archy Lee incident, California's last fugitive slave case, underscored just how precarious life was for African Americans in the Golden State.

Archy Lee, an eighteen-year-old slave from Mississippi, had been brought to Sacramento in 1857 by Charles Stovall, the son of Lee's master. Stovall settled in Sacramento to teach school and hired Lee out for a number of years. Lee, claiming his freedom, ran away, but was arrested. The black and white abolitionist community rallied around him, providing legal aid. After a series of intricate legal maneuvers, the state Supreme Court held that the state's Fugitive Slave Law was valid if the slave owner was sojourning or only temporarily residing in the state. Despite Stovall's lengthy residency in California, the court ruled in his favor, noting that the white man's youth, poor health, and inexperience with the legal process should not be grounds for the forfeiture of his human property. As Stovall prepared to sail out of San Francisco with Lee, however, abolitionists blockaded the ship. Archy Lee won a reprieve while his supporters fought the extradition order in court. After weeks of legal wrangling, Lee was declared free.[29]

Black Californians lived a perilous existence in the shadow of state and national fugitive slave laws. In March of 1858, the California legislature came close to passing a punitive antiblack immigration bill that would have required current black residents to carry registration papers and would have deported blacks who newly entered the state. Therefore, in the spring of 1858, when gold was discovered on the Fraser River, four hundred African Americans (almost 10 percent of the state's black population), began an exodus from California for Victoria, British Columbia, thereby placing themselves farther from the reach of fugitive slave laws. Archy Lee was among those who left.[30]

Though not threatened with slavery, the Chinese experienced equally harsh and uncertain conditions in California. Whites, initially receptive to Chinese immigration as a means to secure cheap labor, quickly acted to curb it when marketplace competition and economic recessions affected white workers and made the Chinese convenient scapegoats. California lawmakers drew on an eighteenth-century federal law that said only "free white persons" could be naturalized. Thus, legislators introduced the short-lived "Act to discourage the Immigration to this state of persons who cannot become citizens thereof," a category into which virtually all Chinese fell. The act imposed a $50 per head tax on all Chinese immigrants and attempted to place a $4 monthly tax on Chinese fishermen. In 1862 San Francisco resident Ling Sing sued the San Francisco tax collector, refusing to comply with a $2.50 capitation tax levied against the Chinese. In the *Ling Sing v. Washburn* decision, the state Supreme Court struck down the tax for being in violation of the constitution.[31]

Even though the court banned most of the anti-Chinese legislation, California legislators persisted in their attempts to forestall Chinese citizenship and residence

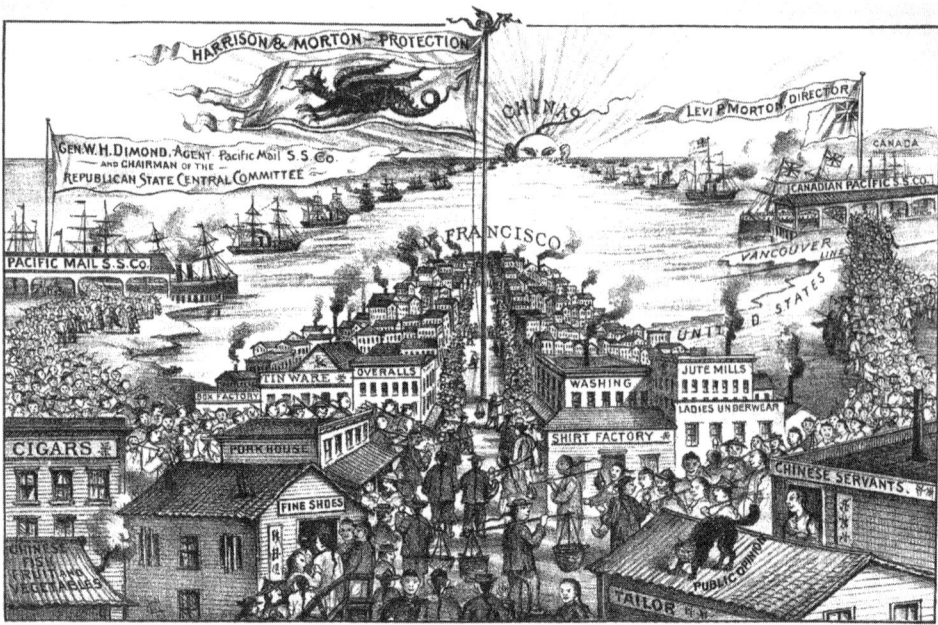

Chinese immigrants faced especially harsh discrimination in California because of the foreignness of their language, dress, and manner. Irish and African American laborers, themselves struggling to survive, provided some of the most strident opposition to Chinese immigration. This lithograph from the late 1860s reflects nativists' fears of being overrun by Chinese "hordes." *California Historical Society, FN-31535.*

in the state. The foreign miners' taxes, the ban on Chinese testimony in court, and the exclusion of Chinese children from the public school system were enacted in the 1850s and 1860s and remained on the books for several decades. In addition, local ordinances (such as San Francisco's infamous Cubic Air Ordinance) regulating boarding houses, sanitation, businesses, and vice were selectively applied and enforced in the Chinese community. Chinese residents and merchants such as the powerful Chinese Six Companies banded together to fight against these outrages, pooling their financial resources to hire white attorneys to challenge the discriminatory measures in court, often successfully, and choosing to fill up the jails rather than pay the fines. Historian Roger Daniels has noted that these acts of nonviolent resistance "foreshadow[ed] the Industrial Workers of the World free speech fights of the early twentieth century and the civil rights movements of the 1960s."[32]

Anti-Chinese hostility reached the boiling point in the 1870s, when economic depressions wracked the country. Alexander Saxton has called the Chinese in California the labor movement's "indispensable enemy." As unemployment rose and labor conditions worsened, white workers in California increasingly blamed the Chinese. In 1877, the emergence of the virulently anti-Chinese Workingmen's Party

Even the California state prison system was not immune to anti-Asian prejudice. At Folsom Prison in Sacramento County, Chinese inmates—considered subhuman—were segregated into the separate, small building shown in this late nineteenth-century photograph. *Courtesy Folsom Prison Museum.*

in San Francisco, led by Irish immigrant Denis Kearney, gave a political voice to unemployed white workers, many of them Irish immigrants. In "sandlot" meetings around the city, the Workingmen's Party denounced political corruption, corporate monopoly, and the Chinese. Kearney made the party's rallying cry "The Chinese Must Go!" When the state constitution was revised in 1879 the Workingmen's Party had garnered enough influence and support to have anti-Chinese provisions inserted into the document: Chinese were prohibited from working for private corporations and for public works, and "coolie" labor was restricted from entering the state. The anti-Chinese backlash that began in California culminated nationally when the United States Congress passed the Chinese Exclusion Act in 1882.[33]

Equal access to the judicial process was another critical issue for California's minority populations, but here too the system established racial barriers that prevented people of color from achieving justice in court. Anti-testimony laws, which California legislators modeled on southern slave codes, had been established as early as 1850. These laws precluded the testimony of people of color in litigation dealing with whites. In 1852, the law stated that "no black or mulatto person, or indian [*sic*], shall be permitted to give evidence in any action to which a white person is a party, in any Court of this State."[34]

The 1852 murder of African American barber Gordon Chase by a white thief in San Francisco underscored the vulnerability of all people of color. In the Chase matter, critical testimony of an eyewitness was disallowed because an examination of his hair revealed him to be "one-sixteenth African." In 1854 the California Supreme Court *(People v. Hall)* overturned the conviction of another white murderer because a Chinese witness had been allowed to testify. Ruling that Chinese and Indians were of similar Asian origin and that the statutes barring Indian testimony also could be applied to Chinese, the court sought to protect whites from the "corrupting influence" of the testimony of "degraded and demoralized blacks from Africa, Indians from Patagonia, South Sea Islanders, Hawaiians, Chinese and other peoples of color." In 1857, Manuel Dominguez, a wealthy landowning Los Angeles County supervisor of Mexican and Indian descent, and a delegate to the constitutional convention of 1849, encountered this racial barrier when he took the stand to testify for the defendant in a San Francisco case and was dismissed when the plaintiff's attorney objected that Dominguez's "Indian blood" disqualified him.[35]

In 1869, San Francisco businessman Fung Tang and other Chinese representatives met with a congressional delegation in San Francisco to demand relief from California's discriminatory laws. Tang told the delegation, "We are willing to pay taxes cheerfully, when taxed equally with others.... Most of all—we feel the want of protection to life and property when Courts of Justice refuse our testimony, and thus leave us defenseless, and unable to obtain justice for ourselves." California's anti-testimony law would stand until 1870, when the federal Civil Rights Act, passed to enforce the post–Civil War amendments to the U.S. Constitution, overturned it.[36]

The complexity of California's multiracial political dynamic is apparent in the way people of color sometimes perceived one another and their bids for equality. This dynamic sometimes led people of color to press their demands for citizenship at the expense of other oppressed groups. In a letter to the African American newspaper *The Elevator*, San Franciscan S. P. Clanton chided the Democratic Party for "prejudic[ing] the minds of the people against the negro's [sic] claims for equal rights before the law, by classing us with Chinamen and Digger Indians." Another black correspondent to the newspaper insisted that "We are natives; our knowledge of the laws of government and customs of civilization are not doubtful—they are fact." Similarly, Lai Chun-Chuen, a spokesman for Chinese merchants in San Francisco, rebuked white Americans for treating them "the same as Indians and Negroes," because the Indians knew "nothing about the relations of society." He asked, "Can it be possible that we are classed as equals with this uncivilized race of men?... We doubt whether such be the decision of enlightened intelligence."[37]

Equal access to California's public schools was another area in which people of

Racially integrated first- and second-graders at Lincoln School in Sacramento, ca. 1915, approximately twenty-five years after the state Supreme Court ended segregation in California's public schools. *Courtesy City of Sacramento, History and Science Division, Sacramento Archives and Museum Collection Center, P. Azevedo Collection.*

color suffered discrimination. It was apparent early that public education in California was headed down a segregated path. In 1855, the state superintendent of public instruction, Paul K. Hubbs, announced that "the education of all others, whether negro or mongol [*sic*] or Indian . . . must depend upon the benevolent care of our citizens or upon their own capacity to pay for it." Later that year, the state legislature changed the school code to guarantee that the state's education funds would be appropriated only "in proportion to the number of *white* children as shown by the census taken by the school marshals" (emphasis in the original). By 1858 the legislature enacted the first of several school segregation bills that prohibited "Negroes, Mongolians, and Indians" from attending public schools. With the introduction of the California School Law in 1870, California began separating children of "African or Indian" descent from whites when there were more than ten such children in the school. In a deliberate attempt to discourage Chinese from remaining in the state, and despite petitions from the Chinese community and supportive white clergy, the law was silent about the status of Chinese children. Thus, after 1870, most minority children in California attended publicly supported, legally segregated schools, which were chronically underfunded and suffered from substandard maintenance, inconsistent faculty, and hostility from the white community.[38]

African American parents fought against the legal proscriptions that kept their children from school, filing suits to test the law's constitutionality. In 1871, African Americans pressured the legislature to introduce two bills that would outlaw segregation in the public schools, but they could not muster enough support to pass them. In 1874, A. J. Ward brought suit to enroll his daughter Mary Frances in a San Francisco public grammar school when the segregated school in her district closed. Ward argued that the state's educational policies and those of the local district violated the Fourteenth and Fifteenth Amendments to the U.S. Constitution and the federal Civil Rights Act of 1866. The state Supreme Court rejected the suit, but the landmark *Ward v. Flood* case had chipped away at some of the legal foundation for school segregation. The legislature eventually amended the school code to allow African American children to attend white schools where no black school was available. However, black parents still had to file suits against school districts to force them to comply with the law. In 1880, the legislature finally abolished school segregation, but five years later it amended the code to establish separate schools for "children of Mongoloid or Chinese descent." Not until 1929 did California officially abolish all segregation in the public school system, but remnants of it persisted into post–World War II years.[39]

All these events underscored the political and socioeconomic dilemma of people of color in California. African Americans addressed these problems through concerted action. In 1852, black San Franciscans formed the Franchise League and unsuccessfully petitioned the state legislature for full civil rights. However, the year 1855 signaled a more aggressive approach on the part of the black community when forty-nine male delegates from ten of California's twenty-seven counties met at St. Andrews AME Church in Sacramento to establish the first Convention of Colored Citizens of the State of California.[40]

Convention delegates were well aware of the convention's historic significance and were equally convinced that the estimated $2.4 million net worth of the black community in California amply qualified them for the undertaking. Moreover, the California convention movement was part of the national struggle for abolition and black civil rights. A number of convention participants, such as Jeremiah B. Sanderson, Peter Lester, Frederick Barbadoes, David W. Ruggles, and Mifflin Wistar Gibbs, had been leading abolitionists in their home states before migrating to California in the early 1850s. Behind the scenes, San Francisco businesswoman and ardent abolitionist Mary Ellen Pleasant made generous financial contributions to the convention movement.[41] Sacramentan James Carter rallied support for the first convention, declaring:

> Brethern:—Your state and condition in California is one of social and political degradation . . . Since you have . . . migrated to the shores of the Pacific, with the hopes of bettering your condition, you have met with one continued series of outrages, injustices,

and unmitigated wrongs unparalleled in the history of nations.... [W]e call upon you to lay aside your various avocations and assemble yourselves together... for the purpose of devising the most judicious and effectual ways and means to obtain inalienable rights and privileges in California.[42]

The first convention in 1855 gave its highest priority to anti-testimony laws. The colored convention movement mounted a series of impressive petition campaigns demanding the elimination of racial restrictions on testimony and voting. Convention delegates authorized the "State Executive Committee," which was the "political arm of the Colored Convention movement," to oversee a statewide anti-testimony petition campaign directed at the legislature. The convention voted to raise $20,000 to finance the operation. Subsequent conventions in 1856, 1857, and 1865 targeted public school segregation, provided legal defense for runaway slaves who were captured under the state's Fugitive Slave Law, and challenged Jim Crow segregation in public conveyances. In 1856, Mifflin Wistar Gibbs's *Mirror of the Times*, California's first black newspaper, was adopted by the convention as "the State Organ of the colored people of California," to disseminate information about their cause and serve as an advocate in the public arena.[43]

The rise of the convention movement in California coincided with the increasing political, sectional, and racial tensions that led to the Civil War. Prior to the Civil War, people of color in California, despite their efforts, found it virtually impossible to gain consideration from a state legislature that was controlled by pro-southern, "Chivalry," Democrats. As early as 1851 the Chivs, led by Senator William Gwin, a former Mississippian, dominated state politics. Proslavery Democrats had unsuccessfully attempted to divide California and open the southern half of the state to slavery. Chiv forces attempted to ban blacks from the state, proposed enslaving all blacks who had entered the state before 1850, thwarted every attempt to overturn racially proscriptive legislation, supported laws that discriminated against Chinese immigrants and workers, and voted for legislation that reduced Indians to a state of land peonage. These political conditions held little promise for harmonious race relations in California. For example, the colored convention movement continued its fight for abolition, suffrage, testimony, and education, but the continued domination of pro-southern political forces caused the third convention in 1857 to be "convened in an atmosphere of discouragement." Bleak future prospects led delegates to seriously consider emigration to Canada or Mexico. Indeed, within a year, Mifflin Wistar Gibbs and some four to six hundred African Americans left California to settle in Canada.[44]

African Americans had won a number of whites to their cause, but not until the early 1860s and the defeat of the pro-southern forces did things begin to improve. The Civil War and Reconstruction years brought intensified efforts and mixed results for people of color in California. For example, African Americans increased their challenges to laws that excluded them from public conveyances and accommodations. In 1863, William Bowen filed a civil suit in San Francisco District Court and won $10,000 after being ejected from a streetcar in North Beach. Charlotte Brown, another black San Franciscan, had filed a similar suit two months earlier that resulted in a jury award of five cents, the cost of the streetcar fare. Mary Ellen Pleasant filed suit against the North Beach and Mission Railroad Company in 1866, when she and another black woman were ejected from a streetcar, but her victory was reversed on appeal by the state Supreme Court in 1868. While none of these challenges ended segregation in public transportation, they helped undermine the legal foundation on which the laws rested. Finally, in 1893 all racial barriers were legally removed when California legislators enacted an equal public accommodations law.[45]

With the election of the antislavery Republican Abraham Lincoln to the presidency in 1860 and the advent of a more tolerant administration led by Republican governor Leland Stanford in 1861, African Americans began to experience some relief. For example, in March 1863, two months after Lincoln's Emancipation Proclamation went into effect, San Francisco state senator Richard F. Perkins successfully introduced a bill that repealed the ban against black testimony. The mood of the Colored Convention in 1865 was more optimistic, given the sweeping changes brought about by the Civil War. Delegates pressed their demands for suffrage and education, linking their cause to the rise of the "copper-colored nations of China and Japan." They urged blacks to take advantage of western homestead laws and called for the employment of forty thousand freedmen on the construction of the transcontinental railroad that was to terminate in Sacramento. In a show of "international solidarity," African American delegates passed a resolution that pledged aid and support to anyone struggling to "free themselves from bondage, whether it is personal servitude or political disfranchisement." They specifically noted the struggle of the Poles and Hungarians with Russia and pledged support for the Irish fight for independence from Britain.[46]

Despite Reconstruction optimism, however, racial advancements were uneven. The Republican regime and the Democrats who resumed control of state government after the Civil War continued anti-Chinese agitation. Governor Stanford's inaugural address denounced the presence of the Chinese in California and called for "any constitutional action, having for its object the repression of the immigration of Asiatic races." The 1863 Perkins Bill legalized black court testimony, but it continued the prohibition against Indians, and it specifically barred "Mongolians" and Chinese from testifying. On the other hand, the Chinese community gained some benefit from Reconstruction-era legislation that aided the freed people. They received federal protections under the Fourteenth Amendment (ratified in 1868), which prohibited states from depriving anyone of due process and equal legal

This cartoon from the November 27, 1869, issue of *Harper's Weekly* mocked the opportunities enjoyed by Irish Americans in California. "Ah, Mike, me boy, you're just in time to Vote," the prosperous man tells the newly arrived Irishman. "Come away with me and get Naturalized. Yer may be an Alderman soon yerself, if yer like." Numerous Californians of Irish descent did rise to positions of political and economic power during the nineteenth century, including Governor John G. Downey, Workingmen's Party president Denis Kearney, U.S. senator James D. Phelan, labor leader Frank Roney, and *Sacramento Bee* editor James McClatchy. *Courtesy California State Library.*

protection. Similarly, the Civil Rights Act of 1870 forbade racial discrimination in the courts and banned the imposition of taxes on any specific immigrant group. In addition, the Burlingame Treaty, which had become federal law in 1868, allowed for free immigration from China. In 1872, California, bowing to federal laws, finally removed all racial bans on testimony. In 1880, the legislature struck down all laws providing for separate schools for blacks; a decade later the state Supreme Court upheld the ruling. Chinese children would be excluded from public schools until the 1920s. The federal Chinese Exclusion Act of 1882, however, would not be repealed until 1943.[47] Many of these post-1860s victories had been achieved through activism by California's people of color, especially African Americans and Chinese, via litigation, lobbying, and publicly exposing inequities.

While post–Civil War legislation provided people of color in California with the beginnings of legal relief, their daily reality revealed that de facto and de jure segregation and discrimination would continue to make them vulnerable to violence and exploitation. African Americans, Asian Americans, Mexican Americans, and Native Americans of the nineteenth century conducted their struggles in an environment where politics had long been conditioned by race and ethnicity. They would be compelled to carry their fight into the twentieth century, when succeeding generations would devise new strategies to overcome both old obstacles and new ones.

NOTES

1. For discussion of the romanticized history of California, see Douglas Monroy, "The Creation and Re-creation of Californio Society," in *Contested Eden: California before the Gold Rush*, ed. Ramón A. Gutiérrez and Richard J. Orsi (Berkeley: University of California Press, 1998), 175–76; and Patricia Nelson Limerick, *The Legacy of Conquest: The Unbroken Past of the American West* (New York: W. W. Norton, 1987), 254–57. Also see Lisbeth Haas, *Conquests and Historical Identities in California, 1769–1936* (Berkeley: University of California Press, 1995), 13–44, 171–74; and Leonard Pitt, *The Decline of the Californios: A Social History of the Spanish-Speaking Californians, 1846–1890* (1966; reprint, Berkeley: University of California Press, 1998), xiii.

2. See Hubert Howe Bancroft, *History of California*, vol. 6, *1848–1859* (1888; reprint, Santa Barbara, Calif.: Wallace Hebberd, 1970), 251–57. People of Montezuma quote from Bancroft, "Personal Observations during a Tour through the Line of Missions of Upper California," in Haas, *Conquests and Historical Identities in California*, 172. In her 1914 history of the state, California novelist Gertrude Atherton proclaimed that "California's historic period began very late. When New England was burning witches on the green . . . this vast and lovely tract . . . was peopled by a few Indian tribes, so stupid that they rarely learned one another's language, so lethargic that they rarely fought. The squaws did what work was done; the bucks basked in the sun for eight months in the year, and during the brief winter sweated out their always negligible energies in the *temescals* [sweat lodges]." Gertrude Atherton, *California* (New York: Harper and Brothers, 1914), 15.

3. For a discussion of the role that the concept of Manifest Destiny played in Anglo-American conquest and hegemony in California, see Monroy, "Creation and Re-creation of Californio Society," 174–76, and Albert L. Hurtado, *Indian Survival on the California Frontier* (New Haven: Yale University Press, 1988), 72–85.

4. Bancroft, *History of California*, vol. 6, 256.

5. Some recent, groundbreaking, and provocative scholarship in this field includes: Limerick, *Legacy of Conquest;* Hurtado, *Indian Survival on the California Frontier;* Haas, *Conquests and Historical Identities in California;* Douglas Monroy, *Thrown among Strangers: The Making of Mexican Culture in Frontier California* (Berkeley: University of California Press, 1990); Quintard Taylor, *In Search of the Racial Frontier: African Americans in the American West, 1528–1990* (New York: W. W. Norton, 1998); Albert Broussard, *African-American Odyssey: The Stewarts, 1853–1963* (Lawrence: University Press of Kansas, 1998); Sucheng Chan, *Asian Americans: An Interpretive History* (Boston: Twayne Publishers, 1991); Sucheng Chan, Douglas Henry Daniels, Mario T. Garcia, and Terry P. Wilson, eds., *Peoples of Color in the American West* (Lexington, Mass.: D. C. Heath, 1994); Elizabeth Jameson and Susan Armitage, eds., *Writing the Range: Race, Class, and Culture in the Women's West* (Norman: University of Oklahoma Press, 1997); Gutiérrez and Orsi, *Contested Eden;* Malcolm J. Rohrbough, *Days of Gold: The California Gold Rush and the American Nation* (Berkeley: University of California Press, 1997). For groundbreaking older scholarship on California, see also Robert F. Heizer and Alan F. Almquist, *The Other Californians: Prejudice and Discrimination under Spain, Mexico, and the United States to 1920* (Berkeley: University of California Press, 1971), and Pitt, *Decline of the Californios.*

6. Taylor, *In Search of the Racial Frontier,* 18–19; Pitt, *Decline of the Californios,* 14–15, 309; Monroy, *Thrown among Strangers,* 174–75. Pitt notes that the term "Anglo" was "unknown in nineteenth-century California." I use the term here aware of its limitations. Strictly speaking it is not interchangeable with the term "white." The European Americans (another imprecise description) who flooded into California after the war with Mexico brought with them a diversity of ethnic, national, and religious heritages. Those of English or "Anglo" descent comprised only some of the white newcomers to California.

7. For a brief discussion of first contact and Pablo Tac, see James A. Sandos, "Between Crucifix and Lance: Indian-White Relations in California, 1769–1848," in Gutiérrez and Orsi, *Contested Eden,* 196–98. Pablo Tac quote from Haas, *Conquests and Historical Identities in California,* 15–16.

8. Limerick, *Legacy of Conquest,* 256–57; Haas, *Conquests and Historical Identities in California,* 26–29; Hurtado, *Indian Survival on the California Frontier,* 23–26; Heizer and Almquist, *The Other Californians,* 4–10; James J. Rawls and Walton Bean, *California: An Interpretive History,* 6th ed. (New York: McGraw-Hill, 1993), 34–39; Sandos, "Between Crucifix and Lance," 204–205.

9. For discussion of *gente de razon* and *gente sin razon,* see Haas, *Conquests and Historical Identity in California,* 2, 13–44; Hurtado, *Indian Survival on the California Frontier,* 23. For a discussion of indigenous sociopolitical systems and the impact of the mission system on them, see Haas, *Conquests and Historical Identity in California,* 16–18, and Sandos, "Between Crucifix and Lance," 206–207. See also Bruce W. Miller, "Chumash Village Life and Social Organization," in Chan et al., *Peoples of Color in the American West,* 221–23.

10. For a discussion of diseases and the death rates of converts, see Rawls and Bean, *California: An Interpretive History,* 38. See also Hurtado, *Indian Survival on the California*

Frontier, 197–98. For a thorough but succinct account of mission life for Indians, see Monroy, *Thrown among Strangers,* 51–80.

11. Population figures in Hurtado, *Indian Survival on the California Frontier,* 1.

12. Heizer and Almquist, *The Other Californians,* 17–22; Hurtado, *Indian Survival on the California Frontier,* 123–29 (Narciso Duran quote, 127); Monroy, "Creation and Re-creation of Californio Society," 186–88, 191; Haas, *Conquests and Historical Identities in California,* 32–37; Monroy, *Thrown among Strangers,* 163–65.

13. Monroy, *Thrown among Strangers,*" 165–69; Pitt, *Decline of the Californios,* 15–18; Richard Henry Dana, Jr., *Two Years before the Mast,* quoted in Monroy, *Thrown among Strangers,* 166; Alfred Robinson, *Life in California,* quoted in Pitt, *Decline of the Californios,* 15.

14. Rawls and Bean, *California: An Interpretive History,* 69–80. For a brief description of José María Amadór, see Monroy, "Creation and Re-creation of Californio Society," 186. For the Amadór quote from his memoirs and a discussion of the designs of American Manifest Destiny in California, see Monroy, *Thrown among Strangers,* 173–80. See also Hurtado, *Indian Survival on the California Frontier,* 72–85. For a discussion of occupied California, see Rawls and Bean, *California: An Interpretive History,* 96–97.

15. Almquist and Heizer, *The Other Californians,* 96–100. For Article 9 of the Treaty of Guadalupe Hidalgo and Californio land losses, see Monroy, *Thrown among Strangers,* 204; see 205–18 for a discussion of the "criminalization" of Mexicans. Articles 8, 9, 10, and 11 of the Treaty of Guadalupe Hildalgo are quoted in Haas, *Conquests and Historical Identities in California,* 56–58.

16. Rohrbough, *Days of Gold,* 10; Heizer and Almquist, *The Other Californians,* 92; Rick Moss, "Not Quite Paradise: The Development of the African American Community in Los Angeles through 1950," *California History* 75 (Fall 1996): 25–26; also see 96–102. For a discussion of "bonanza capitalism," see Monroy, *Thrown among Strangers,* 199–201.

17. Rawls and Bean, *California: An Interpretive History,* 97, 99; Heizer and Almquist, *The Other Californians,* 97, 116–17, also especially 105, for discussion of "degrading labor," and 115, for discussion on barring nonwhites from voting. For an intriguing discussion of the notion of "whiteness" in California, see Haas, *Conquests and Historical Identities,* 168–74. For an insightful examination of the political and social implications of the notion of "whiteness" in antebellum America, see Walter Johnson, "The Slave Trader, the White Slave, and the Politics of Racial Determination in the 1850s," in *The Journal of American History* 87 (June 2000): 13–38.

18. Heizer and Almquist, *The Other Californians,* 94 (Declaration of Rights quote), 96, 105–106 (Wozencraft quote), 115–19; Kenneth G. Goode, *California's Black Pioneers: A Brief Historical Survey* (Santa Barbara, Calif.: McNally and Loftin Publishers, 1973), 44–54. For attempts to bar slaves from the gold fields, see also Odell A. Thurman, *The Negro in California before 1890* (M.A. thesis, College of the Pacific, 1945; reprint, San Francisco: R and E Research Associates, 1973), 29–32; Larry George Murphy, "Equality before the Law: The Struggle of Nineteenth-Century Black Californians for Social and Political Justice" (Ph.D. diss., Graduate Theological Union, Berkeley, 1973), 35–45; James Adolphus Fisher, "A History of the Political and Social Development of the Black Community in California, 1850–1950" (Ph.D. diss., State University of New York, Stony Brook, 1971), 14–19.

19. Quote from Malcolm Edwards, "The War of Complexional Distinction: Blacks in Gold Rush California and British Columbia," *California Historical Quarterly* 56 (Spring

1977): 36. See also Rudolph M. Lapp, *Blacks in Gold Rush California* (New Haven: Yale University Press, 1977), 191–93; Moss, "Not Quite Paradise," 225; Goode, *California's Black Pioneers*, 75; Thurman, *Negro in California*, 44; Jack D. Forbes, *Afro-Americans in the Far West: A Handbook for Educators* (Berkeley: Far West Laboratory for Educational Research and Development, 1969), 23–24; Taylor, *In Search of the Racial Frontier*, 81–82; Susan Bragg, "Knowledge Is Power: Sacramento Blacks and the Public Schools, 1854–1860," *California History* 75 (Fall 1996): 215–21.

20. Hurtado, *Indian Survival on the California Frontier*, 104–24.

21. Roger Daniels, *Asian America: Chinese and Japanese in the United States since 1850* (Seattle: University of Washington Press, 1988), 34; Hurtado, *Indian Survival on the California Frontier*, 129–36, 140–48. See also Heizer and Almquist, *The Other Californians*, 76–90, for discussion of treaties, Modoc Wars, and Indian reservations.

22. *San Francisco Californian*, May 29, 1848, quoted in Rawls and Bean, *California: An Interpretive History*, 85.

23. For a vivid, albeit ethnocentric, description of the international character of the California Gold Rush, see Bancroft, *History of California*, vol. 6, 221–25. For an equally vivid but more balanced description, see Rohrbough, *Days of Gold*, 220–29. For 1850 census figures, see Lapp, *Blacks in Gold Rush California*, 49. Lapp notes that the 1850 census included Sandwich Islanders, or "Kanakas," in this figure, as well as blacks from Latin America, chiefly Mexico and Chile. For Chinese population figures, see Allyn Campbell Loosley, "Foreign Born Population of California, 1848–1920" (master's thesis, University of California, Berkeley, 1927; reprint, San Francisco: R and E Research Associates, 1971), 2, 4, 7, 33; Elmer Clarence Sandmeyer, *The Anti-Chinese Movement in California* (1939; Urbana: University of Illinois Press, 1991), 12–13 (in 1973 edition). For the population of the gold fields, see Heizer and Almquist, *The Other Californians*, 120–21, 144; and Liza Ketchum, *The Gold Rush* (New York: Little, Brown and Company, 1996), 96.

24. Heizer and Almquist, *The Other Californians*, 121, 141–45. For population figures on Chinese miners, also see Ronald Takaki, *Strangers from a Different Shore: A History of Asian Americans* (Boston: Little, Brown, 1989), 82; Carlos U. Lopez, "The Chilenos in the California Gold Rush," *The Californians* 6 (March–April 1988): 29, 32–33; Ketchum, *Gold Rush*, 96; Martin Ridge, "Disorder, Crime, and Punishment in the California Gold Rush," *Montana, the Magazine of Western History* (Autumn 1999): 20–22; Rawls and Bean, *California: An Interpretive History*, 120–21, 126; Rohrbough, *Days of Gold*, 28.

25. Goode, *California's Black Pioneers*, 75; Thurman, *Negro in California*, 44. For a discussion of the black fight for education in California, see Bragg, "Knowledge Is Power," 215–21.

26. Thurman, *Negro in California*, 25; Rohrbough, *Days of Gold*, 211–15; Lapp, *Blacks in Gold Rush California*, 21–22, 64–65, 75; Murphy, "Equality before the Law," 35–45; Fisher, "The Political Development of the Black Community," 14–19.

27. Almquist and Heizer, *The Other Californians*, 122–23.

28. Rawls and Bean, *California: An Interpretive History*, 132–33; Taylor, *In Search of the Racial Frontier*, 72 (Judge Hayes quoted on 78, 79–80, 90); Lapp, *Blacks in Gold Rush California*, 120–21; Judith Freeman, "Commemorating an L.A. Pioneer," *Angeles*, April 1990, 58–60; Goode, *California's Black Pioneers*, 90–91.

29. Lapp, *Blacks in Gold Rush California*, 147–52; Heizer and Almquist, *The Other Californians*, 121–28.

30. Lapp, *Blacks in Gold Rush California*, 239–54; Heizer and Almquist, *The Other Cali-*

fornians, 160–77. See also Herbert Patrick LePore, "Exclusion by Prejudice: Anti-Japanese Discrimination in California and the Immigration Act of 1924" (Ph.D. diss., Brigham Young University, 1973), 14–28.

31. Takaki, *Strangers from a Different Shore*, 80–82, 113; Rawls and Bean, *California: An Interpretive History*, 126–27; Sandmeyer, *Anti-Chinese Movement in California*, 40–56; LePore, "Exclusion by Prejudice," 23–24.

32. Takaki, *Strangers from a Different Shore*, 82, 113; Rawls and Bean, *An Interpretive History*, 126–27; Sandmeyer, *Anti-Chinese Movement in California*, 40–56; LePore, "Exclusion by Prejudice," 23–24; Daniels, *Asian America*, 33–39. Daniels discusses some of the most egregious local ordinances, such as San Francisco's Cubic Air Ordinance, which required each tenement to have at least five hundred cubic feet of air for each inhabitant, and the Laundry Ordinance, which imposed a fee calculated by the number of delivery horses used by the laundry. The highest fee of $15 was levied against laundries that made no deliveries and thus used no horses—as was the case for most Chinese laundries.

33. Saxton is quoted in Russell M. Posner, "The Lord and the Drayman: James Bryce vs. Denis Kearney," in *Neither Separate nor Equal: Race and Racism in California*, ed. Roger Olmstead and Charles Wollenberg (San Francisco: California Historical Society, 1971), 57, 58–59; Takaki, *Strangers from a Different Shore*, 115–16.

34. Daniels, *Asian America*, 34; the 1852 law is quoted in David L. Snyder, *Negro Civil Rights in California: 1850* (Sacramento: Sacramento Book Collectors Club, 1969), 1. See also Heizer and Almquist, *The Other Californians*, 47.

35. Goode, *California's Black Pioneers*, 77; Almquist and Heizer, *The Other Californians*, 128–33; Daniels, *Asian America*, 34–35.

36. Takaki, *Strangers from a Different Shore*, 114.

37. *The Elevator*, November 1, 1867, August 16, 1867; Lai Chun-Chuen, "Remarks of the Chinese Merchants of San Francisco," in Takaki, *Strangers from a Different Shore*, 112–13.

38. Paul K. Hubbs is quoted in Bragg, "Knowledge Is Power," 215–16; Almquist and Heizer, *The Other Californians*, 133–34, 175–76; Sandmeyer, *Anti-Chinese Movement in California*, 50. The 1858 school segregation act is quoted in Daniels, *Asian America*, 36; see also Taylor, *In Search of the Racial Frontier*, 215–16.

39. Heizer and Almquist, *The Other Californians*, 134, 176; Goode, *California's Black Pioneers*, 84–85; Clarence Caesar, "The Historical Demographics of Sacramento's Black Community, 1848–1900," *California History* 75 (Fall 1996): 206; Sandmeyer, *Anti-Chinese Movement in California*, 50.

40. Goode, *California's Black Pioneers*, 74–75; Forbes, *Afro-Americans in the Far West*, 28; Caesar, "Historical Demographics of Sacramento's Black Community," 202; Taylor, *In Search of the Racial Frontier*, 90–92; Rawls and Bean, *California: An Interpretive History*, 132.

41. Taylor, *In Search of the Racial Frontier*, 91; Caesar, "Historical Demographics of Sacramento's Black Community," 202, 204.

42. James Carter is quoted in Thurman, *Negro in California*, 43–44.

43. Caesar, "Historic Demographics of Sacramento's Black Community," 202; Forbes, *Afro-Americans in the Far West*, 28; Taylor, *In Search of the Racial Frontier*, 91–94; Lapp, *Blacks in Gold Rush California*, 91, 203, 209.

44. Goode, *California's Black Pioneers*, 77; Forbes, *Afro-Americans in the Far West*, 27–28; Heizer and Almquist, *The Other Californians*, 76–85, 124–26, 134–37; Hurtado, *Indian Survival on the California Frontier*, 198.

45. Taylor, *In Search of the Racial Frontier*, 93, see esp. 331, note 27; Goode, *California's Black Pioneers*, 87–88; William Loren Katz, *The Black West: A Pictorial History* (Seattle: Open Hand Publishing, 1987), 139; Susheel Bibbs, "Chautauqua Enactment of the Life of Mary Ellen Pleasant," unpublished time line and biographical sketch. Fisher, "Political Development of the Black Community," 39.

46. Caesar, "Historical Demographics of Sacramento's Black Community," 209; Rawls and Bean, *An Interpretive History*, 177; Takaki, *Strangers from a Different Shore*, 114; Taylor, *In Search of the Racial Frontier*, 94.

47. Stanford is quoted in Daniels, *Asian America*, 36; Caesar, "Historical Demographics of Sacramento's Black Community," 209; Rawls and Bean, *An Interpretive History*, 177; Takaki, *Strangers from a Different Shore*, 114; Fisher, "Political Development of the Black Community in California," 39.

5

Capturing California

Joshua Paddison

Late in the evening of May 3, 1851, as San Francisco was once again easing from boisterous Saturday night to quiescent Sunday morning, a fire started somewhere among the hotels, gambling houses, and saloons of its crowded downtown plaza. The flames spread quickly through the city, licking at canvas and devouring wood. The first major blaze in more than seven months, it caught even the fire-hardened residents of gold-rush San Francisco by surprise. A twenty-nine-year-old German visitor named Heinrich Schliemann, many years before archeological discoveries in Troy would propel him to international fame, outran the fire from his plaza hotel to the top of Telegraph Hill, where he watched the city burn. "It was a frightful but sublime view, in fact the grandest spectacle I ever enjoyed," he wrote later. "[T]he whole beautiful city was burned down. The roaring of the storm, the cracking of the gunpowder, the cracking of the falling stonewalls, the cries of the people and the wonderful spectacle of an immense city burning in [the] dark all joined to make this catastrophe awful in the extreme."[1] The fire raged all night and into the morning, traveling from block to block by way of wooden sidewalks and sewers. "The insatiable flames came roaring and rushing onward, darting its thousand-forked tongues of fire far up into the midnight sky," reported witness Mrs. D. B. Bates.[2] Eighteen city blocks, including more than fifteen hundred buildings, were destroyed; dozens of people died, some trapped in "fireproof" brick houses, others crushed by falling debris.[3]

For survivors (as well as for subsequent historians), the temptation to view San Francisco's many fires as metaphors has been strong. William Taylor, a Methodist minister from Virginia who spent seven years proselytizing the sailors, miners, and prostitutes who thronged San Francisco in the early 1850s, saw the holocaust of May 3–4, 1851, as a physical representation of California's spiritual corruption. The city still smoldering around him, Taylor preached from the porch of his adobe church to about one thousand tired, soot-covered listeners. He condemned the gambling, drinking, adultery, swearing, and Sabbath-breaking he routinely observed in the frontier port, warning, "Let the citizens of San Francisco beware! God is dealing with them. This disaster, dreadful as it appears to be, is but a premonition of judgment to come, in consequence for their sins." He called the fire a "disciplinary measure for the correction and improvement of our morals," caused by "the gas of carnal enmity against God, manifesting itself in so many horrid forms in our midst."[4]

William Taylor's sermon was more than hellfire-and-brimstone theatrics; it reflected his palpable disappointment in San Francisco, unleashed by the night's devastation. As Kevin Starr has pointed out, eastern ministers such as Taylor saw California as a "city on a hill," a possible spiritual utopia to guide the rest of the wayward world.[5] Just as the state's mountains "burst" with gold and its fields with agricultural bounty, Protestant missionaries envisioned a flowering of Christianity in California that might well spread to Latin America and Asia. "Let Christians, therefore, everywhere pray for the conversion of California," wrote Taylor, for "very soon we will control the whole empire of darkness, and, under the banner of the cross, will march to the conquest of the world."[6]

Taylor's talk of "conquest" is echoed by the popular nineteenth-century lithograph *Allegorical View of the Conquest of the Continent* (plate 1), based on John Gast's 1872 painting *American Progress*. Widely distributed by western travel writer and promoter George Crofutt, the lithograph glorifies the inexorable advance of European-American culture and technology across the continent. Clearly, ministers were not the only ones to look hopefully toward California. Ever since the earliest descriptions of California had trickled east from the pens of such travelers as Richard Henry Dana, Jr., and John C. Frémont, Americans had dreamt of the region's agricultural possibilities and coveted its furs, hides, and other natural resources.[7] The discovery of gold in January 1848 only fulfilled expectations. In California—land-rich, full of gold, pregnant with promise—a young nation saw itself. In the words of Walt Whitman, California was "the true America."[8]

Yet gold-rush California satisfied few of those dreamers. Gold proved to be not only scarce but physically and mentally punishing to extract. Ministers, lawyers, merchants, and other members of the middle and upper classes complained unremittingly of California's social unruliness, its lawlessness, its multiethnic tumult. "[W]e know of no country in which there is so much corruption, villainy, outlawry, intemperance, licentiousness, and every variety of crime, folly and meanness," lamented southern writer Hinton Helper after three years in California. "Words fail us to express the shameful depravity and unexampled turpitude of California society."[9] From their perspective, elite and bourgeois Californians struggled to erect the foundations of order and decorum in a horrifying sea of vice and crime. For William

Taylor, fire stood as a symbol of California's disorder; for others, the symbol was Joaquín Murieta (plate 2), a most likely mythical Mexican bandit who purportedly terrorized Anglo mining camps. Murieta, representing criminality as well as California's thousands of nonwhite residents, was hunted down and beheaded by Harry Love—or so the story goes.[10]

A tension between order and chaos ran through gold-rush society. Clergymen, businessmen, and entrepreneurs spoke of the need to "tame" wild California—to pacify its itinerant working classes, to subdue its nonwhite groups, to establish recognizable governmental and financial systems. One such institution was the mail. By the end of 1849, the U.S. Post Office Department had established branches in San Francisco, Monterey, San Diego, and other ports, while private companies carried mail to the mining camps of the Sierra Nevada.[11] However, artist H. F. Cox's lithograph of the San Francisco post office (plate 3), ca. 1852, illustrates how quickly mayhem threatened to engulf order during the Gold Rush: queues splinter, men jostle, fights break out. In his book *Eldorado; or, Adventures in the Path of Empire*, Bostonian journalist Bayard Taylor recorded a near-riot outside the office on Halloween night in 1849, as thousands waited for the mail to be sorted:

> Every avenue of entrance was barricaded; the crowd was told through the keyhole that the Office would be opened that day to no one: but it all availed nothing. Mr. Moore's Irish servant could not go for a bucket of water without being surrounded and in danger of being held captive. . . . Towards evening [on November 1] the impatience of the crowd increased to a most annoying pitch. They knocked; they tried shouts and then whispers and then shouts again; they implored and threatened by turns; and not seldom offered large bribes for the delivery of their letters.[12]

The vagrant, desperate, overwhelmingly male character of gold-rush California society produced a level of bedlam odious to its reform-minded middle and upper classes.

By the 1860s, however, those reformers had largely succeeded in their efforts to restrain turbulent California. The depletion of easily harvested placer gold had stemmed the tide of fortune seekers and forced most transient Forty-niners to return home or find steadier work in California's growing cities. Immigration continued, but the institutions of "civilized" society were now firmly in place. Schools, public libraries, and churches, with Sunday schools, women's groups, and benevolent societies, dotted the landscape. The emergence of stable banks encouraged commerce and industry while the economy boomed once again from the discovery of silver in the nearby Comstock Lode in 1859. Agriculture and cattle ranching consumed millions of acres of once uncultivated land, and manufacturers, speculators, and merchants looked forward to the arrival of the transcontinental railroad (completed in 1869).[13] In bustling San Francisco, the state's commercial center, impressive financial and governmental institutions stood alongside other symbols of American urban life, including a high school, about twenty-five elementary schools, two orphanages, a branch of the YMCA, a women's relief society, and no less than eighty-nine benevolent organizations.[14] California missionary Timothy Dwight Hunt, a Presbyterian who had lived through the frustrating gold-rush years, happily reported to the general convention of the American Home Missionary Society in the late 1850s: "I have come from the frontier, and were I asked, 'Watchman, what of the night?' I would at once reply: 'The morning cometh.'"[15]

The establishment and growth of government was the single greatest component of California's transformation from pioneer outpost to industrialized, urbanized, thoroughly American state in the decades following the Gold Rush. Local and state governments, operating with federal sanction, regulated California society, gave it organization, law, and hierarchy. In its myriad forms, American government brought order to California—but not without costs.

From the perspective of California's native peoples, the arrival and expansion of American government meant subjugation and elimination. The state's Indian population, estimated at more than 300,000 before Spanish contact, fell to about 30,000 by 1870. The overwhelming majority died from disease or starvation, but thousands were murdered by white militia groups financed by local, state, and federal governments.[16] The Spanish-speaking Californios, heirs of the first conquerors of California, also suffered financial hardship and discrimination under American rule. The Land Act of 1851 created a special commission to adjudicate land disputes, which heard more than eight hundred cases in the mid-1850s. The average case lasted a whopping seventeen years (including appeals), by which time many once-proud Californio families were bankrupt from attorneys' fees.[17] The Peralta family (plate 4) won legal title to their vast lands in the East Bay but ended up losing all but seven hundred of their original forty-nine thousand acres to speculators, squatters, and lawyers. In southern California, Andrés Pico was elected a state assemblyman in the American regime but lived humbly in ramshackle ex–Mission San Fernando, supported by friends and family members. Bavarian amateur artist Edward Vischer titled his 1865 portrait of Pico *A Californian Magnate in His Home* (plate 5), reflecting a lordly reputation the former don strove to maintain despite his financial hardships. One visitor recorded that Pico was eternally "smiling and bowing and saying in his broken English 'I am de gentleman always'—and such we always found him to be."[18]

Andrés Pico had been one of eight Californios invited to the state constitutional convention of September 1849, a year before California joined the Union. From the perspective of today, the constitution the delegates hammered out is a curious document, a product of committee to be sure, containing both progressive and conservative elements. The document required "all laws, decrees, regulations, and provisions" to be published in both Spanish and English, gave married women the right to own property in their own names, and outlawed slavery (more because of the protestations of miners that slaves were unfair labor competition than because of the delegates' abolitionist sentiments). On the other hand, while acknowledging that "all political power is inherent in the people," the constitution denied suffrage to women, American Indians, African Americans, Asian Americans, "idiots," "insane persons," and individuals convicted of "any infamous crime." The delegates actually passed a provision outlawing free blacks from entering the state, but later decided to exclude it in fear of violating federal law and thereby delaying admission to the Union. The delegates' hastily written, paradoxical constitution undergirded state government in California for thirty years.[19] The conventioneers also adopted a state seal (plate 6), featuring the Roman goddess Minerva (who had been born fully formed from the head of Jupiter) in the hopes that California would likewise escape a lengthy territorial infancy.

Political winds buffeted the seat of California state government from place to place in the early 1850s. After stints in Monterey, San Jose, Vallejo, and Benicia, the capital settled permanently in Sacramento in 1854. Two years later, the legislature created the Board of State Capitol Commissioners, charged with designing and constructing an elegant capitol building befitting the burgeoning state.[20] Their choice for superintending architect, Reuben Clark, expressed his vision for the "neofederalist" capitol in an idyllic watercolor (plate 7), complete with genteel passersby, trotting horses, and a high-stepping dog. However, a chronic lack of funds and two devastating floods delayed construction for years, driving Clark to a mental breakdown and, in 1866, death. Finally completed in 1874, the capitol was widely admired for its imposing Roman Corinthian architecture, stately lawns, and well-kept gardens. "The white dome of the State Capitol rises like a pale planet above the green surges and waving banners of semi-tropic luxuriance," enthused one observer in 1878.[21] A half century later, when a fruit company adopted the capitol for its logo (plate 8), the edifice still reverberated as a symbol of California greatness.

The U.S. federal government had a hand in California affairs as early as 1837, when President Andrew Jackson offered to buy a large portion of the state from Mexico for $3.5 million. Federal troops provided the region's only official government from the outbreak of the Mexican War in May 1846 until California joined the United States in September 1850. Thereafter, the U.S. military remained a constant presence in California's culture and economy. Taking stock of the state's strategic location on the Pacific and its abundant natural resources, the federal government constructed dozens of bases, depots, training centers, and prisons in California. To help protect San Francisco Bay, in 1853 the U.S. Army imported granite from China to build a fortress on forbidding Alcatraz Island, eventually equipping it with more than one hundred cannon. In 1854, the government erected on Alcatraz the Pacific Coast's first lighthouse, visible in painter Joseph Whittle's vivid *San Francisco Bay with Alcatraz and Steamship Princess* (plate 9). The island fortress—called by one

Plate 1. George Crofutt, lithographer, *Allegorical View of the Conquest of the Continent,* 1873, from John Gast, *American Progress,* 1872. Color lithograph, 12 × 16 in. *California Historical Society.*

Plate 2. Unidentified artist, *Mexican Bandit Joaquín Murieta,* undated. Oil on canvas mounted on board, 36 × 18¾ in. *Courtesy Bancroft Library.*

Plate 3. H. F. Cox, *Post Office, San Francisco, California*, ca. 1852. Color lithograph, 16²⁄₅ × 23²⁄₅ in. *Courtesy California State Library.*

Plate 4. Unidentified photographer, *Members of the Peralta Family, Oakland, California*, ca. 1856. Hand-tinted half-plate ambrotype. *Courtesy Peter E. Palmquist.*

Plate 5. Edward Vischer, *A Californian Magnate in His Home*, 1865. Watercolor on paper, 5¾ × 8¼ in. *Courtesy Bancroft Library.*

Plate 6. The Great Seal of the State of California, California State Capitol, Sacramento. Stained glass. *California Historical Society.*

Plate 7. Reuben Clark, *State Capitol of California*, ca. 1860. Watercolor on paper, 14¾ × 19⅜ in. *Courtesy California State Archives.*

Plate 8. Unidentified artist, Capital Pak fruit label, ca. 1930s. Print on paper. *Courtesy California State Library.*

Plate 9. Joseph Whittle, *San Francisco Bay with Alcatraz and Steamship Princess,* ca. 1860. Oil on canvas, 14 × 20 in. *Courtesy Bancroft Library.*

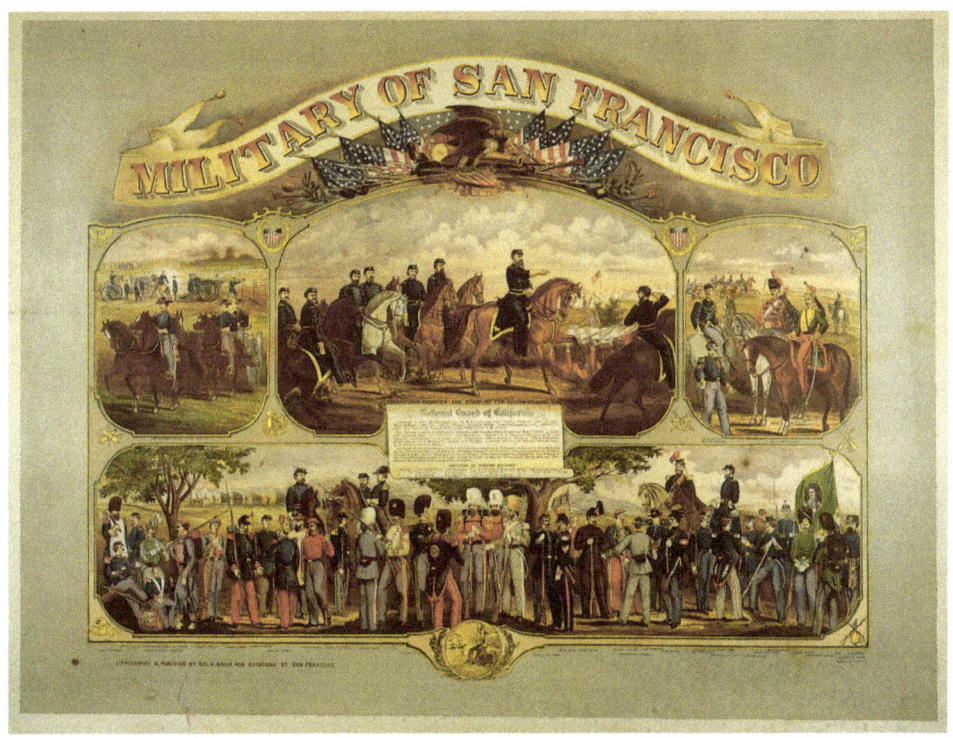

Plate 10. George Holbrook Baker, lithographer, *Military of San Francisco,* ca. 1870. Color lithograph, 17¼ × 22⅛ in. *California Historical Society, FN-32058.*

Plate 11. Nathaniel Currier, lithographer, *Grand National Republican Banner*, 1856. Hand-colored lithograph, 14¾ × 11 in. *Courtesy Bancroft Library.*

Plate 12. William Hahn, *Sacramento Railroad Station*, 1874. Oil on canvas mounted on board, 53¾ × 87¾ in. *Courtesy The Fine Arts Museums of San Francisco, gift of the M. H. de Young Endowment Fund.*

Plate 13.
Theodore Wores, *New Year's Day in San Francisco's Chinatown*, 1881. Oil on canvas, 29 × 22 in. *Courtesy Dr. A. Jess Shenson.*

Plate 14. William Hahn, *Yosemite Valley from Glacier Point*, 1874. Oil on canvas, 27¼ × 46¼ in. *California Historical Society, gift of Albert M. Bender.*

Plate 15.
Edward Keller, *The Sacramento River in the Future,* from *The San Francisco Illustrated Wasp,* December 4, 1880. Print on paper. *Courtesy City of Sacramento, History and Science Division, Sacramento Archives and Museum Collection Center.*

Plate 16. Bosqui Engraving & Print Company, *Untitled* (Horse-drawn fire engines passing in front of San Francisco Mint), ca. 1880s. Color lithograph, 13¼ × 20⅞ in. *California Historical Society, FN-32061.*

The state capitol in Sacramento, photographed here ca. 1865 during construction, cost almost two and a half million dollars and took fourteen years to build (1860–1874). Gordon P. Cummings, superintending architect for eight of those years, called it "the most perfect combination of stone, iron, brick, and mortar I have ever seen and seems intended to last all time and ages." *Courtesy California State Library.*

onlooker "a Siberia, surrounded by water"—became the Department of the Pacific's military prison in 1860.[22] In succeeding decades, Alcatraz was also used to incarcerate civilians, including Indians involved in land disputes and supporters of the Confederacy during the Civil War.[23] Shortly thereafter, lithographer George Holbrook Baker attempted to cash in on postwar patriotism with his *Military of San Francisco* (plate 10), depicting in glorious color the exploits of selected local heroes.

Federal politics likewise influenced the course of California affairs. The state's admission to the Union was delayed for months until a new balance between free and slave states could be reached. National political parties transplanted themselves to California with varying degrees of success. Six of California's first seven governors were Democrats; the lone exception was nativist Know-Nothing John Neely Johnson, elected in 1855. The Whigs, on the other hand, never managed to elect a governor or senator. The Republican Party, which emerged in the mid-1850s, actually chose a California man for its first presidential nominee in 1856—"Pathfinder" John Charles Frémont, whose reports of western expeditions had thrilled eastern readers in the 1840s. A larger-than-life figure in California lore, he had helped instigate the Bear Flag Revolt of 1846, accepted Mexico's surrender at Cahuenga in 1847, and served as the state's first U.S. senator. He lost the presidency to Democrat James Buchanan in 1856 but carried most of the north. Frémont wore a beard during the campaign, as illustrated by the lithograph *Grand National Republican Banner* (plate 11), perhaps to help remind voters of his role in exploring, conquering, and redeeming the American West.[24]

The completion of the transcontinental railroad in 1869 ended California's isolation and further helped bring it into the mainstream of American society. An astonishing feat of engineering, the Central Pacific's daring path through the Sierra Nevada would not have been possible without extensive financial support from federal, state, and county governments. The federal Pacific Railroad Acts of 1862 and 1864 provided the Central Pacific with nearly $28 million in loans and more than 11 million acres of valuable public western lands touched by the railroad. Leland Stanford, one of the Central Pacific's Big Four, was elected governor in 1861, the first Republican to hold the office, and he used his influence to add state and county subsidies to the federal money. The power of Stanford and the other members of the Big Four would only grow after the completion of the railroad in 1869, such that their aggressive control of transportation, agriculture, commerce, and politics would spawn the railroad's vitriolic nickname "the Octopus." However, the railroad did bring undeniable opportunities to many California cities. *Sacramento Railroad Station* (plate 12) by William Hahn, one of the most popular California painters of his era, is a romanticized depiction of the railroad's effect on the state capital, hub of the Central Pacific and home of the Big Four until the early 1870s. Travelers both aristocratic and shabby debark while, in the background, the cosmopolitan city pulses with economic activity. British traveler J. G. Player-Frowd observed in 1872 that the arrival of the railroad "changed the nature of the city. It is no longer the depot for the northern mines. No more heavily laden teams block up the streets. The train drops the goods at every station as it passes over the line, and the storekeeper of the interior now sends his orders direct to Chicago or San Francisco." He added, "The arrival and departure of trains creates a certain bustle."[25]

Although Leland Stanford himself harbored adamant anti-immigration convictions, his Central Pacific was built on the backs of its more than ten thousand Chinese workers. White railroad engineers working along the San Joaquin River in 1873 told travel writer Charles Nordhoff that "Chinese make, on the whole, the best road-builders in the world" because they "learn all parts of the work very quickly" and "do not drink, fight, or strike."[26] In the 1870s, Chinese workers' willingness to accept low wages and dangerous working conditions exacerbated already formidable anti-Asiatic sentiments in California. Dozens of "anti-coolie clubs" formed around the state, paralleled by the rise of the xenophobic Workingmen's Party in local and state politics. City, state, and federal laws reflected the anti-Chinese excitation. San Francisco, for example, passed an ordinance aimed at Chinatown's crowded tenements requiring at least five hundred cubic feet of air per inhabitant. The new state constitution of 1879 forbade any corporation or government agency from employing "any Chinese or Mongolian" and gave the legislature the authority to protect California from "the burdens and evils arising from the presence of aliens who are or may become vagrants, paupers, mendicants, criminals, or invalids afflicted with contagious or infectious diseases." The federal Congress in turn passed the Exclusion Act in 1882 prohibiting immigration from China.[27] Theodore Wores's *New Year's Day in San Francisco's Chinatown* (plate 13), painted at the height of nativist fervor in California, offered a surprisingly sympathetic portrayal of a people vilified by labor leaders and politicians alike.

Like anti-Chinese crusaders, environmental conservationists and preservationists successfully turned to the power of the federal and state governments to further their causes. In 1864, the U.S. Congress designated resplendent Yosemite Valley a protected park (the first such federal designation in American history) and turned its administration over to the state of California. William Hahn's famous *Yosemite Valley from Glacier Point* (plate 14), one of hundreds of late-nineteenth-century Yosemite paintings and photographs, suggests the possibility of a harmonious balance between tourism and preservation (although the discarded wine bottles in the lower left corner imply that a more conscientious stewardship was required).[28] In 1884, the federal judiciary came to the aid of environmentalists in the form of the groundbreaking case *Woodruff v. North Bloomfield Gravel Mining Co.*, which effectively ended hydraulic mining in California. Critics of hydraulicking had for years decried its destructive impact on the gold country and on Sacramento Valley farmland inundated by mining debris. In the pages of *The San Francisco Illustrated Wasp* in December 1880, bombastic cartoonist Edward Keller offered an extreme vision (plate 15) of what hydraulic mining would eventually bring—a Sacramento River clogged with "tailings." Looking on the bright side, *The Wasp* noted, "There would be good 'prospecting' in the bed of the Sacramento, should it ever be uncovered."[29] Previously, state laws had unabashedly encouraged exploitation of California's mineral resources; *Woodruff v. North Bloomfield* was a landmark decision precisely because it offered a new model of environmental policy through governmental regulation.

The rise and expansion of government in California during the decades after the Gold Rush represented one aspect of middle- and upper-class reformers and entrepreneurs' efforts to "tame" the frontier state. Not surprisingly, the benefits of government were not evenly spread across the strata of California society—those with access to the corridors of power profited more than those without. Other groups—especially Indians, Californios, and Chinese—actively suffered. Some advantages of order were undeniable, however. One reason the terrible fire of May 3–4, 1851, had burned so much of San Francisco was the city's lack of an organized fire department. Volunteer groups existed but were scattered throughout the city; furthermore, San Francisco had only four cisterns with which to extinguish fires. In the years following the May 1851 blaze, the city government constructed sixty cisterns and tightly organized the city's network of volunteer firefighters.[30] Thirty years later, San Francisco boasted an efficient, professional fire department, bolstered by privately funded fire patrols such as the Underwriters, which was jointly sponsored by more than ninety insurance companies and the subject of a rousing lithograph (plate 16) issued by the San Francisco–based Bosqui Engraving & Print Company.[31] Of course, fire came again to San Francisco in 1906, just as California's moral and racial unruliness was never completely suppressed by reformers and indeed persists today. Captured by missionaries, businessmen, and artists alike, California continues to inspire utopian dreams of all kinds and to reflect the best and worst aspects of human nature.

NOTES

1. Heinrich Schliemann, *Schliemann's First Visit to America, 1850–1851* (Cambridge: Harvard University Press, 1942), 63–65.

2. Mrs. D. B. Bates, *Incidents on Land and Water; or, Four Years on the Pacific Coast* (Boston: J. French and Co., 1857), 103.

3. Frank Soulé, John H. Gihon, and James Nisbet, *The Annals of San Francisco* (New York: Appleton & Co., 1855), 329–33.

4. William Taylor, *Seven Years Street Preaching in San Francisco, California* (New York: Carlton & Porter, 1856), 114.

5. Kevin Starr, *Americans and the California Dream, 1850–1915* (New York: Oxford University Press, 1973), 69–109.

6. Taylor, *Seven Years Street Preaching*, 349.

7. Joshua Paddison, ed., *A World Transformed: Firsthand Accounts of California before the Gold Rush* (Berkeley: Heyday Books, 1999).

8. Walt Whitman, "Song of the Redwood-Tree," *Leaves of Grass*, 1892 ed. (New York: Bantam, 1983), 170.

9. Hinton R. Helper, *The Land of Gold: Reality versus Fiction* (Baltimore: H. Taylor, 1855), 36–37.

10. For the latest in a long line of interpretations of the probably fictitious Joaquin Murieta, see Susan Lee Johnson, *Roaring Camp: The Social World of the California Gold Rush* (New York: W. W. Norton, 2000), 25–53.

11. For details, see J. S. Holliday, *The World Rushed In: The California Gold Rush Experience* (New York: Simon and Schuster, 1981), 310–11.

12. Bayard Taylor, *Eldorado; or, Adventures in the Path of Empire* (New York: G. P. Putnam; London: R. Bentley, 1850), 210.

13. On the religious development of frontier California, see Steven M. Avella, "Phelan's Cemetery: Religion in the Urbanizing West, 1850–1869, in Los Angeles, San Francisco, and Sacramento," in *Rooted in Barbarous Soil: People, Culture, and Community in Gold Rush California*, ed. Kevin Starr and Richard J. Orsi (Berkeley: University of California Press, 2000), 250–79; Sandra Sizer Frankiel, *California's Spiritual Frontiers: Religious Alternatives to Anglo-Protestantism, 1850–1910* (Berkeley: University of California Press, 1988); Harlan E. Hague, *Prophets and Paupers: Religion in the California Gold Rush, 1848–1869* (San Francisco: International Scholars Publications, 1996); and Laurie F. Maffly-Kipp, *Religion and Society in Frontier California* (New Haven: Yale University Press, 1994). On the rise of public libraries, see Hugh S. Baker, "'Rational Amusement in Our Midst': Public Libraries in California, 1849–1859," *California Historical Society Quarterly* 38 (December 1959): 295–320. On commercial banking, the silver boom, ranching, and agriculture, see James J. Rawls and Richard J. Orsi, eds., *A Golden State: Mining and Economic Development in Gold Rush California* (Berkeley: University of California Press, 1999).

14. Roger W. Lotchin, *San Francisco, 1846–1856: From Hamlet to City*, 2d ed. (Urbana and Chicago: University of Illinois Press, 1997), 348–49; Roberta J. Park, "San Franciscans at Work and at Play, 1846–1869," *Journal of the West* 22, no. 1 (1983): 47.

15. Quoted in Starr, *Americans and the California Dream*, 73.

16. James J. Rawls, *Indians of California: The Changing Image* (Norman: University of Oklahoma Press, 1984), 171–86. See also Sherburne F. Cook, *The Population of the California Indians, 1769–1970* (Berkeley: University of California Press, 1976); Albert L. Hurtado, *Indian Survival on the California Frontier* (New Haven: Yale University Press, 1988); and Ramón A. Gutiérrez and Richard J. Orsi, eds., *Contested Eden: California before the Gold Rush* (Berkeley: University of California Press, 1998).

17. See James A. Sandos, "'Because He Is a Liar and a Thief': Conquering the Residents of 'Old' California, 1850–1880," in *Rooted in Barbarous Soil*, ed. Starr and Orsi, 86–112; Leonard Pitt, *The Decline of the Californios: A Social History of the Spanish-Speaking Californians, 1846–1890* (1966; reprint, Berkeley: University of California Press, 1998); Douglas Monroy, *Thrown among Strangers: The Making of Mexican Culture in Frontier California* (Berkeley: University of California Press, 1990); and Lisbeth Haas, *Conquests and Historical Identities in California, 1769–1936* (Berkeley: University of California Press, 1995).

18. Quoted in Monroy, *Thrown among Strangers*, 227–28.

19. See J. Ross Browne, *Report of the Debates in the Convention of California, on the Formation of the State Constitution, in September and October, 1849* (Washington, D.C.: J. T. Towers, 1850), and David Alan Johnson, *Founding the Far West: California, Oregon, and Nevada, 1840–1890* (Berkeley: University of California Press, 1992).

20. See Board of State Capitol Commissioners Records, 1856–1911, in the California State Archives, Sacramento. The capitol was designed by architect Miner Frederick Butler.

21. Benjamin F. Taylor, *Between the Gates* (Chicago: S. C. Griggs and Co., 1878), 64.

22. George W. Bryan, *The Lure of the Past, the Present, and Future* (Los Angeles: E. G. Newton Co., 1911), 87.

23. See Robert J. Chandler, "Fort Alcatraz: Symbol of Federal Power," *Periodical: Journal of the Council on America's Military Past* 13, no.2 (1984): 27–47.

24. See Andrew Rolle, *John Charles Frémont: Character as Destiny* (Norman: University of Oklahoma Press, 1991), and Ray R. Albin, "Edward D. Baker and California's First Republican Campaign," *California History* 60 (Fall 1981): 280–89.

25. J. G. Player-Frowd, *Six Months in California* (London: Longmans, Green, and Co., 1872), 13.

26. Charles Nordhoff, *California for Health, Pleasure, and Residence: A Book for Travellers and Settlers* (New York: Harper & Brothers, 1873), 189.

27. See especially Sucheng Chan, *This Bittersweet Soil: The Chinese in California Agriculture, 1860–1910* (Berkeley: University of California Press, 1986); Alexander Saxton, *The Indispensable Enemy: Labor and the Anti-Chinese Movement in California* (Berkeley: University of California Press, 1971); Andrew Gyory, *Closing the Gate: Race, Politics, and the Chinese Exclusion Act* (Chapel Hill: University of North Carolina Press, 1998); and Robert W. Cherny, "Patterns of Toleration and Discrimination in San Francisco," *California History* 73 (Summer 1994): 130–41.

28. For a perceptive analysis of "wilderness" painting in nineteenth-century California, see Claire Perry, *Pacific Arcadia: Images of California, 1600–1915* (New York: Oxford University Press, 1999), 99–133. For the history of Yosemite National Park, see especially Alfred Runte, *Yosemite: The Embattled Wilderness* (Lincoln: University of Nebraska Press, 1990).

29. *The San Francisco Illustrated Wasp*, December 4, 1880, 274.

30. Lotchin, *San Francisco*, 174–81.

31. For two contemporary descriptions of the Underwriters Fire Patrol, see Solomon Mead, *Notes of Two Trips to California and Return, Taken in 1883 and 1886–7* (Greenwich, Conn.: n.d.), 40, and C. F. Gordon-Cumming, *Granite Crags* (Edinburgh and London: W. Blackwood and Sons, 1884), 20–22.

6

"Officialdom"

California State Government, 1849–1879

Judson A. Grenier

An overview of California government in the three decades between the first and second constitutional conventions reveals clear patterns of change. At the outset (including the first two legislative sessions), government was creative and generally responsible; relationships between the branches were relatively harmonious. However, as the decade of the 1850s progressed, the legislative and executive branches increasingly were caught up in the partisan bickering that accompanied the rise of political parties and rancor over the spoils of office. The period of the Civil War was a clear watershed for government, as the founding fathers were ushered out and a new breed of official emerged, ready to use the mechanisms of state to encourage the growth of industry, corporations, and large-scale agriculture. Excesses in all of these areas created a political backlash in the 1870s, as the voting public came to view jobholders and especially legislators as captives of special interests, thus fomenting the disillusionment with government that led to the second constitutional convention. Yet during all of these years, serving as a state officer often meant relinquishing a more lucrative career. Given the acquisitive culture of the time, California probably was fortunate that most of its officials were responsible men.[1]

In the state's first election, on November 13, 1849, although the state had not yet been admitted to the Union and its government was extralegal, voters approved the new constitution, elected Peter H. Burnett governor and John McDougal lieutenant governor, and chose the members of the legislature and congressional representatives. The other state officers were chosen by the legislature after it convened in San Jose, the first state capital, on December 17, 1849. On December 20, Governor Burnett took the oath of office, and that afternoon the legislature in joint session elected United States senators. Two days later they met in convention to cast ballots for state treasurer, controller, attorney general, surveyor general, and three justices of the state Supreme Court, and to approve the governor's nominee for secretary of state. (Future holders of these offices would be elected by the public.) During the following month, legislative committees defined the duties of the executive officers. By the end of January 1850, the structure of California government was in place.[2]

The basic elements of state government, with some additions, remained stable throughout the subsequent thirty years, and even thereafter, for the constitutional convention of 1878–79 did little to alter the structure, except for the judicial branch. In spite of the radical rhetoric of some of the members, most delegates at the second convention, according to Carl Swisher, "looked on them as matters which were settled." What follows may be considered the state's "officialdom":

LEGISLATURE: The bicameral body consisted of a Senate and an Assembly, elected by district throughout the state for two- and one-year terms, respectively. At first, the legislature met annually for about four months (early January to the end of April). These sessions put the capital in the public spotlight, as the press dispatched correspondents to cover debates over new legislation. However, the sessions easily were the greatest drain on the annual state budget, for legislators received travel and per diem pay that were excessive in comparison with that paid in other states. In part to reduce expenses, in 1862 voters approved amendments to the state constitution that established biennial sessions and increased the terms of assemblymen to two years and senators to four.[3]

GOVERNOR: The chief magistrate of the state's original term was two years, but it was increased to four by an 1862 constitutional amendment. Chief of the executive branch, he made all formal appointments, supervised civil and military officers, headed the state militia, pardoned prisoners, addressed or forwarded messages to the legislature, approved or vetoed legislation, and served on a variety of boards. ("Too many" was a frequent complaint.)

LIEUTENANT GOVERNOR: Terms were the same as those for governor, and if the governor left office, he assumed that role, as did John McDougal in 1851, John G. Downey in 1860, and Romualdo Pacheco in 1875. As president of the Senate, he could vote on legislation to break a tie. During these years he served on various state boards, such as the Prison Commission and Trustees of the Burial Grounds.

SECRETARY OF STATE: Originally appointed by the governor with the consent of the Senate, his office was made elective and the term fixed as the same as that of the governor by constitutional amendment in 1862. His duties included keeping records of the executive and legislative branches; in essence, he was chief archivist, as spelled out in the 1850 legislature's first act, which created the state's public archives. But over the years he was assigned special tasks, some of which required agencies to fulfill them, such as head of the State Library and sealer of

Tennessee-born attorney Peter Hardeman Burnett was one of the first gold seekers to emigrate to California from Oregon in 1848. In November 1849 voters elected him California's first governor, ten months before the region officially became a state. A stern conservative, Burnett advocated the death penalty for thieves and refused to allow the penniless state legislature to procure loans. He resigned in January 1851 after less than thirteen months in office and moved to San Francisco, where he eventually became a wealthy lawyer and banker. *California Historical Society, FN-23248.*

weights and measures. Another 1850 law required him to record and issue certificates of incorporation, so he was also involved in the growth of business.

TREASURER: His election and term were the same as that of the governor and varied accordingly. His office was the official bank of the state, clearing all checks and warrants. He received and stored the state's income and paid its bills on warrants from the controller. He also redeemed and paid interest on state bonds. Although the state's income was scarce in the 1850s and some of the early treasurers were novices at finance, most performed competently. An exception was Henry Bates, who in 1857 was impeached and convicted of malfeasance; the Senate forbade him from holding future state office.

CONTROLLER: His term was the same as that of the governor. He kept the state's accounts, issued warrants for claims against the state, and oversaw tax collectors, as well as county assessors and treasurers engaged in the state's business. Also his responsibility was preparation of an annual report to the governor and legislature on the state's financial health, together with recommendations for reducing expenses. John Stroud Houston, the first "comptroller" (as it was spelled then) developed procedures and forms for collecting money statewide that served as a model for the rest of the century.

ATTORNEY GENERAL: The length of his term was the same as that of the governor. As the state's chief attorney, his duties were to prosecute or defend all cases to which California was a party, to institute suits in the name of the state, and to advise state agencies on legal matters. He regularly attended sessions of the state Supreme Court and supervised district attorneys and other law enforcement officers. The first two attorneys general were criticized for pursuing legal matters far from the capital and being thus absent when their advice was needed.

SURVEYOR GENERAL: A constitutional officer, the person in charge of surveying and mapping the state was elected at two-year intervals. His duties were expanded in 1858 to serve as register of the state land office and to keep records and maps of all lands to which the state was entitled (especially state school lands).

SUPERINTENDENT OF PUBLIC INSTRUCTION: Although the constitution provided for this office, his power and duties were spelled out by the legislature in 1851. The following year a state Board of Education was created, consisting of the governor, superintendent, and surveyor general, with the superintendent serving as executive officer.

MINOR OFFICES PRIOR TO THE CIVIL WAR: In 1850 the legislature created the office of state printer; at various times the holder of this position was named by the governor or legislature, elected by the voters, or even selected under contract bidding—always to great controversy, because the job of printing minutes of the legislature, statutes, and executive announcements was considered a financial plum.

Like the British Parliament and U.S. Congress, California's state legislature is bicameral, with an upper house of senate and a lower house of assembly. Artist Edward Jump's illustration of the California House of Assembly for 1865 to 1866 includes, in addition to eighty assemblymen, various clerks, secretaries, translators, attorneys, and sergeants at arms. *Courtesy Bancroft Library.*

The office finally was replaced in 1872 by a superintendent of state printing. In 1850 the first act creating a California militia provided for the offices of adjutant-general and quartermaster-general, to be elected by the legislature for a term of four years (an early quartermaster, Joseph Morehead, was fired and prosecuted for collecting state arms for a filibustering expedition); when the term ended, the quartermaster position was melded into that of the adjutant. In 1851, the legislature provided for appointment of a superintendent of the state prison and a three-man Board of Inspectors of the State Prison, offices that constantly evolved during the decade until culminating (1858) in a Board of Directors and a Board of Examiners of the State Prison, both of which were composed of state executive officers. The inspectors, together with the superintendent of public buildings, in 1852 were named to a commission charged with selecting a site for erection of a state prison;

they chose Point San Quentin, north of San Francisco. The first state Board of Examiners (governor, secretary of state, attorney general) was created in 1856 to examine the books of the controller and treasurer and pass on any claims against the state; this body was the ancestor of the 1911 Board of Control. An 1856 law named the secretary of state, controller, and a Sacramento resident to a Board of Capitol Commissioners to contract for erection of a state capitol building in Sacramento, but not until 1860 was money for construction of the capitol authorized.[4]

With this cast of characters in place, we can examine the highlights of the first three decades of state government.

The first legislature ranks as the most creative and probably the most competent. It included many members of the constitutional convention and was faced with the daunting challenge of creating a new government. In a few months' time, legislators had to develop statute law, civil and criminal; establish courts to administer justice; set up county governments to serve as the local arm of the state; design procedures for selling public land, building roads, and draining swamps; stimulate and regulate economic growth; devise mechanisms for dealing with the federal government and other states; construct prisons and hospitals; introduce a public school system; provide mechanisms for incorporating cities and towns; and find the money to pay for it all. Revenue measures chiefly were drafted by the Senate Committee on Finance, headed by Thomas Green, and included taxes of 50 cents on each $100 worth of taxable property, a poll tax of $5 on every male inhabitant between twenty-one and fifty years of age (unless otherwise exempted), and a foreign miners' fee of $20 per month. The last, reflecting racial tensions in the mining regions that were home to many of the legislators, was aimed principally at curtailing the competition of Hispanics. Widely ignored, it proved to be a money-raising failure. Other bills authorized the state treasurer to issue $300,000 worth of bonds, bearing interest of 3 percent per month, and appropriated $750,000 from the general fund to pay state expenses. These measures created a financial straitjacket that crippled the government's ability to function when income failed to match expectations. Everyone involved in the birth of state government—legislature, executive officers, even the former military governor and secretary of state—believed that the federal government would come to the aid of California (as it had other territories and states) by remitting to it those monies collected by customs officers at local ports of entry in 1848–49, the so-called "civil fund." But in spite of almost continual correspondence with Washington and the later efforts of California's congressional delegation, no such money ever was provided. It was a grave handicap for the fledgling state.[5]

Regarding government structure, the first legislature passed measures establishing twenty-five original counties, standardizing the officials required for each (judge, clerk, attorney, surveyor, sheriff, recorder, assessor, coroner, treasurer), providing for the incorporation of cities and for the appointment of harbor pilots in San Francisco and port wardens at every California port of entry, and establishing marine hospitals. Sweeping away the old Spanish-Mexican judicial system, the legislature created a state Supreme Court, district courts, and courts of session in every county. It failed to select a permanent site for the state capital but set up a mechanism to tabulate voter-preference sentiment in a subsequent election.[6]

In regard to its own composition, the legislature established committees in ten areas: finance, judiciary, militia, counties, privileges, engrossed bills, a state library, printing, public buildings, and commerce. Probably the most influential leaders were the chairmen of the Senate and Assembly judiciary committees, Elisha Crosby and Alexander P. Crittenden: they crafted the state's long-term governmental framework. Presiding officers of the two bodies were Lieutenant Governor McDougal in the Senate and Speaker John Bigler in the Assembly, both of whom were conciliatory figures. Most of the legislators were young men who had recently arrived in California, were optimistic about the state's economic growth, and were unencumbered by partisan political pressures. In four months' time, they passed nineteen joint resolutions and 146 acts, some of which, in effect, endure to the present.[7]

Four months after adjournment of the legislature—on September 9, 1850—California was admitted to the Union as its thirty-first state. Therefore, when the second legislature convened on January 6, 1851, again in San Jose, its legitimacy no longer was in question. The leaders had a year's experience under their belts and were determined to present a more disciplined image to the public than that of their predecessors. The majority of the sixteen senators were returnees. On the other hand, the Assembly, which had undergone an election in the interim, sustained considerable change in its thirty-six-man membership. The "old guard" (including some former delegates to the constitutional convention) was substantially reduced; but a few of the newcomers, such as Stephen J. Field, Joseph McCorkle, and Samuel Merritt, were equally talented lawmakers. Bigler again served as Speaker of the Assembly, but when Lieutenant Governor McDougal replaced Burnett as governor early in the session, David Broderick of San Francisco was elected president of the Senate. The second legislature faced the task of evaluating operation of the processes set in motion by the first, identifying problems, and adjusting the machinery of state accordingly. Most of the laws they passed were revisionist rather than innovative. However, Field's committee drafted measures regulating proceedings in civil and criminal legal cases that lasted a generation; notable sections of the Civil Practices Act were a provision for exemption of debtors' property from forced sale and an order to the courts to consider local customs in cases involving miners. An act granting tidal water lots to the city of San Francisco for ninety-nine years generated considerable controversy. More popular were measures creating state institutions to

After years of heated debate in the state legislature, California's seat of government moved permanently to Sacramento in 1854 following brief stints in San Jose, Vallejo, and Benicia. This cartoon, which appeared in the literary journal *Golden Era* in April 1854, mocked the legislature's apparent capriciousness at moving the capital to "the other side of Jordan." *Courtesy California State Library.*

serve the population's sick and criminal persons. The sum effect of the work of the second legislature was to stabilize and substantiate state government, while curtailing the challenges to its authority that were common during the first year.[8]

The accomplishments of the first two legislatures were not appreciated by the contemporary press for a number of reasons. Most of the correspondents represented San Francisco newspapers and considered both the location (San Jose) and the participants to be rather crude. As newsmakers and idealists, they were quick to find fault with proceedings and to openly criticize results. Finally, they tended to reflect the views of friendly executive officers, particularly Controller John Stroud Houston and Secretary of State William Van Voorhies, who considered the legislators profligate and feuded with them over expenses and printing contracts.[9]

To be sure, behavior in the capitol was not formal. While debating, members could be found whittling, smoking, and toying with guns amid what an observer considered "a turbulent dinning colloquy." During the first session, as the time of adjournment drew near each day, the genial chair of the Senate Committee on

Finance, Thomas Green, would proclaim, "Well, boys, let us go take a thousand drinks." The invitation would be accepted by most, for camaraderie relieved the tension of the day's work. As a result, the body was dubbed the "Legislature of a Thousand Drinks," a reputation it could not shake. The milieu did not significantly change during the second session. According to an English visitor, "It is of the style of rump parliament, with very little dignity, very little sense, and still less honesty, judging from the imputations of the members against each other." Clearly, too, these men were racially prejudiced, as indicated by their passage of a foreign miners' tax and their readiness to mount military campaigns against Native Americans in the mining regions. However, their deliberations were not marked by the anti-Chinese fervor of subsequent legislatures, and they rejected the governor's plea to restrict immigration of free blacks into the state. In retrospect, they accomplished as much as could have been expected of that time and place. Many years later (1883), in a dialogue with former governor Frederick F. Low, the historian Hubert Howe Bancroft suggested that the first legislature may have been the purest and best. Low responded, "Very likely it was. It was a small body and . . . they had no money to spend and no schemes to pay money for. It is the conjuring up of these things that corrupts the legislature. It really was self denial in one sense to leave their diggings, where they could make $10 or $15 a day." Of the year 1851, another scholar, Josiah Royce, commented, "[It] is the manly year, the year of clearer self-consciousness, of lost illusions, of bitter struggles, of tried heroism, of great crimes and blunders indeed, and of great calamities, but also of the salvation of the new state." The second legislature played a role in his assessment.[10]

Subsequent California legislatures were less creditable (except for those of 1862–64, when the Civil War provided a focus). Reasons for the decline in their reputation and accomplishments are these: (1) The rise of political parties created extreme partisanship and diverted interest from legislating to campaigning. (2) Legislators devoted excessive attention to one of their roles to the exclusion of others, namely, the election of United States senators, which was also a contest for federal patronage (jobs, contracts), thus corrupting the process. (3) The personal feud between two powerful Democrats, David Broderick and William Gwin, further eroded compatibility and introduced a system of payoffs for support, so that thereafter many legislators were in the pockets of political factions. (4) The rise of corporations and special interests, such as Comstock Lode tycoons, agricultural monopolists, railroads, and banks, led to increasingly intensive lobbying in the capitol. Lobbyists often had a hand in drafting legislation and in rewarding those who voted in their favor. "Conflict of interest" was not a commonplace concept. Instead, the line between what was public welfare and what was private gain was nearly everywhere blurred.

It was common, however, for political parties out of power to attack state governments controlled by the opposition. Some examples of that rhetoric follow.

In the mid-1850s, as the country headed toward the Civil War, a new national political party called the Know Nothings (officially the American Party) rose to power on a platform of nativism and anti-Catholicism. Know-Nothing candidates won remarkable victories in New England, New York, Maryland, and even California, where John Neely Johnson took advantage of a split in the state's Democratic Party in 1855 to win the governorship. After a single term, he—along with the national Know-Nothing movement—receded from the public arena. *Courtesy California State Library.*

The Whig Party meeting in convention on July 6, 1857, proclaimed that "We most heartily disapprove and condemn the administration and government of the state since the organization thereof, the results of which have eventuated in squandering $1,500,000 by the official cormorants who have been a constant curse upon the state." The Republican Party convention, on June 28, 1871, denounced "the scandalous abuse of power exhibited by a democratic legislature in the creation of useless offices, boards and commissions, and the exorbitant increase of salaries and fees, for partisan purposes." The Independent People's Party convention on September 25, 1873, declared, "The abominable and infamous practice of securing election to office by the corrupt use of money at the polls, and in bribing members of legislative bodies, which has become so prevalent in late years, is an evil which strikes at the very foundation of free government."

But though it might direct searing criticism during campaigning, when a new party came to power, it fell into the same pattern of patronage and payoffs as its predecessor. For example, when the American Party (dubbed the "Know Nothings") captured the legislature in 1856, it was expected to curtail political corruption. Instead, according to a student of the party's rise and fall, "Believing from the start that the Know Nothing organization was temporary, the politicians and their friends gave no consideration to its future and cared nothing for its accomplishments in office, but in the customary 'log-rolling' manner, dealt out the spoils of office for private gain." Reflecting on why, after the first two sessions, California legislators were so easily contaminated, former governor Frederick Low in 1883 told Bancroft:

> The first venality developed itself in the state when Broderick fought for the Senate.... Most legislators when they begin are well meaning simple-minded men—the mass of them intend to do what is right. Their poor pay don't support them; they see others voting and getting paid for it, and they do the same. They get discouraged and say, "Oh, what is the use?" and before the legislature adjourns the lobbyists have a ring made up and you can count on it just as surely as you can count on your fingers.... You can buy a man sometimes with a good dinner quicker than you can with a thousand dollars. They study a man's character.

That first political factions and then special business interests compromised the integrity of the state legislature was recognized by most nineteenth-century historians and contributed to the public disaffection that led to the second constitutional convention.[11]

In the three decades between the first and second constitutional conventions, thirteen men served as governor of California (see table 6.1). The first two ran in nonpartisan elections and nominally were independents, but in actuality were Democrats. Prior to the Civil War, all except one, J. Neely Johnson (a Know Nothing), were Democrats. Beginning in 1862, four of the state's six governors were Republican. The time that each served in office varied dramatically. The state's first two governors served only a year; the third, four years (two two-year terms). Four of the next five governors were in office for two years, the remaining one only five days. After the length of terms changed to four years in 1863, most of the remaining governors were in office for one four-year term, the exception being Newton Booth, who resigned with ten months remaining to accept appointment to the United States Senate, thus promoting Lieutenant Governor Romualdo Pacheco to head of state for that brief period. To serve one term or less was the norm (only John Bigler was reelected); this practice guaranteed a rapid turnover in a leadership role where experience usually is considered an attribute.[12]

The first governor, Peter Burnett, was a rather enigmatic figure. Politically ambitious, but reserved and aloof, he often played the role of judge rather than innovator. Born in Tennessee and reared in Missouri, Burnett absorbed the culture of the Old South before traveling to Oregon and becoming a state supreme court justice. Joining the Gold Rush, he administered business matters for John Sutter and son in Sacramento, acquired real estate investments, and for a brief time served as a superior judge in California's military government. As governor, he refused to commit himself on the pressing issues of the day, either to the press or to the legislature. His two gubernatorial messages were concerned with the costs and mechanisms of government, drafting the legal code, and immigration of free blacks (which he opposed unless African Americans were granted full citizenship rights, which he also opposed). In August 1850, he called out the state militia to suppress a squatter riot in Sacramento.

Burnett depended upon the other executive officers to administer state government, used the veto power rarely, and pardoned only one lawbreaker. After he delivered his message to the second legislature, he resigned on January 9, 1851, citing the need to tend to his personal affairs (he was very much in debt). Contemporaries believed that he was offended by increasing criticism of his governance style from both the legislature and the press, and that public life had become distasteful to him.

Evaluations of Burnett's administration vary widely. To Elisha Crosby, Burnett was honest but lacked confidence in himself: "He hadn't *backbone* enough to retain his position and to fulfill what might be required of him in emergencies." Oscar Shuck considered him "cautious, reflective, laborious, and in morals stainless... a business governor." Frederic Low was less praiseworthy: "He was very much overrated... one of those men who make considerable reputation by looking wise and not saying much." But as the pioneer governor with no precedents to follow, Peter Burnett was a pathfinder; he had no reservations about creating a state government even before California had been admitted to the Union, and he enhanced the respectability of the office with his statesmanlike demeanor.[13]

TABLE 6.1
Principal California Executive Officers, 1849–1879

Governors

Name	Term of office
Peter Burnett	Dec. 20, 1849–Jan. 9, 1851
John McDougal	Jan. 9, 1851–Jan. 7, 1852
John Bigler	Jan. 8, 1852–Jan. 9, 1856
J. Neely Johnson	Jan. 9, 1856–Jan. 8, 1858
John B. Weller	Jan. 8, 1858–Jan. 9, 1860
Milton S. Latham	Jan. 9–14, 1860
John G. Downey	Jan. 14, 1860–Jan. 10, 1862
Leland Stanford	Jan. 10, 1862–Dec. 10, 1863
Frederick F. Low	Dec. 10, 1863–Dec. 5, 1867
Henry F. Haight	Dec. 5, 1867–Dec. 8, 1871
Newton Booth	Dec. 8, 1871–Feb. 27, 1875
Romualdo Pacheco	Feb. 27–Dec. 9, 1875
William Irwin	Dec. 9, 1875–Jan. 8, 1880

Lieutenant Governors

Name	Date inaugurated
John McDougal	Dec. 20, 1849
David Broderick (acting)	Jan. 9, 1851
Samuel Purdy	Jan. 8, 1852; Jan. 7, 1854
Robert Anderson	Jan. 9, 1856
Joseph Walkup	Jan. 8, 1858
John G. Downey	Jan. 9, 1860
Issac Quinn (acting)	Jan. 20, 1860
Pablo de la Guerra (acting)	Jan. 7, 1861
John F. Chellis	Jan. 10, 1862
T. N. Machin	Dec. 10, 1863
William Holden	Dec. 5, 1867
Romualdo Pacheco	Dec. 8, 1871
William Irwin (acting)	Feb. 27, 1875
James A. Johnson	Dec. 9, 1875

(continued)

TABLE 6.1 *(continued)*

Secretaries of State

Name	Date took office
William Van Voorhies	Dec. 21, 1849; Jan. 9, 1852
James W. Denver	Feb. 19, 1853; Jan. 9, 1854
Charles H. Hempstead	Nov. 5, 1855
David F. Douglass	Jan. 10, 1856
Ferris Forman	Jan. 9, 1858
Johnson Price	Jan. 10, 1860
William Weeks	Jan. 11, 1862 (died in office)
A. A. H. Tuttle	Aug. 17, 1863
Benjamin B. Redding	Dec. 7, 1863
H. L. Nichols	Dec. 2, 1867
Drury Melone	Dec. 4, 1871
Thomas Beck	Dec. 6, 1875

Treasurers

Name	Date took office
Richard Roman	Dec. 22, 1849; Jan. 5, 1852
Selden A. McMeans	Jan. 2, 1854
Henry Bates	Jan. 7, 1856 (impeached and removed from office)
James L. English	Feb. 13, 1857
Thomas Findley	Jan. 4, 1858; Jan. 2, 1860
Delos R. Ashley	Jan. 6, 1862
Romualdo Pacheco	Oct. 10, 1863; Dec. 7, 1863
Antonio F. Coronel	Dec. 2, 1867
Ferdinand Baehr	Dec. 4, 1871
Jose G. Estudillo	Dec. 6, 1875

Controllers

Name	Date took office
John Stroud Houston	Dec. 22, 1849
Winslow S. Pierce	Jan. 5, 1852
Samuel Bell	Jan. 2, 1854
George W. Whitman	Jan. 7, 1856
Aaron R. Meloney	Feb. 4, 1858

Controllers *(continued)*

Samuel Brooks	Jan. 1860
James S. Gillen	Nov. 20, 1861
Gilbert R. Warren	Jan. 6, 1862
George Oulton	Dec. 7, 1863
Robert Watt	Dec. 2, 1867
James Green	Dec. 4, 1871
James W. Mandeville	Dec. 6, 1875 (died in office)
William B. C. Brown	Feb. 7, 1876

Attorneys General

Name	Date took office
Edward J. C. Kewen	Dec. 22, 1849
James A. McDougall	Jan. 6, 1851
S. Clinton Hastings	Jan. 5, 1852
John R. McConnell	Jan 2, 1854
William M. Stewart	June 7, 1854 (temporary appointment)
William T. Wallace	Jan. 7, 1856
Thomas H. Williams	Jan. 4, 1858; Jan. 2, 1860
Frank Pixley	Jan. 6, 1862
John G. McCullough	Dec. 7, 1863
Jo Hamilton	Dec. 2, 1867 (returned to office Dec. 6, 1875)
John Lord Love	Dec. 4, 1871

Surveyors General

Name	Year took office
Charles Whiting	1849
William Eddy	1852
Samuel Marlette	1854
John Brewster	1856
Horace Higley	1858
James F. Houghton	1862
John W. Bost	1867
Robert Gardner	1871
William Minis	1875

(continued)

TABLE 6.1 *(continued)*

Superintendents of Public Instruction

Name	Year took office
John G. Marvin	1851
Paul K. Hubbs	1854
Andrew J. Moulder	1857
John Swett	1863
O. P. Fitzgerald	1867
Henry Bolander	1871
Ezra S. Carr	1875

California's second governor, John McDougal, presented a total contrast in style. Gregarious and earthy, he shared many of the traits of his fellow veterans of the Mexican War and the miners who elected him to the constitutional convention and the office of lieutenant governor. The legislature elevated him to the governorship on January 9, 1851, and he made a brief inaugural address professing humility. He was popular at the start of his administration for his affability, but that very familiarity undermined his reputation as the months passed. When his wife was not around, he drank and gamed with the legislators and then quarreled with them over minor matters. He vetoed five bills (and was sustained twice) and made greater use of the pardoning power than Burnett had (eighteen pardons). Recurring Indian wars occupied much of his attention; he made special pleas to the legislature to fund the state militia and personally traveled to some of the troubled areas. He suffered great disappointment when the first state convention of the Democratic Party in May 1851 refused to nominate him for reelection, turning instead to Assembly Speaker John Bigler.

Later in his term McDougal became embroiled in disputes with citizens of Napa and Sacramento over reprieves granted to criminals and with San Francisco's first vigilance committee over the hanging of two prisoners. In San Francisco he issued a gubernatorial proclamation condemning the vigilantes and calling upon citizens to obey elected authorities, but with no power to prevent hangings or enforce the proclamation, he was ignored. In his final message to the legislature, McDougal successfully advocated establishment of a federal mint, a public school system, and a state prison, but failed in his call for a state university, tax relief for southern counties, and the forced removal of California's Native Americans. Some commentators believe that McDougal has been treated unfairly by historians because of their sympathies for the vigilance committee with whom he tangled; others dismiss

Government employees—portrayed in this 1883 *Wasp* cartoon titled "Our Public Servants" as simpering, fiendish, and sullen—served as popular targets for nineteenth-century satirists. *Courtesy City of Sacramento, History and Science Division, Sacramento Archives and Museum Collection Center, Eleanor McClatchy Collection.*

him as "a whiskey bum." His lasting legacy probably is his support of legislation that revised and stabilized the legal codes and his use of the governor's office to protest local usurpations of authority.[14]

The administration of John Bigler had four years to top the accomplishments of its predecessors but failed to do so; it may be regarded largely as a four-year holding action. Bigler won two gubernatorial elections by narrow margins, and after the press printed charges of election irregularity, a legislative joint committee in 1854 launched an investigation, but eventually validated the returns. Bigler, a native of Pennsylvania, won repute as a champion of small farmers, those who claimed preemption (often dubbed "squatters"). As such, he was an opponent of the landed gentry, especially those who held Spanish and Mexican land grants. Bigler also was the first governor to advocate the restriction of Chinese immigration, an issue that would fester until the second constitutional convention and beyond. His greatest efforts were devoted to reducing the state's debt by revising tax laws, cutting government expenses, and redeeming outstanding bonds. Yet he was only marginally successful, as costs remained high throughout his two terms. His accomplishments included revising the state hospital and prison systems, an act making Sacramento the permanent seat of government, and the establishment of 221 schools. Bigler issued seventy-one pardons but did little to change the state's administrative structure. His suggestions to reduce the cost of government failed in part because of enmity he engendered among those affected.

In retrospect, Frederick Low gave Bigler a lukewarm endorsement: "I rank him among the Democratic politicians here as a good, fair, average man, and for the time he made a fairly good executive officer." Bancroft considered him a governor who was good-natured and approachable but who could not control his associates or the legislative process. The historian was more critical of the dispersal of public lands that began during Bigler's years in office. The state had received from the federal government five million acres of swamp and overflowed lands and five hundred thousand acres for internal improvements; in 1853 the public lands in California were admitted to preemption rights. The state also was granted two townships for the use of a seminary of learning (to be selected by the governor from the public domain) and ten sections for aid in erecting public buildings. Bancroft claimed that by 1869 most of these grants had been sold, and of the money gained, "a large part of it [was] dissipated by the extravagance of the early legislators, or fraudulently disposed of by political tricksters in collusion with dishonest officials."[15]

Some other early governors had noteworthy accomplishments. During J. Neely Johnson's administration, the state debt was accumulated into one fund and reduced regularly, especially after the federal government agreed in 1856 to pay $924,260 of the Indian war debt. Like McDougal, Johnson clashed with a new San Francisco vigilance committee, with much the same result. A gubernatorial proclamation on June 4, 1856, declared the city to be in insurrection and called on the state militia to suppress the committee, but the militia deserted to the opposition, and Johnson's proclamation languished without the means of enforcement. However, Johnson did sign into law a later measure, promoted by vigilance committee sympathizers, consolidating San Francisco city and county government.[16]

Governor John B. Weller brought to the attention of the legislature a problem about which most of his predecessors had informally complained, namely, that his membership on a variety of boards and commissions sapped his energies. Specifically, he stated in a special message on March 7, 1859, that he had devoted two months of his time to his role as director of the state prison, and he asserted that "in no other State are the duties of the Governor so varied and arduous as in California." During his administration, the anti-Chinese agitation surged again; Weller sent a company of the state militia to Shasta County to put down rioting miners. Also, as a consequence of an act he had signed, six southern California counties voted to separate from the state and form a "territory of Colorado." Weller's successor, Milton S. Latham, forwarded the act to President James Buchanan in Washington with the recommendation that it be presented to Congress, but no action was taken on the measure, because of the looming crisis over secession by southern states. When Latham himself was elected to the United States Senate in 1860 after only five days in the governor's office, Lieutenant Governor John G. Downey was elevated to the governorship. Downey was the first southern Californian to occupy the chair, and his wife, Maria Guirado, member of an early Californio family, became the state's first lady at age twenty-one. According to Bancroft, "[Downey's] administration as governor was universally commended." Downey won accolades and the hearts of San Franciscans for vetoing a notorious bulkhead bill, which would have formed a monopoly to build a seawall with piers and docks along the city's waterline and would have given the favored company the right to appropriate all public and private property to carry out its scheme. Downey was cursed by the developers, but praised by the city and historians of the era.[17]

Downey was the first of three men to serve as governor during the Civil War, the others being Leland Stanford and Frederick F. Low. The war subtly altered the role of governor in that these men were more regularly called upon to deal with the federal government and to make decisions regarding the state militia. But more important, the war created an economic boom and stimulated new industries that called for their attention. As far as the office of governor itself is concerned, both Stanford and Low broke new ground: Stanford was the first Republican to occupy the office, and Low (also a Republican) was the first governor to be elected to a four-year term. With the legislature meeting only biennially, and Low in office for a longer period, the governor's office assumed greater state leadership, at least in the public perception. All three wartime governors fulfilled federal War Department requisitions for troops, Downey in raising units to guard the overland mail route and suppress Confederate sympathizers in southern California, Stanford and Low in keeping those units properly staffed, supplied, and fed, as well as enlisting new volunteers to confront Indian uprisings. (The southern California force evolved into the renowned California Column, which traversed the desert to halt a Confederate army penetrating the Southwest.)

A Chinese American placer miner pans in Amador County in the late nineteenth century. Chinese immigrants found both economic opportunity and legal discrimination in California. During the Gold Rush, the state legislature passed a foreign miners' tax in 1852, specifically aimed at discouraging Chinese prospectors. Chinese Californians were also prohibited from testifying against whites in court and were denied the right to become naturalized citizens. Anti-Chinese xenophobia reached its height in California during the depression of the 1870s, when the nativist Workingmen's Party rose to prominence, "anti-coolie clubs" emerged, and mobs lashed out at Chinese communities throughout the state. *Courtesy California State Library.*

All three governors corresponded with Washington on the state of readiness of California's defenses against prospective invaders. All three responded to federal calls for funds to help finance the war, especially a direct tax with quotas assigned to each state; however, Stanford wrangled (to no avail) with state treasurer Delos R. Ashley over the latter's decision to pay part of California's quota in paper currency that was worth less than coin. Both Stanford and Low worked harmoniously with the legislature during sessions that largely focused on war measures, such as curbing sedition and financing a soldiers' relief fund. Stanford vetoed only five of more than 430 bills passed in 1862 and only one of 530 in 1863. Low used the veto pen much more regularly, chiefly on special legislation he considered none of the state's responsibility. Both Stanford and Low supported measures aiding business, such as forming savings and loan corporations, paying bonuses for new industries in agriculture and manufacturing, and granting road-building materials and rights of way, but they differed over the degree of state aid to railroads. Stanford, who was president of the Central Pacific Railroad at the same time he was governor, lobbied for and approved several subsidies of his own corporation. Low vetoed several similar measures, largely because he considered them raids on the state treasury at a time when he was preaching frugality. However, he did agree to the assumption by the 1864 legislature of interest on $1.5 million in railroad bonds at 7 percent for twenty years—a commitment that historians estimate was worth $2.1 million. The state debt was reduced during all three wartime administrations because of the surge in business; in Stanford's term alone, it was cut in half. Low was especially proud that all the wartime expenses, including bounties for volunteers, resulted in no debt against the state.[18]

The postwar governors—two of them, Henry Haight and William Irwin, Democrats, and two, Newton Booth and Romualdo Pacheco (only one term together), Republicans—were slowly but surely affected by the gathering political winds that led to the second constitutional convention. Democrats Haight and Irwin were perceived to be sympathetic to workingmen and farmers, Booth to business interests. But these were the years of corporate ascendancy, and the role of governors was marginalized. It may be said of the state, as William Issel and Robert Cherny have written of San Francisco, that "the era was one of minimal government by any criterion"—entrepreneurs, rather than government, made decisions about development. Conversely, the machinery of government was growing, and governors spent much of their time on various boards and commissions, engaged in, to use a modern term, "micromanagement." These duties constituted a major handicap, as John W. Dwinelle emphasized in an address to the California Supreme Court on September 25, 1878, memorializing former governor Henry Haight, who had just died after being elected to the second constitutional convention. According to Dwinelle, Haight had complained about the "physical, moral and political strain of exercising the pardoning power" and urged "elevation of the Governor of the State from being the mere chairman of committees to the position of Grand Censor and Inquisitor." Dwinelle continued his oration, which was, in effect, a charge to the newly elected members of the convention to reexamine the role of governor:[19]

> Haight's matured opinion was, that instead of being a component member of the Prison Directors, Board of Regents of the University, the State Normal School, the Board of Examiners, the Board of State Capitol Commissioners, and the like, where he can be overturned by a bare majority vote, and thus held responsible by public opinion for action in which he does not concur, he should rather be the officer to whom all such bodies should make report of what they had done, and be vested with large powers of supervision, suspension and removal.

From 1850 to 1878, state government was swelled by a variety of offices and agencies, some of which existed fleetingly, others permanently in sundry incarnations. Some of the more important ones were the following:

STATE ARCHIVES: The first act passed by the first legislature dealt with the state's public archives, both those of the new state and of the former Spanish-Mexican government, delegating to the secretary of state responsibility for obtaining and preserving the archives. The Spanish-Mexican papers were released to the federal government in 1858, but the records of past state administrations traveled with the secretary of state to each successive state capital in the 1850s and eventually to Sacramento. The archives originally included the papers of the governor, secretary of state, and legislature and was expanded to include Supreme Court cases and some record books of other departments, chiefly the controller and treasurer. Newly created departments were in charge of their own records, with discretion to keep or destroy anything but their record books, a largely hit-or-miss operation throughout the nineteenth century; even the record books were protected by tradition, not law. The most common users of the archives were legislators and their aides, justices and their clerks, lawyers, land agents, and, eventually, historians.[20]

STATE LIBRARY: The State Library was born on December 24, 1849, with a gift of five books to the Senate. Three weeks later, John C. Frémont donated a hundred volumes. The 1850 legislature formally created the State Library, to be kept in the office of the secretary of state, who was ex-officio librarian. In 1852, a library fund for making purchases was created, along with a board of directors composed of the governor, treasurer, controller, president of the Senate, and Speaker of the Assembly. Funds were raised by requiring every state officer to pay $5 on receipt of commission and reserving $5 from the pay of each member of the legislature. Most of the early expansion was in legal texts; in 1856 a collection composed of thirty-five hundred law books was purchased for $17,000 from San Franciscan William Olds and became the basis for the library's law department. In 1861 the State Library was separated from the secretary of state's office and placed under the control of a five-man board of trustees (the governor, chief justice, and three members named by the legislature), which had the power to appoint a librarian. The first designated state librarian they appointed was W. C. Stratton, who served from 1861 to 1870. R. O. Cravens served from 1870 to 1882. During these years, it was not a lending library or open to the public; primarily it was used by legislators and jurists, but gradually it grew into a major public institution.[21]

BOARD OF EDUCATION: The first school law passed by the legislature in 1851 defined the duties of the superintendent of public instruction. A second law in 1852 created a state Board of Education composed of the superintendent, gover-

The California State Library, created by the legislature in 1850, grew to become one of the West's premier public research institutions. Once located in the Capitol in Sacramento, it moved in 1928 to a nearby Library and Courts Building with a main reading room featuring a mural by famed California artist Maynard Dixon. *Courtesy California State Library.*

nor, and surveyor general (included because the board supposedly would manage and sell school lands), and provided a state school tax of five cents on each hundred dollars of assessed valuation. Until the mid-1860s, the Board of Education's principal function was to apportion, annually, the state school moneys. Legislation in 1860 authorized the board to adopt a state series of textbooks and empowered the superintendent to appoint a state Board of Examiners with the power to grant state teachers' certificates. Thanks to the influence of John Swett, who took office as the fourth superintendent on January 2, 1863, the state school structure was revised. (In 1866 Swett served as secretary to both the Senate and Assembly education committees, so every bill passed through his hands.) The legislature set up a free school system supported by taxation and reorganized both the Board of Examiners and the Board of Education. The former now would be composed exclusively of educators empowered to issue diplomas and certificates. The latter now would consist of the governor, the superintendent, the principal of the State

Normal School, the school superintendents of four counties, and two professional teachers, a structure that (with revision) remained in effect until 1880; it was authorized to adopt rules for the conduct of schools, courses of study, and a uniform state series of texts.[22]

STATE HOSPITALS AND SPECIAL SCHOOLS: In the early 1850s three state hospitals existed—at San Francisco, Sacramento, and Stockton—supervised by a board of trustees of six members chosen by the legislature. The government scraped for funds to support their maintenance until 1853, when the Senate's Hospital Committee criticized great extravagance at institutions that benefited chiefly local residents. The hospital at Sacramento was abandoned, that at San Francisco designated a marine hospital (until it, too, was abolished in 1855), and that at Stockton converted to an insane asylum. Captain C. M. Weber of Stockton donated one hundred acres of land to the state for construction, and management of the insane asylum was entrusted to a board of five trustees appointed by the legislature. Over time, the board's membership was altered to include Stockton residents and representatives from each of the state's congressional districts. A correspondent of *Hutchings' California Magazine* in 1859 provided a detailed description of the asylum. He found the building's exterior "imposing and inviting," the grounds "well laid out and cleanly kept, the work of the patients themselves." Inside, "milder cases" wandered the first floor; on the second floor, those "more malignant" were confined behind locked doors. The asylum that year housed 280 men and 66 women; their insanity was caused, according to the staff, by masturbation, intemperance, want of chastity, and incontinence. The reporter observed, "It is a depressing sight, indeed, to witness either man or woman when reason is dethroned; but it is a wise provision of the State that such should be well cared for, and by kind and suitable treatment, both physical and mental, restored to their former sanity." Another state effort at rehabilitation undertaken in 1859 lasted only a brief time. The governor was authorized to appoint a board of commissioners to find a site for construction of a State Reform School, which subsequently was established at Marysville. When the act was repealed in 1868 and the institution abandoned, the boys of the reform school were dispersed to locations ineligible for state funding. More permanently, the California School for the Deaf and Blind was created in 1860, when a five-member board of trustees was charged with erecting an institution for educating and caring for the indigent blind and deaf. A board of managers subsequently was added to administer the school. Initially located in San Francisco, the school moved to Berkeley in 1869.[23]

PORT AND HARBOR COMMISSIONERS: Because seagoing transportation was vital to California's economic and social development, state government from the start gave special attention to licensing pilots for guiding shipping at various

Artist B. F. Butler's 1855 lithograph of the state insane asylum in Stockton depicts the institution as dark and menacing, but some contemporary observers praised its cleanliness and gentle methods. "There is not a single cell in or about the establishment," boasted the state asylum superintendent in the mid-1850s. "Many cases recover without much medicine. The great object is to support the system, to compose the mind and induce sleep." *Courtesy Bancroft Library.*

coastal harbors. The legislature passed in 1850 both a general law providing standards and qualifications and special acts regulating individual ports. To carry out the provisions, the legislature created a panoply of regulatory bodies: Boards of Pilot Commissioners for San Francisco Bay (1850), Mare Island and Benicia (1856), Humboldt Bay and Bar (1860), and San Diego (1853, formalized in 1872); two port wardens for San Francisco, and one for every other port of entry in the state (1850). Qualifications for membership on the various boards of pilot commissioners changed over the years, but the governor made the appointments after receiving recommendations from residents of the affected ports, such as shipmasters or chambers of commerce. Expenses of each board were funded by charging local pilots 5 percent of their earnings. Port wardens were appointed by the governor with the consent of the Senate; they were required, when requested, to survey any ship arriving in distress or that had suffered damage at sea. In 1863 the legislature created a Board of State Harbor Commissioners (three men with staggered four-year terms), which, despite its name, was concerned primarily with the bay waterfront of San Francisco and the management of its wharves, seawalls, piers, rents, and tolls. In effect, the state took over operation of the harbor and became a large-scale entrepreneur. With the creation of this body, the legislature hoped to put an end to the constant political turmoil, corruption, charges, and countercharges that waterfront development had generated during the preceding decade. However, the three commissioners had little experience in confronting the immense problems of managing the harbor and in the 1870s were themselves compromised by charges of corruption.[24]

STATE BOARD OF EQUALIZATION: Since the first attempt to assess property and collect taxes from Californians in 1850, controversy raged over differing standards used by county officials in various parts of the state. The belief of southern California residents—largely accurate—that they were being treated unfairly led to the movement for state division in the 1850s and rankled even after the Civil War. Partially in response, on April 4, 1870, the legislature created a State Board of Equalization, consisting of the controller and two members appointed by the governor to four-year terms. Their task was to investigate methods of assessment used locally and to equalize tax collection throughout the state; within a year, total assessments more than doubled. These provisions were incorporated into the Political Code of 1872 (the controller was made ex officio), and in 1876 the attorney general was added to the board. In January 1874, the raison d'être of the Board of Equalization was undermined by the state Supreme Court, which declared that section of the Political Code unconstitutional. The court held that the state constitution mandated that valuation must by made by locally elected assessors and that the power to change it could not be delegated to a state board. This decision also provided impetus to the call for a convention to revise the constitution.[25]

A review of California officialdom would be incomplete without reference to a variety of minor bodies created prior to the second constitutional convention. (Growth of the state prison system is covered in chap. 2 in this volume.) In 1860, the legislature named a board of commissioners to select a tract of land to be known as the State Burial Grounds; it became a board of administrative trustees in 1866. In 1870 an act created a Board of Fish Commissioners—three persons appointed by the governor to establish "fish breederies" to preserve fish in the state's waters, regulate length of the fishing season, and introduce new types of fish (many new species were brought from the eastern United States in aquarium cars). The legislature in 1854 established a State Agricultural Society, with the power to buy land for an experimental farm. Although the society was not officially part of government, it received $5,000 in support annually and often functioned as an arm of the state. This relationship was solidified in 1863, when the legislature added a Board of Agriculture to administer society affairs. The society sponsored annual fairs, and during the Civil War its president awarded premiums for experiments to foster agricultural production. Membership in the Board of Capitol Commissioners changed periodically after its organization in 1856, but despite war, flooding, cost overruns, and contractors' malfeasance, the new capitol building finally opened in Sacramento on November 26, 1869.

For a brief period of time (1861–1866), a Board of Swamp Land Commissioners existed to undertake reclamation of swamp, overflowed, and salt-marsh land acquired by the state from the federal government; in partnership with landowners, this board hired engineers and construction companies to drain surplus water. In 1868 and 1870, the legislature created two Code Commissions to review laws passed between 1850 and 1868 and to recommend legislation for clarification; as a result of their deliberations, newly revised Political, Civil, and Penal codes and a Code of Civil Procedure were passed in 1872. Included in the Political Code was a state Board of Health (first established in 1870)—seven physicians from throughout the state appointed by the governor to four-year terms, with solely advisory functions.[26]

Faced with increasing political criticism that government was beholden to corporate interests, legislators took steps that may be considered precursors to a second constitutional convention. In 1868 the office of Insurance Commissioner was created to regulate insurance companies incorporated in California; the 1872 Political Code specified that the head of this department be appointed by the governor with the consent of the Senate. The first two commissioners were more aggressive in restricting activities of out-of-state companies and weeding out smaller firms than in supervising the local market. A Board of Bank Commissioners was established in 1878; its duties included licensing and examining California's banks. All banks were required to make annual reports and were subject to semiannual visitations. In 1876, the legislature took its first step to regulate the state's railroads by authorizing the governor to appoint three commissioners of transportation to fix maximum charges for freights and fares and prevent extortion in the operation of steam railroads. Although all of these agencies gathered useful information about the status of their fields, they were hampered by the refusal of many companies to provide the required data and ultimately were largely ineffectual, because little was done to protect them from being captured by the very interests they were intended to regulate. Finally, in 1878, foreshadowing what someday would become a department of public works, the legislature created the position of state engineer to improve irrigation, drainage, and river navigation. Among the tasks of the first engineer, the capable William Hammond Hall, was to devise a workable water plan for the state and to mitigate disputes between those claiming riparian rights to water (because their land lay alongside a source) and those seeking appropriation and transportation of water for agricultural development.[27]

An on-again, off-again governmental position was that of state geologist. In 1851 legislators awarded that honorary title to John B. Trask and published a pamphlet

James T. Gardiner, Richard D. Cotter, William H. Brewer, and Clarence King (from left), members of the field party of the California Geological Survey of 1864. The men traveled from San Francisco through the San Joaquin Valley to Visalia and along the Kings River into the Sierra, eventually reaching Virginia City, Nevada. During its thirteen-year existence, the survey contributed significantly to scientists' and geographers' understanding of California's topography and geology. *Courtesy California State Library.*

based on his studies of the Sacramento Valley; two years later they appropriated $2,000 for Trask to examine the Sierra Nevada and coast ranges and valleys, which resulted in three additional pamphlets. By the late 1850s public pressure had risen for more comprehensive surveys. At the urging of Justice Stephen Field and well-known scientists throughout the nation, the legislature in 1860 appointed Josiah D. Whitney to be state geologist and lead a geological survey of California. Whitney served until the office was abolished in 1874. His team of reputable assistants, some of whom became leading scientists of the era, produced an immense amount of useful scientific data regarding the state's topography, geology, economic resources, botany, and zoology. However, he antagonized the legislature by not concentrating on mineral and oil exploitation, and his relations with various governors (especially Downey and Booth) were icy. And thus, according to historian Gerald Nash, because of a conflict between pure and applied science, "the most ambitious attempt of state government to promote agriculture and mining by research came to an end."[28]

For an overview of the effect of public policy on economic growth in California during the years 1849 to 1879, no study is more thorough and reflective than Nash's *State Government and Economic Development*, which has stood the test of time since it was published, in 1964. Nash argued that in the years after 1850, Californians were eager to exploit natural resources but needed investment capital and knowledge about mining and agriculture, for which they turned to government. Lawmakers in turn created a legal framework to attract entrepreneurs, extended direct financial subsidies and other incentives, imposed restraints on various groups, and created research facilities and agencies. Functions assigned to government in California were very similar to those inherited from other states because "the pattern of their political and administrative inheritance was flexible enough to meet their economic needs" until agricultural specialization and industrial growth transformed the dynamic after 1870. Thereafter, "governments at all levels found existing methods wanting and began to experiment with alternate means to deal with new economic problems." Other observers have recognized this shift. Historian David Alan Johnson points out that in its first thirty years, the state changed in many ways: it became urban, and heavy and light manufacturing, finance, and retail grew dominant, as did large-scale ranching and grain production, with a concomitant demand for consumer goods. By the end of the Civil War, only half of the members of the first constitutional convention still lived in California; by the mid-1870s, "the state's founding fathers had become relics of a bygone age." Yet, for English visitor James Bryce, summarizing his observations of California in 1881, the traits of the Argonauts—their temper, character, and expectation of success—were passed on to the capitalists and laborers who confronted one another in the conflicts that led to the second constitutional convention; and the corporate regime of the 1870s was the culmination of the individualist order of the Gold Rush. In like manner, California's governing officers—"officialdom"—were far different in motivation from those predecessors who gathered at the state capital in San Jose in December 1849, but the structure in which they operated and their assumptions about governance were in a direct line of descent.[29]

NOTES

1. Very few studies have been devoted to early California government. Those nineteenth-century historians who tackled the subject were largely negative, reflecting the views of the press that they relied upon as sources; see, for example, Hubert Howe Bancroft, *History of California*, vols. 6 and 7 (San Francisco: The History Company, 1890), and Theodore H. Hittell, *History of California*, vol. 4 (San Francisco: N. J. Stone and Co., 1898). More objective overviews include William Henry Ellison, *A Self-Governing Dominion: California, 1849–1860* (Berkeley and Los Angeles: University of California Press, 1950); H. Brett Melendy and Benjamin F. Gilbert, *The Governors of California: Peter H. Burnett to Edmund G. Brown* (Georgetown, Calif.: The Talisman Press, 1965); and David Alan Johnson, *Founding the Far West: California, Oregon, and Nevada, 1840–1890* (Berkeley: University of California Press, 1992). Published after this chapter was written was Mary Jo Ignoffo, *Gold Rush Politics: California's First Legislature* (Sacramento: California State Senate, and Cupertino: California History Center and Foundation, De Anza College, 1999); it reviews proceedings of the 1849 constitutional convention and 1849–1850 legislature, presents capsule biographies of the first members of the Senate and Assembly, and concludes that these mostly American men imposed on California the traditions of the United States, replacing the Mexican heritage.

2. Bancroft, *History*, vol. 6, 308; *Alta California*, December 23, 1849; Herbert C. Jones, *The First Legislature of California* (Sacramento: California Assembly, 1949), 11–12; Ellison, *Dominion*, 56; *Journal of the Senate, 1st Session* (San Jose: J. Winchester, State Printer, 1850), 23–24.

3. Ellison, *Dominion*, 59–60; Carl Brent Swisher, *Motivation and Political Technique in the California Constitutional Convention, 1878–79* (New York: Da Capo Press, 1969), 93; Melendy and Gilbert, *Governors*, 120.

4. Information on the legislature and executive branch officers is taken from Elsey Hurt, *California State Government: An Outline of Its Administrative Organization, 1850 to 1939*, vol. 1 (Sacramento: Supervisor of Documents, 1936), 36–39, 69, 75, 77, 78, 180–82; Hurt, *California State Government: An Outline of Its Administrative Organization, 1850 to 1939*, vol. 2 (Sacramento: Supervisor of Documents, 1939), 5, 7, 9–10, 12, 17, 21, 23; Melendy and Gilbert, *Governors*, 120; C. F. Curry, ed., *California Blue Book or State Roster* (Sacramento: State Printer, 1907), 635–38.

5. Ellison, *Dominion*, chapter 7; Judson Grenier, *Golden Odyssey: John Stroud Houston, California's First Controller* (Spokane: The Arthur H. Clark Company, 1999), chapter 5; E. W. McKinstry, "Report from the Select Committee Appointed to Examine into the Nature of Certain Claims of the State of California," San Jose, March 13, 1850, 7–12.

6. Ellison, *Dominion*, 66–68; Jones, *Legislature*, 12–13.

7. Curry, *Blue Book*, 537–38; Jones, *Legislature*, 9–12, 14; *Journal of the Assembly, 1st Session* (San Jose: J. Winchester, State Printer, 1850), 624, 632–38.

8. Curry, *Blue Book*, 534–628; Melendy and Gilbert, *Governors*, 42–44; *Dictionary of American Biography*, s.v. "Field, Stephen Johnson."

9. Survey of the *Alta California, San Francisco Daily Herald, Evening Picayune, Daily Pacific News,* and *Sacramento Transcript* clearly demonstrates correspondents' propensity for legislative criticism and sympathy for the views of the controller and secretary of state. Of course, these two officers also dispensed the state's printing contracts, which may have won them friends in the press.

10. William Kelly, *An Excursion to California* (London: Chapman and Hall, 1851), 308–309; Mary Joan Elliott, ed., "The 1851 California Journal of M.V.B. Fowler," *Southern California Quarterly* 50 (September 1968): 229–33; Bancroft, *History*, vol. 6, 311; Robert H. Becker, ed., *Some Reflections of an Early California Governor Contained in a Short Memoir by Frederick F. Low . . . and Notes from an Interview between Governor Low and Hubert Howe Bancroft in 1883* (Sacramento: Book Collectors Club, 1959), 47; Josiah Royce, *California from the Conquest in 1846 to the Second Vigilance Committee* (1886; reprint, New York: Alfred A. Knopf, 1948), 242.

11. Winfield J. Davis, *History of Political Conventions in California, 1849–1892* (Sacramento: California State Library, 1893), 27, 308, 329–32; Becker, *Reflections*, 46–47; Bancroft, Royce, and Hittell, although they disagreed on many issues, were alike in their criticisms of later legislatures.

12. Curry, *Blue Book*, 640–41.

13. Royce Delmatier et al., *The Rumble of California Politics* (New York: John Wiley & Sons, 1970), 13; Peter Burnett, *Recollections of an Old Pioneer* (New York: D. Appleton & Co., 1880), 1–5; Melendy and Gilbert, *Governors*, 29–35; Elisha Crosby, *Memoirs: Remembrances of California and Guatemala from 1849 to 1864* (San Marino, Calif.: The Huntington Library, 1945), 46–47; Oscar T. Shuck, *Bench and Bar in California* (San Francisco: The Occident Printing House, 1888), 88–89; Becker, *Reflections*, 29.

14. *Journal of the Legislature, 2nd Session* (San Jose: Eugene Casserly, State Printer, 1851), 47, 842–43; Barbara Pickett, "The Life of John McDougal, the Second Governor of California" (seminar paper, March 14, 1939, in the California State Library), 3–7; Melendy and Gilbert, *Governors*, 42–47; Becker, *Reflections*, 29. Melendy and Gilbert make the charge of historians' unfairness; they probably were referring to Bancroft and Hittell.

15. Melendy and Gilbert, *Governors*, 52–64; Becker, *Reflections*, 29–30; Bancroft, *History*, vol. 6, 638–42.

16. Melendy and Gilbert, *Governors*, 70–72; Bancroft, *History*, vol. 6, 710. The Democratic-controlled legislature in 1857 brought impeachment proceedings against Henry Bates, treasurer, and George Whitman, controller. Bates was charged with illegally giving $88,000 to a San Francisco law firm to pay interest on state bonds (which was not paid), of illegally lending money, and of purchasing state warrants with state coin and "pocketing the difference in value." Whitman was charged with obstructing the board of examiners and refusing to provide information about the Bates affair. Bates was convicted and declared forever disqualified from holding office; Whitman, who fought his charges "inch by inch," was acquitted on all points. See Hittell, *History*, vol. 4, 199–200; Peyton Hurt, "The Rise and Fall of the 'Know-Nothings' in California," *Quarterly of the California Historical Society* 9 (June 1930): 111.

17. Melendy and Gilbert, *Governors*, 86–87, 95, 103–105; Bancroft, *History*, vol. 7, 279; Charles Russell Quinn, *History of Downey: The Life Story of a Pioneer Community and of the*

Man Who Founded It—California Governor John Gately Downey (Downey, Calif.: Elena Quinn, 1973), 33, 41.

18. Melendy and Gilbert, *Governors*, 109, 121–25, 134–35; Norman E. Tutorow, *Leland Stanford: Man of Many Careers* (Menlo Park, Calif.: Pacific Coast Publishers, 1971), 52–56; Spencer C. Olin, *California Politics, 1846–1920* (San Francisco: Boyd & Fraser Publishing Company, 1981), 30; William Issel and Robert W. Cherny, *San Francisco, 1865–1932: Politics, Power, and Urban Development* (Berkeley and Los Angeles: University of California Press, 1986), 120; Becker, *Reflections*, 12.

19. Curry, *Blue Book*, 640; Olin, *Politics*, 31; Issel and Cherny, *San Francisco*, 207; John W. Dwinelle, "Address to the Supreme Court of California," printed in "Address Delivered by Rev. Rodney L. Tabor at the Funeral of Henry Huntley Haight, Sept. 4, 1878" (San Francisco: Francis and Valentine, 1878), 18.

20. J. N. Bowman, "Preservation of the State Archives," *California Historical Society Quarterly* 28 (1949): 143–49.

21. State Librarian, compiler, *Descriptive List of the Libraries of California* (Sacramento: Board of Trustees of the State Library, 1904), 7, 12; *Journal of the Legislature, 1st Session*, 56, 96–97; Hugh S. Baker, "Public Libraries in California," *California Historical Society Quarterly* 38 (December 1959); Hurt, *Government*, vol. 1, 42.

22. Hurt, *Government*, vol. 1, 36–39, 43; John Swett, *Public Education in California* (New York: American Book Company, 1911), 154, 170; Roy W. Cloud, *Education in California* (Stanford: Stanford University Press, 1952), 24, 38, 40–42.

23. Hittell, *History*, vol. 4, 162–64; Hurt, *Government*, vol. 1, 43, 107–109, 113; "State Asylum for the Insane," *Hutchings' California Magazine* 9 (September 1859), reprinted in R. R. Olmsted, ed., *Scenes of Wonder and Curiosity from Hutchings' California Magazine, 1856–1861* (Berkeley: Howell-North, 1962), 369–71.

24. Hurt, *Government*, vol. 2, 95–104; Gerald Nash, *State Government and Economic Development* (1964; reprint, New York: Arno Press, 1979), 114–16, 215.

25. Nash, *Development*, 208; Hurt, *Government*, vol. 2, 34–35.

26. Hurt, *Government*, vol. 1: 77–78, 199; vol. 2: 77, 151–52; Curry, *Blue Book*, 692–95; Nash, *Development*, 68–69.

27. Nash, *Development*, 161–62, 179–80, 182–83, 189–90; Curry, *Blue Book*, 639; Hurt, *Government*, vol. 1: 121, 123, 216; vol. 2: 117.

28. Nash, *Development*, 98–103.

29. Nash, *Development*, 351–57; Johnson, *Founding*, 237–39; James Bryce, *The American Commonwealth*, 3d ed., vol. 2 (New York: Macmillan, 1897), 373–74. This essay on "officialdom" includes nothing on the contributions of women to California government because during these years, denied suffrage, they were virtually invisible, except in the field of education, where some became school principals; Jeanne Carr became deputy to her husband, School Superintendent Ezra Carr. Toward the end of the period, some women were employed as government clerks or secretaries. Clara Shortridge Foltz of San Jose drafted legislation to eliminate gender and racial discrimination for admission to the legal profession, which became law in 1878 after she lobbied the governor for his signature. See Joan M. Jensen and Gloria Ricci Lothrop, *California Women: A History* (San Francisco: Boyd & Fraser Publishing Co., 1987), 23, 44; and Cloud, *Education*, 61.

7

"None Could Deny the Eloquence of This Lady"

Women, Law, and Government in California, 1850–1890

Donna C. Schuele

Although women played no direct role in California law and politics until 1870, both their interest in law reform and their later entry into the political arena can be traced in part to two sections of the constitution that went into effect at statehood in 1850, one excluding women from the franchise and the other purporting to grant wives liberal property rights. Around 1870, California women joined their eastern sisters in organizing for suffrage rights and began seeking as well a more equitable implementation of the constitutional guarantee to marital property rights. This chapter will explore the circumstances that led California women to become involved in law reform, and their persistent fight over the next twenty years for equal political, property, and occupational rights, waged of necessity within the masculine arenas of law and politics.

WOMEN IN THE FORMATION AND DEVELOPMENT OF STATE GOVERNMENT

The Constitutional Convention of 1849

While the inaugural constitution excluded women (and nonwhite men) from suffrage, it did grant married women certain property rights by providing that "All property, both real and personal, of the wife, owned or claimed by her before marriage and that acquired afterwards by gift, devise or descent, shall be her separate property, and laws shall be passed more clearly defining the rights of the wife, in relation as well to her separate property as that held in common with her husband. Laws shall also be passed providing for the registration of the wife's separate property."[1]

At the point when California's constitutional convention met, in 1849, two very different systems of marital property law were in force across the United States. One, operating most notably in Louisiana and Texas, could be traced to the civil law of European continental countries, including Spain and France, which had governed these regions before the United States acquired them. California, as a Spanish (and then Mexican) territory, was also governed by this system. In the civil law, a woman's status was unaffected by marriage. Both spouses retained separate ownership of all property acquired prior to marriage, while property acquired during marriage through the efforts of either spouse was considered to be owned by the marital community, in which each spouse held an equal interest. Upon the death of either spouse, this marital property, known as common or community property, was kept intact and managed by the survivor, after which it descended to the couple's heirs. Spouses had testamentary power over only their separate property, yet they had equal power, as wives were allowed to execute wills. Under the community property system, the spouses' contributions to the marriage were equally valued, and widows exercised real power over marital property.[2]

The other system, holding sway in most American jurisdictions, was an outgrowth of the common law of England and was part of that system's law of coverture. Under these rules, a woman's legal status changed dramatically upon marriage. She became invisible in the eyes of the law, her identity subsumed under (or covered by) that of her husband. Lacking a legal identity, a wife could not own property. Consequently, the husband acquired ownership of any property the wife brought to the marriage and owned as well any property (such as wages) that her efforts might produce during the marriage. In exchange, a wife was given limited rights in a set portion of the husband's property, known as dower rights, regardless of the duration of the marriage or how or when the property was acquired. These rights could not be defeated by the husband during his lifetime or by will, but they were meant only to protect a wife in her widowhood.[3]

By the mid-nineteenth century, the law of coverture concerning marital property was coming under attack for its harsh treatment of women as well as its inability to guard families against financial ruin stemming from a husband's debts. By the 1850s and 1860s, a preferred avenue of reform emerged from the state legislatures that involved giving married women specific rights over certain property, designated as their separate property, through the passage of Married Women's Property Acts (MWPAs). These statutes treated the wife as if she were unmarried for the purpose of rights to her inheritances, gifts, and, later, wages, but otherwise left the system of coverture intact. In the context of the nineteenth-century world of separate spheres, where wives rarely worked outside the home, MWPAs were more effective in protecting women from intemperate or unfortunate husbands in an increasingly commercial economy than in empowering them as individuals.[4]

In the mining town of Big Oak Flat in Tuolumne County, Lucinda Stocking watches while her husband and his partners take a break from working their long tom to pose for this 1856 daguerreotype. Though often scarce in the gold country, women found employment as cooks, innkeepers, teachers, stagecoach drivers, entertainers, merchants, and miners. The letters of Mary Ballou, a New Hampshire woman who managed a boardinghouse in a mining district near Sacramento, delineated the many tasks she was forced to perform to scrape together her living expenses, including washing, ironing, cooking, placer mining, and raising hogs. "Sometimes I am taking care of Babies and nursing at the rate of Fifty dollars a week," she told her sons, "but I would not advise any Lady to come out here and suffer the toil and fatigue that I have suffered for the sake of a little gold—neither do I advise anyone to come." *Courtesy Oakland Museum of California, gift of Concours d'Antiques.*

However, in the years just prior to California's constitutional convention, Louisiana's legal system gained attention from common-law jurisdictions such as New York, leading these jurisdictions to toy with embracing the civil law's concept of joint ownership of property acquired as a result of efforts by either the husband or the wife. Ultimately, these jurisdictions settled for the more limited MWPAs, partly in order to avoid eroding the husband's exclusive rights to his earnings, but not before the issue was extensively debated.[5]

It was within this complex context that the California constitutional convention confronted the issue of married women's property rights in 1849.[6] Referencing property "held in common," the proposal put before the delegates was borrowed nearly verbatim from the Texas state constitution, and it differed little from that which had been rejected in New York.[7] Paradoxically, the provision could at once be understood as a static retention of the law inherited from Spain and as a dynamic reform of the law of coverture in force in most of the United States. While one representative of a district primarily populated by native-born Californios praised the proposal for protecting settled expectations in joint property rights born of indigenous law, another delegate opposed the measure as an unwise departure from common law. Recently arrived from New York, he sought to alert fellow delegates to the radical potential of female joint property ownership:

> I have lived some years in countries where the civil law prevails, and where such a separate right of property is given to the wife. If there is any country in the world which presents the spectacle of domestic disunion more than another, it is France. There the husband and wife are partners in business, raising the wife from head clerk to partner. The very principle is contrary to nature and contrary to the married state.[8]

However, his dire warning was ignored, as the debate shifted to the issue of the wife's separate property. It seems that most of the delegation read the proposal as calling for a reformed common-law system that would accord the wife limited rights without impinging on the husband's interests in property he acquired during the marriage, notwithstanding the provision's joint property language and the fact that the common law governing marital property had never been in force in California.[9]

In addition, the debates failed to settle the purpose of the provision—whether to protect women or empower them. One delegate predicted the difficulties that the new state would encounter if families were left to their own devices in the volatile gold-rush economy: "Any cool, dispassionate man, who looks forward to California, as she will be in five years to come, who does not see that wildness of speculation will be the characteristic of her citizens, is not, I think, gifted with the power of prophecy. I claim that it is due to every wife, and to the children of every family, that the wife's property should be protected."[10] But another representative, responding to the keenly felt scarcity of marriageable Anglo-American women in California, promoted the provision as empowering women and thereby encouraging their emigration: "Having some hopes that I may be wedded . . . I shall advocate this section in the Constitution, and I would call upon all the bachelors in this convention to vote for it. I do not think that we can offer a greater inducement for women of fortune to come to California. It is the very best provision to get us wives that we can introduce into the Constitution."[11]

In sum, the discussion indicated that the measure could be, and was, read in

Members of the Peralta family relax on their front porch in Alameda County, ca. 1856. Under Mexican law, Spanish-speaking California women enjoyed the right to testify in court, inherit property on an equal basis with male siblings, and own land (about sixty land grants went to women). After the American conquest, Californianas faced discrimination based on their gender as well as their language and race. Nineteenth-century American common law forbade married women to own land in their own name and limited property inheritance mostly to male offspring. *Courtesy Peter E. Palmquist.*

three very different ways: most simply, as requiring the retention of indigenous law; more complexly, as adopting civil law rules of joint property ownership in order to effect far-reaching reform of inequitable common-law principles; or, least controversially, as no more than part of the growing eastern-based trend toward limited common-law reforms. Within each of these interpretations, the measure appeared more or less empowering, more or less protective, of women. Nevertheless, a consensus emerged whereby the constitutional guarantee of married women's property rights was viewed as a progressive enactment boldly distinguishing the Golden State from eastern jurisdictions struggling to emerge from the grips of antiquated notions of law and patriarchy.

Development of Married Women's Property Rights

Unfortunately, the unfocused and incomplete discussion at the convention provided little guidance for translating the constitutional guarantee of property rights for wives into a comprehensive, workable statutory scheme. The common-law sensibility that reigned during the first legislative session squelched the progressive intentions of the convention. In complete derogation of the express constitutional guarantee, and contrary to Spanish or Mexican law, the Anglo-American-dominated legislature gave the husband full lifetime control over both the common property and the wife's separate property, and even prohibited the wife from willing her separate property. Yet the new law remained faithful to the historical and theoretical bases of the community property system by continuing the Spanish-Mexican practice of leaving the common property intact during the lifetime of the surviving spouse, and calling for a fifty-fifty division of the common property upon divorce, without regard to fault.[12] In these ways, the system appeared to recognize the spouses' equal ownership rights in the marital community.

However, according the wife an ownership interest in property an Anglo-American husband considered himself alone to have earned would not survive in an increasingly commercial, wage-based economy where a woman's appropriate place was in the home. In 1857, the legislature ended equal, no-fault division of common property upon divorce by granting judges certain discretionary powers. Meanwhile, the state Supreme Court and the legislature worked in tandem to accord the husband, but not the wife, testamentary control over half of the common property. Eliminating these indications of equal right to the common property allowed the Supreme Court eventually to conclude that the wife's interest in the common property was nothing more than a "mere expectancy," which would mature into a legally protectable right only if and when she survived her husband.[13]

The ramifications of these changes, added to the control already given to husbands, were staggering for married women. Already, a husband was not precluded from disposing of his wife's separate property during his lifetime. Now, with the husband considered the full owner of the common property, he was free to dispose of any or all of it during the marriage, thereby leaving the wife penniless at his death. And while the wife's death had no impact on a widower's rights to the common property, the husband's death was what triggered the widow's rights. Not only did the wife's right to half of the common property mature upon her husband's death, but a widow could gain the other half of the common property only through her husband's testamentary generosity. Consequently, a widow had to submit herself to the onerous probate process in order to gain title to any of the common property. More generally, with their ability to exercise control over their separate property severely restricted and their claim to the common property denied, California wives

Actress Adah Isaacs Menken, photographed here ca. 1863, enjoyed a degree of freedom and fame unknown to most nineteenth-century women. Born in New Orleans to a French mother and an African American father, Menken traveled to San Francisco in 1863 as the star of the melodrama *Mazeppa*, during the course of which she seemingly stripped to the nude (actually a flesh-colored bodysuit) and rode offstage on horseback. The *Sacramento Union* complained, "Not an actress, she is an exhibition—a voluptuous experiment on American taste for amusement. And it pays." Menken married and divorced often, danced, painted, wrote poems, traveled widely, and reportedly won the friendship of Mark Twain, Bret Harte, Joaquin Miller, Charles Dickens, and Alexandre Dumas. *California Historical Society, FN-19626.*

witnessed the withering of the legal concept of the marital community, where the lifetime contributions of spouses were equally valued.[14]

By 1870, the marital property system, intended as a reform, actually rendered California wives worse off than their eastern sisters, who were protected in their dower rights and were increasingly benefiting from the enactment of MWPAs that served to segregate other property from the husband's control.[15] California's system did nothing to empower wives, did little to protect families, and in fact, blatantly violated the state's constitution. As it happened, whether women would be able to battle these legal inequalities would come to depend on their ability to mount an organized fight in the political arena.

CALIFORNIA WOMEN PRESS FOR EQUAL RIGHTS

Organizing for Equal Rights

In July 1869, a small cadre of women established the San Francisco Woman Suffrage Association (SFWSA). This triggered a statewide movement, resulting in the formation of the California Woman Suffrage Association (CWSA) six months later. The membership of California's suffrage societies—white, Protestant, and middle class—mirrored groups forming in other parts of the country. However, the broad platform of the California movement, calling for economic, marital, occupational, and political rights, set it apart from the national movement, which had begun to narrow the broad focus expressed in the 1848 Seneca Falls Declaration of Sentiments to the single issue of suffrage. California reformers' extensive agenda resulted from two interconnected factors that distinguished women's experience in the Golden State during the 1850s and 1860s: pervasive labor-market discrimination and the significant influence of Spiritualism.[16]

From the outset, California's subsistence frontier environment drove many Anglo-American female émigrés, middle class included, into the employment market, and finding work was especially difficult in San Francisco's volatile economy.[17] Beginning in the mid-1850s, a few women, armed with their own printing presses, began publishing newspapers and magazines geared toward a female audience, in which they increasingly commented on gendered employment discrimination. Hitting closest to home were the antics of the all-male San Francisco typographical union, which waged a vicious battle to exclude female typesetters from the higher-paying jobs. As a result, female publishers spearheaded the formation of a women's cooperative printing enterprise, one of the earliest organizational efforts by California women.[18]

But recognition of labor-market discrimination alone would not have led to the adoption of a women's rights platform extending beyond suffrage. Another crucial impetus came from the influence of Spiritualism, a religion founded around the same time and place as the Seneca Falls convention in 1848, which embraced individualism and empiricism in a way that propelled its adherents toward a radical social program dedicated to female equality and autonomy.

During the antebellum period, Spiritualism, women's rights, and radical abolitionism were closely intertwined. However, during the 1860s, the course of women's rights within abolitionism and Spiritualism began to diverge. In the East, the women's rights movement developed in reaction to abolitionists' post–Civil War fight for suffrage for the freedman, causing its agenda to narrow to female voting rights. In California, meanwhile, with abolitionism never taking root and Spiritualism holding particular appeal, Spiritualism's broad view of female emancipation came to be reflected over the next twenty years in the multifaceted agenda of the state's women's rights movement.[19]

Spiritualism also played a crucial role in the development of women's movement leadership in California. Spiritualist direction was provided by mediums, female as well as male, who were called to the position by the spirits. With no church in which to preach, mediums employed public meeting places, allowing them to address the faithful and skeptics alike. At a time when the issue of female public speaking was dividing the abolitionist movement, female mediums authoritatively addressed large gatherings, and by the 1860s, the most successful Spiritualist lecturers in San Francisco were women.[20] One of America's foremost trance speakers, Laura de Force Gordon, came to California in 1867, a few months later delivering the first speech dedicated to the topic of women's rights.[21] The connection between Spiritualism and public support for women's rights grew to the point where nearly all of the founding members of the SFWSA had ties to Spiritualism.[22]

In the 1860s, individuals, many of them Spiritualists, began to urge support for female enfranchisement in general circulation newspapers, although mainstream women's publications continued to espouse support for equal occupational rights only.[23] Finally, in January 1869, newspaper owner and Spiritualist sympathizer Emily Pitts Stevens stepped forward to proclaim her commitment to women's political equality as well, dedicating her weekly publication, renamed the *Pioneer*, to advancing a broad equal rights agenda.[24]

Although ties to Spiritualism proved uniquely advantageous for the development of California's women's rights movement, they came to have negative ramifications as well, causing dissension and division between the movement's more radical and more conventional adherents during the 1870s. From the start, the CWSA wrestled with whether to affiliate, if at all, with the Stanton-Anthony National Woman Suffrage Association (NWSA), which insisted on female leadership and espoused suffrage rights guaranteed by the federal constitution, or the Stone-Blackwell American Woman Suffrage Association (AWSA), with its inclusion of male leadership and a more conservative, state-based approach.

The San Francisco Spiritualists' sympathies rested with the more radical NWSA,

Feminist and Spiritualist Laura de Force Gordon emigrated to California in 1867, where she spent the remainder of her life toiling for women's suffrage as a lecturer, lawyer, and newspaper editor. In 1870 she stood before the state legislature and called for a "true democracy" where "white and black, red and yellow, of both sexes, can exercise their civil rights," one of the earliest public appeals for equal rights for women in the American West. Gordon helped found the California Woman Suffrage Association in 1870 and nine years later became one of the first women admitted to the state bar. She also helped draft a clause added to the 1879 California constitution guaranteeing women the right to pursue any "lawful business, vocation or profession." In 1883 Gordon became only the second woman admitted to practice before the U.S. Supreme Court. She died in Lodi in 1907, her dream of women's suffrage in California still unrealized. *Courtesy California State Library.*

while the city's Unitarians favored the AWSA. Trading on the support of the San Jose and Santa Cruz Spiritualists (who chafed under the San Franciscans' disproportionate influence), the AWSA sympathizers split off from the CWSA in January 1871. A little over two years later, the CWSA suffered another split, when radical Emily Pitts Stevens and her supporters ousted a more conservative Spiritualist male leader who had attempted to tar the Stevens faction with charges of support for free love (a perennial thorn for Spiritualists, with their trenchant critique of traditional Victorian marriage).[25] While the organized movement survived, Spiritualist influence was driven underground to such a degree over the next decade that no mention of this unique factor was made in the first account of the rise of the California women's rights movement, published in the mid-1880s by Stanton and Anthony.[26]

Yet, enough California suffrage leaders rose above these organizational disruptions to carry on the task of law reform, with a broad-based and interconnected agenda shaped by early Spiritualist influences and women's labor-market experience.

The Campaign for Political Rights

With the organization of suffrage societies gaining steam across the state in late 1869, optimism ran high that female voting rights could be achieved quickly, notwithstanding a general consensus that enfranchising women would require a difficult two-step process of first enacting a measure calling for a referendum to amend the state constitution and then gaining voter support for the issue.[27] Over three thousand signatures (more than half from men) were gathered on suffrage petitions presented to the legislature in January 1870, and in 1872, petitions totaling five thousand signatures, including that of former governor Leland Stanford, were submitted.[28] In both sessions, the most eloquent of the activists were sent to address lawmakers, nearly all having honed their public-speaking skills as Spiritualist mediums. Of Laura de Force Gordon's speech in 1870, one Sacramento newspaper reported, "none could deny the eloquence of this lady. . . . The Senate Chamber has heard nothing superior. There was a hush universal in this place during the hour she consumed speaking[,] . . . discussing questions of constitutional and parliamentary law with an ease and familiarity which many of the most potent, grave and reverend Senators could themselves have envied."[29] In the following session, when known rabble-rouser Emily Pitts Stevens addressed the legislators, another local newspaper praised her speech as "Pitts-Stevenism in the best style of the art. She railed against class legislation, walked the stand, and in an off-hand, defiant way told the audience a good many wholesome truths."[30]

The speakers advanced both rights-based and expediency arguments for the vote, viewing suffrage as just one part of an integrated agenda for equal treatment of men and women.[31] To correct the multitude of wrongs visited upon women, one speaker implored, "give us the ballot, the key to all civil rights, and *it* will

Leland Stanford, photographed here ca. 1863 with his wife, Jane Lathrop Stanford, helped found the Republican Party in California and became its first Republican governor in 1862. In the 1870s he signed petitions to the state legislature supporting women's suffrage. *California Historical Society, FN-07381.*

redress them, for the root of them all is the fact that man claims the right to be our representative."[32] Others focused on women's civic obligations, ranging from taxpaying to motherhood, as the basis for extension of suffrage.[33] Attacking the worn argument that the right to vote flowed to men as the result of military duties, theirs alone, one speaker slyly asserted that "it was rather too much to ask women to bear soldiers and arms also."[34]

In both 1870 and 1872, special legislative committees, established to consider women's rights petitions and bills, argued in favor of female enfranchisement. The 1872 committee cleverly attempted to mute criticism by playing down the boldness of its position, going so far as to assert that nothing about woman suffrage was "either of a revolutionary character or in opposition to the spirit and genius of Government." At the same time, it tried to curry support by appealing to the Golden State's progressive reputation. Both committees recommended passage of the suffrage bills before them, but the measures stalled in both houses before reaching a vote.[35]

In 1874, however, activists achieved a related goal—declaring women eligible for seats on school boards and as superintendents. After the officeholding bill was introduced, three women, led by Sallie Hart, an outspoken San Francisco public school teacher, devoted six weeks of "indefatigable efforts" to lobbying the cause in Sacramento. Perturbed by her effectiveness, one senator complained of Hart "going from seat to seat, like some blazing comet, shaking a kind of fascination from her twirled hair."[36]

Detractors viewed the measure as an opening wedge for suffrage and questioned the constitutionality of nonelectors holding educational offices. Supporters meanwhile appealed to women's particular suitability to oversee children's schooling and promoted the bill as merely declaratory of rights already held, given that the state constitution had virtually nothing to say about female officeholding. Interestingly, the proposal was also advocated as one to advance men's rights, specifically to elect officeholders of their choice. In truth, the bill probably passed thanks to the support of pragmatic lawmakers who understood how difficult it was becoming to persuade good men to run for these minor school offices and to treat the positions as more than just stepping stones to higher office.[37] Further indicating that practical, rather than ideological, concerns carried the day was the fact that legislators seemed unbothered by the irony that women would nonetheless be precluded from casting a ballot for these same educational offices.

In subsequent sessions during the 1870s, the legislature avoided the suffrage issue by resorting to the excuse that a constitutional convention would soon be called, where the question could be better addressed. By the time this occurred, in 1878, anti-Chinese sentiment had reached a fever pitch in California. Many Caucasians, as well as some members of other racial groups, were determined to keep those of

San Francisco–based reformer Marietta L. Stow helped form the California Woman Suffrage Association in 1870 and worked throughout the late nineteenth century for a variety of causes, including racial and gender equality, probate law reform, and communitarianism. She refused to wear the "long, uncouth drangling bag called a dress skirt," preferring instead a dress-trousers hybrid of her own design, shown here. In 1884, independent-minded Stow became the first woman ever nominated for vice president of the United States, in her case by the tiny National Equal Rights Party. *Courtesy Oakland Museum of California.*

Chinese descent from exercising any rights of citizenship, especially suffrage. In this light, white women's votes had the potential to counterbalance those of Chinese men. As a result, progressive delegates who genuinely supported women's rights were joined by opportunistic representatives to force extensive consideration of the issue.

While in one sense, then, the timing of the convention was advantageous for women, in another it occurred too late in the decade. By 1878, the infrastructure of California's organized women's rights movement, established earlier in the decade, had deteriorated. Rivalries and internal dissensions had taken their toll, no doubt. But more important, the lobbying efforts expended over eight years on a range of issues had worn down activists already taxed by family and other responsibilities. This led to the absence of an organized lobbying force at the convention, causing some delegates to wonder whether women really desired suffrage. Local Sacramento women finally sprang into action, but they were unwilling to do what was necessary to make an impact in the few short weeks before the convention adjourned. Believing that the original movement had foundered because of overly radical behavior and beliefs, these women refused assistance from experienced lobbyists, considering overt persuasion unladylike. The convention ultimately rejected woman suffrage, with even sympathetic delegates fearing that a provision extending the franchise might imperil ratification of the new constitution.[38]

In the wake of missed opportunities and defeat, veteran suffragists reevaluated the postconvention political landscape and concluded that the legislature would refuse to place a referendum before the electorate so soon after ratification of the new constitution. Consequently, in the 1880s, activists turned from their commitment to universal suffrage toward the alternative goal of partial suffrage, which they maintained could be achieved through a majority vote in the legislature without resort to a constitutional amendment. In some forms, limited suffrage would grant women the right to vote in school and/or municipal elections, while in other forms it would grant only taxpaying women the right to vote.

School suffrage seemed a natural starting point, given that women were now avidly running for educational offices. A bill to that end was lobbied and heavily debated in 1880, coming close to passage in the Assembly before the session closed. In 1881, the CWSA reappeared as an organized force, submitting numerous petitions and seeing to it that three school suffrage bills were introduced, but by then the issue had become mired in questions of constitutionality.[39]

By 1883, the organized movement had again faded, while the legislature appeared to be growing weary of the suffrage issue, pressed this session by Laura de Force Gordon alone. Some lawmakers called for a popular referendum, but only so "the 'vexed question' would be settled."[40] No suffrage measures were presented again until 1889, when Gordon pressed a revised version of the 1883 school suffrage bill. She lobbied it to passage in the Assembly, but the proposal foundered in the Senate, again as time ran out. In nearly twenty years of agitation, this was the closest the legislature ever came to passing a woman suffrage proposal.[41]

Advocating for Property Rights

Marital property law reform vied with suffrage as the most sought-after goal of the California women's rights movement in the 1870s and 1880s. Founding suffragists were keenly aware of the system's failure to treat marriage as a partnership in which each spouse's contribution was equally valued. Many leaders themselves had experienced the unfairness of California's scheme, having been denied equal treatment upon widowhood or divorce, the sting made greater for those who had helped to support their families financially while married. Given that marital property reform, "being within the province of ordinary legislation," could be granted without resort to a constitutional referendum, advocates could hardly be faulted for believing that statutory change in this area was quite achievable.[42]

Reformers were most concerned with repairing the damage that flowed from the California Supreme Court's determination that wives had no lifetime interest in the common property, that their interest was nothing more than a "mere expectancy."[43] They particularly sought to equalize the treatment of widows and widowers and to end the probate system's control over the widow. In doing so, activists might have argued that the law ought to be returned to its Spanish-Mexican roots, or even that such a return was constitutionally required. Instead, they drew upon the joint property rhetoric that had developed in the East beginning in the 1840s—the same arguments that had propelled New York lawmakers to consider adopting a community property scheme.[44] However, unlike back East, in California activists did not have to push for an altogether new system in order to gain joint property rights. Instead, they faced the seemingly easier task of convincing the legislature to fulfill the purpose of the plan already in place.[45]

Addressing representatives in Sacramento in 1872, Nettie Tator, a law-trained Santa Cruz suffragist, forcefully staked out the wife's claim to the common property:

> When a man and his wife commence life poor, and struggle along together in the acquirement of property, by good right half of that property and whatever income accrues from it is hers. But does she get it? No! And if she dies he continues on just the same with all his business relations . . . ; while on the other hand, if he dies, she cannot do anything until the property has been administered upon by law. . . . You say this is necessary to protect the interest of her children. Who, I ask, looks after the interest of children more closely than mothers do?[46]

In 1876, the recently widowed Marietta Stow emerged to repeat Tator's charges as part of an iconoclastic but far-reaching reform crusade motivated by her personal experiences. According to Stow, the San Francisco probate bench and bar had conspired

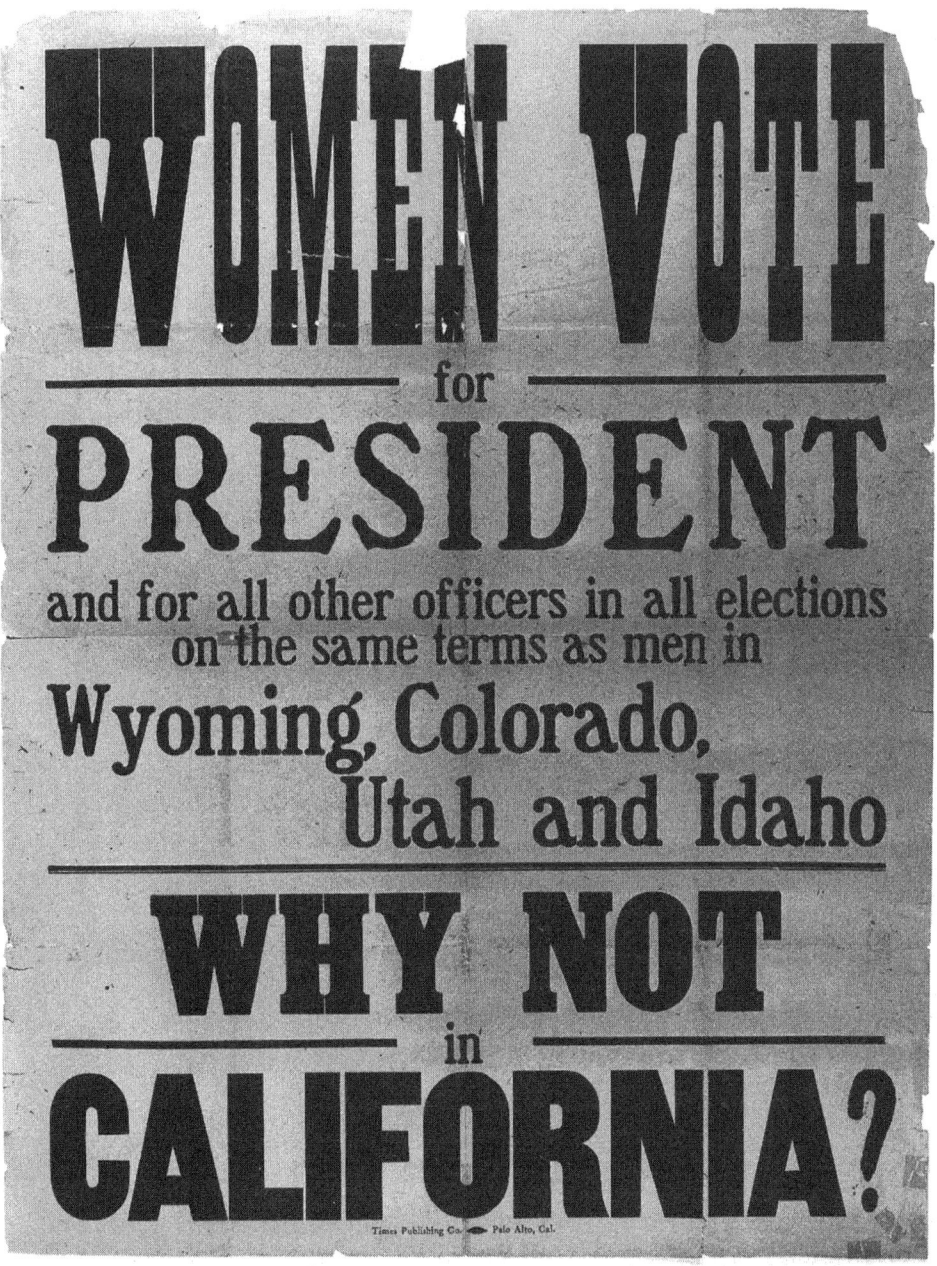

In 1869, Wyoming became the first American territory to extend suffrage to women, and Colorado, Utah, and Idaho followed by 1896. "Why not in California?" asked this turn-of-the-century suffragist poster. However, Californians emphatically voted down a women's suffrage amendment in 1896; ironically, the strongest opposition came from San Francisco and Oakland, two of the state's most progressive cities throughout the twentieth century, because their residents correctly feared that female voters would favor prohibition. California finally enfranchised women by initiative in 1911, the culmination of more than forty years of feminist activism. *Courtesy Bancroft Library.*

to rob her of her husband's $200,000 estate.[47] To advance her cause, Stow penned a polemic, entitled *Probate Confiscation*, which included her perspective on wives' status under California law:

> [T]here is no such thing as a partnership relation in the marriage union. . . . [I]n wedlock woman is still a slave. . . . She cannot use a dollar of the common property which she has helped to earn, without the husband's consent. . . . You may say that making the wife a legal partner will embarrass and cripple the business transactions of the husband. . . . Nothing but recognition of the importance of the wife's consent will lift her out of the position of a legal nonentity.[48]

For all of the force of Tator's and Stow's rhetoric, however, their words hinted at an entrenched belief that would prove to be the major roadblock to marital property reform.

The legislative process began promisingly enough when, following Tator's speech in 1872, the Assembly's special committee on women's rights came out in favor of the equalization of marital property law. The members did so on the basis that the wife's contribution to the marital community deserved to be equally valued and equally rewarded. However, its wholesale acceptance of the Victorian ideology of separate spheres led the committee to characterize the wife's contribution as noneconomic.

According to the committee, the wife contributed to the marriage through "embellishment of the home, . . . the cultivation of her mind, the refinement of her taste, and the protection of her health," which would allow her to "bear . . . well formed and beautiful and healthy children," whom she would properly raise, "and thus honoring [her husband's] name, transmit it to the future untarnished." The committee contended that the contributions of the spouses were equal unless, it posited rhetorically, "money is more valuable than the mind of man, and coin than character."[49]

However, in the later nineteenth century, in an increasingly commercial economy, this rhetoric proved to be far from convincing. In its anxiousness to declare the value of wives' noneconomic contributions, the committee nonetheless seemed to realize its inability to refute the argument that an economic contribution was in fact more valuable and thereby granted the husband a greater claim over the common property. As the committee itself put it, "he earned it by virtue of his own persona, foresight, enterprise, perseverance and business energy, and . . . therefore it belongs to him."[50]

Beyond this entrenched belief that the wife did not truly earn any portion of the common property, another stumbling block to reform proved to be the difficulty attendant with drafting bills that would achieve equal treatment but still mesh with California's complex and contradictory marital property scheme. The first bill to address unequal treatment regarding the common property, possibly drawn up by the San Jose offshoot of the CWSA, simply gave all the common property to the surviving spouse. The measure passed the Assembly quickly with no debate in 1872, but foundered in the Senate as time ran out.⁵¹

In 1876, Stow drafted a bill equalizing the rules of property distribution upon death of either spouse and giving the survivor broad administrative powers meant to lessen the confiscatory involvement of the probate court and attorneys.⁵² However, her proposal was never introduced in either house; working outside of the channels of the organized women's movement probably undercut her influence in Sacramento.⁵³ Instead, the two bills that were introduced during that session were probably drafted by CWSA stalwart Sarah Wallis. Thrice married, Palo Alto–based Wallis had successfully supported herself and a son after being abandoned by one husband, and eventually wed a women's rights sympathizer who served in the state Senate in the 1860s.⁵⁴ Her bills proposed to equalize the spouses' claims over the community property, but by reducing the husband's rights to the level of those of the wife. Again, debate centered around the issue of whether the wife had fairly "earned" any rights to that property. No surprise, both the Senate and Assembly Judiciary committees recommended against passage, and the measures died.⁵⁵

In 1881, Wallis returned to the strategy of stepping up rights for widows to the level of those enjoyed by widowers, this time seeking out citizen support. With the issue of marital property reform lacking the simple appeal of the suffrage question, as early as 1869 activists had enlisted the help of sympathetic male attorneys and judges to educate eastern-bred émigrés regarding the complexities and inequities of the state's community property law and rally them to the cause.⁵⁶ In 1876, Stow herself had traveled California to alert wives to the dangers ahead as widows, widely circulating four editions of her book and giving newspaper interviews.⁵⁷ Now Wallis canvassed the state, collecting more than ten thousand signatures on petitions calling simply for passage of "an Act to confer upon the wife the right to succeed to the community property on the death of the husband."⁵⁸

Six bills of varying effect were submitted over three sessions, in 1880, 1881, and 1883. Although they all proposed to improve the wife's position vis-à-vis the common property, not all guaranteed equal rights. Those that bore Wallis's imprint suffered from poor drafting and failed to advance in 1880 and 1881. Then, in 1883, an elegant proposal was introduced, calling for the repeal of the particular statute governing the widow's rights to the community property, and making the statute governing the widower's rights gender neutral. Yet, it too went nowhere after the Assembly Judiciary Committee recommended against passage. The only bills receiving favorable committee treatment were the two of most minor effect, seeking to improve but not equalize the widow's rights in the common property, and these bills were probably introduced to draw support away from Wallis's measures.⁵⁹

Following these setbacks, the author of the 1872 special committee report, John M. Days, returned to Sacramento as a senator in 1885 and renewed his call for equal

Clara Shortridge Foltz, widowed at a young age with five children to support, moved to San Jose in 1872 hoping to establish a law practice. In 1879, she and Laura de Force Gordon became the first women admitted to the University of California's Hastings School of Law and successfully opened the state bar to women. In addition to her groundbreaking legal career, Foltz worked as a newspaper editor, women's suffragist, and penal reformer. *Courtesy Bancroft Library.*

treatment for the wife and widow, proclaiming that the present state of the law, denying married women an interest in the community property, constituted "an injury to the children, a robbery to the wife, and a disgrace to the statutes."[60] Days introduced a measure similar to both his 1872 bill and the 1883 proposal, to equalize the claim of the surviving spouse to the common property. Membership on the Judiciary Committee failed to gain Days a favorable review for his bill, but it allowed him to issue a blistering minority report.[61]

Continuing to wrestle with the entrenched belief that the wife did not deserve to share equally in the community property because it "was earned by the husband . . . and . . . therefore it belongs to him," Days now discarded romantic notions about the marriage relationship in favor of acknowledging the wife's *economic* contribution:

> Who does not know that hundreds of wives in California have not only performed the household duties . . . , but have actually done as much as the husband in earning the means of livelihood, and more, in saving and acquiring the community property? Who does not know that hundreds of wives in California, by their skill, industry, affection and love for their husbands and families, not only acquire the community property but support children and husbands besides.[62]

Days doggedly moved his bill toward passage, but time ran out before it could come up for a vote on the merits, these efforts closing out reform attempts for that decade.[63] Instead, his success in the Assembly in 1872 continued as the high-water mark for equalization of the survivorship interest in the common property.

However, activists were more successful in achieving for wives full control over their separate property, albeit almost accidentally, and due more to eastern influence rather than any recognition of the civil law's treatment of separate property. Charged by the legislature with codifying California statutory and common law, a commission of prominent attorneys unveiled a Civil Code in 1872 that included a provision giving the wife the power to manage her separate property. Its insertion in the draft of the Civil Code most likely reflected both the increasing popularity of MWPAs and the fact that the codification movement began in New York. Reform of the wife's separate property rights became law with no active intervention from female activists, as the legislature adopted the Civil Code in total, with virtually no debate. Nevertheless, suffragists widely publicized the reform, and when a repeal attempt was made in the next session, activists rushed to Sacramento and successfully lobbied for its retention.[64]

The Fight for Occupational Rights

During the 1870s and 1880s, activists sought not only political and marital-property rights for California women, but occupational rights as well. Advocating not special treatment but a level playing field, reformers targeted appointive offices and other government employment, public school teaching, and law practice. The movement's strategy was circumscribed by the times, as there were fewer appropriate points for government intervention in the labor market in an era of laissez-faire political economy. However, activists seemed to realize that the legislature could be more willing to step in when government itself caused or contributed to the particular occupational inequality. Interestingly, lawmakers were more receptive to women's demands for equal occupational treatment than they were to demands for equal political or marital rights, as women secured, in less than a decade, constitutional protection of the right to pursue any lawful occupation free from gendered restrictions.

Responding to the dearth of women in government employment, sympathetic legislators in 1870 pushed colleagues to accord women greater opportunities. However, barriers to women's participation in this labor market were not directly law related, as few if any regulations prohibited women from holding appointive office or other paid government employment. This led some lawmakers to question the appropriateness of legally sanctioned "encouragement," and others to contend that supporters were actually seeking preferential treatment that would lead to a requirement to hire women. The measure was ultimately rejected as an unwarranted governmental intrusion into the employment marketplace. Later, when a proposal was introduced into the constitutional convention to designate particular government positions for women, such as state librarian, the measure was given no consideration.[65] Lawmakers were apparently unwilling to enact proposals that could lead, in today's parlance, to a set-aside or quota system.

On the other hand, in the one area of public employment where women had gained a foothold, school teaching, state legislators were willing to remedy and preclude unequal treatment originated by local government. When the San Francisco school board instituted a system of unequal pay within the school levels, female teachers in the city became emboldened to seek salary equalization not just for themselves, but for public school teachers statewide. Led by Sallie Hart, educators descended on Sacramento during the 1872 and 1874 sessions, leading an opponent to complain sarcastically, "We must take our lessons, rules and orders from these young ladies who have been teaching perhaps six months, perhaps nine months, and as soon as they get a husband quit."[66] Nonetheless, the San Franciscans' lobbying was positively received overall, as the teachers succeeded, with little debate or dissension, in gaining first city- and then state-level protection against unequal salaries at elementary schools.[67]

Yet, the legislature was less amenable to remedying the exclusion of women from the legal profession, an unequal treatment mandated by state law. The United States had a long-standing tradition of local and state-based regulation of the legal profession, and in California, women's exclusion was accomplished by way of a statute restricting bar membership to white males. However, with control over entrance into the profession far less formalized and centralized than it is today, by the 1870s

The University of California, chartered by the state legislature in 1868, admitted its first female students two years later. Three UC Berkeley coeds pillow fight in their dormitory in this photograph, ca. 1900. *Courtesy Bancroft Library.*

women in California and elsewhere began studying under sympathetic male lawyers and then seeking admission to the bar nonetheless. When denied, these women drew on their legal training to fight back. Elsewhere would-be lawyers brought suit for admission, most famously Myra Bradwell of Illinois, who took her case all the way to the United States Supreme Court in 1873.[68] In California, women uniquely turned to the legislature.

Although California lawmakers had given some consideration to women's bar membership as early as 1872, the issue was not pressed in earnest until Laura de Force Gordon and Clara Shortridge Foltz decided to seek admission in 1878. Both divorced with dependents, they had determined that the practice of law would allow them to provide more lucratively for their families. Rather than seek redress from the courts, Foltz and Gordon decided to lobby the legislature to change California's restrictive statute, an unprecedented move. With the impending constitutional convention, the women's rights movement spent little time that session lobbying the suffrage issue or marital property reform, thus leaving the field open for Gordon, a veteran suffragist, newspaperwoman, and lobbyist, and Foltz, a more recently arrived suffragist, to push their agenda.[69]

San Jose–based Foltz drafted what became known as the "Woman Lawyer's Bill" and had her district's senator, who was sympathetic to women's rights, introduce it early in the session. Attending the proceedings as a newspaper reporter, Gordon was in a unique position to advance the bill. Assisted by other suffragists, the would-be lawyers astutely garnered statewide support from members of the bar, especially prominent attorneys. Although the bill passed handily in the Senate, Foltz and Gordon had to navigate a variety of institutional hurdles in the Assembly, thrown up most ungallantly by attorney lawmakers.[70] According to one legislator, final consideration of the bill was full of drama: "The fight came on this afternoon, and a real lively time it was, so far as parliamentary tactics were concerned. I never knew before how much pluck and energy there was in a woman—how they could urge their claims, plead for the privilege of making the battle of life—for such our friend Mrs. Foltz did, gently and eloquently."[71] The measure passed by a margin of two votes and was signed by the governor literally in the waning minutes of the session, only after additional lobbying by Gordon and Foltz.[72]

Realizing, however, that this hard-fought victory could be snatched away by any subsequent legislature, Foltz and Gordon wasted little time celebrating their victory. With the constitutional convention opening a scant six months after the Woman Lawyer's Bill was enacted, Foltz and Gordon took advantage of the chance to safeguard their investment in a legal career by constitutionalizing their right to practice law. They drafted a provision which stated simply that no person would be disqualified from entering into or pursuing "any lawful business, vocation or profession on account of sex," and demonstrated once again a talent for navigating the political arena, by having their proposal introduced late in the convention, in place of an unrelated provision that had been voted down. Whether delegates at that point were feeling the need to make up for having denied numerous other provisions of benefit to women, or simply didn't notice the substitution, the new measure was accepted without debate as part of a package of miscellaneous articles. Upon ratification of the new constitution, California women ostensibly became protected from gender-based discrimination in their choice of occupation.[73]

However, even while seeking these reforms, activists believed that, ultimately, it was the vote that would be the key to eliminating barriers to women's occupational equality. Addressing the predicament of those women who lacked a male breadwinner, Nettie Tator in 1872 argued that the only realistic remedy was "to open the doors to every honorable employment to woman; giving her equal chances with man, and equal pay for the same labor." But, Tator proclaimed, "*this will not be done, until the ballot is put into her hand to compel it.*"[74]

Over the course of twenty years of agitation, reformers were most successful in achieving occupational rights for women; they scored one victory in securing political rights and were thoroughly disappointed in their efforts to correct marital prop-

After almost six months of debate between Democrats, Republicans, and Workingmen, the 152 delegates to the state constitutional convention of 1879 produced what was at the time the world's longest written constitution. In this cartoon by Edward Keller from *The Wasp*, a Workingmen's mason adds a few building blocks to the new constitution, including "the land grabbers must go" and "society must support its poor," while Republican and Democratic masons wait to add their bricks. Feminists Laura de Force Gordon and Clara Shortridge Foltz managed to add a provision to the lengthy new constitution outlawing gender-based occupational discrimination. *Courtesy Bancroft Library.*

erty law. Why? Perhaps the most satisfying explanation lies in the varying power of these proposals to threaten the social order. For example, equalization of teachers' salaries at the elementary school level left untouched the gender and salary differentials existing between the feminized elementary and male-dominated high school levels. And clearing away legal barriers to women's employment, where they existed, did nothing to address the more significant *de facto* forces that barred women from more remunerative employment. Moreover, even the symbolic value of these laws was limited in an era when a woman's ideal place was thought to be in the home.

Meanwhile, the lone victory in the realm of political rights is easily explained as an exercise in pragmatism. Although a high value was placed on local governance of schools in the nineteenth century, men's decreasing interest in filling educational offices meant that women had to be called upon to keep the system functioning. But there was no corresponding need for women's votes; men were not averse to casting their ballots for school offices. And while, as it later turned out, women's enfranchisement failed to give rise to expected reforms, the perceived symbolic value of woman suffrage was enough at this time to prevent the enactment of female voting rights.

Reforming California's marital property system so as to give real force to the notion of joint property rights threatened to reach beyond the public and symbolic sphere into the private lives of husbands and wives. Granting the wife rights at the expense of the husband over property he felt he alone had earned—rights that would survive her death, rights that would empower and not merely protect her— was a far more radical proposition than that which was offered to eastern women through MWPAs, which provided wives with separate rights to property they would have owned had they remained unmarried. In the 1870s and 1880s, California legislators proved hostile to these reforms, even when they would have been in the interest of a state operating with a volatile economy and offering little in the way of a system of social welfare to aid its most vulnerable citizens.

NOTES

1. California Constitution, article 11, section 14 (1849). For the suffrage provision, see article 2, section 1.

2. See William Q. deFuniak, *Principles of Community Property*, vol. 1 (Chicago, 1943). There is no comprehensive exposition of the community property system, particularly as it existed historically, written for laypersons. However, treatment of the subject can be found in Carole Shammas, Marylynn Salmon, and Michael Dahlin, *Inheritance in America from Colonial Times to the Present* (New Brunswick, N.J., 1987), and Helen S. Carter, "Legal Aspects of Widowhood and Aging," in *On Their Own: Widows and Widowhood in the American Southwest, 1848–1939*, ed. Arlene Scadron (Chicago, 1988), 271–300.

3. For a description of the rules of coverture and their operation from colonial times through the antebellum period, see Marylynn Salmon, *Women and the Law in Early America* (Chapel Hill, 1986); Norma Basch, *In the Eyes of the Law: Women, Marriage, and Property in Nineteenth-Century New York* (Ithaca, 1982), esp. ch. 2; Joan Hoff, *Law, Gender, and Injustice: A Legal History of U.S. Women* (New York, 1991), esp. pp. 82–90, 106–16.

4. Regarding Married Women's Property Acts, see Richard Chused, "Married Women's Property Law: 1800–1850," *Georgetown Law Journal* 71 (1983): 1359–1425; Hoff, *Law, Gender, and Injustice*, 121–24, 127–35, 187–91; Basch, *In the Eyes of the Law*, esp. chs. 5 and 6. Regarding the concept of separate spheres, see Barbara Welter, "The Cult of True Womanhood: 1820–1860," *American Quarterly* 18 (1966): 151–74.

5. Regarding New York's consideration of civil law, see Peggy Rabkin, "The Origins of Law Reform: The Social Significance of the Nineteenth-Century Codification Movement and Its Contribution to the Passage of the Early Married Women's Property Acts," *Buffalo Law Review* 24 (1974): 683–760. Regarding New York and Wisconsin, see James W. Paulsen,

"Community Property and the Early American Women's Rights Movement: The Texas Connection," *Idaho Law Review* 32 (1996): 660–67.

6. The text of the debate is set forth in J. Ross Browne, *Report of the Debates in the Convention of California, on the Formation of the State Constitution, in September and October, 1849* (Washington, D.C., 1850), 257–69. For further discussion of the debates, see Donna C. Schuele, "Community Property Law and the Politics of Married Women's Property Rights in Nineteenth-Century California," *Western Legal History* 7 (1994): 248–60; Susan Westerberg Prager, "The Persistence of Separate Property Concepts in California's Community Property System, 1849–1975," *UCLA Law Review* 24 (1976): 8–24; Donald E. Hargis, "Women's Rights: California, 1849," *Southern California Quarterly* 37 (1955): 320–34; and Ray August, "The Spread of Community Property Law to the Far West," *Western Legal History* 3 (1990): 35–66.

7. Regarding the New York–Texas–California connection, see Paulsen, "Community Property," and Donna C. Schuele, "'A Robbery to the Wife': Culture, Gender, and Marital Property in California Law and Politics, 1850–1890" (Ph.D. diss., University of California, Berkeley, 1999), 42–44.

8. Browne, *Debates,* 258, 261.

9. Prager, "Persistence of Separate Property Concepts," 10–11.

10. Browne, *Debates,* 258.

11. Ibid., 259.

12. For further discussion regarding the initial enactment of community property law in California, see Schuele, "Robbery to the Wife," 57–72; Prager, "Persistence of Separate Property Concepts," 25–34.

13. For further discussion of the development of California community property law in the 1850s and 1860s, see Schuele, "Robbery to the Wife," 72–100; Prager, "Persistence of Separate Property Concepts," 34–49.

14. Schuele, "Robbery to the Wife," 57–100; Prager, "Persistence of Separate Property Concepts," 25–49.

15. Prager, "Persistence of Separate Property Concepts," 28.

16. For further discussion of the rise of an organized women's rights movement in California, see Schuele, "Robbery to the Wife," ch. 3; Roger Levenson, *Women in Printing: Northern California, 1857–1890* (Santa Barbara, 1994), esp. chs. 4–6; Reda Davis, *Woman's Republic: The Life of Marietta Stow, Co-operator* (San Francisco, 1969), 201–32.

17. See JoAnn Levy, *They Saw the Elephant: Women in the California Gold Rush* (Norman, Okla., 1992), 92–103.

18. See Levenson, *Women in Printing,* chs. 4 and 5; Robert J. Chandler, "A Woman Printer Battles an All-Male Union," *The Californians* 4 (1986): 44–47.

19. Regarding the connection between Spiritualism and the women's rights movement, particularly in California, see Ann Braude, *Radical Spirits: Spiritualism and Women's Rights in Nineteenth-Century America* (Boston, 1989), esp. chs. 3–5 and conclusion; Robert J. Chandler, "In the Van: Spiritualists as Catalysts for the California Women's Suffrage Movement," *California History* 73 (1994): 189–201.

20. Braude, *Radical Spirits,* 84–98, 193–95.

21. Elizabeth Cady Stanton, Susan B. Anthony, and Matilda J. Gage, eds., *History of Woman Suffrage,* vol. 3 (New York, 1886), 751.

22. Braude, *Radical Spirits,* 193.

23. Schuele, "Robbery to the Wife," 109–12.

24. Regarding Emily Pitts Stevens, see Levenson, *Women in Printing*, ch. 6; Sherilyn Cox Bennion, *Equal to the Occasion: Women Editors of the Nineteenth-Century West* (Reno, 1990).

25. For further discussion of the dissensions within the California women's movement during the 1870s, see Schuele, "Robbery to the Wife," 134–61.

26. This account is contained in Stanton, Anthony, and Gage, *Woman Suffrage*, vol. 3, 751–65.

27. During this time, California women also took part in the New Departure strategy, whereby women attempted to vote, or at least register to vote, on the basis that the newly ratified Fourteenth and Fifteenth Amendments to the federal constitution conferred suffrage on women as well as the freedmen. See Schuele, "Robbery to the Wife," 326 n. 224.

28. "Petition for Woman's Suffrage. In the Senate, March 2, 1870," in Women's Rights Pamphlets, Bancroft Library, University of California, Berkeley; State of California, "Report of Special Committee in Relation to Granting Women Political Equality," in *Appendix to Journals of the Senate and Assembly*, 19th sess., 1871–72, no. 3.

29. "Woman-Suffrage. The Meeting in the Senate Chamber," *Pioneer*, March 19, 1870, at 1 (reprint from the *Capital Reporter*).

30. "Woman Suffrage Meeting," *Sacramento Weekly Union*, March 16, 1872, at 8.

31. For further discussion of the types of arguments advanced in support of woman suffrage, see Aileen S. Kraditor, *The Ideas of the Woman Suffrage Movement, 1890–1920* (New York, 1981), esp. ch. 3.

32. "Plea on Behalf of Woman-Suffrage, before the Assembly Committee, Sacramento, California. March 18, 1870," *Pioneer*, April 2, 1870, at 2.

33. Regarding taxpaying as the basis for the right to vote, see Carolyn Jones, "Dollars and Selves: Women's Tax Criticism and Resistance in the 1870s," *University of Illinois Law Review* (1994): 265–309; Linda K. Kerber, *No Constitutional Right to Be Ladies: Women and the Obligations of Citizenship* (New York, 1998): 81–120.

34. "Woman Suffrage Meeting," at 8.

35. "Report of Special Committee," 5; Schuele, "Robbery to the Wife," 173–74, 193–94.

36. "The Education Bill," *San Jose Weekly Mercury*, February 26, 1874, at 2; "Sacramento," *San Francisco Chronicle*, February 18, 1874, at 3.

37. Schuele, "Robbery to the Wife," 208–15.

38. Regarding the battle over woman suffrage in the 1879 constitutional convention, see Barbara A. Babcock, "Clara Shortridge Foltz: Constitution Maker," *Indiana Law Journal* 66 (1991): 879–94; Schuele, "Robbery to the Wife," 259–88.

39. Schuele, "Robbery to the Wife," 296–309, 316–21.

40. *Senate Journal*, February 17, 1883, at 211.

41. Schuele, "Robbery to the Wife," 358–59. Regarding woman suffrage efforts in the 1890s, particularly the referendum battle of 1896, when the issue was narrowly defeated, see Susan Scheiber Edelman, "A Red Hot Suffrage Campaign: The Woman Suffrage Cause in California, 1896," *California Supreme Court Society Yearbook* 2 (1995), 49–131; and Gayle Gullett, *Becoming Citizens: The Emergence and Development of the California Women's Movement, 1880–1911* (Chicago, 2000), 83–84, 93–106.

42. "Report of Special Committee," 3.

43. Regarding the development of the "mere expectancy" doctrine in California commu-

nity property law, see Prager, "Persistence of Separate Property Concepts," 34–39; Schuele, "Robbery to the Wife," 77–84.

44. For further discussion of the use of joint property rhetoric within the women's rights movement, both in the East and West, see Reva Siegel, "Home as Work: The First Woman's Rights Claims Concerning Wives' Household Labor, 1850–1880," *Yale Law Journal* 103 (1994): 1073–1217.

45. Schuele, "Community Property Law," 264, 271–72.

46. "Address of Mrs. Nettie C. Tator before the Joint Committees of the Senate and Assembly of the State of California on the Subject of Extending the Right of Suffrage to Women, Sacramento, March 13, 1872," in Women's Rights Pamphlets, Bancroft Library.

47. For further discussion of Stow's experiences with the probate of her husband's estate and her efforts to reform California law, see Schuele, "In Her Own Way: Marietta Stow's Crusade for Probate Law Reform within the Nineteenth-Century Women's Rights Movement," *Yale Journal of Law and Feminism* 7 (1995): 279–306.

48. Marietta L. Stow, *Probate Confiscation; or, the Unjust Laws that Govern Women* (reprint, New York, 1974), 232–33.

49. "Report of Special Committee," 10.

50. Ibid., 3, 5, 10.

51. Schuele, "Robbery to the Wife," 193–94.

52. Stow, *Probate Confiscation*, 13–14.

53. Regarding Stow's relationship to the California women's rights movement, see Schuele, "In Her Own Way," 281.

54. Regarding Sarah Wallis, see Dorothy Regnery, "Pioneering Women: Portraits of Sarah," *The Californian (Magazine of the California History Center, De Anza College)* 8 (1986): 6–8.

55. Schuele, "Robbery to the Wife," 235–38.

56. For further discussion regarding the rise of legal consciousness among California women in the 1870s, see Schuele, "Community Property Law," 263–67.

57. Schuele, "In Her Own Way," 285–86.

58. Printed petition form entitled "Petition for Equal Rights," Laura deForce Gordon Collection, Bancroft Library; Schuele, "Robbery to the Wife," 310, 316–18; Schuele, "Community Property Law," 276.

59. Schuele, "Robbery to the Wife," 309–11, 318, 321–22, 337–38.

60. *Senate Journal,* January 26, 1885, at 142.

61. Schuele, "Robbery to the Wife," 339–40, 343–47.

62. *Senate Journal,* January 26, 1885, at 142–43.

63. Schuele, "Robbery to the Wife," 347–50.

64. Ibid., 194–203, 218–20. For further discussion of the influence of the codification movement on California marital property law, see Schuele, "Community Property Law," 270–71.

65. Schuele, "Robbery to the Wife," 177–78, 292.

66. "Sacramento," *San Francisco Chronicle,* March 14, 1872, at 1.

67. Schuele, "Robbery to the Wife," 179, 216–17.

68. *Bradwell v. Illinois,* 83 U.S. 130 (1873); Schuele, "Robbery to the Wife," 242–45. For further discussion of women's entrance into the legal profession, see Virginia Drachman, *Sisters in Law: Women Lawyers in Modern American History* (Cambridge, Mass., 1998).

69. Barbara A. Babcock, "Clara Shortridge Foltz: 'First Woman,'" *Arizona Law Review* 30 (1988): 613–717; Schuele, "Robbery to the Wife," 242–44.
70. Babcock, "First Woman," 686–94; Schuele, "Robbery to the Wife," 240–41.
71. "A Victory in California," *Woman's Journal,* April 20, 1878, at 124.
72. Babcock, "First Woman," 692.
73. Babcock, "Constitution Maker," 894–99; Schuele, "Robbery to the Wife," 292–94.
74. "Address of Mrs. Tator," 12.

8

The Beginnings of Anglo-American Local Government in California

Edward Leo Lyman

California local government in the Anglo-American period did not get off to a particularly auspicious start. For a short time during the United States military occupation and thereafter, some of the Hispanic institutions, especially the office of alcalde, a position that existed in many localities, mainly in northern California, continued in effect. This office combined legislative, judicial, executive, and law enforcement functions in one person. But there was little patience among newcomers with the lack of separation of powers and checks on the power inherent in the position, and the rapidly increasing throng of citizens from the United States demanded prompt instituting of offices and procedures with which they had more confidence. Sometimes this impatience ran roughshod over existing officials and the rights of people who had been in the region much longer. Yet in an amazingly short time the structure and functions of local government as they would continue to operate were successfully established throughout the state.

In southern California the transition from the Mexican forms of local government to that of the United States was sufficiently gradual to be generally less painful for Spanish-speaking residents, who supposedly were assured full rights of citizenship by the recent Treaty of Guadalupe Hidalgo, than was often the case in northern California. In the huge Los Angeles County, which in 1850 stretched east to the Colorado River and into what would later become southern Nevada, the first County Court of Sessions met June 24, 1850, with Augustin Olivera serving as presiding judge.[1] Since he could not speak English and at least one of the associate justices knew no Spanish, G. Thompson Burrill, who was also the sheriff, was appointed county interpreter at an additional salary of fifty dollars per month. By June 1852, the state legislature had provided for a five-member county commission or board of supervisors in a few of the larger counties, including Los Angeles. There

Los Angeles plaza, photographed here in 1865, served as a public meeting place and civic center during both Mexican and American control of the region. Though dwarfed by San Francisco to the north, Los Angeles grew steadily throughout the nineteenth century, attracting merchants and homesteaders with its hospitable weather and rich soil. James Clarke, a lawyer who headed to Los Angeles in the mid-1850s after failing to establish a practice in northern California, reported that "Our Climate is that of France yet we have every Tropical production in abundance," including "Oranges, Sweet & Sour Limes, Lemons, figs, prunes, Citron, Peaches, Pears, Apples, Grapes, Quince, Olives, etc. etc." *Courtesy Seaver Center for Western History Research, Natural History Museum of Los Angeles County.*

the positions were first occupied by two men with Hispanic surnames and three with Anglo-American names, including Jefferson Hunt, representing the new Mormon settlers at San Bernardino.[2]

The process of Americanizing the predominantly Hispanic population of the California southland was no easy task even without the aggressiveness prevailing farther north. This was partly because the existing laws were in a chaotic condition and partly because most Latinos understood neither the language nor the customs of the new rulers. And many Anglo-Americans residing there had but little patience for the older Mexican ways of conducting law and government. Maintaining peace and harmony between the two groups required a tact difficult to attain on either side. Fortunately, there were a few crucially placed individuals who assisted immeasurably in bridging the gaps.[3]

In Santa Barbara, Colonel Benton, of the occupying army, questionably—but with some fairness—issued a private manifesto assuring Hispanic residents that they were now American citizens with a constitutional right to help make laws for themselves. The first county government there went into effect in August 1850, a month before California statehood, with Joaquin Carrillo as county judge. Eugene Lies, formerly of New York, was appointed interpreter and translator. Some confusion under the new system arose because several elected officials were not qualified for their tasks and never actually occupied the offices. The majority of potential voters had long been accustomed to deferring to the directions of a few patriarchs of powerful families. The son of one of these, Joaquin de la Guerra, at first refused to relinquish his records from the old Mexican Court of First Instance. He probably held the new system in contempt and was demonstrating his disregard in this manner. But his brother, Pablo, who inherited a large measure of the trust and prestige enjoyed by the family, was supportive of and fully involved in the new government. First marshal for the southern district, then state senator and president of that body, he eventually served as lieutenant governor of California. Pablo also served as mayor of Santa Barbara and was elected to the county's first board of supervisors. In these positions, and less officially, he gradually taught his Latino countrymen the importance of trusting the courts for settlement of issues, while also encouraging others to be patient and considerate during the transition period. Always a conciliator and advisor, he later served as district judge. During the American Civil War he was a powerful advocate for the Union cause in the region.[4]

Probably even more significant in this transition process was Benjamin I. Hayes, who had arrived in southern California from Missouri in late 1850. A devout Catholic who was fluent in Spanish, he not only served as the first Los Angeles County attorney, but also helped translate into Spanish the initial statutes enacted by the California legislature. In 1852, Hayes was able to generate widespread support for his successful candidacy for judge of the district, which included San Diego and soon the new San Bernardino County. He was equally cordial with Latino, Mormon, and southern Democratic segments of the region's population, and his consistent fairness and commitment to helping accomplish true assimilation immeasurably enhanced progress in that direction.[5]

Another who contributed immeasurably to better relations between Anglo newcomers and Mexican Americans in the California southland was Andrés Pico. This former Californio cavalry officer and brother of the last Mexican governor led the most effective posse of more than forty men, primarily Hispanic, in successful pursuit of the Juan Flores gang, which in January 1857 had ambushed and killed Los Angeles sheriff James Barton and several of his men. The Pico brothers' examples of friendship and cooperation with their new neighbors significantly enhanced the accommodation process.[6]

An example of how a typical California county initially organized is El Dorado

Pablo de la Guerra, a powerful ranchero and civic leader from Santa Barbara, adapted to the changes wrought by the American conquest of California better than most Spanish-speaking residents. The son of influential Californio patriarch José Antonio Julián de la Guerra y Noriego, Pablo learned English, won title to his family's lands, and served in the California Senate. *California Historical Society Collection at the University of Southern California: Title Insurance and Trust Photo Collection.*

County, in the center of the gold fields. In May 1850, the Hon. Vinal Daniels, presiding judge, had given notice for all fifteen justices of the peace functioning within the county to gather at the county seat, Coloma—especially appropriate, as Coloma is where gold had first been discovered two years before, thus sparking the great influx of Anglo-Americans that had occurred in the region. The stated purpose of what was called a "convention of justices of the peace" was to select two of their number to serve as associates with Judge Daniels on the County Court of Sessions. They elected William Rolfs and Henry Waldo, who immediately commenced functioning as the first official government of the new county. Each of the original counties, and a few soon created, was governed by such a body, which originated as a derivative of English common law in the colonial American period. Other states and territories then getting started, including Utah, utilized the same system. The California legislature soon adjusted this governmental structure by providing boards of supervisors with broader functions. The associate justices of the early courts of sessions were certainly not full-time positions. In El Dorado County, Rolfs and Waldo were paid sixteen dollars per day for the six days they served on the court in their first three weeks in office. Judge Daniels, who performed some administrative duties and conducted much of the judicial business of the county, apparently received the seemingly generous sum of a thousand dollars per month salary for closer to full-time work.[7]

The subjects addressed in the first months of the El Dorado County Court of Sessions are doubtless typical of many other more heavily populated counties in the early period. Immediately pressing were the claims for services rendered during the first state elections, particularly by precinct judges. Virtually all of the huge leather-bound record books still extant in the region contain numerous pages of claims by persons seeking such remuneration. The court promptly instituted a countywide poll tax of three dollars per person, certainly to recoup the funds just dispersed for election purposes. Since the supervisors later served as a canvassing board attesting to the validity of elections within their county, the courts of sessions probably also functioned in this manner. Similarly, funds were immediately allocated for grand jurors and witnesses involved in court proceedings.

One of the most demanding early functions of these county governments was construction and maintenance of roads and bridges. There had been some of each built and operated elsewhere in the earlier Mexican period, but hardly any in the newly settled mining country. Even prior to commencement of official government operations at the local level there were numerous entrepreneurs among the miners—as there had been in the East and among emigrants coming west across the plains—building toll roads and bridges to operate as private businesses. Again, El Dorado County illustrates this situation with literally dozens of individuals and partnerships applying for licenses to conduct such enterprises. Invariably, bonds were required to assure faithful compliance, and rates were specified, providing for recouping construction costs and some profits.[8] Most toll bridge contracts were renewed annually, although spring floods undoubtedly discouraged and dissolved more than a few such ventures. John F. Little and original gold discoverer James W. Marshall operated several toll bridges on branches of the American River and naturally asserted their rights to protect those businesses. In one case, they successfully enjoined William Riley and James McKee from further operation of a ferry in competition with their bridge at Coloma. Little was less successful in his protest against another bridge license being granted with the same rates as theirs just a mile upstream from the one he and his partners operated at Salmon Falls.[9]

In a similar manner, franchises were frequently granted for toll roads, some operated until after the new California constitution went into effect in 1879, but usually for a much shorter duration. Except where maintenance costs were exceptionally high, within just a few years, county officials declared most of these to be public highways, sometimes designating a committee to determine which of the several existing roads through a given area should be favored with continual maintenance. Occasionally there were later grants of permission to build additional public roads to places of special need, sometimes "provided that [the appointed supervisors urging such roads] perform said service [constructing them] without compensation from the county." More frequently the Court of Sessions responded to petitions from interested citizens for a specific new road to be considered by appointing the advocates to work with the county surveyor to "look over" the proposed route and lay it out in the most efficient manner before reporting back to the county officials, usually at the next month's sessions. Within a year after the Board of Supervisors took over the primary functions of governing El Dorado County, it acted to prevent ill-conceived petitions for opening new roads by ordering a deposit to defray all expenses for laying out such roads. If the county actually proceeded with construction, the funds were reimbursed, but if the investigation process determined the proposed road to be unfeasible, the money deposited "would be appropriated to the payment of the costs of surveying and locating said road and in reporting thereon." Doubtless this curbed many, but not all, requests for new roads.[10]

Usually, when a particular road was declared a public highway, a county road supervisor was appointed and a road district created. All able-bodied men residing in a given district were required to work two to four days each year maintaining the roads, if notified to do so by their district supervisor. Very soon, counties allowed persons so assessed to pay the road tax in cash rather than labor. In Nevada County and many others this fee amounted to four dollars per annum, with the road supervisors authorized to grant receipts for that year's road tax, specifying whether it had been paid in money or labor. Accounting for the totals of each category was a prerequisite for the supervisors' taking their own quarterly pay from the funds col-

Downtown Auburn, shown in this idyllic 1876 drawing, housed Placer County's courthouse (right), constructed in 1854, and jail, built three years later. An iron bridge connected the buildings' second floors. A main supply center during the Gold Rush, Auburn prospered in subsequent decades thanks to the arrival of the transcontinental railroad in 1865. A grandiose three-story domed structure built nearby replaced the gold-rush-era courthouse in 1898. *Courtesy Placer County Department of Museums.*

lected. They were also empowered to levy fines for noncompliance. Sometimes the supervisor was allowed to expend all taxes collected on the roads of his district, and sometimes a portion was paid into the county general fund. The road supervisors usually had an allocated number of hours of labor that had to be expended on their roads in any given quarter, themselves doing whatever work was not accomplished through tax-levied labor. They were also responsible for making emergency repairs and for pointing out future projects needed. This system persisted, at least in the more rural areas of the state, well into the twentieth century.[11]

Another original function of county government was granting licenses for other business enterprises. The right to sell liquor in quantities of less than one pint was usually granted for periods of up to six months at rates varying with the volume of business. In El Dorado County, for example, the Marshall House Hotel at Coloma had to pay thirty-five dollars for two months, while a tavern in Placerville was charged just thirty dollars for six months and a store in Georgetown paid fifteen dollars for three months. What were called in some places "auctioneer's licenses" were usually granted for one year, allowing permission to conduct business in retail sales of merchandise. The fact that this obligation to pay fees for business operation was accepted virtually everywhere but San Francisco is no compliment to early businessmen of that city.

By early 1852 there was already a state general hospital functioning at Stockton, which was converted in July 1853 to an asylum solely for the insane. Outside larger cities, there appears to have been little, if any, official acknowledgment of responsibility for most indigent ill persons until after formation of boards of supervisors in the smaller counties in 1855. Certainly, private funds were known to have been raised and expended for such purposes. Among the first to address the need for care of the indigent ill were El Dorado County officials, in the spring of 1854. They allocated funds to individuals for boarding and medical attendance for several poor and sick persons, including the burial expenses for at least one who died. By the end of the year, they had created a special county indigent sick fund, with persons in the various population centers designated to care for those in that qualifying category in their areas. Soon after, Calaveras County supervisors specified that only "regular" physicians within the county could submit proposals for care and maintenance of the indigent sick, including furnishing a "substantial building" for that purpose. About that time, Nevada County officials also contracted with physicians in three towns each to provide medicine and attendance, along with board and lodging, for such persons in their vicinity.[12]

By the mid-1850s, the state legislature provided funds for the indigent sick, and county treasurers drew at least partly on state money for that purpose. El Dorado County consolidated its services, which had been provided by eleven individuals, by contracting with two Placerville physicians at just over a thousand dollars per month "for taking care of and providing for the indigent sick of the county." A committee investigated the facility and reported that the "subjects [were] properly cared for," hearing no cause for complaint. Later, the operating fee was raised to $3,750 per quarter, with the managers posting adequate bond. These arrangements were similar in other counties throughout the period. About a decade later, Nevada County paid Dr. R. M. Hunt eighty-five cents per day for each person placed in his charge. That county was at the time levying a tax of fifteen cents per one hundred dollars of assessed property valuation specifically for its indigent sick fund, besides funds still coming from the state. In Amador County, Samuel Page was paid seventy-five dollars per month to furnish medical care to the patients of the county hospital and jail. The monthly amount allocated by the county thereafter varied, probably with the number cared for, from a high of eighty dollars in 1868 to fifty-nine dollars in 1870. San Francisco, Sacramento, and perhaps some other more urbanized counties offered more extensive services, but overall, most had come to consider care for the indigent ill as a legitimate county function, a precursor of the later welfare system.[13]

Certainly the various county governments were not slow in levying the usual taxes, nor in directing either the county treasurer or sheriff to collect them. Frequently, notice was posted and published as to when the official would be in each given area for the purpose of receiving such taxes. For at least the less urban counties, the sheriff usually acted as tax collector for some state funds as well. Most made at least annual "statements of accounts" along with reports to state and county officers as to the amount of various taxes collected. For some years the supervisors also met occasionally as boards of equalization to adjust some tax assessments.

The foreign miners' tax enacted, repealed, and reenacted by the state legislature in the early 1850s caused the various counties to authorize "deputy collectors," allowing them to retain a percentage as personal fees for their service. El Dorado County had some difficulty determining what was proper in this regard. The law provided that the collector should receive 15 percent of the funds, but the judges of the Court of Sessions deemed this insufficient compensation and added another 10 percent, making the total one quarter of all money collected. Soon, the new Board of Supervisors cut the collection fee back to the original 15 percent, but almost immediately raised it to 22 percent. At least for a time, some counties had fond hopes that this questionable source of revenue would solve many of their fiscal problems. In the summer of 1853, El Dorado County allocated its share of the foreign miners' tax "for the payment of the current expenses of the county." It was also ordered that the county treasurer take any revenues from that source exceeding a surplus of five thousand dollars to be "used in the payment of outstanding county indebtedness."[14]

With so many local justices of the peace levying fines and other county officials handling various funds, it was not difficult to lose monies through negligence and malfeasance. Early in 1852, the El Dorado County Court of Sessions ordered the district attorney to institute suits against all magistrates who had received county funds and neglected to pass such money to the county treasurer, as required by a recent order. It directed that similar suits be aimed at "delinquent officers" holding funds belonging to the county. Later that spring the same officers complied with a grand jury mandate to appoint two men, presumably qualified in accounting, "to examine the public offices of the county and report to the court the following month." The auditors were charged to examine the "condition of the books and the fidelity with which county officers have discharged their duty." All was reported well regulated. In 1855, the supervisors of the same county appointed other auditors to examine the account books of an assessor who had just left office. They discovered deficiencies of almost seven hundred dollars each to the county and the state. While these funds were ordered paid, there is no mention of further reprisals for the oversight.[15]

In San Bernardino's first year as a separate county, the Court of Sessions felt constrained to order a former member of that body, Louis Rubidoux, whose term had expired, to relinquish his docket books to the new justice of the peace, José Gallego. Later, the neighboring justice of the peace, Julian Trujillo, of the town of San Salvadore, was ordered to report and "account for all fines collected during his term of service." At that same time, the court refused to recognize the bill submitted by the county assessor, former mountain man Valentine "Rube" Herring, for sixty days' services performed. Having concluded that "there being no evidence of him being faithful in the discharge of his duty," the court allowed him only thirty-five days' pay at the rate of eight dollars per day. There were doubtless mitigating circumstances, since Herring had attempted to assess the undeveloped city lots of San Bernardino at a higher rate than the Mormon leaders of that community deemed fair. The majority of the county's Court of Sessions, also faithful Latter-day Saints, were clearly expressing the disdain of the church hierarchy toward the defiant assessor. Later, as the majority of dedicated Mormons were moving back to Utah, the San Bernardino County Board of Supervisors refused to recognize the full amount of rent assessed on rooms used for county purposes, paying a far lesser amount—perhaps for similar retaliatory reasons.[16]

One of the most complex matters undertaken by several county courts of sessions was funding earlier county debts. In the spring of 1853, the Tuolumne County court appointed a three-man board of fund commissioners to procure the necessary bonds to fund forty thousand dollars of county indebtedness. The board was directed to publish notice in the local newspapers to inform holders of warrants due from the county to present such bills, apparently with the option of either receiving cash payment or exchanging them for new bonds carrying a very high rate of interest. These days, many people have no idea of the interest rates that prevailed in the gold-rush era, but 3 and 4 percent interest per month was considered moderate, and most of the interest paid in connection with Tuolumne County's bonds over the subsequent years of the 1850s remained just under 90 percent interest annually.[17]

Nevada County, which had to cope with the loss of records when a new courthouse was destroyed by fire in the summer of 1856, called for those holding warrants against the county to present what evidence they had of the debt, with the Board of Supervisors clearly granting the benefit of the doubt. Early the following year, reconstruction costs compelled the board to order that a "sufficient amount of county warrants be sold at public auction at the court house . . . to realize the sum of five thousand dollars in cash" for the purpose of paying the cost of construction and repair.[18]

The year after California statehood, about five hundred Mormons from Deseret, Utah, emigrated to southern California and commenced establishing what became

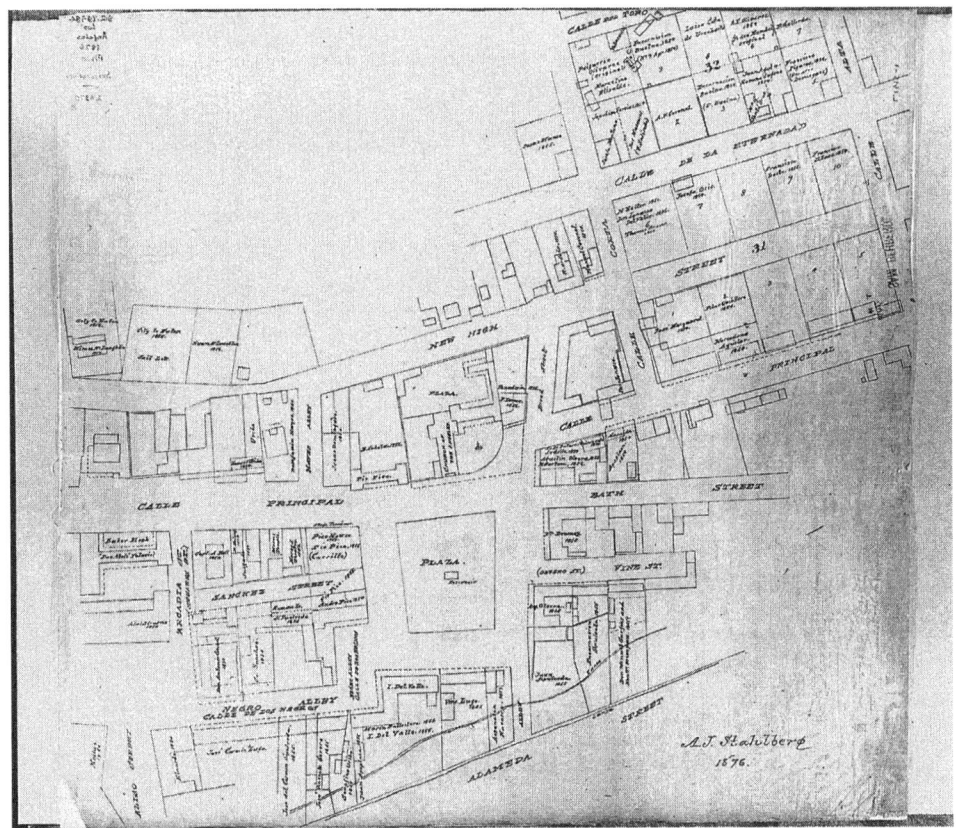

A. J. Stahlberg drew this map of downtown Los Angeles in 1876, the year the Southern Pacific Railroad finally connected the city to San Francisco. Los Angeles's population would more than quadruple in the next decade, overrunning much of the Mexican presence evident in Stahlberg's map. *Courtesy Seaver Center for Western History Research, Natural History Museum of Los Angeles County.*

the largest Anglo-American community in the entire southland, San Bernardino. Los Angeles County granted the new citizens one of the five seats on the county Board of Supervisors. Jefferson Hunt, well known in the region as the ranking church member in the so-called Mormon Battalion serving garrison duty at San Diego and Los Angeles at the end of the Mexican War, held that position. The county was already saddled with considerable debt, and the *Los Angeles Star* urged citizens to take advantage of new state legislation authorizing funding of such debts. In the fall election of 1852, in which Hunt was elected one of the state assemblymen, the Mormon voters helped defeat the proposition to fund the debt. It is likely they hoped to escape from the county before such action took place, assuming the refinanced obligations would be substantially larger than the existing one.[19]

By that time, another leading Latter-day Saint political activist, county judge Daniel M. Thomas, was circulating a petition requesting formation of a separate county. Early in the 1853 state legislative session, Hunt introduced the document and a bill authorizing the new county. The committee assigned to consider the proposal promptly recommended division, with no known opposition at any stage of the process (unlike the later San Bernardino County, which has resisted each time a segment of the county, still the largest in the state, has attempted similar division). The law passed on April 26, 1853, making San Bernardino one of the first nonoriginal counties in the state. The first act of the new Court of Sessions, headed by Thomas, was to appoint Hunt and fellow Mexican War officer Alden A. M. Jackson as a committee to confer with their counterparts from Los Angeles for the purpose of "apportioning the amount of indebtedness of Los Angeles chargeable to San Bernardino County." The new county's proportion of $4,500 was certainly fair, and payments were made regularly at least in the years when the Mormons maintained control, through 1857. In that year the annual payment was $844.41.[20]

Even as the eastern segment of the county was essentially seceding, efforts were mounted once again to fund the Los Angeles County debt. This time a bill was submitted to the state legislature for that purpose. It passed and was signed by the governor, leaving the local steps of implementation mainly to the county clerk. He had to recall outstanding warrants, pay some, and replace the remainder with new ones payable at acceptable intervals and interest.[21]

Partly because the Latter-day Saints were such law-abiding citizens, and partly because such public affairs as probate courts were dominated through ecclesiastical officials, there was but a minimum of county government required in San Bernardino. There had been a jail contracted through another Mormon Battalion officer, Jesse D. Hunter, at a cost of seven thousand dollars while the area was yet within Los Angeles County. It appears to have been the epitome of an inside pork-barrel arrangement. What adobe structure had been erected collapsed during a rainstorm. The building was never completed, and the community never had a jail during the six-year Mormon period. Prisoners, usually but not always "outsiders," were incarcerated from time to time in private apartments or a local hotel, with the property owners reimbursed for lodging and food provided. Similarly, there was no courthouse, with such business conducted at a hotel, the sheriff's residence, or the office building also used by the leading ecclesiastical authorities, Amasa M. Lyman and Charles C. Rich, with their clerk, Richard R. Hopkins, usually functioning in a like county capacity along with the district judge and others.

In commitment to education, even when it was an infant county, as before, San Bernardino emerged as an exemplary sector of the state. While still in a temporary camp as their leaders searched for a permanent location, the Mormons had conducted several schools under sycamore trees at the mouth of Cajon Pass. Similarly, when the Mormon settlers moved into their newly erected fort in San Bernardino, a corner covered by a tent served as a school. And the year they moved out of the fort and built at least a hundred individual residences, church officials, who also conducted most school affairs, including hiring teachers and establishing salaries, formulated plans for two adjacent adobe structures for schools to be erected near the center of town. Another school was already being conducted some miles south in an old building left over from a Franciscan attempt to establish a mission in the valley prior to 1834.

As late as 1855, these schools received no state funds, but they were expanding nevertheless. Residents of sectors some distance from the schools petitioned the Board of Supervisors to organize schools closer to them, and districts were promptly established at Warm Creek to the northeast, the mill district to the southwest, and what became Mt. Vernon due west, along with one some distance to the southeast in the San Gorgonio Pass area. According to the most careful student of the subject, Hazel Miller Croy, this school system was at the time the best in the state by several measures. The percentage of school-age children enrolled and attending was the highest in the state, and the ratio of pupils to teachers was the lowest of those submitting such figures, which would have been at least the main districts at the time. While there are no comparative studies of the proportionate wealth that other communities expended on their schools, San Bernardino, with its poor grain harvests and large debt from its purchase of the former Lugo rancho, exhibited an impressive public commitment to its schools.[22]

Most other California counties struggled with educational matters during the first years of statehood. Early in 1852, the *Los Angeles Star* chided that there were no public schools in that county and that many children were suffering from the negligence of both city and county officials. Later that year the Board of Supervisors ordered a tax of three cents on each hundred dollars of assessed valuation for support of county schools, with the county assessor charged by state law to also serve as superintendent of such schools as were established. In 1853, the Los Angeles city common council resolved to support the movement, and three schools were established, some seeking state funds to enroll poor children. In 1854, Los Angeles mayor Stephen Foster made education his highest priority, complaining that three-quarters of the five hundred school-age children in the city still had no means of schooling. It was no better the next year, with the population growing rapidly. There were 1,191 school-age children then in Los Angeles, El Monte, San Gabriel, and adjacent areas, and the *Star* alleged that not more than 150 of them were yet attending school. Half of these were in the largely former Texan community of El Monte. That year, A. H. Hoyt of the Methodist Episcopal church opened a school for boys, and Los Angeles city promptly made an appropriation enabling the proprietor to lower tuition substantially, but that did not help those families with no means at all for paying tuition.[23]

According to the *Star*, by the end of 1855, a "brick school house" had been erected or purchased in Los Angeles, and the next year, four schools operated in the area. But in March of 1856, two of them closed for lack of funds, with the *Star* charging that officials had been too lavish in paying teacher salaries ($125 per month instead of $75) and renting some classrooms ($25 instead of $15). There were still two schools in operation on the predominantly Anglo-American west side of town, with children—mainly Latino—on the north side denied educational opportunities at least for the remainder of that school year. The next year, sixty school pupils of the "district school" conducted by Mrs. Hoyt were examined in the traditional public recitals along with an undisclosed number examined at a "female school" and a similarly unknown number at the "boy's school" directed by Mr. McKee.[24]

Certainly the fact that so few children resided in the Mother Lode mining camps during the state's first few years helps explain the low priority of counties there assigned to educational pursuits. This was also partly the fault of the state legislature for being slow in mandating such matters. Finally, in 1854, some mining counties, including El Dorado, allocated a portion of their property tax for school purposes. Doubtless there had been by that time more of an influx of insistent mothers as well as potential pupils. The public school system thereafter commenced to expand and flourish in that section. In the next decade the county tax apportionment devoted to school purposes was more typically twenty-five to thirty cents on each hundred dollars assessed valuation. In that era, another phenomenon arose, particularly in mining districts where paying ore had played out, of older separate school districts consolidating into new ones as the population declined in some formerly booming areas.[25]

Another of the first acts of the new San Bernardino County officials was to appoint several "judges of the plains," a carryover from the Hispanic period that remained fully operational in southern California for at least thirty years after statehood. A judge of the plains served a very important function in the livestock-raising region of the southland. It was this official's duty to call for cattle roundups and to be present at these annual or semiannual rodeos for cattle and *recojedas*, or gatherings of horses. His seat of justice was in the saddle, where he determined who the unmarked young animals belonged to, presumably by observing the brand or mark on the cow or mare offering milk to the animal in question. From his decision there was little appeal, and all stock-ownership disputes were settled before him. Most of the rules applying were probably never codified into state law, although the institution was recognized there. In 1850 there were a dozen judges of the plains acting in Los Angeles County at a salary of one hundred dollars each per year. Usually, as in San Bernardino County, each election precinct had its own appointed judge, functioning similarly to the urban justices of the peace. An act of 1857 gave these officials power to make arrests for stealing livestock.[26]

Local officials were also soon charged to regulate the often controversial matter of water rights. In 1854 the California legislature enacted a law providing for a "board of commissioners . . . to regulate water courses" and apportion irrigation water, including authority for the construction of ditches. The San Bernardino County Board of Supervisors appointed three prominent Mormon men to those offices early in 1856, and that year they stood firmly against the wishes of Charles C. Rich of the Mormon hierarchy, deciding that their right to continuous use of Lytle Creek had lapsed through negligence and that non-Mormon claimants recently settled in the later community of Rialto possessed superior rights. They similarly intervened to prevent Rich and his associates from utilizing water south from the Santa Ana River when others had diverted that same stream flow earlier to lands on the opposite side of the river. These decisions remained crucial precedents in one of the first successful Anglo-American irrigation regions of the state and fully demonstrated the value of county water commissioners.[27]

Unlike many other areas of the new state, San Francisco inherited little earlier Hispanic governmental structure on which to build. The commercial settlement there had been dominated from the beginning by non-Latino merchants. Probably none of them was more influential than Samuel Brannan, who in the limited confines of this study will serve as a focal point on which to demonstrate the self-interested power often wielded by businessmen in this unfortunate period of the city's infancy. From the beginning of the Anglo-American era, Brannan's *California Star* probably overstated the amount of crime in the city, partly because Brannan supported a rival candidate to the person then serving as constable. After the gold-rush exodus from San Francisco to the mining districts, stimulated largely by merchandiser Brannan for obviously selfish reasons, there was little crime, because so few potential victims or perpetrators remained in town. But even later, with the influx of new population, the city almost ended the year 1848 without a murder, though one was committed on Christmas Day.

In the San Francisco legislative body, still called the ayuntamiento, member Brannan in October 1849 introduced a resolution that city-owned lots be sold at auction, supposedly to generate funds to build a hospital, city hall, and public wharves. Of more interest to him was the fact that individual officeholders purchased 120 such parcels largely near the waterfront, and he helped appropriate three hundred thousand dollars of the funds derived therefrom to construct the wharf in an area where he and other city officials held at least fifty lots. Certainly their inside information about the location of the wharf, as well as what lots were available, was an invaluable and questionable advantage in these transactions.

As the population and related problems of San Francisco mushroomed, the new state legislature enacted a charter providing for a typical mayor-council form of government with eight aldermen and eight assistant aldermen drawn from eight city districts. An elected recorder served as police court judge, with powers similar to a justice of the peace. The marshal functioned as chief of police. John Geary was the first mayor, and though not often criticized, he amassed the considerable sum of two hundred thousand dollars in less than three years apart from his private business profits.[28] Within a year, the usually biased *Alta California*, with more than a little justification, denounced the government's "shameless profligacy" and "unblushing selfishness," which demonstrated "less public spirit than any other group of men that ever pretended to act for public good." The editor concluded that the officials "saw good in nothing that did not put money into their own pockets." Yet in this they were hardly different from their predecessors, who had almost never been criticized by the same newspaper.[29]

San Francisco simply experienced in more concentrated form what was happening in other cities in the nation and elsewhere. Great social upheaval occurred as migrants from rural areas and a flood of foreign immigrants with alien value systems converged as a teeming horde. The machinery of government was suited for an earlier, more neighborly environment, and it would take many years for the proper adjustments to be made. Yet the city did have a regularly constituted governmental structure, and it will always remain debatable whether the drastic vigilante actions of 1851 and 1856 were justified. San Francisco's urban vigilante movements were unprecedented in the nation's history, although there was abundant similar activity that appeared more justified in places where organized governments were lacking.

In February 1851, prior to the first major outbreak of San Francisco vigilantism, the *Alta California* proposed that the city should eliminate more than sixty government positions and reduce the salaries of those remaining. This, the newspaper argued, could enable reduction in the expense of municipal government to a cost of some $235,000 annually, instead of almost a million dollars. There was doubtless some waste and much profiteering in city government, but even as matters stood at that time, the police were not paid that month, which was not uncommon. (When they were paid, it was often in depreciated scrip rather than cash.) The critics of government did not yet resort to the allegation that crime and lawlessness were rampant in an effort to bring down the constituted government. But if there was such a condition, it might well have been partly the responsibility of the outside critics pressing unreasonably for economizing measures.[30]

Certainly, among the greatest deficiencies of San Francisco municipal government in the early statehood period was the lack of adequate fire protection. As elsewhere, fire service depended on volunteer companies, whose members, upon hearing an alarm, dropped what they were doing and rushed to where their fire-fighting equipment was housed. Each company was largely independent of the others, although a chief engineer was sometimes elected to assure that the various segments worked together. But often there was conflict and competition among the companies, even to the detriment of fighting fires. There were some efforts by firemen to get the state legislature to grant an official united fire department power to enforce rules and regulations at the fire scene and during fire alarms, but nothing came of the matter in the crucial period of 1851. Firemen also urged the creation of a fund to be used for the benefit of those injured on the job. Unfortunately, such ideas were contrary to the prevailing laissez-faire philosophies of the day, and it would take much more property loss and suffering before professionalization finally occurred, between 1864 and 1866.[31]

During the period from December 1849 to June 1851, the city was devastated by six major fires. With hindsight, one might question the lack of any building or safety codes or restrictions on the use of flammable materials for rebuilding. Historian Kevin J. Mullen quotes a contemporary correspondent who warned that the risk of fire was great, with the town appearing to be "one great tinder box." Although some of the prisoners who were forced to confess transgressions during the vigilante activity admitted to incendiarism, Mullen asserts that despite all of the allegations, most of the fires were probably started by accident. In late February 1851, members of the fire companies held a public meeting at which they considered resigning and turning their engine equipment over to city officials. The expressed reason for their frustration was that each communication they sent to the common council "for sustenance of [the] fire department" had been disregarded even after four of the great fires had already occurred. Lack of attention to fire-fighting matters appears to be the epitome of poor governance, which was typical of the city during the era, no matter who was in power.[32]

One of the main reasons for the fire companies' failure was that the water contained in the city's small cisterns was quickly exhausted during each conflagration. There were a few springs, rills, and wells scattered about the city, but no abundant or reliable water supply. In early 1851, a private entrepreneur, Arzo D. Merrifield, proposed to spend more than $750,000 to bring water from Mountain Lake, near the Presidio, to various portions of the city. He also proposed installing sufficient fire hydrants and water pressure—whose use would be free during times of crisis and for other public purposes—to markedly improve fire protection. The common council passed an ordinance granting him a franchise for twenty-five years, later reduced to five years of exclusive rights with possible forfeiture any time his company could not supply performance adequate to the council's specifications. Private rates would be set by a commission appointed by the council. By 1858 the system included sixty-one large cisterns capable of storing more than a million and a half gallons for fire-fighting purposes. This capacity would be later expanded by the City Water Works Company and Spring Valley Water Company. Even as the *Alta California* urged initial approval of the Merrifield proposition, the newspaper questionably

Franklin E. R. Whitney, San Francisco volunteer firefighter and temperance leader, ca. 1852. As ferocious fires repeatedly ravaged San Francisco in the 1850s, merchants and property owners—with assistance from city government—funded a loosely organized network of volunteer firefighter companies. Firemen were required to provide their own uniforms and equipment, thereby excluding all but the city's wealthy from participating. Whitney, longtime fire chief of Howard Engine Company on Montgomery Street, hailed from an affluent Bostonian family. In 1859 he founded the Dashaway Association, a fraternal temperance organization aimed at persuading firefighters to "dash away the intoxicating cup." *California Historical Society, FN-25844.*

also argued that it would justify eliminating much of the expense of maintaining the fire department.[33]

The San Francisco public school system, or more accurately the absence thereof, was even more a subject for legitimate complaint. In the fall of 1850, Mr. and Mrs. John C. Pelton commenced a school supported primarily from their own funds. Finally the common council allocated some depreciated scrip to help support the school, but there was no state assistance. By the following spring, the family had mortgaged their home to maintain the facility, which was then serving, with assistant teachers, up to five hundred students. But when Mrs. Pelton became ill, her husband was compelled to discontinue the project, reportedly still with no hope of relief or reimbursement from the city. This negligent situation persisted despite a rapid growth in school-age population. It would be more than a decade before the state legislature fully supported public education.[34]

There is no question of the large degree of venality and inefficiency in San Francisco government during the early years of California statehood. It is easy to understand the frustration and anger of the supposed "better class" of citizens, who claimed to despair of any lawful remedy to their situation. Yet it can be argued that many merchants and other businessmen were so preoccupied with protecting their own profit margins that they made few demands for government efficiency that would cost them more taxes, such as seeking redress for the often unpaid policemen and schoolteachers. In fact, one of the causes of the depleted municipal treasury was the lack of license fees required of merchants for doing business in the city during much of the period. Similarly, some of the criticisms aimed at city officials for the poor condition of many streets would actually have been better directed at property owners, who successfully refused to pay their share of the expense for improvements. Samuel Brannan and Joseph L. Folsom, who owned two of the largest landholdings in the city, were prominent on the lists of street-assessment nonpayers in 1855. The *Alta California* was referring to the vigilante excitement when it stated, "Our people have been aroused from the dangerous lethargy into which they had strangely fallen," which is an apt observation. It is unfortunate that the influential newspaper, along with other natural (and perhaps honest) leaders of the community, could not have awakened the citizens earlier and channeled their energies into more regular political solutions.[35]

The four city charters in San Francisco's first five years appear to have accomplished little in the way of governmental reform. But when the state legislature passed the so-called consolidation act, which combined San Francisco city and county government in late April 1856, it signaled a subtle but significant transition. Among the first such actions in the nation, the law eliminated serious duplication of duties, and by creating twelve supervisorial districts it may have partly diffused some of the tendency to concentrate influence for questionable purposes. The changes were already under way before the drastic vigilante committee actions of mid-1856. Although the questionable activity of that extralegal body certainly chastened some who might have been more visibly opposed to the new consolidated government, the vigilantes were not at all active in the process of electing or instituting the significant new regime. The provisions of the new charter were aimed primarily at economizing in local government, specifically prohibiting the use of scrip and most borrowing of additional funds. Many informed citizens preferred this "legal straitjacket" to what had so often been the case previously. Even during the interim period prior to institution of the new combined government, expenditures had declined by more than two-thirds, from $2,646,190 in 1854–55 to $856,120 in 1855–56. One of the first acts undertaken after consolidation went into effect was the adoption of strict taxation limits, which placed severe restrictions on city expenditures. As usual, the less-vocal schoolchildren and indigent sick bore more than their share of the cuts.[36]

Among those repudiated in the fall election of 1856 were the Democratic Party, led by David Broderick, and the political club or machine associated with him in San Francisco. The American, or "Know Nothing," Party, led by the pathetically weak Governor J. Neely Johnson, was discredited as well. A local "People's Party" entered the field with all of the advantages of no prior tarnishing record among its leaders. The *Alta* observed that "there are no political hacks, no men who make politics a business and a profession" among the People's Party candidates for county office. Actually, all three parties' candidates for president of the city Board of Supervisors, an office that was essentially the mayor, were considered clean and capable businessmen. E. W. Burr, longtime city merchant and People's standard-bearer, was the victor, as were the others on his ticket.[37]

The *Alta California* editors spoke for many in stating that the new slate of officials then taking office "inaugurates a new era in the history of San Francisco." They hoped "no longer will office be made the mere means of self-aggrandizement" but would be used to serve the people and the welfare of the city. Affirming that "confidence will be restored" and "villainy and fraud no longer command a premium," the newspaper conceded that the new officers would have to clean out "much filth and corruption" that had accumulated for a long time around the seat of government. The editors were most appreciative of the newly mandated economizing, and they encouraged citizens to continue to be vigilant in ensuring that such aims were adhered to.[38]

A careful student of this period of San Francisco history, Roger W. Lotchin, is correct in his conclusion that with the new government "no regeneration or purification occurred. San Francisco in 1857 did not differ markedly from what it had been in 1855, except politically." As he asserts, the change had already been taking place, without vigilantes. The normal evolution of municipal government, never easy in most burgeoning American cities of the era, and probably not as bad as was often assumed in

San Francisco, considering the city's amazingly rapid growth, solved most challenges in the natural course of maturity. As the grand jury report of the time indicates, many of the existing problems were on their way to solution even as the new consolidated government took over. One significant boost offered this infant government was a respite from the hostility toward municipal affairs so prevalent earlier among the press and many citizens. The *Alta* cited the inaugural wish of supervisor president Burr that all would "bury the dead past," including bitterness toward city government, and work together for civic betterment. The newspaper called on the people and other newspapers to "cease instilling anger and resentment into the bosoms of the citizens of this youthful city [and allow them] to grow with its growth and strengthen with its strength." In large measure this policy was implemented, a significant key to the long-term greater success of the new city-county government.[39]

Few, if any, California counties faced a more formidable challenge than did Sacramento County in the need to protect its people from the flood ravages of the Sacramento and American rivers. The problem was not new, with epochal inundations in 1805, 1825–26, and 1846–47, prior to organization of the county government. In the first year of the new county, 1850–51, however, the storm-swelled Sacramento not only flooded most of the town but destroyed many of the structures recently erected there. During the fearful flood, what privately constructed levees existed demonstrated the potential of such structures as a solution to the problem. There was subsequently considerable discussion of the matter, and a committee was formed to conduct feasibility surveys. Directed by committee member Hardin Bigelow, the city commenced construction of more levees. This soon helped save the city from more severe damage from a second flood, after which Bigelow was promptly elected mayor of Sacramento. The city council passed resolutions authorizing appointment of a four-person commission to act with the city engineer to locate spots for other proposed levees. Citizens backed the project by approving a quarter-million-dollar additional tax for the purpose. A levee at least three feet high was thus erected from the high ground along the Sacramento past its confluence with the American River and up that stream bank some two and a half miles to higher ground.

However, the floods of 1852 were not contained by the new levees, and citizens worked feverishly to throw up a temporary embankment along I Street. There was still much flooding, but not as severe as two years previously. After that, some levees were relocated and more were built, but at the end of 1852 city residents were again disappointed when a large break occurred in the barrier during another flood, followed by still another early in January 1853. Fortunately, although the water level actually rose higher, there was far less damage to city property than in the 1850 episode. That summer Sacramento city officials passed ordinances to widen and heighten the levee system, which by that time had clearly proven to be an essential facet of city and county government responsibility. The structure soon stood more

After a series of devastating floods in the early 1850s, the Sacramento city council authorized the construction of numerous levees along the nearby Sacramento and American rivers. Heavy rains in December 1861, however, swelled the American River—already choked with hydraulic mining detritus—until it burst through its levee. This picture from the *Illustrated London News* in 1862 shows the corner of L and Fourth streets in Sacramento submerged by the raging flood. "The amount of rain that has fallen is unprecedented in the history of the state," recorded geologist William Brewer in January 1862. "Thousands of farms are entirely under water—cattle starving and drowning." *Courtesy City of Sacramento, History and Science Division, Sacramento Archives and Museum Collection Center, Eleanor McClatchy Collection.*

than twenty-two feet above the low-water marks of the rivers. It would be eight years before this levee enclosure would be tested by further floods.[40]

After some flooding in late March 1861, the most destructive flood yet hit on December 9. The levee east of the city gave way, and the American River swept in with devastating force. The other levees actually served to retain the water within the city, which did more damage than any preceding flood. Property losses approached two million dollars. Two weeks later, still another flood inundated Sacramento. After that, the levee commissioners engaged a construction crew of some thirty men to repair the damaged embankments. These men were themselves threatened by a flood on January 9, 1862. Their work was essentially destroyed in yet another event on January 22, when the business section of the city was flooded, as it was again in February in the fifth inundation in three months. After these devastations, Sacramento authorities "bent all their energies to the task of ensuring a better protection for the future." At a cost of almost a quarter million dollars, the levee system was further elevated, and streets, buildings, and homes for several blocks east of the river were raised. This proved adequate for the next sixteen years.

On the first of February 1878, the gopher-weakened levee along the Sacramento River broke, flooding some of the sector south of R Street. Work crews closed the breach as the river reached more than twenty-five feet above its low-water mark, higher than had ever been known. Several weeks later, assisted by gale winds, the river, almost a foot higher, again endangered the levee. Large numbers of willing citizens made the structure secure, and further work continued for several months. By late spring the project was again completed and the city pronounced safely enclosed by "an admirable system of protective levees" that usually thereafter assured the safety of the citizenry. This was doubtless one of the most extensive undertakings of any municipal government during the period when the first California state constitution was in effect. Other municipalities and counties would also be challenged over the years in flood-control matters, which had been a legitimate local-government function since the beginning of the state.[41]

The propensity of United States citizens to innovate and adapt their governmental machinery to the needs of the time and place is well demonstrated in the first years of California statehood. There was naturally some chaos at the beginning, particularly because of the unprecedented influx of people associated with the Gold Rush and differences between their governmental preferences and the already existing forms established in the Spanish-Mexican era. Yet both the voters and the officials they selected to govern them generally resolved the challenges they faced and rather quickly laid the institutional and infrastructural foundation for local government in the Golden State.

NOTES

1. The court of sessions, an old English governmental body, was composed of a presiding judge and two associate justices.
2. J. M. Guinn, *Historical and Biographical Record of Southern California* (Los Angeles: Chapman Publishing Co., 1902), 132, 134.
3. Guinn, *Southern California*, 147–48.
4. Thompson & West, *Santa Barbara County, California, with Illustrations and Biographical Sketches of Its Men and Pioneers* (Oakland: Thompson & West, 1883), 79, 80–81, 96, 144.
5. Leland Ghent Stanford, *San Diego's Legal Lore and the Bar: A History of Law and Justice in San Diego County* (San Diego: San Diego County Bar Association, 1968), 69.
6. *Los Angeles Star*, January 31 and February 7, 14, 21, 1857.
7. Court of Sessions Record Book, El Dorado County, May 21 and June 14, 1850, July 14, 1851, County Government Complex, Placerville, Calif.
8. Hubert Howe Bancroft, in *History of California*, vol. 6, *1848–1859* (1888; reprint, Santa Barbara, Calif.: Wallace Hebberd, 1970), 483, states that the first of fifteen bridges in El Dorado County cost $20,000, but yielded $250 per day, which would easily recoup construction costs in one season.
9. El Dorado Record Book, June 13 and July 8, 1850. It is probable that all of the bridges authorized that season were intended to replace others washed out in the devastating floods of the previous January.

10. El Dorado Record Book, August 19, 1850, February 11, 1852, February 17 and June 15, 1854.

11. El Dorado Record Book, January 15, 1853, November 12, 1855; Nevada County Court of Sessions Minutes, Nevada City, Calif., February 12, 1855.

12. El Dorado Record Book, July 10, 1850, April 17, 1852, April 27 and December 6, 1854; Board of Supervisors Minutes, vol. A, Calaveras County, San Andreas, Calif., August 21, 1855, May 27, 1857; Nevada County Board of Supervisors Minutes, September 8, 1856.

13. El Dorado Record Book, November 12, 1855, March 21 and June 20, 1856; Nevada County Minutes, March 3 and December 12, 1864, May 6, 1865; Amador County Board of Supervisors Minutes, March 7, 1864, April 4, 1865.

14. El Dorado Record Book, July 16, 1853.

15. El Dorado Record Book, February 14 and April 17, 1854, November 19, 1855.

16. Court of Sessions, regular term, 1853, San Bernardino County, in middle of Record Court of Sessions, October 4, 1858–June 1868, San Bernardino County Archives, San Bernardino, Calif., October 2, 1854, May 6, 1856, December 18, 1857; Edward Leo Lyman, *San Bernardino: The Rise and Fall of a California Community* (Salt Lake City: Signature Books, 1996), 108.

17. Minutes Board of Supervisors, Board of Fund Commissioners, Tuolumne County, Tuolumne County Museum and Historical Society, Sonora, Calif., March 1 and June 8, 1853, February 16 and May 7, 1855, February 15 and November 28, 1856, April 7 and September 29, 1857, February 4 and May 10, 1858.

18. Nevada County Records, August 5, 1856, February 4, 1857.

19. *Los Angeles Star,* August 7 and November 6, 1852. Much of the outstanding scrip was then marketable at a third of its face value. If all of what was outstanding had been collected and funded at full face value, that would have substantially increased the county's indebtedness.

20. Lyman, *San Bernardino,* 90; Guinn, *Southern California,* 131; San Bernardino Court of Sessions Minute Book, November 2, 1857.

21. *Los Angeles Star,* April 2, 1853.

22. Lyman, *San Bernardino,* 269–71; Hazel Miller Croy, "A History of Education in San Bernardino during the Mormon Period" (Ph.D. diss., University of California, Los Angeles, 1955), 82–98.

23. *Los Angeles Star,* February 28 and August 7, 1852, May 11, 1853, May 6, 1854, February 1 and 8, April 28, 1855.

24. *Los Angeles Star,* December 22, 1855, March 1, 1856, December 26, 1857.

25. El Dorado Record Book, February 17, 1854; Nevada County Supervisors Minutes, August 6 and December 12, 1864.

26. Guinn, *Southern California,* 132–33; Bancroft, *California History,* 194.

27. Lyman, *San Bernardino,* 222–23.

28. Kevin J. Mullen, *Let Justice Be Done: Crime and Politics in Early San Francisco* (Reno: University of Nevada Press, 1989), 8, 25, 44, 92–96, 118.

29. Ibid., 105–18; *Alta California,* January 27, 1851.

30. *Alta California,* February 11, 1851; Mullen, *Early San Francisco,* 118–19; see Theodore H. Hittell, *History of California,* vol. 3 (San Francisco: N. J. Stone & Co., 1897), 397–98, for a discussion of scrip.

31. Hittell, *California,* vol. 3, 361–65; *Alta California,* January 27, 1851.

32. Mullen, *Early San Francisco,* 83–87; *Alta California,* February 26, 1851.

33. Hittell, *California*, vol. 3, 361, 366; *Alta California*, March 19 and April 4, 1851.

34. *Alta California*, March 20, 1850, January 27 and 28, February 28, March 3 and 13, 1851.

35. Roger W. Lotchin, *San Francisco, 1846–1856: From Hamlet to City* (New York: Oxford University Press, 1974), 150, 275; *Alta California*, October 10 and 31, 1856. It was hardly a joke when the *Alta* warned that if pedestrians were not on their guard, they could "turn *down* missing" from falling through the plank streets into the surf below. Some had actually drowned, and many others were narrowly rescued from this well-publicized municipal deficiency, for which both public and private interests were responsible.

36. Lotchin, *San Francisco*, 137–40.

37. *Alta California*, October 27 and 30, 1856.

38. *Alta California*, November 6 and 22, 1856.

39. Lotchin, *San Francisco*, 271; *Alta California*, October 1 and November 17, 1856.

40. Thompson & West, *History of Sacramento County, California, with Illustrations* (1880; reprint, Berkeley: Howell-North Press, 1960), 50–51, 66–69, 73.

41. Marysville was equally challenged with flooding and in 1861–62 raised funds by subscription for a levee extending from the foot of D Street to F Street. Later citizens would organize a flood control district and appoint commissioners to oversee such matters. See Peter J. Delay, *History of Yuba and Sutter Counties, California, with Biographical Sketches* (Los Angeles: Historical Record Co., 1924), 103–104.

9

An Uncertain Influence

The Role of the Federal Government in California, 1846–1880

Robert J. Chandler

Did rugged individualists tame the West, or did pioneers merely arrive at a well-ordered colony of the federal government? Popular myth enshrines the first view. In 1991, however, "New" Western historian Richard White, building on more than a half century of research, argued that "The West has been historically a dependency of the federal government." Moreover, he observed, "the West itself served as the kindergarten of the American state," teaching it the governing skills needed to develop a sparsely settled land. In a 1999 article, Karen R. Merrill called on New Western historians to specifically distinguish how federal aid to the West differed from benevolence to other regions. What has been the federal role in dynamic California?

White concentrated on the less populated territories and states. He excluded the largest and most populous western states, Texas and California, as their "early statehood place[s] them in a different category," which renders his theory dubious for the Golden State between 1846 and 1880. During the pioneer period, when residents quickly needed the most rudimentary federal services, the national government did not provide. Through the nineteenth century, in fact, the federal government's participation in California was more a product of happenstance than it was activist, but growing more sure of itself, the government gradually laid the foundation for a dominant role building the West in the twentieth century.

Historian William Henry Ellison argues that through the 1850s, when southern strict constructionists dominated, the federal government did too little, too late. The national government failed in any actions that required speed. Question and answer between Washington and San Francisco took up to three months, leading the San Francisco newspaper *Alta California* to remark, "The Golden State is the only one which, in consequence of its isolation, is forced to work out her own destiny."

Congressional neglect spurred Californians to establish a state government, immigrant roads, mining law, circulating coinage, and letter delivery.[1]

In California, the federal government slowly fulfilled its constitutional mandate to "establish justice, insure domestic tranquillity, provide for the common defence, [and] promote the general welfare." Through the fortunes of war, it provided able military governors before statehood in 1850. By the mid-1850s, the federal government had authorized subsidies for the operation of steamships, stagecoaches, telegraphs, and railroads; the exploration, surveying, and distribution of public lands; the building of forts, harbor defenses, lighthouses, and dry docks; and the establishment of a rudimentary postal system and branch mint. The federal government built an infrastructure—but it brought along corrosive political patronage.

Mixed federal success came with important issues during the 1850s, when politics determined action and the government was unable to broker lasting solutions. Whether stopping filibusters, deciding ownership of Mexican land grants and mineral lands, preserving peace between whites and Indians, negotiating with Native Americans, or establishing reservations to contain them, the federal government made few people happy. For instance, settlers and the state "took care" of Indians with brutal precision, and during the Civil War, California Volunteers supplied enough troops to finally crush Native American resistance.

With more activist Republican control in the 1860s, California gained from the federal government daily overland mail service, an overland telegraph, and the long-sought transcontinental railroad. During the Civil War, civil authorities, by inclination, the ballot box, and presidential proclamation, smothered any secessionist threat to the three hundred thousand Californians. Four successive commanding generals of the military Department of the Pacific kept the peace, occasionally sending heated Democrats to cool off on frigid Alcatraz, while the secret Union League, which counted the governor and army adjutant among its grand council members, watched closely. National stamp, license, and income taxes showed federal presence as never before.

After the war, the federal government began to exceed some state and private efforts in economic affairs and assert more influence over politics, but the same imprecision existed. In the 1870s, California's enormous and powerful economic entity, the Central and Southern Pacific Railroad, called into being by congressional subsidies and land grants, equaled state efforts and surpassed the federal government in selling land, developing crops, and promoting conservation. Of course, this same mighty Southern Pacific Railroad chose the laissez-faire federal government as a refuge from the angry regulatory state of California.

At the same time, the national government did promote civil rights and encourage conservation and forestry. Beginning in the late 1860s, during Reconstruction, Radical Republicans passed civil rights legislation enabling the federal courts to thwart the public will and actively protect the Chinese in California. These courts also favored farmers over miners to prevent hydraulic debris from destroying cropland, but irrigation remained a tangled state issue. As late as 1901, for instance, federal irrigation expert Elwood Mead issued a four-hundred-page report on California's chaotic allocation of water, arguing that federal intervention was not "either possible or desirable." Symbolically, in 1902, the year after Mead's report was published, Congress passed Nevada congressman Francis Newlands's famed Reclamation Act. Twentieth-century Progressives brought an interventionist national government.[2]

SETTING POLICY

The Military's Role in Birthing State Government

In the beginning, agents of the federal government presided over California. From July 7, 1846, until December 20, 1849, five military officers ruled the just-conquered province: Commodore John D. Sloat (July 1846); Commodore Robert F. Stockton (July 1846–January 1847); General Stephen W. Kearny (January–May 1847); Colonel Richard B. Mason (June 1847–April 1849); and General Bennett Riley (April–December 1849). Distant from Washington, these governors interpreted customs regulations, inaugurated local government, and kept the peace.

Theirs was a thankless job. On August 19, 1848, Colonel Mason wrote Washington: "No other officers exist in the country, save the alcaldes confirmed or appointed by myself." Yet, he asked, under the Constitution, "what right or authority have I to exercise civil authority?" As Congress continually abrogated its responsibility to create a civil government for the province, General Riley declared on June 3, 1849, that "imperative duty" required him to inaugurate a civil government. Elections on August 1 would select delegates to devise a constitution, which the citizens promptly passed. Military governor Riley stepped aside on December 20, with new "state" officials in place: "The principal object of all his wishes is now accomplished," he declared to Californians, "the people have a government of their own choice." Amid a gold-mad population, a handful of military officers had honored the credo of West Point: "Duty, Honor, Country."[3]

Formal statehood, belatedly approved by Congress in 1850, cemented traditional civil government, and the Army assumed a subordinate role. Crusty General John E. Wool, age seventy, summed up California conditions on March 1, 1854, when he had only a thousand men—a tenth of the peacetime Army—to "keep the peace in the immense territory of California, Oregon, Washington, and Utah," to prevent filibustering "expeditions fitting out against Mexico, and to protect the whites and the Indians against each other." To emphasize, Army officers knew duty called them to protect peaceful Indians from settler mayhem, just as much as it did to protect farm-

After months of virulent debate in Congress, President Millard Fillmore signed a bill admitting California into the United States on September 9, 1850. According to one observer, the news, which reached the state more than a month later, "was received on all hands with demonstrations of joy. Balls, processions, illuminations, fireworks, all testified to the general sentiment which prevailed." British Argonaut Frank Marryat captured the mood of excitement in this drawing of an October 29 parade celebrating California's statehood down Montgomery Street in San Francisco. *California Historical Society, FN-00616.*

ers and ranchers from mountain raiders. "We have too few troops to do either the one thing or the other," Wool concluded.[4]

When hostilities had broken out with Mexico in 1846, the Army had seized the presidios at San Francisco and Monterey. A supply depot established at Benicia on April 30, 1849, for the Army's mere six hundred men was expanded in August 1851 to include an extensive arsenal. Through the 1850s, the Army built additional forts to watch hostile Indians and protect peaceful ones, while engineers planned and slowly constructed elaborate forts for defenseless San Francisco Bay.[5]

Politics limited Army action. The Compromise of 1850 that admitted California as a state limited the number of slave states. Southerners looked south to Cuba and Mexico, and California became a staging ground for private filibustering expeditions against Mexico. General Ethan Allen Hitchcock, who had special presidential instructions to stop such hostile expeditions, on October 1, 1853, seized William Walker's filibuster brig *Arrow*. However, with the connivance of proslavery federal officers, arms and men transferred to the *Caroline*, and Walker sailed away. On January 9, 1854, pro-southern, petulant secretary of war Jefferson Davis replaced Hitchcock with the opinionated Wool, who assumed he had full power to stop filibustering expeditions. In March 1854, Wool arrested leading men, seized ships, had the

More than five hundred U.S. naval vessels have been built, housed, or maintained at the Navy yard at Mare Island, drawn here by J. B. Dunlap in 1855. Situated near Vallejo in San Pablo Bay, the Mare Island shipyard set a naval record for speed of construction during World War I, when it built the USS *Ward* in seventeen days. *Courtesy Bancroft Library.*

Mexican and French consuls tried for abetting the expedition, and gloried that he had been "the means of breaking up the filibustering schemes." In April, however, the secretary of war also reined in Wool and ordered Army headquarters moved from San Francisco to the more isolated Benicia. While these orders were in transit, French threats provoked Wool on May 1, 1854, to order the first guns mounted for harbor defense—ten heavy guns for Alcatraz and another ten for Fort Point. Thanks to future Confederate States president Jefferson Davis, Wool's adjutant concluded, "Filibusters now go and come as they choose and no one cares a straw."

Having had his hand slapped once, Wool was cautious when the San Francisco Committee of Vigilance formed in May 1856. By law, only the president could issue arms, so Wool and his Navy counterpart declined the California governor's repeated requests for military assistance and ordered officers to remain "perfectly neutral." The Navy, on the other hand, showed federal might with a warship anchored off downtown San Francisco. Although Governor J. Neely Johnson fumed over the "duplicity and falsehood" of "Old Granny Wool," President Franklin Pierce maintained there were "insuperable obstacles" to federal intervention.[6]

The Navy had its special role in California, and especially San Francisco. In the mid-nineteenth century, French and British imperialists eyed Mexican instability, while the United States fought a war to acquire Mexico's northwestern provinces. The Pacific might not remain pacific, the Navy's theory went, and United States warships needed a base for regular maintenance and numerous repairs of damage caused by normal operations at sea or enemy shot and shell.

In 1850, President Millard Fillmore reserved Mare Island, near Vallejo, for government purposes. "A new empire has, as by magic, sprung into existence," Secretary of the Navy William A. Graham exclaimed, and "a navy yard is very much needed in California." In 1854, a prefabricated floating sectional dry dock went into operation. Commercial sailing ships, Pacific Mail Company ocean steamers, and California Steam Navigation riverboats used it far more often than the half-dozen warships of the Pacific Squadron. That autumn, David Glasgow Farragut, who knew the Pacific from his days aboard the frigate *Essex* during the War of 1812, wrote in the Navy Yard log for September 16, 1854, that he "took command of the Island this day, and [reflecting confused land titles] forthwith warned off all the Squatters, viz. Turner, Roy, Vera, Gilbert and Antonio Pinto. Weather very fine but warm."

On March 3, 1859, the Mare Island Shipyard launched the first of 513 vessels it built before decommissioning in April 1996. Petaluma white oak went into the 155-foot, four-gun, sidewheeler *Saginaw*. Eleven years later the ship was providing typical peacetime Navy duties: helping construct a coal station on Midway Island for the Pacific Mail's China steamers and plotting the location of nearby Ocean Island while searching for shipwrecked sailors. But on October 29, 1870, a strong current drove the vessel onto a reef, and the *Saginaw* became the third wreck in the atoll.[7]

Constructing Transportation and Communications Systems

Federal assistance, including by the armed services, was vital in building California's transportation system. The U.S. Coast Survey helped navigators. Scientist George Davidson, who arrived in 1850 and served the Coast Survey through 1895, was a workaholic with tremendous physical stamina. From Mexico to Puget Sound, and then on to Alaska, he traveled four hundred thousand miles producing maps, while sensitively preserving Native American names for geographical features. Davidson was also on the federal Lighthouse Board, which chose locations for building lighthouses to aid navigation along the treacherous shore. In June 1854, Fort Alcatraz had the first light in California, and nine others quickly followed. In 1880, twenty-two beacons lit the California coast.[8]

Land routes were another matter. Journeying overland to California in the late 1840s and early 1850s was a do-it-yourself proposition, from choosing equipment and selecting a route to developing a traveling organization. In late August 1849, Army commander General Persifor F. Smith had to dispatch rescue parties with provisions for eight thousand amateur Argonauts stuck far out on the trails as winter closed in. Civilians, rather than the Army, however, assumed the most active roles in transportation improvements, as through the 1850s isolated Californians demanded better roads, faster mail, speedier communications, and above all, a railroad.

Scientist and engineer George Davidson led a seven-year U.S. survey of the Pacific Coast in the 1850s, recorded here by renowned California photographer Carleton E. Watkins. The Davidson Expedition established accurate latitude and longitude measurements for several prominent California landmarks, chose sites for numerous lighthouses, and published the *Directory of the Pacific Coast,* which established the standard for the authoritative nine-volume Coast Pilot series of nautical books, written by various authors and describing the coasts and waterways of the entire United States. *California Historical Society, FN-29050.*

Yet to succeed, private interests depended on federal encouragement and especially federal subsidies to spur development.

Just in time for the Forty-niners, Army topographical engineer John Charles Frémont published a map of California and Oregon with an explanatory geographical memoir. His information became part of numerous guides and descriptions, with mixed results. In 1856, Charles T. Blake, a supporter of Frémont, now the Republican presidential candidate, wrote home: "Many a time in '49 and '50 have I heard Frémont cursed roundly" because his maps "are very incorrect and will not do to travel by." After the Gold Rush was over, California senator John B. Weller and seventy-five thousand Californians petitioned "for the Construction of a Wagon Road across the Plains." His 1856 law transferred road-building from the War Department to the Department of the Interior, and appropriations for the Pacific Wagon Road Office came on February 17, 1857. Field parties, filled with those showing "service to the Democracy," began work, and through 1860, engineer Frederick W. Lander improved the central route.[9]

To the delight of Californians, on March 3, 1857, Weller also inserted a semi-weekly overland mail subsidy into the Post Office appropriation bill, and of course, the southern postmaster general picked a southern route. Mail between St. Louis and San Francisco, via El Paso, Texas, and Los Angeles, crossed the fiefdoms of four large express companies: American, Adams, United States, and Wells Fargo. Together they formed the Overland Mail Company to bid successfully to supply the three-week stage and mail service, and the first coaches on this regularly scheduled overland mail and passenger service departed in September 1858. Hostile Indians and Texas rebels blocked the mail coaches in March 1861, however, causing service to shift to the central route, which traveled through Salt Lake City to Sacramento.[10]

From 1857 to 1859, California senators John Weller and David C. Broderick, powerful northern Democrat Stephen A. Douglas of Illinois, and the foremost Republican, William H. Seward of New York, fought for an overland telegraph to produce virtually instantaneous communication. On June 16, 1860, President James Buchanan finally signed California senator William M. Gwin's bill, which gave the contract to the Western Union Telegraph Company. In July 1861, a subsidiary began building west from the Mississippi Valley toward Salt Lake City, while concurrently the California State Telegraph Company made the same arrangement to head east. The lines joined on October 24, 1861, connecting the state to the rest of the nation, and with the Atlantic cable in 1866, to the rest of the world.[11]

The railroad, the third of California's requests, was first in desirability. As the newspaper *Alta California* phrased it, Californians demanded "the iron band which will create an adhesiveness of common interest." In January 1853, Senator Gwin introduced the first of many Pacific railroad subsidy bills, yet Californians knew that under the limited constitutional construction by Gwin's southern cronies, it would never be. When John B. Weller read the southern Democratic Party railroad resolution at a San Francisco ratification meeting on July 28, 1860, the crowd "fairly shouted with mirth." The Republican revolution in the 1860 election—bringing in a Republican president, a Republican-dominated Congress, and soon a Republican state governor and legislature—brought life to California's railroad dreams. Fulfilling one promise, the new Lincoln administration authorized a quicker, daily overland mail on the central route through Salt Lake City beginning July 1, 1861.

The next year, Republicans fed a steam-puffing iron horse. The mighty *Sacramento Union* exulted on July 4, 1862, that "the President has signed the Pacific Railroad bill (*laus Deo!*)." This bill, and an even more generous one in 1864, provided essential federal monetary subsidies and land grants from the public domain to assist in the construction of California's Central Pacific Railroad and the eastern-based Union Pacific Railroad. The two lines joined in a dramatic golden-spike ceremony in the northern Utah desert on May 10, 1869, opening up new opportunities in agriculture and business to California's residents.[12]

Indian Policy

Complicating the federal role in Indian policy, intense conflict erupted in California after 1846. Native peoples had long called the land home before citizens of the United States arrived, and the federal government was forced to mediate the conflicting claims of ownership. Initially, a massive influx of agricultural and industrialized Americans and Europeans, crazed by the search for gold, generated conflict with more than a hundred thousand hunter-gatherer native inhabitants. One Forty-niner summed up a general hostile feeling among the miners in Clear Creek: "We have an Indian hunt here in our neighborhood about once every two weeks," he wrote. Within ten years, the Indian population, due to violence directed against them and even more because of disease, had dropped to about thirty thousand. Native Americans have fared better in recent scholarship than they did physically in the 1850s. Even a century later, many writers saw Indians only as "murderous savages"; more often now, that epithet is applied to their opponents, and contemporary scholars view Native Americans as active participants in historical events, rather than passive victims.[13]

In April 1847, military governor Stephen W. Kearny appointed Mariano G. Vallejo and John A. Sutter as Indian subagents to work to pacify Indian-settler relations, but strife in the Southern Mines led in late 1850 to the dispatch of three additional commissioners. George Barbour, Oliver M. Wozencraft, and Redick McKee joined James D. Savage, a local Indian negotiator, to establish a series of Central Valley reservations to separate Indians from the aggressive newcomers. This new policy had high hopes, but poor results. First, in 1852, Congress, to no one's surprise, refused to ratify the reservation treaties that tribes had been coaxed into signing, which would have set aside one-seventh of the state. In 1853, Congress began fitfully to establish federal reservations on which to concentrate and isolate Indian populations. One was in southern California (Tejon), followed by three in the north (Nome Lackee, Klamath River, and Cape Mendocino). Not only did this arrangement disrupt the habits and food supply of the Indians, who were moved into unfamiliar territories, but it also brought no peace. In July 1852, Chief Pasqual mourned, "When in the mountains we were hunted like wild beasts; here [on our Kings River reservation] we are shot down like cattle."

"As far as anyone can see, the whole system is turned into a speculation for the benefit of the [Indian] Agents," Major Edward D. Townsend, the California military department's adjutant general, concluded in 1855. Little improvement came in the next decades, as the federal government proved unable to discipline patronage-appointed officials, who continued to commandeer Indian property, women, and supplies. Sometimes, the perspective of a madman—but one devoted to civil rights— is the clearest: on April 23, 1873, His Imperial Majesty Norton I, the self-proclaimed

Emperor of the United States and a notorious San Francisco street character, decreed: "It is our intention to have publicly punished, before as many Indian chiefs as can be assembled together, all the Indian agents and other parties connected with frauds against the Indian tribes."[14]

Significantly, contemporary historian George Phillips has declared that the state of California (as well as Oregon and Washington territories) took "advantage of a weak federal presence" to handle Native Americans by funding volunteer quasi-military companies to decimate or relocate them. In 1853, the California legislature condemned federal inefficiency: "Families were being daily most inhumanely massacred by ruthless savages. No protection had been furnished by the officer in command of the United States forces." Michele Shover's fine scholarship centered on Butte County reveals the complexity. Her analysis foreshadows the epic battle of "gold versus grain," or miners against farmers. Mountain Indians formed alliances with gold miners, who furnished protection and firearms for valley raids on farmers, who were interfering with debris-causing mining operations. Valley settlers, working marginal wheat farms and cattle ranches, saw to their own security, as county officials had no duty to protect them. The retributive cycle of attack and counterattack became continuous and resulted in the scattering or annihilation of many Indian groups.[15]

The Civil War ended Indian-settler conflict in California. General George Wright, an Indian fighter from the Pacific Northwest, provided Army leadership, while the California Volunteers supplied needed manpower. With the exception of occasional skirmishes, violence between Indians and settlers subsided. The federal government concentrated California's Indians, now sharply reduced in population, on a few reservations, and most Army posts did not remain open past mid-1865.

The 1873 Modoc War is surely misnamed as a "war." Kientipoos, or Captain Jack, as whites called him, led a mere two hundred Modoc men, women, and children from a reservation in Oregon, where they had been confined with enemy tribes, back to a small portion of their desolate homeland in far-northern California. Indian treachery through murdering a general at a peace conference brought conflict, but Army ineptness created a drawn-out crisis. The untrained soldiers fought so poorly that His Imperial Majesty Norton I offered a suggestion to the bumbling federal government: rather than hang the Modoc captives, Norton I suggested that they "all be pardoned and sworn into the service of the United States army" where their skills would be of benefit. The government chose to hang its captives.[16]

Conflicting Policies on Mining and Land

When the cry of "Gold!" resounded around the world, the federal government treated its California mineral lands with benign neglect. It ignored Governor Richard B. Mason's suggestion to license miners, contained in his famed report of August 17, 1848, announcing the gold discovery. Instead, itinerant miners, drawing on Spanish precedent and English frontier self-determination, established extralegal, locally devised administrations and imposed regulations for placer and lode mines, which state courts ultimately enforced.[17]

Other voices spoke otherwise, however. "Mineral lands should be sold," John S. Hittell, the commercial editor of the *Alta California* avidly argued from March 1858 forward. "Ownership makes the people permanent, and induces men to get wives and comfortable homes." In 1861, the formidable challenge of paying for the Civil War effort made the federal government his ally. Secretary of the Interior Caleb Smith suggested in his report that year that miners should "pay a reasonable amount" to exploit public lands and resources, and in 1862, the commissioner of the General Land Office asserted that taxing the mines would bring "an immense revenue." Accustomed to free access to harvest the riches of the public domain, however, Californians thought the idea preposterous.[18]

Civil War finance, greed, corruption, activism, President Abraham Lincoln's meddling, and the gubernatorial election compounded a complicated crisis on the mineral lands in 1863. At stake was the New Almaden Quicksilver Mine near San Jose, founded before the Mexican War and now claimed under Spanish-Mexican land and mining law. On March 10, 1863, a confused U.S. Supreme Court ruled that the mine was on federal property. Two months later, on May 6, 1863, Interior Secretary John P. Usher, backed by Attorney General Edward Bates, proposed an unprecedented deal to Samuel F. Butterworth, president of the Quicksilver Mining Company and one of the claimants to the New Almaden. This arrangement would give the government a third of the mine's yearly income as lease rent. If agreeable, Leonard Swett, an Illinois attorney and good friend of the president, would take "immediate possession of the mine" and operate it. Swett and Butterworth arrived in California on June 29, presented the presidential writ to the mine superintendent, and called on General George Wright for federal troops to install them in possession. Soon a detachment from Company F, Second Cavalry, California Volunteers, departed for San Jose "fully prepared for active service."

On July 8, Frederick F. Low, Collector of the Port of San Francisco and the first of many Californians worried about implied government control of all mines, telegraphed Washington that the seizure "will be terrible." Ira P. Rankin, the former collector, stated the problem: "Many are already inquiring anxiously, if the government may with the strong hand take possession of the Almaden mine, why not of the Ophir the Gould & Curry or any other of the richest silver or gold mines of California and Nevada?" While Butterworth worked out a deal with the occupying mine company, opposition Democrats had a field day. Former Governor John G. Downey, running again for governor, denounced the "unmitigated evil" of federal interference and issued a ringing declaration: "To the miners belong the mines." President Lincoln, meanwhile, laid low and opined that in California land cases, "I do not think I should meddle as a volunteer."[19]

The federal government, though, continued to assert that mines were "the property of the nation" and could be taxed, and a 0.5 percent levy on assayed gold bars became part of the revenue law of June 30, 1864. In 1866, eastern congressmen, seeking to place a larger share of the cost of supporting federal operations on westerners, pushed strongly for the sale of mineral lands, but Senators John Conness of California and William M. Stewart of Nevada thwarted what westerners perceived as misguided ignorance. Stewart's bill, which became law on July 26, 1866, allowed for the sale of lode mines but incorporated local custom, which generally provided for free claims. Once the federal government assured investors it would not disturb current practices, the controversy died. Congress added placer mines on July 9, 1870, while on May 10, 1872, Senator Stewart pushed through the present mining law, which provides for mineral claims to be made on federal lands for only token fees.[20]

In a generous mood, the federal government turned over public lands to the states, but national and state bureaucracies often prevented benefits from reaching intended recipients. On September 28, 1850, the government, through the Arkansas Act, gave the states control of swamp and overflow lands, provided they reclaimed them. However, in California, for the next fifteen years, the federal land commissioner quibbled over definitions and characteristics of this allegedly worthless acreage, and the federal government transferred only small amounts of such land.

In another area, the state took the blame. In 1852, the federal government, under an 1841 law, donated five hundred thousand acres of public land to the state, which California in article 9, section 2, of its 1849 constitution declared would go "for the support of schools." On March 3, 1853, the national government added sections 16 and 36 from each of the townships on federal land that it surveyed and prepared for sale to farmers and other settlers. The state, however, by a law of May 3, 1852, accepted depreciated state scrip at par value for payment on school lands and placed the minimal proceeds into the general fund, rather than the school fund. In 1862, for instance, impoverished schools did not receive their allotted frugal budget "on account of pressing demands on the Treasury."[21]

General federal land law for California became more troublesome than that governing mineral lands. A prime federal duty since the Continental Congress's Land Ordinance of 1785 and Northwest Ordinance of 1787 was to disburse public land to farmers and investors. Even before federal surveying, settlers in possession of land, but lacking actual titles, could preempt or buy their holdings. For the Golden State, on March 3, 1853, Congress obliged with "An Act to provide for the survey of Public Lands in California, the granting of pre-emption rights therein, and for other purposes." Government surveyors plotted land into six-mile-square townships, subdividing them into thirty-six sections of one square mile, or 640 acres, each. Between

1857 and 1860, President James Buchanan reduced the federal debt through the sale of eleven million acres in the Central Valley. The federal Homestead Act of May 20, 1862, allowed settlers to claim a quarter section, or 160 acres, at essentially no cost. "Good Land for Nothing," the *Visalia Delta* trumpeted on Christmas Day 1862, and in less than four months after the law went into effect on January 1, 1863, the local land office handled sixty-eight homestead claims. Furthermore, various land laws later transferred several million acres of additional federal land free or at very low prices to farmers and land-development companies, who subdivided and brought the land into production. The Central-Southern Pacific Railroad also worked mightily through the 1870s and 1880s to get its government-granted farmland into the hands of settlers.[22]

In California's first decade of statehood, only white men could gain public land. In 1858, Democrat A. C. Bradford, register of the General Land Office in Stockton, reaffirmed Justice Roger B. Taney's Dred Scott decision. "By the laws of the United States," he ruled, "colored men are not entitled to the right of pre-emption." Yet times were changing. During the Civil War, on November 29, 1862, U.S. attorney general Edward Bates declared that African Americans were indeed "citizens," and Republican A. J. Snyder of the Marysville Land Office agreed. When squatters attempted to oust sixty-seven-year-old Benjamin Berry, who had arrived a slave in 1850 but purchased his freedom through three thousand dollars' worth of labor, Snyder appealed to Washington. Acting federal Land Commissioner Joseph S. Wilson replied quickly on March 12, 1863: "The man Berry," Wilson said, "will be entitled to the benefit of the pre-emption laws, as also of the Homestead Law."[23]

Women, too, benefited from both acts, as a Nevada case shows. Deserted by her husband, Francis Straskel and her two children fled to Nevada, where in 1861 she married a man squatting on unsurveyed land. Her husband turned out to be a bigamist, and following his death in 1865, his children claimed the now-surveyed homestead. The Carson City Land Office investigated: "Mrs. Straskel was really the head of the family," it found. She had "worked out of doors, and by keeping cows, raising chickens and vegetables, taking care of the sick and practicing mid-wifery, raised the greater share of the funds necessary for putting up said improvements [of a dwelling house] and supporting the family." On May 10, 1867, the General Land Office "affirmed" the decision of its Nevada branch. Many women homesteaded, or preempted, or otherwise acquired, federal land in California through the nineteenth century.[24]

The most contentious and controversial policy concerned the status of some eight hundred huge Mexican land grants, which the federal government had promised to respect under the terms of the 1848 Treaty of Guadalupe Hidalgo. Two conflicting reports advised Congress of the situation. The first, by Captain Henry W. Halleck, secretary of state under the region's military government, on March 1, 1849, declared that many grants, and certainly those granted in the final days of Mexican rule, were "very doubtful, if not entirely fraudulent." A year later, William Carey Jones, son-in-law of influential Missouri senator Thomas Hart Benton, who, like Benton's other son-in-law, John C. Frémont, had gained large holdings from Mexican ranchers, saw things differently: "The grants in California, I am bound to say, are mostly *perfect titles*."[25]

At the urging of California senator William M. Gwin, who wished to protect "a princely national domain" for "hardy enterprising settlers," Congress on March 3, 1851, passed "an Act to Ascertain and Settle the Private Land Claims in the State of California." Unlike with previous contested claims in the expanding United States, which Congress had handled amid great uncertainty and conflict, a three-man commission would first rule on the legitimacy of Mexican titles, with the right of appeal to either of the two United States District Courts in California and then to the Supreme Court in Washington.[26]

The effect of the California Land Commission remains highly controversial, with division among historians still following the logic of the Halleck and Jones reports. All agree the process was time consuming and costly. "The result is delay upon delay," John S. Hittell fumed in 1858, as attorneys "made out like bandits." In Los Angeles, Hittell claimed, "two fifths of the land has gone to pay the fees of the lawyers employed." Attorney Elisha Oscar Crosby, whose firm handled one-eighth of the cases, denounced the United States Supreme Court for "the grossest outrages upon equity and common honesty." Even the law firm of Henry W. Halleck, Archibald C. Peachy, and Frederick Billings, which argued at least 120 of the 800 cases, was often baffled. In 1865, John Rowland despairingly wrote Halleck after thirteen years of battle to patent an uncomplicated southern California grant. General Halleck, then chief of staff of the Army, cited his comparable frustrations on June 2: "There seems but one way to expedite business in that [General Land] office—hire an agent and give him plenty of money." That government deceit and confusion robbed grantees of their patrimony is a mantra of contemporary California historians.[27]

The great land historian Paul W. Gates almost alone opposed the Jones position, until historian Donald J. Pisani later intellectually joined him. Gates firmly backed "the settler interest," and after thoroughly studying the cases, he found areas of gray. Gates and Pisani ably supported Crosby's conclusion that the rancho system worked to place lands "into the hands of speculators." Men of power and wealth, whether Californios or grant purchasers, floated boundaries to cover settler-improved land assumed to be in the public domain, while squatters occupied the best rancho lands hoping grants would not be confirmed.[28]

Christian G. Fritz, biographer of federal district judge Ogden Hoffman, emphasized the politics behind the determination of land ownership, from the appointment of the commissioners to the decisions of the United States Supreme Court. District

Judge Hoffman scrutinized grants critically until Jones and Benton personally appeared before the Supreme Court to appeal the rejection of Frémont's Mariposa grant, which had filled none of the conditions of Mexican law. Chief Justice Taney, showing the questionable legal acumen later appearing in the Dred Scott case, ruled in December 1854 that Mexican governors had made grants solely "in consideration of the previous public and patriotic services of the grantee," and none of the regulations needed to be followed. A bewildered Hoffman admitted he "did not understand the decision of the Supreme Court," but felt bound to apply it, and confirmed eighty-five of the next ninety grants appealed from the commission, including blatantly fraudulent ones.[29]

A political shift came in 1857, when Jeremiah S. Black became U.S. attorney general and looked askance at the "pretended titles" in the Golden State. Crusty attorney Edwin M. Stanton found proof to convince Black of "an organized system of fabricating land titles carried on for a long time." By 1860, the Supreme Court agreed, and grant-holders suffered losses in some cases. But the final turn arrived in 1863. President Lincoln appointed the dominating California justice, Stephen J. Field, to the U.S. Supreme Court, and Field held the right to property sacred; subsequently, most claims to Mexican grants were confirmed. Nevertheless, confusion over prior Mexican land titles deterred agricultural development for decades after the Gold Rush.[30]

FEDERAL PATRONAGE

Influence of U.S. Treasury Department

Normal government services relied on patronage. Politicians raised the support needed to gain and hold office by parceling out jobs to friends. Competence for positions was secondary, and through alliances, patronage became a unifying party machinery. For patronage, no other department could top the U.S. Post Office, with its network of party animals scattered through the hinterlands. In California's dominant city, San Francisco, however, the U.S. Treasury Department reigned supreme. There, the Treasury Department ran—besides the obvious customs houses (in San Francisco, Benicia, Monterey, Sacramento, San Diego, San Pedro, and Stockton) and branch mint—the Revenue Cutter Service, Light House Department (both later merged into the Coast Guard), and the U.S. Marine Hospital. The San Francisco Customs House had 120 employees, and the collector of the port pulled down a salary of $10,400 a year, compared to $4,500 for the superintendent of the branch mint and assistant treasurer of the United States. The customs house collector ruled the offices of collector, auditor, appraiser, naval officer, surveyor, weigher and measurer, superintendent of warehouses, and gauger, plus the thirty $150-a-month inspectors. Even laborers in the agency received what was

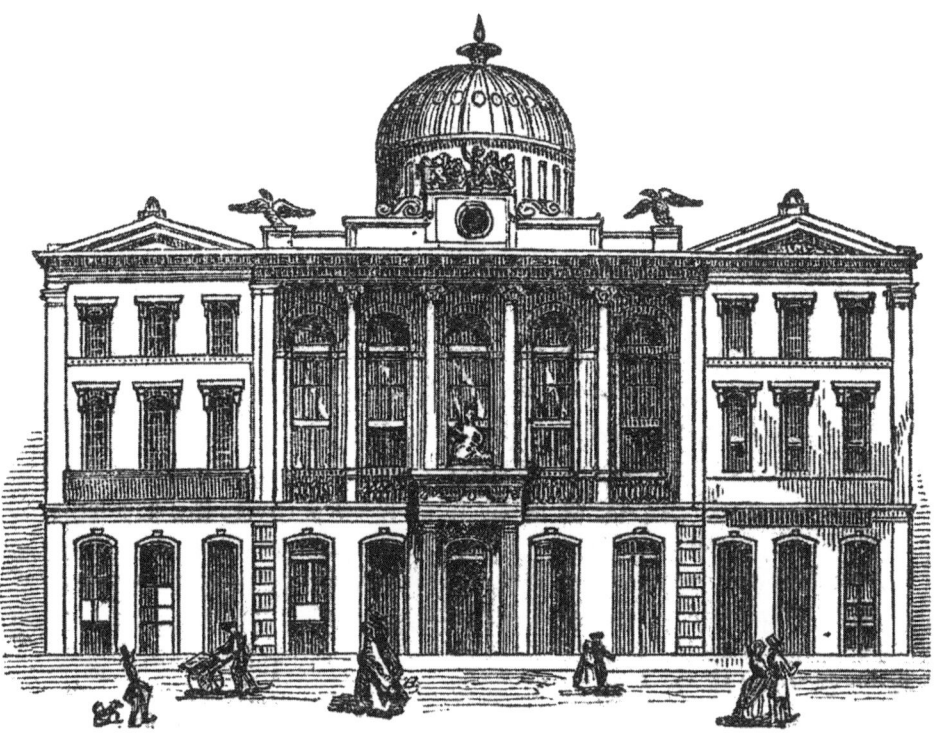

An important aspect of the U.S. government's role in shaping pioneer California was its establishment of a federal court system in the 1850s. This drawing of the U.S. District Courtrooms, on Battery Street in San Francisco, appeared in the 1859 *San Francisco Almanac*. The building housed both a district court (for the prosecution of federal crimes) and a circuit court of appeals. *California Historical Society, FN-19510*.

then a princely wage of $100 monthly. The branch mint had thirteen highly paid employees, with six clerks starting at $2,000 per year, but employment there required a knowledge of chemistry and metallurgy. The Marine Hospital, which opened in 1854 to care for indigent seamen, provided opportunities to award lower-paying jobs. Its staff consisted of two surgeons, a steward, and an apothecary, plus seventeen nurses, cooks, washmen, watermen, and laborers.[31]

Through southern Democratic control of the state during the 1850s, Californians knew the customs house as "The Virginia Poor House," but in 1860, victorious Republicans quickly lost any claim to being reformers. "Sir, the Election is over and I have for once in my life, Voted for the successful Candidate," a Californian declared, "and now I am one of the Many that want an office." Throughout the 1860s and 1870s, California Republicans and Democrats battled over spoils, embarrassing presidents, citizens, and themselves. Corruption became the greatest when the legislature picked the United States senators to represent the state in Congress. The manner of choice in caucus led to widespread bribery. The story of the occupants of one seat will do.[32]

Northern Democrat David C. Broderick lusted for a U.S. Senate seat and finally bested California's senior senator, William M. Gwin. In his infamous "Scarlet Letter," Gwin complained in 1857 of the debilitating effects of patronage, where those he appointed "should be my supporters instead of enemies, and it is being used for my destruction." However, President James Buchanan, a southern toady, spurned Broderick's recommended appointments. The feud festered into the 1859 state election, which saw a southern Democratic sweep, Milton S. Latham's election as governor, and Broderick's death in a duel. The *San Francisco Bulletin* observed, "The Gubernatorial chair has no special charm for Mr. Latham, except as a means to an end." Inaugurated governor of California on January 9, 1860, Latham served only five days before becoming Broderick's successor in the U.S. Senate.[33]

In 1863, many candidates wished to warm this seat. One contestant reportedly "boasted that he would be Senator, if it cost him $150,000," and his emissary wrote a friend to "secure two or three men [supporting other candidates] as soon as possible. Work hard; don't stop on account of price, but secure them as best you can." Meantime, the federal postal agent tendered a bribe to an assemblyman to vote for his Republican candidate in caucus, while two state senators stood hidden in the hotel room wardrobe. The explosive revelation sent uncorrupted northern Democrat John Conness to the Senate and produced a hit play at Sacramento's Metropolitan Theater: *King Caucus, or the Senatorial Muddle,* complete with a facsimile of the original wardrobe.

As Conness's term drew to close in 1868, Democrat Eugene Casserly, who had supported the war effort, received the prize, while another dramatic production appeared as a pamphlet: *Bribery; or, the California Senatorial Election: A Comedy, in Three Acts.* Continuing charges forced Casserly's resignation on November 29, 1873, and through a deal, Republican governor Newton Booth pulled a Latham, resigning to accept a full term in the U.S. Senate. So the story played out in California, with the Central Pacific Railroad owning the deepest pockets, until the 1913 ratification of the Seventeenth Amendment to the U.S. Constitution, which required the statewide popular election of senators.[34]

In addition to helping elect politicians, offices had assigned jobs. The customs house provided the federal government's main source of revenue in the state. In 1846, Captain James L. Folsom became the first military collector of the port. Military governors modified customs regulations to fit California's needs, and duties financed their government. On March 10, 1849, Congress finally placed California under the general revenue laws, establishing a customs district, and on November 12, James Collier became the first civilian collector. Checking ships and passengers proved to be laborious work. A ledger at the Huntington Library reveals, for example, that on June 19, 1854, the French ship *Notre Dame des Victoires* arrived with thirty-five baskets of champagne and other cargo listed in 347 manifests. Not until August 3 did officials finally finish their report on that ship.[35]

However, private enterprise expedited customs matters for those importers who wished to pay higher express charges in order to receive their merchandise sooner and be first in the market. Whereas individual shippers had to clear boxes individually, Wells, Fargo & Co. arranged with customs officials in New York to clear eight thousand packages at a time. When the Wells Fargo consignment reached the Isthmus of Panama, express company agents placed all of the small boxes into protective, locked packing trunks and sent the shipment on under the watchful eye of a messenger.[36]

More energy in the customs house went into detecting fraud. Since colonial days, avoiding customs duties had been a matter of course, and until the mid-1860s, the free port of Victoria, British Columbia, served as the conduit for smuggled goods. In 1866, Panama became the place where foreign goods could be slipped among through-merchandise from New York to San Francisco. "It is not much of a [golden] shower that is necessary to enable importers to fee [bribe] a man at Panama," said Joseph W. Stow, president of the San Francisco Commercial Association. Still, prejudice distorted the minds of some customs officials. A San Franciscan declared in 1869 that "the Israelites [were] a little more prone to that sort of business," while a New Yorker affirmed that a Panama miscreant was "a Jew, like nine-tenths of the smugglers." The transcontinental railroad rerouted imports away from such "free" foreign ports, and Jewish stereotyping seems not to have been an issue any longer in the 1870s.

By 1868, San Francisco was "the distributing point for drugs, and especially opium, for the Pacific Coast," special agent Samuel Purdy reported, as Chinese evaded a 100-percent tariff on these products. Ingenious smuggling methods included slipping eight hundred copper shells filled with opium into barrels containing a thousand eggs preserved with a coating of tar and sand, and placing common five-tael (about a half pound) tin boxes filled with drugs into the soles of imported shoes.[37]

The Arrival of the U.S. Mint

The U.S. Constitution declared that "Congress shall have Power . . . to coin Money, regulate the Value thereof, and of foreign Coin" (Article 1, Section 8). California, with its surfeit of gold dust, massive influx of population, and huge importation of goods, with their accompanying tariff duties, needed this service badly. Characteristically, the federal government responded with too little, too late.

In July and August 1848, military governor Richard B. Mason wrestled with "the almost entire absence of gold and silver coin" in a booming economy of the early Gold Rush. First he allowed merchants to pay customs duties in gold dust valued at sixteen dollars a troy ounce, and then with assayed ingots, revoking his orders each time when informed of their illegality under 1846 customs regulations. Gold was only a commodity; customs duties, according to federal law, had to be paid in recognized coin. Soon, foreign coins flowed in to be accepted at the value of comparably sized U.S. coins, regardless of their bullion content. This further added to the instability of monetary value.[38]

Californians themselves tried to solve their coin shortage. By the summer of 1849, San Francisco's private minters, following a precedent from the North Carolina gold fields, were in full production, eventually striking gold coins ranging from 25 cents to $50, based on the U.S. Mint standard of $20.67 per troy ounce of gold. Still, such coins circulated at uncertain values, which was debilitating for commerce. Bankers accepted or discounted the privately minted coins—which were not illegal until 1864—according to their metallic value, and in 1851, federal customs officials furthered the confusion. In payment of tariffs, they accepted only the unwieldy United States Assay Office's $50 octagonal slugs, while Treasury Department officials quibbled that the coins were only 884 to 887 fine, and not the regulation 900—even though they assayed at $50.10 in gold.[39]

In the East, the mint at Philadelphia used California gold to begin coining twenty-dollar gold pieces. It struck 1.3 million of them in 1850, 2.4 million in 1851, and 2.2 million in 1852. As usual, though, an official U.S. mint for the area that produced the gold came only much later. Not until February 8, 1851, three years after James Marshall's discovery of gold and the worldwide rush to the new El Dorado, did Senator Gwin introduce a bill to establish a branch mint. The legislation did not clear a dawdling Congress until seventeen months later. Merely remodeling a cramped assayer's office took until April 3, 1854, and the branch mint's operations were slow and careful thereafter. Only after Agoston Haraszthy took charge in 1855 did it begin to meet demand for "Mint Drops," the twenty-dollar double-eagles of commerce, and payroll-standard silver half-dollars. In late 1856, the private minters shut down for good. However, Haraszthy's unbridled energy ran the inadequate plant so hard, losing gold up the chimneys, that the government rewarded his enterprise with a charge of embezzlement. Of course, evidence and the courts cleared Haraszthy, but by then, this talented Hungarian had turned his energies to wine production.[40]

The Commercial Street mint facility also provided respectable jobs for women, and many of them served as adjusters, weighing coins to determine if they fit within legal tolerances, as well as performing clerical jobs. Similar employment continued when operations moved in 1875 to a spacious new building at Fifth and Mission streets, now known as the "Old Mint." When it came to turning gold dust into bars, San Francisco's private assayers and refiners were faster and cheaper than the U.S. Mint. With borrowed money worth 2 to 3 percent interest a month, dust-buyers in the mining districts did not wish to tie up their funds in a two- to four-week wait for the U.S. Mint, and into the twentieth century, private refiners, such as Contra Costa's Selby Smelting and Lead Company, did a huge business.[41]

The Civil War brought a new monetary problem to California. In December 1861, the government suspended specie payments. No longer would it redeem paper money in gold. In 1862, it had presses running off treasury bills, or paper money, to pay war expenses, and in 1863, Congress established national banks, which also issued currency. All federal paper money fluctuated wildly in exchange value with gold, especially according to the Union Army's successes or defeats. However, in November 1862, hard-money Californians resolved to accept paper only at its gold value, defying the central government. Merchants' bills quickly came to carry the notation "Payable in U.S. Gold Coin." When borrowers began paying depreciated "greenbacks" on loans made in gold, the 1863 state legislature passed the Specific Contract Act, permitting a lender to designate the money. Currency reached a low value of thirty-nine cents to the gold dollar in the summer of 1864, as General Ulysses S. Grant stalled before Richmond, and the San Francisco Chamber of Commerce dryly stated that "Our people are not in the habit of carrying Treasury notes in their pockets."[42]

If two values of United States money were not enough, the 1870s brought a third: silver. Prior to the 1870s, silver dollars did not circulate, since they contained more silver than their face value, and purchasers gobbled them up to melt down for bullion. In 1873, Congress discontinued their minting ("the Crime of '73"), and authorized a slightly heavier silver Trade Dollar for use with China. When European governments also stopped coining silver and the big bonanza of Nevada's Comstock Lode came into production, the price of silver plummeted. Trade Dollars, then worth ninety-five cents, circulated extensively in the West, and in February 1876, San Francisco merchants resolved to accept them only at market value. As a result, bank customers could—and did—keep accounts in three kinds of money until 1878–1879, when the federal government resumed coining standard silver dollars and greenbacks reached par value with gold. However, controversy over the 16:1 ratio of silver to gold coinage, which inflated silver money and deflated gold coinage, continued long after, unsettling investments and commerce.[43]

The Bumpy Ride of the Mail Services

Congress, on August 14, 1848, provided for a California mail service, but until the completion of the transcontinental railroad, its performance was poor. Before the Gold Rush, the U.S. Post Office had grown accustomed to slow, orderly westward settlement, contracting for new mail routes at the cheapest possible cost. Washington officials had no precedents for facilitating mail for a distant land, where money lay everywhere and where the population was booming. Californians would just have to keep within the eastern scale of expenses.

On November 1, 1848, Postmaster General Cave Johnson chose William Van Voorhies as the special agent to establish mail services and appoint postmasters at the coastal ports where congressionally mandated mail steamers called—but which initially had little population, and which gained little population. Revenues alone would have to pay for unauthorized routes into the populous mining regions. Two politically appointed postmasters never showed up in San Francisco, and Van Voorhies himself established the San Francisco post office upon his arrival on February 28, 1849. Not only were operational expenses "exorbitant" among the Golden State's great distances, scattered population, and inflated economy, he reported on March 13, but "No one in California seems at present disposed to take upon himself the trouble of public office." However, unknown to Van Voorhies, he had been replaced on March 30.

The new special agent, R. T. P. Allen, arrived on June 13, 1849, and late that month established seven interior post offices at the supply centers of Vernon, Sacramento, and Stockton, as well as at Benicia, Sonoma, and San Jose; Coloma became the first gold-country office. On receipt of this news, the postmaster general chastised Allen for his high expenses and his failure to have contracts "executed in triplicate," and he "withheld" approval for all Allen had done. As late as 1854, the state legislature memorialized Congress to establish more frequent delivery and institute service over forty detailed routes.[44]

However, only the federal government could and did subsidize transportation of the mails, from specially built mail steamers commanded by naval officers to stagecoach lines. Monthly steamer mail between New York and San Francisco by way of the Isthmus of Panama began in 1849, and service to the Orient came in 1865. Congress authorized a five-hundred-thousand-dollar annual mail subsidy, and the *Colorado*, the first of the monthly sidewheel steamers, left San Francisco on January 1, 1867, for Hong Kong and Yokohama. When the government doubled payments in 1872, the shipping company doubled the frequency of sailings, using modern iron, screw-propeller steamers. Flour and quicksilver (mercury) became prized exports. On land, mail contracts kept stage companies alive. Stagecoaching was a hard, time-consuming, often barely profitable business, and many times when the mail contract changed, so did the ownership of the stage line.[45]

Again, in the dearth of public service, private enterprise took up the slack and entered California mail delivery. In October 1849, beginning with Alexander H. Todd in the Southern Mines, individual expressmen compiled lists of subscribers, carried their outgoing mail to San Francisco, picked up incoming letters, and charged one to two dollars a letter. In November, energetic Adams & Co., the first of the eastern expresses, arrived. In the frantic express business, owners changed frequently, little companies became bigger ones, and rates came down. In 1852, when a faction of the dissension-ridden American Express Company came to California as Wells,

Constructed in 1874, this lighthouse at Point Fermin guided ships into Los Angeles's San Pedro Bay for almost seventy years. The federal government built twenty-two lighthouses in California between 1854 and 1880. *Courtesy California State Library.*

Fargo & Co., express letter fees stood at twenty-five cents, compared to three cents for U.S. postage. Still, the Sacramento *Californian* remarked on December 30, 1852, "Wells, Fargo & Co. and Adams & Co. have entirely monopolized the Post Office business. We never receive a paper or letter except by one or other of the expresses." The well-traveled editor of the *California Farmer* charged in 1861 that "If the Postmaster-General could look into some of his Post-Offices of California, he would hardly wish to have the 'U.S.A.' placed over the door, unless it should be interpreted— *Useless, Scandalous, Affair.*" By then, Wells Fargo handled three-quarters of all letters within California. On July 1, 1863, the government rewarded California patriotism by dropping the ten-cent rate to the Atlantic states and making postage three cents per half ounce within the entire nation.[46]

San Franciscans soon had more than enough of patronage politics. In April 1864, northern Democratic senator John Conness secured the replacement of Republican San Francisco postmaster Samuel H. Parker with Robert F. Perkins, who promptly sacked fifteen of twenty-five clerks, brought in untrained Conness supporters from the countryside, and assigned them to distribute incoming mails. The mostly Republican Chamber of Commerce then howled about "the general mismanagement of postal affairs" and wished the Post Office to establish "the same promptitude" as Wells Fargo. Wells Fargo sorted letters on steamers and railroads and used post boxes and letter carriers—unknown to government service until a congressional act of March 3, 1863. Not until November 15, 1869, did the San Francisco postmaster appoint the first seventeen carriers, while free letter delivery came only in 1872.[47]

The 1870s brought increased population, settled agriculturists, and above all, a railroad network to carry the mails to and from and within the state. Postal efficiency increased, while the number of letters Wells Fargo carried between the 1860s and 1890s remained stable at two hundred thousand monthly. In 1880, the government, while admitting that "the Express Company handles the mails more efficiently than the postal authorities," unsuccessfully attempted to close it down. Fifteen years later, in May 1895, Wells Fargo discontinued its legendary but by then unprofitable Letter Express, but not until January 1, 1913, did the federal government's Parcel Post challenge express package delivery.[48]

"THE HIGH ARM OF MILITARY TYRANNY"

National affairs disrupted any routine the three hundred thousand Californians enjoyed. When Civil War followed Republican electoral victory and southern secession in the winter of 1860–61, stark ideology divided California's three political parties. Southern Democrats, dominant through the 1850s, held firm to white supremacy and state sovereignty; Republicans believed in federal supremacy and equality under the law; northern Democrats combined the racism of the southern Democrats with the nationalism of the Republicans. Each side would have to destroy the opposing ideology to triumph, or, as one orator stated, "The issue is slavery first and Union afterwards; Union first and slavery nevermore."[49]

That winter, the California congressional delegation proved the unreliability of the Democrats when all boldly or covertly supported California's secession as an independent Pacific Republic, and one of the four led Rebel troops at Bull Run. The U.S. Army, though, quickly secured federal property in California. In January 1861, General Albert Sidney Johnston took command of a military department with seventeen hundred troops in California and nineteen hundred in Oregon—about a quarter of the Army nationwide. Fort Alcatraz alertly protected shipping, while at recently completed Fort Point, newly mounted heavy guns faced landward to protect against attack by local Rebels. General Edwin Vose Sumner arrived by sea on April 24, the same day the news of the fall of Fort Sumter came through by Pony Express and telegraph, and took command quietly the next day. Johnston left for the Confederate Army and death at Shiloh.[50]

General Sumner set policies his successors followed. He actively worked with Unionist civil and political leaders, stationed troops in disaffected southern California, where secessionist and pro-southern sentiment was strong, and made arms available for militia companies. Three days following the battle of Bull Run on July 21, the federal government called for the first regiments of California troops.

Unitarian minister Thomas Starr King, photographed here with his wife, Julia Wiggin, worked tirelessly on behalf of the cause of national unity from the time of his arrival in California in 1860 until his death from diphtheria and pneumonia four years later. He campaigned for Abraham Lincoln, served as a spokesman for the U.S. Sanitary Commission during the Civil War, and traveled widely, using his pulpit to urge Californians to see themselves as an inseparable part of the Union. *Courtesy California State Library.*

General Patrick Edward Connor commanded those protecting the Central Overland Mail Route and watching the Mormons in Utah, some of whom also harbored anti-Union sympathies, while General James H. Carleton had the responsibility for the Butterfield stage route into Texas. Ultimately, California funded eight regiments of infantry and the First Battalion of California Mountaineers of six companies, two regiments of cavalry, and the First Battalion of Native California Cavalry of four companies. At least sixteen African Americans served as cooks and in other auxiliary positions in the California units, while two hundred black sailors served aboard ships of the Pacific squadron. The national government enrolled men in the far West, but unlike in the East, never instituted the draft there. The federal government still has not paid the Golden State's $2.5 million direct outlay for raising and equipping 15,725 men, and in 1997, the state legislature passed a resolution asking for the money.[51]

In July 1861, the southern Democratic Party went on record saying that, since the federal government had failed to end "the horrors of civil war" through "Constitutional guarantees," it was "in favor of the recognition of the independence of the Confederate States." Not surprisingly, Republicans, as a result, captured the state offices open for election that year. On February 15, 1862, Postmaster General Montgomery Blair told his San Francisco subordinate to ban the pro-Confederate *Los Angeles Star* and an Oregon newspaper from the mails to curtail their paid subscriptions. In late spring 1862, battlefield losses staggered the Union, and that summer, President Lincoln called for six hundred thousand more troops, threatened to institute a nationwide draft, and concurrently wished to emancipate southern slaves. To silence vociferous Democratic opponents to these measures, on August 8, 1862, the president ordered the secretary of war to suspend the writ of habeas corpus and allow Army officers, U.S. marshals, and chiefs of police to arbitrarily arrest those "discouraging voluntary enlistments" or for "any other disloyal practice."

Rather than being telegraphed to California, these commands arrived by slow boat on September 8, 1862. "Leading Secessionists will be confined at Alcatraz," commanding General George Wright told subordinates, and he constructed the first prison building at the fort that in the future would become infamous as a prison island. "Drunken brawlers of no account will be confined to your guard house unless they take the Oath of allegiance." The general exulted that "open mouthed traitors" were now "beyond the reach of civil authorities" and quibbling attorneys.

With local politicians supplying the targets, those quickly arrested and imprisoned were Major W. R. I. McKay of Benicia, a former state office-holder; George P. Gillis, Democratic State Central Committee representative from Sacramento; Assemblyman E. J. C. Kewen; editor Henry Hamilton of Los Angeles; and state senator Thomas Baker from Visalia. In September and October, Wright also excluded from the mails the *Stockton Argus* and its weekly edition, the *Democrat;* the *San Jose*

Tribune; the *Visalia Equal Rights Expositor* and its predecessor, the *Tulare Post;* and the Placerville *Mountain Democrat,* plus four Oregon journals. Although Democrats reacted with only subdued protest, long-term suppression did not appeal to General Wright. He reported to Washington on November 8 that with state militia companies and "a judicious posting of U.S. troops, I can comprehend but little danger." Most prisoners took the oath of allegiance quickly, while newspapers suspended briefly or resumed publishing under new names. On November 22, the secretary of war ordered, again by slow sea mail, the release of all prisoners. McKay and Gillis left Alcatraz on December 20, 1862, the last openly political arrests for more than a year.[52]

The year 1863 became the pivotal one in the East militarily and the West politically. Three secessionist pirates, Ridgely Greathouse, Asbury Harpending, and Alfred Rubery, a British subject, angered over the president's Emancipation Proclamation, precipitated much of the action. On March 15, 1863, customs officials, U.S. Navy sailors, and city police captured the pirates' schooner, the *J. M. Chapman,* which proposed to despoil the gold-carrying mail steamers. An outraged legislature quickly passed legislation banning treasonable practices, requiring loyalty oaths for lawyers and schoolteachers, effectively doubling the militia, and allowing soldiers to vote absentee—which had the potential of increasing the number of Union voters, especially in county elections. The federal circuit court, under Justice Stephen J. Field, quickly convicted the three pirate conspirators of treason, and almost as fast, Rubery received a presidential pardon and district court judge Ogden Hoffman, to great Unionist anger, released the other two under the president's general amnesty proclamation of December 8, 1863.[53]

On April 13, 1863, the secret Union League arrived in California, forming a shadow civil-military government while its 110 local councils inspired Union voters, watched Democrats, and formed legal state militia companies. If conflict broke out, drilled Unionists would have access to arms—kindly supplied to the state by General Wright. The league's Grand Council included two congressmen, the governor, the commander of the state's militia, and a state Supreme Court justice. San Francisco contributed its chief of police, one supervisor, the federal postmaster, the regional revenue assessor, and four customs officers. Of particular importance, Lieutenant Colonel Richard C. Drum, adjutant, and therefore the right-hand man for the U.S. Army's Department of the Pacific commanders, served throughout the league's existence.[54]

In the early 1850s, the California legislature and Supreme Court had banned blacks, Indians, and Chinese from testifying in civil or criminal cases involving whites. Federal judges followed state laws, but district judge Hoffman pushed the limits. When the fusion Union Party–dominated 1863 legislature lifted the ban from black men and women, African Americans filed suits to ride on the street railroads and attend public schools and worked to win acceptance to march in Independence Day parades. The federal government supplied another three important civil rights during the war and Reconstruction that dramatically improved opportunities for black people: the right to homestead and preempt public land, to serve as soldiers and sailors, and finally to vote.[55]

The quest for stronger harbor defenses during wartime evolved into a struggle between department commanders and Washington-based engineers. For three years, General Wright wished to throw up temporary earthen batteries, whereas the Army's Engineer Bureau studied everything to death. By the summer of 1864, Alcatraz Island had mounted ninety guns, including a pair of fifteen-inch Rodmans; one faced the Golden Gate, the other pointed toward San Francisco in case a ship made it past the batteries. New federal port regulations adopted in April 1864 directed ships along the south side of the island fortress, so they could be guarded by cross fire from a new battery at Fort Mason (now partially restored). Ships straying along the north side of Alcatraz would meet a similar cross fire from Angel Island batteries, partially built by Humboldt War Indian prisoners.[56]

Concurrently, civilians provided an ironclad warship for the Navy. In 1862, Humboldt County state senator James T. Ryan persuaded the Navy to allot an armored monitor to San Francisco harbor. The *Camanche*, one of the ten *Passaic*-class monitors, had two hundred feet of decking almost at the waterline and two fifteen-inch guns in a revolving turret that fired 460-pound solid shot. Ryan, Frances Secor, a New Jersey shipbuilder, and Peter Donahue of San Francisco's Union Iron Works contracted to prefabricate the ship in the East and reassemble it in California. The ship carrying the monitor arrived safely but then sank in a freak storm on November 16, 1863, while moored to a wharf. Salvagers had raised all pieces by June 1864, but parties wrangled over liability. Finally, on July 21, the San Francisco Board of Supervisors pledged sixty thousand dollars in gold to begin reassembly, which the federal government never reimbursed. On November 14, 1864, twenty-five thousand people watched the *Camanche* slide down the ways. The city of San Francisco had built "the 'prophylactic' which warded off the attacks of pirates," remarked supervisor Isaac Rowell.[57]

In 1864, military stalemate in the East gave way slowly to grinding, costly, approaching military victory. The presidential election heightened tensions, and in the Golden State, the Union League dominated Democrats and commanding generals. On May 3, a week before the Democratic State Convention was due to meet in San Francisco, John S. Chipman, a former Michigan congressman, called on Democrats to "rise up" and "put down the military despotism under which we are at present groaning," and then establish "a Republic on the Pacific." A few important Unionists visited General Wright, and Chipman, as his nephew phrased it, was given lodging at the "Army's Bastille Boarding House of Alcatraz." As Democratic delegates from

Modeled after Fort Sumter in Charleston, Fort Point was built by the U.S. Army Corps of Engineers in the late 1850s to guard San Francisco Bay against enemy intrusion. It served as a defense installation during the Civil War, manned by a U.S. artillery regiment, and continued to house troops until 1886. *California Historical Society Collection at the University of Southern California: Title Insurance and Trust Photo Collection.*

the interior counties on their way to San Francisco steamed past the grim, cold, island fortress, convention proceedings remained subdued.[58]

Like the French Bourbons, Democrats forgot nothing and learned nothing. On July 21, 1864, Charles L. Weller, chairman of the state central committee and second in command of the Knights of the Columbian Star, a laughable counterpart to the Union League, repeated Chipman's message to the same Democratic club. Fearing that the Union League would prevent Democrats from voting, Weller called on party members to arm themselves and form secret societies to "resist the high arm of military tyranny in California." The grand secretary of the Union League notarized a newspaper reporter's account, and Weller soon had his own island vacation for several weeks. General Irvin McDowell, who took over as the Union military commander in California on July 1, questioned "whether the public safety will admit of Mr. Weller's release to join his friends, or will require," the general slyly added, "his friends shall be sent to join him."[59]

At the same time, in response to a civil war in Mexico, coupled with the French

Although California had no compulsory military draft during the Civil War, a battalion of Californians volunteered to fight with the Second Massachusetts Cavalry in Virginia. This collage of photographs includes sixty-one members of the so-called California Hundred, who helped the Union Army capture Richmond in 1865. *Courtesy California State Library.*

invasion and the establishment of a puppet empire there, United States customs officials and Army generals were made agents of the State Department so they could fight to preserve American neutrality in that conflict. Throughout 1864, General Plácido Vega, a Mexican citizen taking refuge in California, sought to send arms and men south to help President Benito Juárez's popular Liberal cause. In a situation similar to what Generals Hitchcock and Wool had faced ten years earlier, in July and August 1864, federal authorities seized some fifteen thousand of Vega's muskets. Meanwhile, ex-senator Gwin proposed to Napoleon III that he colonize the mineral-rich northern states of Mexico with settlers from California and hold those territories in trust until the French-controlled Mexican emperor, Maximilian, paid off his war debt. From January through March 1865, Unionists ridiculed "El Duque de Güino," while important Democratic newspapers supported this haven for "the friends of free white government, the persecuted, outraged, down-trodden Democracy." General Irvin McDowell booted out Gwin's two immigration agents, and with the aid of the Liberal Mexican consul on February 11, 1865, required passports for Mexican-bound travelers.[60]

John Wilkes Booth's assassination of President Lincoln on April 14, 1865, shattered the nation's exultation at the surrender of Confederate general Robert E. Lee. Black mourning crepe appeared, and bells tolled throughout San Francisco the next morning. At 3 p.m. on April 15, angry Unionists vented frustration on disloyal newspapers. First, mobsters spread the second-floor office papers and printing material of the *Democratic Press* over Washington Street, followed quickly by that of the British *News Letter,* Irish-Catholic *Monitor* and *Occidental,* and the French Imperialist *L'union franco-americaine. L'echo du Pacific,* organ of the French Imperial consul and housed on the fourth floor of the *Alta California* building, became the final target. As men bent on destruction congregated on Montgomery and Sansome streets, the police and Army provost guard took protective positions in front of the Sacramento Street newspaper office.

About five o'clock, the crowd spotted General McDowell walking to his Portsmouth Square headquarters and called to him. "My Friends," he addressed the mob, a salutation Democrats never forgot, "I have wished to exercise as seldom as possible the military power so apt to become military despotism. I have therefore tolerated many wrong things done in the public press." Approval then followed: "While your course today was very wrong, it was very natural . . . and [you] have perhaps saved me some trouble. Now, I want you to save me further trouble by dispersing." The crowd did, helped along by two thousand militiamen. By evening, five thousand troops from the Presidio occupied the city. Their bonfires blazed at financial district street intersections, and shortly the provost guard occupied the gutted newspaper offices. General McDowell gradually allowed the papers to revive under different names. The destroyed *Democratic Press,* for instance, emerged in June 1865 as the *Examiner.* Minor disturbances continued throughout California, and the mayor of San Francisco, the federal district judge, and others called on General McDowell to preserve the peace. On April 17, 1865, he ordered the arrest of anyone and the suppression of any newspaper "so utterly infamous as to exult over the assassination of the President." From then until June 1, the Army arrested sixty-eight Californians, thereby preventing the calamity Judge Hoffman predicted if "people would have taken vengeance in their own hands." By the end of July 1865, however, the Army had freed all its prisoners.[61]

THE REPUBLICAN REVOLUTION

With peace, the Army withdrew from civil affairs and a semblance of balance returned to the political scene. John McCall, one of the military prisoners, sued General McDowell for illegal arrest, and on April 25, 1867, Circuit Judge Matthew P. Deady of Oregon ruled in McCall's favor. Deady upheld the tenets of the famed 1866

U.S. Supreme Court *Ex Parte Milligan* decision, which determined that only Congress possessed the authority to suspend the writ of habeas corpus. While McDowell had acted on "public necessity," Judge Deady ruled, he did so with "no authority or order from the President." Congress made the question moot, however. A quickly passed law upheld all officers in such cases.[62]

In 1867, with voters repulsed by what they saw as Republican wartime excesses and returning to their traditional political loyalties, the Democratic Party regained control of state offices, leaving Republicans to fight a rear guard action on civil rights. The issues in the gubernatorial election, the *Examiner* declared on July 1, 1867, were "negro and Chinese suffrage" and "railroad swindles." With opposition toward nonwhite groups still strong in the state and growing toward the Chinese, in 1868 a split legislature failed to ratify the Fourteenth Amendment to the U.S. Constitution, which gave some civil rights protections to freed slaves and other nonwhites. The next year, allegations of imminent Chinese suffrage demolished the Republicans in the legislative and state Supreme Court elections. Democrats, now constituting 80 percent of the new legislature, rejoiced in their return to power in 1870 after a decade, and also gleefully "disapproved of and rejected" the Fifteenth Amendment, granting black suffrage.

However, the two constitutional amendments became law despite California's refusal to ratify them and, with the Civil Rights Act of 1870, pushed through Congress by Senator William M. Stewart of Nevada with one section for the particular benefit of the Chinese, had a profound effect on civil rights in the state. Three Code Commissioners revising California's laws removed all bans on court testimony by Chinese and Indians—though a stubborn Democratic state Supreme Court refused to allow such testimony until the codes went into effect on January 1, 1873. Similarly, in January 1871, a federal circuit judge struck down the hated foreign miners' tax, applied exclusively to Chinese since 1860. Then, through the mid-1880s, Democratic and Republican governors alternated in a closely contested state, and support for the Chinese became politically unwise for either party. Urban ordinances and state laws harassed the Chinese, culminating in the federal Chinese Exclusion Act of 1882, prohibiting most immigration to the United States from China. However, the federal district, circuit, and supreme courts used the 1868 Burlingame Treaty permitting free immigration, the Fourteenth Amendment, and numerous congressional civil rights acts to afford the Chinese a measure of redress, striking down the most discriminatory provisions in state and municipal law. Civil War–related changes in federal law ushered in an era of dramatically altered, though slowly developing, opportunity for California's racial minority groups.[63]

Also during and after the Civil War, Republican federal administrations favoring internal improvements encouraged construction of a network of rails throughout California through land grants and subsidies. While shippers groaned about high short-haul rates, passengers at least benefited. From the 1860s to the 1890s, rail fares averaged four cents a mile, compared to a "bit" (12.5 cents) per mile on the other government-subsidized public transportation, the stagecoach.[64]

However, granters of favors attracted lobbyists, and in January 1868, a railroad promoter described how to cultivate congressmen, their staffs, and various Washington departments: "We keep on getting acquainted, for there lies the power, the ability to go to these different men & greet them as friends and acquaintances. A little stock distributed judiciously helps things too, you know." Collis P. Huntington of the Central Pacific, who found the government a friend rather than a regulatory foe, was the best of the best. David Igler argues in a recent article that railroad lands rather than Mexican grants created California's great landed estates—aided by helpful congressmen. Senator Aaron A. Sargent in 1875 exempted British mining investors from anti-alien land laws and then in 1877 pushed the Desert Lands Act through Congress to help James Ben Ali Haggin's Kern County Land Company solidify its holdings.[65]

Angry denunciations of the railroad "monopoly," which to some extent was empowered by federal actions and land subsidies, became a staple feature of state elections from 1867 forward. They became especially virulent at the 1878 constitutional convention. The Central-Southern Pacific Railroad countered attacks on its economic and political influence by using the federal government as a refuge. In 1884, the railroad gained a Kentucky charter to circumvent California's strong anti-railroad restrictions and to switch lawsuits to friendly federal courts. The Southern Pacific went to its grave on September 11, 1996, absorbed by the Union Pacific, its 1869 transcontinental partner and later bitter rival, forever damned as "the Octopus" in Frank Norris's famed 1901 novel for squeezing the life out of wheat farmers. Yet Richard J. Orsi's scholarship shows that the story of the federally subsidized Southern Pacific is a complicated one. Beyond federal and even state efforts, the railroad sponsored immigration, land distribution to actual small-scale farmers, fair-use irrigation, scientific agriculture, energetic marketing of California fruits, forest preservation, and national parks.[66]

Seaborne commerce demanded safe anchorages, and the federal government worked to supply them. In 1866, U.S. Army engineer Major Robert S. Williamson took charge of rivers and harbors in northern California—San Francisco, Napa, Petaluma, and Humboldt Bay. In 1869, at his request, Alexis Von Schmidt blew up Blossom Rock, a navigational hazard in San Francisco Bay, in a spectacular show for San Franciscans. Better known was his successor, Major George H. Mendell, who served from 1871 to 1895, while General Barton S. Alexander saw to the southern California ports of Santa Barbara, Los Angeles, and San Diego.[67]

The state of California and the federal government often shared resources. The national government gave wide distribution to facts and figures on California's pop-

A parade on Montgomery Street in San Francisco celebrates the meeting of the Union Pacific and Central Pacific railroads in Promontory, Utah, in May 1869. Decades in the making, the transcontinental railroad represented a massive cooperative effort between federal and state governments and private industry. *California Historical Society.*

ulation, economy, society, and other glories through the deca-annual census, cabinet secretary reports, and various publications. In 1873, President Ulysses S. Grant appointed General Alexander and Major Mendell of the Army Corps of Engineers and versatile scientist George Davidson of the Coast Survey to examine California's irrigation needs. Building on their work, in 1878, William Hammond Hall, the first state engineer, argued that "the State shall direct and control the diversion of waters from the streams." The legislature, however, refused to publish Hall's studies, and twentieth-century state and Army civil engineers had to redo them. Meanwhile, the federal district court solved the problem of mining debris choking the rivers and ruining farmland. In 1884, Judge Lorenzo Sawyer ordered that hydraulic tailings be impounded, in one of the first major assertions of federal environmental regulatory power.[68]

Federal action also played a role in the restoration of California's fisheries, which had been depleted or destroyed by miners' destruction of streambeds. The state was a year ahead of the federal government when the 1870 legislature established a Fish Commission "for the restoration and preservation of fish," but in 1872, Spencer F. Baird, the United States Commissioner of Fish and Fisheries, dispatched Livingston Stone to set up a salmon hatchery. At the McCloud River site, Stone also recorded the language of his Indian employees, who made the project successful. In 1874, Wells Fargo & Co.'s Express shipped six million salmon eggs to Minnesota and eastward; in 1875, eight million; and in 1878, twelve million. In 1877, Shasta County egg shipments also went to Australia, New Zealand, Canada, and Europe.[69]

Concurrently, a concern for forestry and watershed preservation spread from Europe to the United States, and in late 1879, a federal Division of Forestry emerged, six years before a parallel state agency. In 1880, in response to clamorous Californians, the federal General Land Office adopted limited protection for the Sequoia "Big Trees," and the following year, Senator John F. Miller attempted to create a huge national park to contain major Sequoia groves in the Sierra. When the secretary of interior allowed large stands of the Big Trees to be logged, Californians, including the domineering Southern Pacific Railroad, rallied to the cause of a Sequoia national park. George W. Stewart thundered as much through the columns of his *Visalia Delta*, and victory came on September 25, 1890, with congressional passage of a bill creating and then expanding Sequoia National Park. Golden State precedent existed. Back in 1864, Senator John Conness and President Abraham Lincoln had turned Yosemite Valley over to the state as the nation's first wilderness preserve, and on October 1, 1890, Yosemite, again with strong railroad support, also became a national park.[70]

Overall, what was the federal role in early California? In 1880, thirty years past statehood, most federal operations were almost routine: customs house, mint, post office, harbor improvements, lighthouses, arsenals, Navy yards, systems of mining and land titles, railroad and other transportation subsidies, and Indian control. The Civil War was fast becoming memory, leaving Judge Ogden Hoffman to reflect, "Military authority [was] always strong enough here to discourage resistance; [it would have been] in the highest degree dangerous to have left this state to the civil authority." However, the war's civil rights legacy survived in the federal courts, which, contrary to public will, increasingly exhibited judicial activism by striking down discriminatory city ordinances and state laws. As the twentieth century approached, new economic and environmental areas caused federal government concern. Conservation, land use and water rights, and abuses by huge monopolies such as the government-spawned Southern Pacific Railroad, would bring regulation. The new century would give the national government the dominant role.[71]

NOTES

1. Richard White, *"It's Your Misfortune and None of My Own": A History of the American West* (Norman: University of Oklahoma Press, 1991), 57, 58; Karen R. Merrill, "In Search of the 'Federal Presence' in the American West," *The Western Historical Quarterly* 30 (Winter 1999): 449–73; San Francisco *Alta California*, November 29, 1860, hereafter cited as *Alta;* William Henry Ellison, *A Self-Governing Dominion: California 1849–1860* (Berkeley: University of California Press, 1950); and Joseph Ellison's pioneering *California and the Nation, 1850–1869: A Study of the Relations of a Frontier Community with the Federal Government* (1927; reprint, Berkeley: University of California Press, 1969).

2. Elwood Mead, *Report of Irrigation Investigations in California* (Washington, D.C.: U.S. Department of Agriculture, Office of Experiment Stations, 1901), 20.

3. Theodore Grivas, *Military Governments in California, 1846–1850* (Glendale, Calif.: The Arthur H. Clark Company, 1963), 124, 143, 219. See Will Bagley, ed., *Scoundrel's Tale: The Samuel Brannan Papers* (Spokane: The Arthur H. Clark Company, 1999), 75–130, for government plans in 1845 to have Mormons colonize the West; Donald C. Biggs, *Conquer and Colonize: [Colonel Jonathan D.] Stevenson's [First New York Volunteer] Regiment and California* (San Rafael, Calif.: Presidio Press, 1977); Zachary Taylor, *Message from the President . . . 1850*, House Ex. Doc. 17, 31st Cong., 1st sess.; Josiah Royce, *California from the Conquest in 1846 to the Second Vigilance Committee in San Francisco: A Study of American Character* (Boston: Houghton, Mifflin & Co., 1886); and Neal Harlow, *California Conquered: War and Peace on the Pacific, 1846–1850* (Berkeley: University of California Press, 1982).

4. *Correspondence [1854–1857] between Secretary of War Jefferson Davis and General John E. Wool,* House Ex. Doc. 88, 35th Cong., 1st sess., 1858, 10; Glenn Thomas Edwards, Jr., "The Department of the Pacific in the Civil War Years" (Ph.D. diss., University of Oregon, 1963); William F. Strobridge, *Regulars in the Redwoods: The U.S. Army in Northern California, 1852–1861* (Glendale, Calif.: The Arthur H. Clark Company, 1994); Robert M. Utley, *Frontiersmen in Blue: The United States Army and the Indian, 1848–1865* (1967; reprint, Lincoln: University of Nebraska Press, 1981); and Utley, *Frontier Regulars: The United States Army and the Indian, 1866–1891* (1973; reprint, Lincoln: University of Nebraska Press, 1984).

5. Raphael P. Thian, *Notes Illustrating the Military Geography of the United States, 1813–1880*, ed. John M. Carroll (1881; reprint, Austin: University of Texas Press, 1979); Robert W. Frazer, *Forts of the West* (Norman: University of Oklahoma Press, 1965); Robert Bruegmann, *Benicia: Portrait of an Early California Town: An Architectural History* (San Francisco: 101 Productions, 1997; orig. pub. 1980); Josephine W. Cowell, *History of Benicia Arsenal, January 1851–December 1962* (Berkeley: Howell-North Press, 1963); George W. Stammerjohan, "Fort Tejon State Historic Park: An Interpretive History," *Dogtown Territorial Quarterly* (Fall and Winter, 1997; Spring 1998) Nos. 31–33: 54–63; 4–25 and 31–37; 16–25 and 61–62; Lisa M. Benton, *The Presidio: From Army Post to National Park* (Boston: Northeastern University Press, 1998); Erwin N. Thompson and Sally Woodbridge, *Presidio of San Francisco: An Outline of Its*

Evolution as a U.S. Army Post, 1847–1990 (Denver: National Park Service Special History Study, 1992), and Thompson and Woodbridge, *Defender of the Gate: The Presidio of San Francisco: A History from 1846 to 1995*, 2 vols. (Denver: National Park Service, 1997); John A. Hussey, *Fort McDowell, Angel Island* (1949; reprint, San Francisco: National Park Service, 1981); Francis J. Clauss, *Angel Island: Jewel of San Francisco Bay* (Menlo Park, Calif.: Briarcliff Press, 1982); Erwin N. Thompson, *The Rock: A History of Alcatraz Island, 1847–1972* (Denver: National Park Service, 1979), and Thompson, *Seacoast Fortifications San Francisco Harbor* (Denver: National Park Service, 1979); Edwin C. Bearss, *Fort Point* (Denver: National Park Service, 1973); Aurora Hunt, *Major General James Henry Carleton, 1914–1873: Western Frontier Dragoon* (Glendale, Calif.: The Arthur H. Clark Company, 1958); George R. Stewart, *John Phoenix, Esq., the Veritable Squibob: A Life of Captain George H. Derby, U.S.A.* (New York: Henry Holt and Co., 1937); Charles G. Ellington, *The Trial of U.S. Grant: The Pacific Coast Years, 1852–1854* (Glendale, Calif.: The Arthur H. Clark Company, 1987); Erasmus D. Keyes, *Fifty Years' Observations of Men and Events Civil and Military* (New York: Charles Scribner's Sons, 1884; partially reprinted, 1950); William T. Sherman, *Memoirs*, 2 vols. (New York: D. Appleton & Co., 1875); Langdon Sully, *No Tears for the General: The Life of Alfred Sully, 1821–1879* (Palo Alto, Calif.: American West Publishing Co., 1974); and Ann Swinger, ed., *John Xántus: The Fort Tejon Letters, 1857–1859* (Tucson: University of Arizona Press, 1986).

6. *Correspondence between Jefferson Davis and John E. Wool*, 148, 186, 191; Malcolm Edwards, ed., *The California Diary of General E. D. Townsend, 1851–1856* (Los Angeles: The Ward Ritchie Press, 1970), 91–96 (quote 95); Herbert G. Florcken, "The Law and Order View of the San Francisco Vigilance Committee of 1856," *California Historical Society Quarterly*, parts 1–4, December 1935 to September 1936, in particular, 14 (December 1935): 356–74; 15 (March 1936): 71 (Johnson quote, to state Quartermaster General William C. Kibbe, Sacramento, June 10, 1856), 83–86; and 15 (September 1936): 254–63. Arnold S. Lott, *A Long Line of Ships: Mare Island's Century of Naval Activity in California* (Annapolis, Md.: United States Naval Institute, 1954), 39–44; Joseph Ellison, *California and the Nation*, 125–35 (quote, 132). See also William C. Davis, *Jefferson Davis: The Man and His Hour* (New York: Harper Collins Publishers, 1991), 222–54, and Durwood Ball, "Filibusters and Regular Troops in San Francisco, 1851–1855," *Military History of the West* 28 (Fall 1998): 161–83.

7. John S. Wallace, "The Mare Island Navy-Yard," *Scribner's Monthly* 3 (April 1872): 641–50. Lott, *Long Line of Ships*, 7, 10; Sue Lemmon and E. D. Wichels, *Sidewheelers to Nuclear Power: A Pictorial Essay Covering 123 Years at the Mare Island Naval Shipyard* (Annapolis, Md.: Leeward Publications, 1977); George H. Read, *The Last Cruise of the Saginaw* (Boston: Houghton, Mifflin & Co., 1912).

8. Oscar Lewis, *George Davidson: Pioneer West Coast Scientist* (Berkeley: University of California Press, 1954); Chad Ehlers and Jim Gibbs, *Sentinels of Solitude: West Coast Lighthouses* (Portland, Ore.: Graphic Arts Center Publishing Company, 1981); Herman R. Friis, Director for the Center for Polar Archives at the National Archives, "A Brief Review of . . . U.S. Geographical Exploration . . . of the North Pacific Ocean . . . Prior to 1914," *Proceedings of an Archival Symposium . . . May 21, 1971 [on Alaskan Records]* (San Francisco: National Archives, n.d.), 1–106.

9. Charles T. Blake, Michigan City, November 1, 1856, to his brother, typescript, Wells Fargo Bank, San Francisco. Ferol Egan, *[John Charles] Frémont: Explorer for a Restless Nation* (Reno: University of Nevada Press, 1985); John Charles Frémont, *Geographical Memoir upon Upper California in Illustration of His [1848] Map of Oregon and California*, Senate Misc. Rep.

148, 30th Cong., 1st sess. (1848; reprinted 1964); W. Turrentine Jackson, *Wagon Roads West: A Study of Federal Road Surveys and Construction in the Trans-Mississippi West, 1846–1869* (New Haven: Yale University Press, 1979), 161–217 (quote, 177); Albert H. Campbell, General Superintendent, *A Report upon the several wagon roads constructed under the direction of the Interior Department,* House Exec. Doc. 108, 35th Cong., 2d sess. (1859); Thomas Frederick Howard, *Sierra Crossing: First Roads to California* (Berkeley: University of California Press, 1998).

 10. LeRoy R. Hafen, *The Overland Mail, 1849–1969* (Cleveland: The Arthur H. Clark Company, 1926; reprint 1976); Roscoe P. Conkling and Margaret B. Conkling, *The Butterfield Overland Mail, 1857–1869,* 3 vols. (Glendale, Calif.: The Arthur H. Clark Company, 1947). Historians such as the Conklings who state that the fourth partner was the National Express are in error.

 11. Robert J. Chandler, "The California News-Telegraph Monopoly, 1860–1870," *Southern California Quarterly* 57 (Winter 1976): 459–84.

 12. *Alta,* December 1, 1860; *Evening Bulletin* (San Francisco), July 30, 1860; *Reports of the Explorations and Surveys to Ascertain the Most Practicable and Economical Route for a Railroad from the Mississippi River to the Pacific Ocean,* 13 vols. (Washington, D.C.: U.S. House of Representatives, 1855); David A. White, ed., *News of the Plains and Rockies, 1803–1865,* vol. 6, *Gold Seekers, California, 1849–1859, and Railroad Forerunners, 1850–1865* (Spokane: The Arthur H. Clark Company, 1999); Ward McAfee, *California's Railroad Era, 1850–1911* (San Marino, Calif.: Golden West Books, 1973); George Kraus, *High Road to Promontory* (Palo Alto, Calif.: American West Publishing Company, 1969); and Mead B. Kibbey, *The Railroad Photographs of Alfred A. Hart, Artist* (Sacramento: The California State Library Foundation, 1996).

 13. Clear Creek, January 29, 1850, letter fragment in Robert J. Chandler collection. See Sherburne F. Cook, *The Population of the California Indians, 1769–1970* (Berkeley: University of California Press, 1976). David Henige, in his book *Numbers from Nowhere: The American Indian Contact Population Debate* (Norman: University of Oklahoma Press, 1998), challenges the "high counters" such as Cook. See also Robert J. Chandler, "The Failure of Reform: White Attitudes and Indian Response in California during the Civil War Era," *Pacific Historian* 24 (September 1980): 284–94; James J. Rawls, *Indians of California: The Changing Image* (Norman: University of Oklahoma Press, 1984); and C. H. [Joaquin] Miller, *Life amongst the Modocs: Unwritten History* (1873; reprint, Berkeley: Heyday Books, 1996).

 14. Townsend, *Diary,* 67; Chief Pasqual quoted in newspaper of July 18, 1852, 146; *San Francisco Pacific Appeal,* April 26, 1873. See Albert L. Hurtado, *Indian Survival on the California Frontier* (New Haven: Yale University Press, 1988); George Harwood Phillips, *Indians and Indian Agents: The Origins of the Reservation System in California* (Norman: University of Oklahoma Press, 1997); Michele Shover, "John Bidwell and the Rancho Chico Indian Treaty of 1852: Seduction, Betrayal, and Redemption," *Dogtown Territorial Quarterly,* no. 42 (Summer 2000): 4–24, 32–39; Lynwood Carranco and Estle Beard, *Genocide and Vendetta: The Round Valley Wars of Northern California* (Norman: University of Oklahoma Press, 1981); Todd Benson, "The Consequences of Reservation Life: Native Californians on the Round Valley Reservation, 1871–1884," *Pacific Historical Review* 60 (May 1991): 221–44; Gerald Thompson, *Edward F. Beale and the American West* (Albuquerque: University of New Mexico Press, 1983); J. Ross Browne and James Y. McDuffie, *The Management of the Indians and Their Reservations in California,* Ex. Doc. 46, 36th Cong., 1st sess. (1860); David Michael Goodman, *A Western Panorama 1849–1875: The Travels, Writings, and Influence of J. Ross Browne* (Glendale, Calif.: The Arthur H. Clark Company, 1966); Michael A. Sievers, "Funding the

California Indians Superintendency: A Case Study of Congressional Appropriations," *Southern California Quarterly* 59 (Spring 1977): 49–73; Robert J. Chandler, "José Chico: Bearing a Bi-Cultural Burden," *Dogtown Territorial Quarterly*, no. 32 (Winter 1997): 54–63; and Helen Hunt Jackson, *Ramona* (1884), and see Antoinette May, *The Annotated Ramona* (San Carlos, Calif.: Wide World Publishers, 1989).

15. Phillips, *Indians and Indian Agents*, 186; Royal T. Sprague, *Report of the Committee on Indian Affairs on the Claims of [Captain B.] Wright and [Charles] McDermitt's Command* (Sacramento: George Kerr, State Printer, 1853), Doc. 33 of the Appendix of the Senate Journal, p. 3; Michele Shover, "John Bidwell: Reluctant Indian Fighter, 1852–1856," *Dogtown Territorial Quarterly* (Winter 1998): 32–56; Shover, "The Politics of the 1859 Bidwell-Kibbe Campaign: Northern California Indian-Settler Conflicts of the 1850s," *Dogtown Territorial Quarterly* (Summer 1999): 4–39; *Reports from the Senate Finance Committee, on Senate Bill No. 206 [Concerning Indian War Bonds, 1851–1853]* (Sacramento: Benjamin P. Avery, State Printer, 1862); Joseph Ellison, *California and the Nation*, 54–78; *Majority and Minority Reports of the Special Joint Committee on the Mendocino War*, Rept. 11 in the *Appendix to Journals of Assembly, of the Eleventh Session of the Legislature of the State of California* (Sacramento: State Printer, 1860); Robert A. Anderson, *Fighting the Mill Creeks* (Chico, Calif.: The Chico Record Press, 1909); Sim Moak, *The Last of the Mill Creeks and Early Life in Northern California* (Chico: n.p., 1923); and Theodora Kroeber, *Ishi in Two Worlds* (Berkeley: University of California Press, 1965).

16. *Pacific Appeal*, September 27, 1873. See Carl P. Schlicke, *General George Wright: Guardian of the Pacific Coast* (Norman: University of Oklahoma Press, 1988); Leo P. Kibby, *California, the Civil War, and the Indian Problem* (reprinted from April and July 1965 issues of the *Journal of the West*, 1967); Edwards, "Department of the Pacific"; Keith A. Murray, *The Modocs and Their War* (Norman: University of Oklahoma Press, 1959); and Arthur Quinn, *Hell with the Fire Out: A History of the Modoc War* (Winchester, Mass.: Faber and Faber, 1997).

17. See Rodman W. Paul, *California Gold* (1947; reprint, Lincoln: University of Nebraska Press, 1965); Charles Howard Shinn, *Land Laws of Mining Districts* (Baltimore: Johns Hopkins University, December 1884), and Shinn, *Mining Camps: A Study in American Frontier Government* (1885; reprint, New York: Alfred A. Knopf, 1948); John S. Hittell, *Mining in the Pacific States of North America* (San Francisco: H. H. Bancroft and Co., 1861); Gregory Yale, *Legal Titles to Mining Claims and Water Rights in California, under the Mining Law of Congress, of July, 1866* (San Francisco: A. Roman & Co., 1867); John F. Davis, "The History of the Mining Laws of California," in *History of the Bench and Bar of California*, ed. Oscar T. Shuck (Los Angeles: The Commercial Printing House, 1901), 278–331; Joseph Ellison, *California and the Nation*, 54–78; Ray August, "*Gringos v. Mineros:* The Hispanic Origins of Western American Mining Law," *Western Legal History* 9 (Summer–Fall 1996): 147–75; Donald J. Pisani, "The Origins of Western Water Law: Case Studies from Two California Mining Districts," *California History* 70 (Fall 1991): 242–57, 325, and Pisani, "'I am resolved not to interfere, but permit all to work freely': The Gold Rush and American Resource Law," *California History* 77 (Winter 1998–99): 123–48.

18. Hittell, *Mining*, 212; Davis, "Mining Laws," 304; *Bulletin*, December 30, 1862; John S. Hittell, "The Necessity of Selling the Mineral Lands of California," *Hesperian* 3 (January 1860): 492–502; see also *New York Tribune*, March 17, 1858.

19. Usher correspondence in microfilmed Robert Todd Lincoln Papers, 23343–4, 2357–8; Richard C. Drum, July 8, 1863, telegram to Colonel Henry M. Black, in *The War of the Re-*

bellion: A Compilation of the Official Records of the Union and Confederate Armies, vol. 50 (Washington, D.C.: 1880–1901), pt. 2, 514; Frederick F. Low to Secretary of Treasury Salmon P. Chase, Robert Todd Lincoln Papers, 24721; Ira P. Rankin, July 11, 1863, to President Lincoln, Robert Todd Lincoln Papers, 24757–8; John G. Downey's address is in *Marysville Express,* July 25, 1863; President Abraham Lincoln, August 22, 1863, to General Daniel E Sickles, in Roy P. Basler, ed., *The Collected Works of Abraham Lincoln,* vol. 6 (New Brunswick, N.J.: Rutgers University Press, 1953), 402. See also Samuel C. Wiel, *Lincoln's Crisis in the Far West* (San Francisco: n.p., 1949); Kenneth M. Johnson, *The New Almaden Quicksilver Mine* (Georgetown, Calif.: The Talisman Press, 1963); Milton H. Shutes, "Abraham Lincoln and the New Almaden Mine," *California Historical Society Quarterly* 15 (March 1936): 3–20; and Jimmie Schneider, *Quicksilver* (San Jose: Zella Schneider, 1992).

20. Interior Department memo quoted in Castine [Noah Brooks], Washington, March 14, 1864, in *Sacramento Union,* April 12, 1864; *Sacramento Union,* September 3, 1864; Gary D. Libecap, "Government Support of Private Claims to Public Minerals: Western Mineral Rights," *Business History Review* 53 (Autumn 1979): 364–85. See also J. Ross Browne and James W. Taylor, *Reports upon the Mineral Resources of the United States* (Washington, D.C.: Government Printing Office, 1867); J. Ross Browne, *Mineral Resources of the States and Territories West of the Rocky Mountains, 1868* (San Francisco: H. H. Bancroft and Co., 1869); Rossiter W. Raymond, *Mining Statistics West of the Rocky Mountains,* 8 vols. (Washington, D.C.: Government Printing Office, 1869–1877). Without congressional support, later volumes have limited usefulness.

21. Joseph Ellison, *California and the Nation,* 25–53; Richard H. Peterson, "The Failure to Reclaim: California State Swamp Land Policy and the Sacramento Valley, 1850–1860," *Southern California Quarterly* 56 (Spring 1974): 45–60; John Swett, *Thirteenth Annual Report of the Superintendent of Public Instruction . . . for the Year 1863* (Sacramento: O. M. Clayes, State Printer, 1863), 8, and Swett, *History of the Public School System of California* (San Francisco: A. L. Bancroft and Co., 1876), 19–37, and passim.

22. White, *"It's Your Misfortune,"* 137–54; *Visalia Delta,* April 23, 1863; Richard J. Orsi, "The Octopus Reconsidered: The Southern Pacific and Agricultural Modernization in California, 1865–1915," *California Historical Quarterly* 54 (Fall 1975): 197–220.

23. *Sacramento Union,* October 1, 1858; *Marysville Appeal,* May 21, 1863.

24. General Land Office, May 10, 1867, to Register and Receiver, Carson City, "Case of Frances Straskel vs. Benjamin Sears, Administrator of Richard J. Gilman, deceased," fair copy in Robert J. Chandler collection.

25. Henry W. Halleck, *Report on the Laws and Regulations Relative to Grants and Sales of Public Lands in California,* March 1, 1849, House Ex. Doc. 17, 31st Cong., 1st sess. (1850), 119–22; William Carey Jones, *Report on the Subject of Land Titles in California,* Senate Ex. Doc. 18, 31st Cong., 1st sess. (March 9, 1850), 34 (emphasis in the original); W. W. Robinson, *Land in California* (Berkeley: University of California Press, 1948); Robert H. Becker, *Diseños of California Ranchos: Maps of Thirty-Seven Land Grants (1822–1846) from the Records of the U.S. District Court, San Francisco* (San Francisco: Book Club of California, 1964), and Becker, *Designs on the Land: Diseños of California Ranchos and Their Makers* (San Francisco: Book Club of California, 1969); Crisostomo N. Perez, *Land Grants in Alta California: A Compilation of Spanish and Mexican Private Land Claims in the State of California* (Rancho Cordova, Calif.: Landmark Enterprises, 1996); Robert Glass Cleland, *The Cattle on a Thousand Hills: Southern California, 1850–1870,* rev. ed. (San Marino, Calif.: The Huntington Li-

brary, 1951); and Lawrence James Jelinek, "'Property of Every Kind': Ranching and Farming during the Gold-Rush Era," *California History* 77 (Winter 1998–99): 233–49.

26. *Speech of Mr. Gwin, of California, on Land Claims in California, Delivered in the Senate of the United States, August 2, 1852* (Washington, D.C.: Congressional Globe Office, 1852), 6–7.

27. John S. Hittell, "Mexican Land-Claims in California," *Hutchings' California Magazine* 2 (April 1858): 442–48 (quotes, 446–47); Charles A. Barker, ed., *Memoirs of Elisha Oscar Crosby* (San Marino, Calif.: The Huntington Library, 1945), 115; Barker, "Elisha Oscar Crosby: A California Lawyer in the Eighteen-Fifties," *California Historical Society Quarterly* 27 (June 1948): 133–40; *Donald E. Rowland, John Rowland, and William Workman: Southern California Pioneers of 1841* (Spokane: The Arthur H. Clark Company, 1999), 121; Huntington Manuscript 40520; Leonard Pitt, *The Decline of the Californios: A Social History of the Spanish-Speaking Californians, 1846–1890* (Berkeley: University of California Press 1998), 83–119; Beverly E. Bastian, "'I Heartily Regret that I ever Touched a Title in California': Henry W. Halleck, the Californios, and the Clash of Legal Cultures," *California History* 72 (Winter 1993–94): 310–23, 387–88, expands on Pitt; and Paul Bryan Gray, *Forster vs. Pico: The Struggle for the Rancho Santa Margarita* (Spokane: The Arthur H. Clark Company, 1998).

28. Barker, *Memoirs of Elisha Crosby*, 70; Paul W. Gates, "California's Embattled Settlers," *California Historical Society Quarterly* 51 (June 1962): 99–130, Gates, "Pre-Henry George Land Warfare in California," *California Historical Society Quarterly* 46 (June 1967): 121–48, Gates, "The California Land Act of 1851," *California Historical Quarterly* 50 (December 1971): 395–430, Gates, "Carpetbaggers Join the Rush for California Land," *California Historical Quarterly* 56 (Summer 1977): 98–127, collected in *Land and Law in California: Essays on Land Policies* (Ames: Iowa State University Press, 1991); Joseph M. Petulla, "Paul Wallace Gates: Historian of Public Land Policy," *California Historical Quarterly* 56 (Summer 1977): 170–74; Paul W. Gates, ed. and comp., *California Ranchos and Farms, 1846–1862* [descriptions from the *San Francisco California Farmer*] (Madison: The State Historical Society of Wisconsin, 1967); Donald J. Pisani, "Squatter Law in California, 1850–1858," *Western Historical Quarterly* 25 (Autumn 1994): 277–310.

29. *Frémont v. U.S.*, 58 U.S. (17 Howard) 442 (1854), 558; Hoffman is quoted in Gates, "Embattled Settlers," 126; Christian G. Fritz, *Federal Justice in California: The Court of Ogden Hoffman, 1851–1891* (Lincoln: University of Nebraska Press, 1991), 134–79. See also Ogden Hoffman, *Reports of Land Cases Determined in the United States District Court for the Northern District of California, June Term 1853 to June Term 1858* (San Francisco: Numa Hubert, 1862, and reprinted 1975); Lewis Grossman, "John C. Frémont, Mariposa, and the Collision of Mexican and American Law," *Western Legal History* 6 (Winter–Spring 1993): 16–50; Arthur R. Abel, *Preliminary Inventory of the Records of the United States District Court Northern District of California, San Francisco, 1851–1950* (National Archives, San Francisco Region, 1964); George Cosgrave, *Early California Justice: The History of the United States District Court for the Southern District of California, 1849–1944* (San Francisco: The Grabhorn Press, 1948); and the Ninth District Court's historical journal, *The Historical Reporter*, 1981, and its 1988 successor, *Western Legal History*.

30. *Expenditures on Account of Private Land Claims in California*, House Ex. Doc. 84, 36th Cong., 1st sess. (1860), 30–31; John Norton Pomeroy, *Some Account of the Work of Stephen J. Field* (San Francisco: n.p., 1881; reprinted, 1895; 1986); Carl Brent Swisher, *Stephen J. Field: Craftsman of the Law* (Washington, D.C.: The Brookings Institution, 1930); Paul Kens, *Jus-*

tice Stephen Field: Shaping Liberty from the Gold Rush to the Gilded Age (Lawrence: University Press of Kansas, 1997); Henry George, *Our Land and Land Policy: What It Is, and What It Should Be,* July 27, 1871 (n.p.: W. E. Loomis, 1871); John S. Hittell, *All about California and the Inducements to Settle There* (San Francisco: The California Immigrant Union, 1870); Gordon Morris Bakken, "Mexican and American Land Policy: A Conflict of Cultures," *Southern California Quarterly* 75 (Fall–Winter 1993): 237–62; and KD Kurutz and Gary F. Kurutz, *California Calls You: The Art of Promoting the Golden State, 1870 to 1940* (Sausalito, Calif.: Windgate Press, 2000).

31. William Penn Moody, "The Civil War and Reconstruction in California Politics" (Ph.D. diss., University of California, Los Angeles, 1950); *Register of Officers and Agents, Civil, Military, and Naval, in the Service of the United States, as of September . . .* (Washington, D.C.: Government Printing Office, odd-numbered years); *The State Register and Year Book of Facts: For the Year 1857* (San Francisco: Henry G. Langley, Samuel A. Mathews, and James Queen, 1857), 46–51; Norman E. Tutorow, "A Tale of Two Hospitals: U.S. Marine Hospital no. 19, and the U.S. Public Health Service Hospital on the Presidio of San Francisco," *California History* 75 (Summer 1996): 154–69, 184–87.

32. Leonard Noyes, San Francisco, December 7, 1860, to Richard J. Jaques, Robert J. Chandler collection; see Moody, "The Civil War and Reconstruction in California Politics," 263–71.

33. Gwin quotation, Sacramento, January 11, 1857, in James O'Meara, *Broderick and Gwin* (San Francisco: Bacon & Company, 1881), 212; *San Francisco Bulletin,* June 29, 1859.

34. Thomas Brown, October 28, 1862, to Salmon P. Chase; Chase mss., Library of Congress; *Sacramento Union,* January 28, February 4, 1863.

35. *U.S. Customs and Kindred Services, San Francisco, 1915* (U.S. Customs Service, Historical Study no. 7, March 1988); Arthur R. Abel, *Preliminary Inventory of the Records of the District Director of Customs San Francis District and of the Deputy Collectors for the Ports of Eureka and Monterey* (National Archives, San Francisco Region, 1969); U.S. Customs House, Ledger, 1854–1855, Huntington Library Manuscript 35253, pictured in Peter Blodgett, *Land of Golden Dreams: California in the Gold Rush Decade, 1848–1858* (San Marino, Calif.: The Huntington Library, 1999), 119. See also Katherine Coman, *Economic Beginnings of the Far West* (New York: The Macmillan Company, 1925), and Thomas Senior Berry, *Early California Gold, Prices, Trade* (Richmond, Calif.: The Bostwick Press, 1984).

36. *Report of the Joint Select Committee on Retrenchment,* Senate Rept. 47, 41st Cong., 2d sess. (1870), 58–59, 79, 103–107.

37. *Retrenchment,* 113, 151; The Israelites of San Francisco, *Dr. John T. McLean and the Israelites: Unfounded and Gross Slander* (San Francisco: n.p., 1870), reprinted in Robert J. Chandler, "That Lurking Prejudice, 1869–1870," *Western States Jewish History* 27 (July 1995): 205–13; Samuel Purdy, *Report on Internal Revenue—California,* 41st Cong., 1st sess. House Ex. Doc. 6. (1869), 11; Richard H. Dillon, "J. Ross Browne and the Corruptible West," *American West* 2 (Spring 1965): 37–45.

38. Edgar H. Adams, *Private Gold Coinage of California, 1849–1855: Its History and Its Issues* (New York: Edgar H. Adams, 1913), vi–ix.

39. Donald H. Kagin, *Private Gold Coins and Patterns of the United States* (New York: Arco Publishing, 1981); *The Brasher Bulletin: Newsletter of the Society of Private and Pioneer Numismatics;* Walter Breen and Ronald J. Gillio, *California Pioneer Fractional Gold* (Santa Barbara, Calif.: Pacific Coast Auction Galleries, 1983); and Robert J. Chandler, *San Francisco*

Clearing House Certificates: Last of California's Private Money (Reno: McDonald Publishing, 1986).

40. Brian McGinty, *Haraszthy at the Mint* (Los Angeles: Dawson's Book Shop, 1975); Brian McGinty, *Strong Wine: The Life and Legend of Agoston Haraszthy* (Stanford: Stanford University Press, 1998); *Laws of the United States Relating to the Coinage* (Washington, D.C.: Government Printing Office, 1897, and reprinted); Thomas W. Wadlow et al., *Preliminary Inventory of the Records of the United States Mint Redesignated in 1962, United States Assay Office San Francisco* (National Archives, San Francisco Region, [ca. 1968]); "Coining Money at the San Francisco Branch Mint," *Hutchings' California Magazine* 1 (October 1856): 145–53, and reprinted in Roger R. Olmsted, ed., *Scenes of Wonder & Curiosity* (Berkeley: Howell-North Press, 1962), 61–69; Ira B. Cross, *Financing an Empire: History of Banking in California,* 4 vols. (Chicago: S. J. Clarke Publishing Co., 1927); Q. David Bowers, *The History of United States Coinage as Illustrated by the Garrett Collection* (Los Angeles: Bowers & Ruddy Galleries, 1979); Q. David Bowers, *The Treasure Ship S.S. Brother Jonathan: Her Life and Loss, 1850–1865* (Wolfeboro, N.Y.: Bowers and Merena Galleries, 1999); Bowers and Merena Galleries, "The S.S. *Brother Jonathan* Treasure Coins," Sale, Los Angeles, May 29, 1999; and William A. Bullough, "Eadweard Muybridge and the Old San Francisco Mint: Archival Photographs as Historical Documents," *California History* 68 (Spring–Summer 1989): 2–13, 59–60.

41. Wells Fargo Bank has a collection of letters of recommendation for deserving women from the 1860s and 1870s. None of the applicants were hired, as far as I could determine from the city directories.

42. *Report of the Committee Appointed by the Chamber of Commerce of San Francisco, To Report on the Condition of Our Postal Affairs and to Consider the Feasibility of Improvements and Reforms, San Francisco, September [16], 1864* (San Francisco: Waters Brothers & Co., 1864), 8; Wesley Clair Mitchell, *A History of the Greenbacks* (Chicago: The University of Chicago Press, 1903); Joseph Ellison, *California and the Nation,* 208–30, and "The Currency Question on the Pacific Coast during the Civil War," *Mississippi Valley Historical Review* 16 (June 1929): 50–66; Gordon Bakken, "Law and Legal Tender in California and the West," *Southern California Quarterly* 62 (Fall 1980): 239–59; D. W. Cheesman, *The National Currency . . . An Address . . . on February 8, 1864* (Washington, D.C.: Judd & Detweiler, Printers, 1869).

43. Allen Weinstein, *Prelude to Populism: Origins of the Silver Issue, 1867–1878* (New Haven: Yale University Press, 1970); John M. Willem, Jr., *The United States Trade Dollar: America's Only Unwanted, Unhonored Coin* (New York: 1959; reprinted 1965); and J. Laurence Laughlin, *The History of Bimetalism in the United States* (New York: D. Appleton & Co., 1896).

44. From Zachary Taylor's *Report,* January 24, 1850, 932–52, transcribed in Walter N. Frickstad, *A Century of California Post Offices* (Oakland, Calif.: Philatelic Research Society, 1955), 372–95; *California Statutes 1854,* pp. 272–74. See also Wayne E. Fuller, *The American Mail: Enlarger of the Common Life* (Chicago: University of Chicago Press, 1972); Marshall Cushing, *The Story of Our Post Office: The Greatest Government Department in All Its Phases* (Boston: A. M. Thayer & Co., 1893); James H. Bruns, *Mail on the Move* (Polo, Ill.: Transportation Trails, 1992); Jesse L. Coburn, *Letters of Gold: California Postal History through 1869* (Canton, Ohio: U.S. Philatelic Classics Society, 1984); "The History of a Letter," *Hutchings' California Magazine* 2 (January 1858): 289–300, reprinted in Olmsted, *Scenes of Wonder,* 25–34. See also Harold E. Salley, *History of California Post Offices, 1849–1990,* 2d ed., edited

by Edward L. Patera (Lake Grove, Ore.: The Depot, 1991); Fannie Smith Spurling, ed., *Postmarked Vermont and California, 1862–1864* (Rutland, Vt.: The Tuttle Publishing Co., 1940); and Alan H. Patera, ed., *Your Obedient Servant: The Letters of Quincy A. Brooks, Special Agent of the Post Office Department, 1865–1867* (Lake Oswego, Ore.: Raven Press, 1986).

45. Cedric Ridgely-Nevitt, *American Steamships on the Atlantic [and the Pacific]* (Newark: University of Delaware Press, 1981); Ernest A. Wiltsee, *Gold Rush Steamers of the Pacific* (San Francisco: The Grabhorn Press, 1938; reprinted 1976); Milton S. Latham, *Steamship Line from California to China, April 10, 1862* (Washington, D.C.: McGill, Witherow & Co., Printers, 1862); John Haskell Kemble, *Side-Wheelers across the Pacific* (San Francisco: Museum of Science and Industry, 1942), and Kemble, *A Hundred Years of the Pacific Mail* (Newport News, Va.: The Mariners' Museum, 1950); David J. St. Clair, "New Almaden and California Quicksilver in the Pacific Rim Economy," *California History* 73 (Winter 1994–1995): 278–95, 336–37; Rodman W. Paul, "The Beginnings of Agriculture in California: Innovation vs. Continuity," *California Historical Quarterly* 52 (Spring 1973): 16–27, and Paul, "The Wheat Trade between California and the United Kingdom," *Mississippi Valley Historical Review* 45 (December 1958): 391–412; W. A. Starr, "Abraham Dubois Starr: Pioneer California Miller and Wheat Exporter," *California Historical Society Quarterly* 27 (September 1948): 192–202; Daniel Meissner, "Bridging the Pacific: California and the China Flour Trade, "*California History* 76 (Winter 1997–1998): 82–93, 148–50; Captain William Banning and George Hugh Banning, *Six Horses* (New York: The Century Co., 1930); Oscar O. Winther, *Express and Stagecoach Days in California* (Stanford: Stanford University Press, 1936); Mae Hélène Bacon Boggs, comp., *My Playhouse Was a Concord Coach* (Oakland, Calif.: Howell-North Press, 1942); Ralph Moody, *Stagecoach West* (New York: Thomas Y. Crowell Co., 1967); John M. Townley, *The Overland Stage: A History and Guidebook* (Reno: Jamison Station Press, 1994); and A. C. W. Bethel, "The Golden Skein: California's Gold-Rush Transportation Network," *California History* 77 (Winter 1998–1999): 250–75.

46. *California Farmer,* November 8, 1861. See also Coburn, *Letters of Gold;* Ernest A. Wiltsee, *The Pioneer Miner and the Pack Mule Express* (San Francisco: California Historical Society, 1931); *Western Express,* the quarterly publication of the Western Cover Society; and John F. Leutzinger, *The Handstamps of Wells, Fargo & Co., 1852 to 1895,* 2d ed. (San Francisco: Western Cover Society, 1993).

47. *Report of the Committee Appointed by the Chamber of Commerce,* 4, 18; Diane DeBlois and Robert Dalton Harris, "Letter Boxes: Street and Home," *P.S. No. 21: A Quarterly Journal of Postal History* 6 (January 1984): 20–31; Cushing, *Our Post Office,* 498–99; Roger R. Rhoads, "The Free Delivery System in the Nineteenth Century," *American Philatelist* 113 (November 1999): 1072–77.

48. Postmaster-General T. O. Howe, circular, December 2, 1882, quoted in a Wells, Fargo & Co. circular, March 31, 1883, Orders Relative to Letter Service. See *Report of a Committee [on March 9] Appointed by the Postmaster-General January 5, 1880, to Take into Consideration the Matter of the Letter-Express Business of Wells, Fargo & Co., as Shown by Letter of Special Agent B. K. Sharretts, Dated December 31, 1879* [No publication data]; *Argument before Hon. D. M. Key, Postmaster General, by Hon. Horace F. Page, of California. The Origin, Methods, and Important Public Uses of the Letter Service of Wells, Fargo & Company* (Washington: Judd & Detweiler, Printers, 1880); Wells, Fargo & Co., *Wells, Fargo & Co.'s Letter Express, San Francisco, April 20, 1880, to Hon. D. M. Key.*

49. *Speech of the Hon. F. M. Pixley at the Ratification Meeting Held at Platt's Hall, on Thurs-*

day Evening, September 13, 1864 (San Francisco: n.p., 1864), 6. See Milton H. Shutes, *Lincoln and California* (Stanford: Stanford University Press, 1943); Oscar Lewis, *The War in the Far West, 1861–1865* (Garden City, N.Y.: Doubleday & Co., 1961); Alvin M. Josephy, Jr., *The Civil War in the American West* (New York: Alfred A. Knopf, 1991); Robert J. Chandler, "The Press and Civil Liberties in California during the Civil War, 1861–1865" (Ph.D. diss., University of California, Riverside, 1978), Chandler, "Fighting Words: Censoring Civil War California Journalism," *The Californians* 8 (May–June 1990): 46–57, Chandler, "Democratic Turmoil: California during the Civil War Years," *Dogtown Territorial Quarterly* 31 (Fall 1997): 32–46, and Chandler, "Private Feelings: Californians View the Civil War, *Dogtown Territorial Quarterly* 31 (Fall 1997): 47–53.

50. Robert J. Chandler, "The Velvet Glove: The Army during the Secession Crisis in California, 1860–1861," *Journal of the West* 20 (October 1981): 35–42.

51. See Aurora Hunt, *The Army of the Pacific* (Glendale, Calif.: The Arthur H. Clark Company, 1951); Glenn Thomas Edwards, Jr., "The Department of the Pacific in the Civil War Years" (Ph.D. diss., University of Oregon, 1963), the finest work on military California; *War of the Rebellion*, ser. 1, vol. 50, pts. 1 and 2; *Reports of the Adjutant-General of the State of California* (Sacramento: State Printer) found in Appendices to the Legislative Journals; Richard H. Orton, *Records of California Men in the War of the Rebellion, 1861–1867* (Sacramento: State Printing Office, 1890, reprinted 1978), and J. Carlisle Parker, comp., *A Personal Name Index to . . .* (Detroit: Gale Research Company, 1978); Wayne Colwell, "The California Hundred," *The Pacific Historian* 13 (Summer 1969): 63–75; John Phillip Langellier and Wayne Colwell, "Cavaliers from California," *Gateway Heritage* 5 (Winter 1984–1985): 16–21; The Madera Method [6th grade] Historians of Kentfield, Madera, and Modesto, *The Civil War Diary of Samuel James Corbett* (Madera, Calif.: The Classroom Chronicles Press, 1992); Larry and Keith Rogers, "The California Hundred," forthcoming; Gunter Barth, ed., *All Quiet on the Yamhill: The Civil War in Oregon, the Journal of Corporal Royal A. Bensell, Company D, Fourth California Infantry* (Eugene: University of Oregon Books, 1959); Dorothy Clora Cragen, *The Boys in the Sky-Blue Pants: The Men and Events at Camp Independence and Forts of Eastern California, Nevada and Utah, 1862–1877* (Fresno, Calif.: Pioneer Publishing Co., 1975); *Butte County Historical Society Diggin's* 28 (Spring 1984); Edward Carlson, "The Martial Experiences of the California Volunteers," *Overland Monthly,* 2d ser., 7 (May 1886): 480–96; Lewis Albert Lucian, "Los Angeles in the Civil War Decades, 1850–1868" (Ph.D. diss., University of Southern California, 1970); John W. Robinson, *Los Angeles in Civil War Days* (Los Angeles: Dawson's Book Shop, 1977); Don McDowell, *The Beat of the Drum: The History, Events and People of Drum Barracks, Wilmington, California* (Wilmington, Calif.: Drum Barracks, 1993); Dennis G. Casebier, *Tales of the Mojave Road: Carleton's Pah-Ute Campaign; The Battle at Camp Cady; Camp Rock Spring, California; Fort Pah-Ute, California; The Mohave Road; The Mojave Road in Newspapers* (Norco, Calif.: Tales of the Mojave Road Publishing Co., 1972–1976); *Volunteer Troops for Guarding the Overland and Inland Mail and Emigrant Routes,* Senate Ex. Doc. 70, 50th Cong., 2d sess., 1889; John C. Cremony, *Life among the Apaches, 1850–1868* (San Francisco: A. Roman & Co., 1868, reprinted 1969); Darlis A. Miller, *The California Column in New Mexico* (Albuquerque: University of New Mexico Press, 1982); Robert Lee Kerby, *The Confederate Invasion of New Mexico and Arizona, 1861–1862* (Tucson: Westernlore Press, 1958, reprinted 1981); L. Boyd Finch, *Confederate Pathway to the Pacific: Major Sherod Hunter and Arizona Territory, C.S.A.* (Tucson: Arizona Historical Society, 1996); Lawrence R. Murphy, "The Enemy Among

Us: Venereal Disease among Union Soldiers in the Far West, 1861–1865," *Civil War History* 31 (September 1985): 257–69; E. B. "Pete" Long, *The Saints and the Union: Utah Territory during the Civil War* (Urbana: University of Illinois Press, 1981); James F. Varley, *Brigham and the Brigadier: General Patrick Connor and His California Volunteers in Utah and along the Overland Trail* (Tucson: Westernlore Press, 1989); Brigham D. Madsen, *Glory Hunter: A Biography of Patrick Edward Connor* (Salt Lake City: University of Utah Press, 1990); CAMP *Headquarters Heliogram,* February 1997, p. 5; Hunt, *Carleton,* 305–323, 368–70; *Rebellion War Claims of California, Oregon, and Nevada,* 52d Cong., 1st sess. House Rept. 254, 1892; *The State of California v. The United States,* in the United States Court of Claims, no. 49912, Decided March 2, 1954; Rudolph M. Lapp, "Blacks in Civil War California," in *California and the Civil War 1861–1865,* ed. Robert J. Chandler, Book Club of California 1992 Keepsake Series, no. 2; Chandler, "Press and Civil Liberties," 220.

52. Winfield J. Davis, *History of Political Conventions in California, 1849–1892* (Sacramento: California State Library, 1893), 166–67. *War of the Rebellion,* ser. 2, vol. 4, 359; ser. 3, vol. 2, 321; vol. 50, pt. 2, 211. Department of the Pacific, Letters Sent, vol. 11, 191–93, 206, Record Group 393, National Archives; Robert J. Chandler, "Crushing Dissent: The Pacific Coast Tests Lincoln's Policy of Suppression, 1862," *Civil War History* 30 (September 1984): 235–54; Chandler, "Democratic Turmoil," 32–38; Mark E. Neely, Jr., *The Fate of Liberty: Abraham Lincoln and Civil Liberties* (New York: Oxford University Press, 1991).

53. Robert J. Chandler, "The Release of the *Chapman* Pirates: A California Sidelight on Lincoln's Amnesty Policy," *Civil War History* 23 (June 1977): 129–43, Chandler, "Success to Civil War Tragedy: The Greathouse Brothers of Greathouse & Slicer's Express," *Western Express* 46 (March 1996): 4–13, and Chandler, "California's 1863 Loyalty Oath: Another Look," *Arizona and the West* 21 (Autumn 1979): 215–34.

54. Robert J. Chandler, "Vigilante Rebirth: The Civil War Union League," *The Argonaut: Journal of the San Francisco Historical Society* 3 (Winter 1992): 10–18.

55. Robert J. Chandler, "Friends in Time of Need: Republicans and Black Civil Rights in California during the Civil War Era," *Arizona and the West* 24 (Winter 1982): 319–40; Rudolph M. Lapp, *Blacks in Gold Rush California* (New Haven: Yale University Press, 1977, reprinted 1997); and Quintard Taylor, *In Search of the Racial Frontier: African Americans in the American West, 1528–1990* (New York: W. W. Norton, 1998).

56. Robert J. Chandler, "Fort Alcatraz: Symbol of Federal Power," *Periodical: Journal of the Council on America's Military Past* 13 (May 1985): 27–47; John A. Martini, *Fortress Alcatraz: Guardian of the Golden Gate* (Kailua, Hawaii: Pacific Monograph, 1990), and Martini, "Search and Destroy [Or, the Discovery of 1864 Alcatraz Photographs]," *American Heritage* 43 (November 1992): 98–103.

57. *Alta,* May 22, 1866; John A. Russell, comp., "Monitor 'Camanche,'" in the appendix to *San Francisco Municipal Reports for the Fiscal Year 1880–1881* (San Francisco: Geo. Spalding & Co., 1881), 63–78; Robert Ryal Miller, "The *Camanche:* First Monitor of the Pacific," *California Historical Society Quarterly* 45 (June 1966): 113–24.

58. *San Francisco American Flag,* May 5, 1864; William W. Chipman, Diary, May 21, 24, 25, 1864, Society of California Pioneers, San Francisco.

59. *San Francisco American Flag,* July 22, 1864; Department of the Pacific, Letters Sent, vol. 13, 29–30.

60. *Sonora Union Democrat,* February 18, 1865; Robert Ryal Miller, "Californians against the Emperor," *California Historical Society Quarterly* 37 (September 1958): 193–214; Miller, "Arms

Across the Border: United States Aid to Juarez during the French Intervention in Mexico," *Transactions of the American Philosophical Society*, n.s., 63, pt. 6 (1973); Collector of the Port Charles James, letterbook, "Correspondence &c. Relating to the Attempted Export of Arms from San Francisco, 1864," Bancroft Library, University of California, Berkeley; Plácido Vega, mss., Bancroft Library; Benjamin Franklin Gilbert, "Welcome to the Czar's Fleet," *California Historical Society Quarterly* 26 (March 1947): 13–19; Raphael Semmes, *Memoirs of Service Afloat* (1868; reprint, Baton Rouge: Louisiana State University Press, 1996); James I. Waddell, *C.S.S. Shenandoah*, ed. James D. Horan (New York: Crown Publishers, 1960). Chester G. Hearn, *Gray Raiders of the Sea: How Eight Confederate Warships Destroyed the Union's High Seas Commerce* (Baton Rouge: Louisiana State University Press, 1992), is the best overall work.

61. *Alta*, April 17, 1865; *War of the Rebellion*, vol. 50, pt. 2, 1198; *John McCall v. I. McDowell*, Judge's Note of Evidence, March 15–30, filed April 26, 1867, Record Group 21, Series 8, Box 19, Case 197, National Archives Branch, San Bruno, Calif.; Chandler, "Press and Civil Liberties," 388–409.

62. *McCall v. McDowell*, no. 8,673, 15 Federal Cases, 1235; *Congressional Globe*, 39th Cong., 2d sess., appendix, chap. 155, p. 199 (March 2, 1867).

63. *California Statutes, 1870*, Senate Joint Resolution 10, p. 914; Robert J. Chandler, "'Anti-Coolie Rabies': The Chinese Issue in California Politics in the 1860s," *Pacific Historian* 28 (Spring 1984): 29–42; Charles J. McClain, *In Search of Equality: The Chinese Struggle against Discrimination in Nineteenth-Century America* (Berkeley: University of California Press, 1994); Senator Aaron A. Sargent, *Report of the Joint Special Committee to Investigate Chinese Immigration*, Senate Rept. 689, 44th Cong., 2d sess. (1877).

64. John S. Hittell, *Bancroft's Pacific Coast Guide Book* (San Francisco: A. L. Bancroft & Co., 1882); *Bishop's ABC Guide* 9 (March 1891): 52–96. "Stage fare, where not given, averages about 12½ cents per mile."

65. William B. Hyde, Washington, January 11, 1868, to Henry Bacon of Terminal Central Pacific Railway Company, Robert J. Chandler collection; William Hyde Irwin and Charles A. Chapin, eds., *William Birelie Hyde: The Letters of a California Engineer and [Railroad] Lobbyist of the Eighteen-Sixties and Seventies* (Stockton, Calif.: Augusta Bixler Farms, 1988); David Lavender, *The Great Persuader: The Biography of Collis P. Huntington* (Garden City, N.Y.: Doubleday & Co., 1970, reprinted 1999). Huntington's voluminous letterbooks at Syracuse University are on 115 reels of microfilm; Salvador A. Ramírez, ed., *The Octopus Speaks: The Colton Letters* (1883; reprint, Carlsbad, Calif.: Tentacled Press, 1982); Gerrit L. Lansing, Railroad Secretary and Controller, *Relations between the Central Pacific Railroad Company and the United States Government: Summary of Facts* (San Francisco: H. S. Crocker & Co., 1889); and David Igler, "The Industrial Far West: Region and Nation in the Late Nineteenth Century," *Pacific Historical Review* 69 (May 2000): 159–92.

66. Philip L. Merkel, "Railroad Consolidation and Late Nineteenth-Century Federalism: Legal Strategy in the Organization of the Southern Pacific System," *Western Legal History* 11 (Summer–Fall 1998): 215–57; Richard J. Orsi, "The Octopus Reconsidered: The Southern Pacific and Agricultural Modernization in California, 1865–1915," *California Historical Quarterly* 54 (Fall 1975): 196–220. See also Richard J. Orsi's sections on the railroad era and the confrontation at Mussel Slough in Richard B. Rice, William A. Bullough, and Orsi, *The Elusive Eden: A New History of California*, rev. ed. (New York: Alfred A. Knopf, 1996), 214–90, and his forthcoming book "A Railroad and the Development of the American West: The Southern Pacific Company, 1860–1930."

67. Joseph Jeremiah Hagwood, Jr., *Engineers at the Golden Gate: A History of the San Francisco District Army Corps of Engineers, 1866–1980* (San Francisco: U.S. Army Corps of Engineers, 1982); G. H. Mendell, *Annual Report upon the Improvement of Rivers and Harbors in California, being Appendix HH of the Annual Report of the Chief of Engineers for 1877* (Washington, D.C.: Government Printing Office, 1877); Michael R. Corbett, *Building California: Technology and the Landscape* (San Francisco: California Historical Society, 1998); Engineer Department, U.S. Army, *Report upon United States Geographical Surveys West of the One Hundredth Meridian,* Appendix F: *Memoir Upon the Voyages, Discoveries, Explorations, and Surveys . . . between 1500 and 1880* (Washington, D.C.: Government Printing Office, 1889); William H. Goetzmann, *Army Exploration in the American West, 1803–1863* (New Haven: Yale University Press, 1959); Michael L. Tate, *The Frontier Army in the Settlement of the West* (Norman: University of Oklahoma Press, 1999); Charles M. Scammon, *The Marine Mammals of the Northwestern Coast of North America* (1874; reprint, New York: Dover Publications, 1968); Lyndall B. Landauer, "Charles M. Scammon: From Seaman to Civilized Whaler to Naturalist," *California History* 61 (Spring 1982): 46–57.

68. A sampling of statistical works includes: *U.S. Census,* 1850, 1860, 1870, and 1880, on population, economy, and society; William P. Blake, ed., *Reports of the United States Commissioners to the Paris Universal Exposition, 1867,* 6 vols. (Washington, D.C.: Government Printing Office, 1870); H. D. Dunn, "California: Her Agricultural Resources," in *U.S. Commissioner of Agriculture Report, 1866* (Washington, D.C.: n.p., 1867), 581–610; Eugene W. Hilgard of the University of California, "The Agriculture and Soils of California," in *Annual Report of the Commissioner of Agriculture for the Year 1878* (Washington, D.C.: Government Printing Office, 1879), 476–507; Hilgard, "Report on the Physical and Agricultural Features of the State of California, with a Discussion on the Present and Future of Cotton Production . . ." in *Tenth Census,* 1880, vol. 6 (1883; reprinted San Francisco: Pacific Rural Press, 1883); William Hammond Hall, *Second Report of the State Engineer* (Sacramento: State Printer, 1881), pt. 4, 7; Hall mss., California Historical Society; Charles P. Korr, "William Hammond Hall: The Failure of Attempts at State Water Planning in California, 1878–1888," *Southern California Quarterly* 45 (December 1963): 305–22; Robert Kelley, *Battling the Inland Sea: American Political Culture, Public Policy, and the Sacramento Valley, 1850–1986* (Berkeley: University of California Press, 1989); *Lux, et al., v. Haggin, et al., Majority and Minority Opinions, Water and Water Rights, October 27, 1884, and April 26, 1886* (Sacramento: State Printer, 1886); Jeff R. Bremer, "The Trial of the Century: *Lux v. Haggin* and the Conflict over Water Rights in Late Nineteenth-Century California," *Southern California Quarterly* 81 (Summer 1999): 197–220; John D. Works, "Irrigation Laws and Decisions of California," in *History of the Bench and Bar of California,* ed. Shuck, 100–170; General Barton S. Alexander and Major George H. Mendell, of the Corps of Engineers, and scientist George Davidson of the Coast Survey, *Report of the Board of Commissioners on the Irrigation of the San Joaquin, Tulare, and Sacramento Valleys of the State of California,* House Ex. Doc. 290, 43d Cong., 1st sess. (1874); Mead, *Report of Irrigation Investigations in California.* Robert L. Kelley, *Gold vs. Grain: The Hydraulic Mining Controversy in California's Sacramento Valley* (Glendale, Calif.: The Arthur H. Clark Company, 1959) is classic.

69. *California Statutes, 1870,* chap. 457, p. 663; Livingston Stone, "Reports 1873, 1875–1876, 1877, 1878" in *Annual Reports of the Commissioner of the Fish Commission, 1872–1879,* 377–483, 921–58, 797–810, 741–70.

70. George W. Stewart, "Early Governmental Attempts at Forest Conservation," *Sierra*

Club Bulletin 16 (February 1931): 16–26; Francis P. Farquhar, "Colonel George W. Stewart," *Sierra Club Bulletin* 27 (February 1932): 49–52; Douglas H. Strong, "The History of Sequoia National Park, 1876–1926," *Southern California Quarterly* 48 (1966): 137–67, 265–88, 369–99; Lary M. Dilsaver and Douglas H. Strong, "Sequoia and Kings Canyon National Parks: One Hundred Years of Preservation and Resource Management," *California History* 69 (Summer 1990): 98–117, 219–21.

71. *McCall v. McDowell*, Judge's Note of Evidence.

Contributors

GORDON MORRIS BAKKEN is professor of history at California State University, Fullerton. Holder of both a law degree and a Ph.D. in history from the University of Wisconsin-Madison, Bakken has authored or edited more than a dozen books on legal history, U.S. western history, and California history, including *The Development of Law in Frontier California* (Greenwood, 1985), *Practicing Law in Frontier California* (University of Nebraska Press, 1991), and *Learning California History* (Harlan Davidson, 1999).

JOHN F. BURNS is history and social science consultant for the California Department of Education. For sixteen years he served as the State Archivist of California and was responsible for planning and building the new State Archives facility, Golden State Museum, and Constitution Wall in downtown Sacramento, and for creating the State Government Oral History Program. He has been adjunct professor in the Public History Program at California State University, Sacramento, and in the Library Science Program at San Jose State University. He has also been president of the National Association of Government Archives and Records Administrators, member of numerous local, state and national boards and commissions, and recipient of several awards, including the California Military History Medal. Recent publications include the history essay in *Courthouses of California* (Heyday Books and California Historical Society, 2001) and several articles as well as editing *Sacramento: Gold Rush Legacy, Metropolitan Destiny* (Heritage Media, 1999) and the California History–Social Science Standards issue of *Social Studies Review* (Spring/Summer 1999).

ROBERT J. CHANDLER received his doctorate in 1978 from the University of California, Riverside, for his dissertation "The Press and Civil Liberties in California during the Civil War, 1861–1865." Since then, he has been the senior researcher for Historical Services, Wells Fargo Bank. Bob Chandler has written forty articles on Wells Fargo and Civil War California. He is chairman of the *Quarterly News-Letter* committee of the Book Club of California, a member of the Roxburghe Club of San Francisco, and is in good standing with Yerba Buena no. 1, E Clampus Vitus.

JUDSON A. GRENIER is professor emeritus of history at California State University, Dominguez Hills, where he served as first chair of the history department. A graduate of UCLA, where he collaborated with George Mowry on a study of the muckraking movement of the

Progressive era, he has written extensively about California history, including political figures such as Hiram Johnson and Upton Sinclair, and is the author of *Golden Odyssey: John Stroud Houston, California's First Controller and the Origins of State Government* (Historical Society of Southern California, 1999).

EDWARD LEO LYMAN has been teaching history in California for more than thirty-four years, the last half of that time at Victor Valley College, in Victorville. He received a Ph.D. in history from the University of California, Riverside, in 1981. Among other books and some two dozen journal articles, he has written *A History of Millard County [Utah]* (Utah State Historical Society, 1999) and *San Bernardino: The Rise and Fall of a California Community* (Signature Books, 1996).

ROGER D. MCGRATH, Ph.D., is author of *Gunfighters, Highwaymen, & Vigilantes: Violence on the Frontier* (University of California Press, 1984) and a contributor to *Violence in America: The History of Crime* (Sage Publications, 1989). He has authored some forty articles and book reviews, appearing in historical journals, magazines, encyclopedias, and newspapers. He is featured in twenty-four episodes of *The Real West* and in a half-dozen episodes each of *Biography* and *Tales of the Gun* and was the consultant and technical advisor for *The Young Riders* television series. From 1982 to 1997 he taught the history of the American West and California at UCLA, where he was named "Outstanding Professor" by the Panhellenic Council. In 1999 he was awarded the California Military History Medal.

SHIRLEY ANN WILSON MOORE received her Ph.D. in history from the University of California, Berkeley, and is professor of history at California State University, Sacramento. Her areas of specialty are African American history, U.S. western history, and oral history. She is the author of a number of journal articles and essays. Her first book, *To Place Our Deeds: The African American Community in Richmond, California, 1910–1963*, was published in 2000 by the University of California Press, and she is the coeditor, with Quintard Taylor, of the forthcoming book *Above the Rockies of Prejudice: African American Women in the West*. Dr. Moore serves on the board of the Sacramento African American Historical and Cultural Society and has served on the editorial board of the *Western History Quarterly*, the board of trustees of the California Historical Society, and the Committee on the Status of Women in the Historical Profession of the Organization of American Historians. She is the recipient of the City of Richmond's Historic Preservation Award (2000), and the California State University President's Award for Research and Creative Activity (1999–2000). Dr. Moore is also a singer and songwriter who has performed her one-woman multimedia show, "Women's Lives in Song: Workers, Wives, Mothers, Daughters, Lovers, and Wild Women," for audiences around California.

RICHARD J. ORSI is professor emeritus of history at California State University, Hayward. He is the co-author (with Richard B. Rice and William A. Bullough) of *The Elusive Eden: A New History of California* (McGraw-Hill, 1996; third, revised edition, 2002). He retired in 2000 from a position of twelve years as editor of *California History*, the quarterly journal of the California Historical Society. He is the editor of the California History Sesquicentennial Series and the co-editor of each of the four volumes.

JOSHUA PADDISON is a doctoral student in history at the University of California, Los Angeles. He has worked as a researcher, archivist, or historical consultant for a variety of institutions, including the National Park Service, California Council for the Humanities, California Historical Society, and San Francisco State University. He is editor of *A World Transformed: Firsthand Accounts of California before the Gold Rush* (Heyday Books, 1999).

DONNA C. SCHUELE received her J.D. from the University of California at Berkeley's Boalt Hall in 1985 and her Ph.D. in jurisprudence and social policy from Boalt Hall in 1999. She has taught at the University of California's Berkeley and Santa Barbara campuses and at Whittier College School of Law. In 1997–98, she clerked for the Hon. Alfred T. Goodwin of the United States Court of Appeals for the Ninth Circuit, and she is currently a judicial law clerk in the United States Bankruptcy Court. In addition, she is the executive director of the California Supreme Court Historical Society.

MARLENE SMITH-BARANZINI, associate editor of *California History* from 1990 to 2002, is editor of *The Shirley Letters from the California Mines, 1851–1852* (Heyday Books and Santa Clara University, 2001). She is co-author with Howard Egger-Bovet of the five-volume USKids History Series (Little, Brown, 1994–1998). Ms. Smith-Baranzini is working on a biography of Louise A. K. S. Clappe.

TEENA STERN is an archivist, museum specialist, and historical consultant residing in Citrus Heights, California. She holds a master's degree in American history from California State University, Northridge. Former president of the Los Angeles City Historical Society, the Society of California Archivists, and the California Council for the Promotion of History, she has served as a professional historian with, among other agencies, the Urban Archives Center, California State University, Northridge; El Pueblo de Los Angeles State Park; and the California State Archives. Author of numerous articles and book reviews on California history, she was also co-editor (with Waverly Lowell and Richard J. Orsi) of the "Archives in California" special issue of *California History* (Spring 1996).

Index

abolitionist movement, 109, 111, 116, 177
Act for the Government and Protection of Indians, 81, 105
Adams & Co., 244
African Americans, 7, 9, 12, 20, 59, 81, 114, 130, 145, 148, 248; and American citizenship, 103, 104, 236; and slavery in California, 109, 111; challenge California's Fugitive Slave Law, 109; improved conditions for, 118, 250; in Gold Rush, 105; migrate to Canada, 111, 117; organize first Convention of Colored Citizens, 116
Agua Fria, 42
Ah Goon, 60
Alameda County, 15
Alcatraz Island, 130, 131, 225, 228, 229, 246, 249, 250
Alemany, Most Reverend Joseph Sadoc, 85
Alexander, Barton S., 255, 256
Allegorical View of the Conquest of the Continent (lithograph), 127; see also *Plate 1*
Allen, R. T. P., 244
Alpine County, 11
Alvitre, Felipe, 81, 82
Amador County, 33, 206
Amadór, José Maria, 100
American Express Company, 244
American Home Missionary Society, 129
American ("Know Nothing") Party, 47, 81, 146, 147, 218
American Progress (painting), 127
American River, 204, 220
American Woman Suffrage Association (AWSA), 177, 179
Anderson, Robert, 149
Angel Island, 51
Angels Camp, 33
Anthony, Susan B., 179
Anza Trail, 100
Arkansas Act, 235
Army Corps of Engineers, 256
Arrow (brig), 227
Ashburner, William, photo of, 21
Ashley, Delos R., 150, 156
Asian Americans, 7, 12, 130. See also Chinese
Athearn, Chandler, Hoffman, and Angell (attorneys), 85
Atherton, Gertrude, 120
Auburn, 205
Aurora, 43, 45
Austin, Nev., 44
Averill, Chester, photo of, 21

Bad Company (book), 30
Baehr, Ferdinand, 150
Baird, Spencer F., 257

Baker, George Holbrook, 100, 131
Baker, Thomas, 248
Bakken, Gordon Morris, 18
Ball, Frank, 94
Ballou, Mary, 171
Bancroft, Hubert Howe, 47, 96, 145, 154, 155
bandidos, 28–36, 65, 70
Barbadoes, Frederick, 116
Barbour, George, 232
Barton, James, 82, 201
Bates, Edward, 234
Bates, Henry, 150, 167
Bates, Mrs. D. B., 126
Bear Flag Revolt, 100, 132
Beck, Thomas, 150
Bell, Samuel, 150
Benicia, 130, 227, 228, 244; photo of capitol in, 5
Bennett, Nathaniel, 81
Benton, Colonel, 200
Benton, Thomas Hart, 237
Berry, Benjamin, 236
Big Oak Flat, 171
Bigelow, Hardin, 219
Bigler, John, 143, 148, 149, 152; evaluation of as governor, 153
Billings, Frederick, 84, 85, 237
Black Bart. See Boles, Charles
Black, Jeremiah S., 238
Blair, Montgomery, 248
Blake, Charles T., 230
Board of Agriculture, 162
Board of Bank Commissioners, 163
Board of Capitol Commissioners, 163
Board of Education, 158, 159
Board of Fish Commissioners, 162
Board of State Harbor Commissioners, 161
Board of Supervisors, 204, 207, 208, 209, 211, 218, 250
Board of Swamp Land Commissioners, 163
Bodie, 45, 54, 56, 58
Bolander, Henry, 152
Boles, Charles, 61, 62, 63, 64, 66
Bolton, Charles. See Boles, Charles
Booth, Newton, 148, 149, 157, 240

Bosqui Engraving & Print Company, 134
Bost, John W., 151
Botts, Charles T., 7, 9, 77, 79
Bowen, William, 118
Bradford, A. C., 236
Bradwell, Myra, 191
Brannan, Samuel, 37, 213, 217
Brewer, William H., photo of, 21, 164
Brewster, John, 151
Bridgeport, 60
Broderick, David, 12, 40, 44, 49, 50, 143, 145, 149, 218, 231, 240
Brooks, Samuel L., 151
Brown v. Omnibus Railroad Company (1866), 81
Brown, Charlotte, 118
Brown, David, 81, 82
Brown, Richard Maxwell (historian), 47
Brown, Sam, 42, 44
Brown, William B. C., 151
Bryce, James, 165
Buchanan, James, 132, 155, 231, 236, 240
Buchanan, Robert "Buck", 30
Bull Run, 246
burglary, 53, 56, 83
Burke, Martin J., 40
Burlingame Treaty, 120
Burnett, Peter, Bvii, 137, 149, 152; evaluation of as governor, 148; photo of, 139
Burns, Walter Noble, 30
Burr, E. W., 218, 219
Burrill, G. Thompson, 199
Butler, B. F. (artist), 161
Butte County, 233
Butterworth, Samuel F., 234

Calaveras County, 33, 82, 206
Calaveras River, 38
Calhoun, John C., 11
California, admitted to the Union, 12; and Congress (1849), 3; infrastructure in, 1848, 4; population growth in, 4. See also government in California
California Column, 155
California Fugitive Slave Act. See Fugitive Slave Act of 1852

California Geological Survey (1864), photo of, 164
California Hundred, 252
California Land Commission, 237
California Rangers, 34
California School for the Deaf and Blind, 160
California School Law (1870), 115
California State Archives, 158
California State Geological Survey, photo of, 21
California State Library, 158; photo of, 159
California State Telegraph Company, 231
California Steam Navigation, 229
California Supreme Court, 75, 81, 85, 87, 89, 109, 111, 114, 116, 118, 120, 157, 184, 254; creation of, 143
California Volunteers, 225, 234
California Woman Suffrage Association (CWSA), 176, 177, 178, 179, 182, 183, 186
Californian Magnate in His Home (painting), 129
Californios, Californianas. See Mexican Californians
Camanche (ship), 250
Cantua Creek, 34
Cape Mendocino Indian Reservation, 232
capitol building (photo of), 131; see also *Plates 7, 8*
Captain Jack, 233
Carleton, James H., 248
Caroline (ship), 227
Carr, Ezra C., 152, 168
Carr, Jeanne, 168
Carrillo, Joaquin, 201
Carter, James, 116
Carvalho, Solomon Nuñes, 107
Casey, James P., 47, 49, 53
Cashman, Nellie, 58
Casserly, Eugene, 240
Caughey, John (historian), 11
Central Overland Mail Route, 248
Central Pacific Railroad, 157, 231, 240, 255
Central-Southern Pacific Railroad, 236, 255
Chabolla, Anastacio, 30
Chandler, Robert J., 23

Chase, Gordon, 114
Chattel Mortgage Act (1857), 90
Chellis, John F., 149
Cherny, Robert (historian), 157
Cherokee Flat, 33
Cherokee Indians, 30
"Chilean War", 38, 39
Chileans, 36, 37, 38, 39, 42
Chiletown, 35, 36, 37
Chili Gulch, 37, 38
Chinese, 12, 13, 20, 37, 59, 81, 105, 145, 156, 226, 254; and opium, 241; denounced by Stanford, 118, 132; discrimination against, 111–113, 114, 117, 154, 181, 183; population of during Gold Rush, 108; robbery of, 27, 32, 33. See also Asian Americans
Chinese Camp, 30
Chinese Exclusion Act (1882), 13, 113, 120, 254
Chipman, John S., 250, 251
Chun-Chuen, Lai, 114
Chung, Sam, 59, 60, 61
civil rights, Bviii, 225
Civil Rights Act (1866), 116
Civil Rights Act (1870), 114, 120, 254
Civil War, 12, 117, 201, 225, 233, 243, 246, 248, 249; government in California during, 137, 155, 156
Clanton, S. P., 114
Clark, Reuben, 130
Clarke, Charlie, 27
Clarke, James, 200
Clay, Henry, 12
Clear Creek, 232
Clemens, Samuel, 41, 42
Clifford, Pinckney, 81
Code Commissions, 163
Code of Civil Procedure, 163
Coleman, William T., 45, 49
Collier, James, 240
Collier, Lewis, 38
Coloma, 203, 204, 206, 244
Colorado (steamer), 244
Colorado River, 100
Colton Hall (photo of), 104

Columbia, Calif., 31, 32, 45
communications, 229
Compromise of 1850, 79, 104, 227
Comstock Lode, 42, 128, 145
Conness, John, 235, 240, 245, 257
Connor, Patrick Edward, 34, 248
constitution (1849), 137; and women, 169–173; creation of, 7, 9, 74, 85, 103; Iowa as basis for, 7; sources on, 25
constitution (1879), 9, 10, 15, 146, 157; contemporary effects of, 16, 138; convention for, 13; historical analysis of, 16; initiative and referendum in, 16
Constitution Wall, photo of, 2
Convention of Colored Citizens of the State of California, 116, 117
Copperopolis, 63
Cora, Charles, 47, 49
Coronel, Antonio, 150
Cotter, John, 39
Cotter, Richard D., 164
Court of Sessions, 203, 204, 207, 208, 210
Cox, H. F., 128
Cravens, R. O., 158
Crittenden, Alexander B., 143
Crofutt, George, 127
Crosby, Elisha, 143, 148, 237
Croy, Hazel Miller, 211
Cubic Air Ordinance, 112, 124
Cummings, Gordon P., 131
Cunningham, Thomas, 66, 68

Daly, John, 42, 44, 45
Dana, Richard Henry, 99, 127
Daniels, Roger (historian), 105, 112
Daniels, Vinal, 203
Dashaway Association, 216
Davidson, George (scientist), 229, 230, 256
Davis, Jefferson, 227, 228
Days, John M., 187, 189
de la Guerra y Noriego, José Antonio Julián, 202
de la Guerra, Joaquin, 201
de la Guerra, Pablo, 201; photo of, 202; see also *Plate 5*
de la Guerra, Pedro, 149

Deady, Matthew P., 253, 254
death penalty, 75
Democratic Party, 10, 68, 114, 117, 146, 148, 152, 157, 218, 239, 246, 248, 249, 251, 254
Denver, James W., 40, 150
Desert Lands Act, 255
Dimmick, Kimball, 77, 79
discrimination, 18, 103, 104, 105, 109, 111–112, 117, 120; and the judicial process, 113, 114; and women, 176; codified by law, 108–109, 249
Dixon, Maynard (artist), 159
Dominguez, Manuel, 114
Donahue, Peter, 250
Dorsey, Caleb, 32
Double Springs, 38
Douglas, Stephen A., 231
Douglass, David F., 150
Downey, John G., 119, 138, 149, 155, 234
Dred Scott decision, 236
Drum, Richard C., 249
Dueling, 39, 40
Dunn, John H., 53
Duran, Narciso, 99
Dwinelle, John W., 157

Eddy, William, 151
education, and local government, 211, 212; and race, 116; in San Francisco, 217
El Dorado County, 64, 201–203, 204, 206, 207, 212
El Monte, 211
Eldorado; or, Adventures in the Path of Empire (book), 128
elections, 137; of 1849, 137
Ellison, William Henry (historian), 11, 224
Emancipation Proclamation, 249
Encinos, Prudencia, 60
English, James L., 150
Essex (frigate), 229
Estell, James Madison, 51, 53
Estudillo, Jose G., 150
Ex Parte Milligan, 254
Exclusion Act (1882), 133

Fallon, Malachi, 66, 67, 68
Farragut, David Glasgow, 229
federal government, and California, 224–271
Federal Reserve System, 88
Feliz, Claudio, 30, 31, 32, 36
Feliz, Jesus, 34
Feliz, Reyes, 30, 32
Ferguson & Bigg's California Laundry, 63
Fernald, Charles, 85
Field, Stephen J., 41, 42, 82, 143, 165, 238, 249; photo of, 88
Fifteenth Amendment, 254
Fillmore, Millard, 227, 229
Findley, Thomas, 150
fire, 126, 127, 134
firearms, 41
First Battalion of California Mountaineers, 248
Fisher, Henry, 87, 88
Fitzgerald, O. P., 152
floods, 219, 220
Flores, Juan, 201
Foley, Thomas McFarland, 53
Folsom Prison, photo of, 113
Folsom, James L., 240
Folsom, Joseph L., 217
Foltz, Clara Shortridge, 168, 188, 191, 192, 193
foreign miners' tax, 37, 106, 108, 142, 145, 156, 207, 254
Forman, Ferris, 150
Fort Gunnybags, 49
Fort Mason, 250
Fort Point, 228, 246; photo of, 251
Fort Sumter, 246
Fort Yuma (drawing of), 100
Foster, Stephen, 211
Fourteenth Amendment, 118, 254
Franchise League, 116
Franciscans, 97
Fraser River, 43, 111
Frémont, John C., 127, 132, 158, 230, 237, 238
French Camp, 33
Fritz, Christian G. (historian), 74, 237
Fugitive Slave Act of 1852, 109, 110, 111, 117

Gabb, William, photo of, 21
Gaines, John S. (historian), 16
Gallego, José, 208
Gardiner, James T., 164
Gardner, Robert, 151
Gast, John, 127
Gates, Paul W. (historian), 237
Geary, John, 214
General Land Office, 234
gente de razon, 97, 99, 121
Georgetown, 206
Gibbs, Mifflin Wistar, 110, 116, 117
Gilbert, Edward, 39, 40, 44
Gillen, James S., 151
Gillis, George P., 248, 249
Gold Rush, 1, 4; and native Californians, 102, 105
Gonzales, Pedro, 32
Gordon, Laura de Force, 177, 179, 183, 188, 191, 192, 193; photo of, 178
government in California, article concerning, 137–168; early efforts at, 3, 5, 138; effect of Gold Rush on, 4; in the mining regions, 6; military's role in, 226; original structure of, 138–142; transition from Mexican to American administration, 4, 6
governor, early responsibilities of, 138
Grand National Republican Banner (lithograph), 132; see also *Plate 11*
Grant, Ulysses S., 243, 256
Grass Valley, 45
Gray, Giles H., 85
Greathouse, Ridgely, 249
Green, James, 151
Green, Thomas, 142, 145
Grenier, Judson A. (historian), 3, 11, 20–21
gunfighters, 42, 43, 44
Gwin, William, 12, 77, 117, 145, 231, 237, 240, 252

Haggin, James Ben Ali, 255
Hahn, William, 132, 133
Haight, Henry F., 149, 157
Hall, William Hammond, 163, 256

Halleck, Henry Wager, 7, 77, 84, 236, 237; photo of, 78
Hamilton, Henry, 248
Hamilton, Jo, 151
hanging, 82
Haraszthy, Agoston, 242
Harpending, Asbury, 249
Harrison, William Henry, 10
Hastings School of Law, 188
Hastings, L. W., 75, 79
Hastings, S. Clinton, 151
Hastings, Serranus C., 79, 81
Hayes, Benjamin, 109, 201
Hayes, Thomas, 39
Helper, Hinton, 127
Hempstead, Charles H., 150
Herring, Valentine "Rube", 208
Heydenfeldt, Solomon, 87
Hibernia Savings and Loan Association, 85
Higby, William, 82, 83, 84
highwaymen, 55
Higley, Horace, 151
Hill, Sarah Althea, photo of, 50
Hispanics. See Mexican Californians
Hitchcock, Ethan Allen, 227, 252
Hittell, John S., 47, 234, 237
Hoen v. Simmons (1850), 87
Hoffman, Charles F., photo of, 21
Hoffman, Ogden, 237, 238, 249, 253, 257
Holden, William, 149
Holliday, J. S. (historian), 3
Homestead Act, 236
homicide, 59
Hopkins, Richard R., 210
Hopkins, Sterling A., 41
Hornitos, 33
Houghton, James F., 151
Hounds, 35, 36, 37. See also vigilantism
Houston, John Stroud, 140, 144, 150
Hoyt, A. J., 211, 212
Hubbs, Paul K., 115, 152
Humboldt Bay, 255
Humbug, 31
Hume, James B., 62, 63, 64, 68
Hunt, Dr. R. M., 206
Hunt, Jefferson, 200, 209, 210

Hunt, Timothy Dwight, 129
Hunter, Jesse D., 210
Huntington, Collis P., 255
Huse, Charles, 85
hydraulic mining, 133, 220; photo of, 89

I Am the New Constitution!!!! (lithograph), 14
Igler, David, 255
Independent People's Party, 146
Insurance Commissioner, 163
Iowa Cabins, 37, 38
Irish Americans, 119
Irwin, William, 149, 157
Issel, William (historian), 157

J.M. Chapman (schooner), 249
Jackson, 33, 45, 84
Jackson Creek, 33
Jackson, Alden A. M., 210
Jackson, Andrew, 130
Jackson, Joseph Henry, 30
Jacksonian democracy, 74, 78, 79
jails. See prisons
Jews, 107
Johnson, Cave, 244
Johnson, David Alan (historian), 5, 17, 165
Johnson, James A., 149
Johnson, John Neely, 131, 147, 149, 218, 228; administration of, 154; photo of, 146
Johnson, William, 43
Johnston, Albert Sidney, 246
Jones, J. M., 77
Jones, Sandy, 109
Jones, William Carey, 237
Juárez, Benito, 252
judicial system, 16, 18, 74–95; structure of, 75, 79
Jump, Edward (artist), 141

Kearney, Denis, 15, 113, 119
Kearny, Stephen W., 226, 232
Keller, Edward, 15, 133
Kern County Land Company, 255
Kewen, Edward J. C., 151, 248
Kientipoos, 233

King, Clarence, photo of, 21, 164
King (of William), James, 46, 47, 49, 53
King, Thomas Starr, photo of, 247
Kirgan, John, 60
Klamath River Indian Reservation, 232
Knights of the Columbian Star, 251
"Know Nothing" Party. See American Party

La Grande Ditch, photo of, 91
Land Act of 1851, 102, 129
land grants, 236, 237
Land Ordinance of 1785, 235
Lander, Frederick W., 230
larceny, 75
Last Chance Hill, 43
Latham, Milton S., 149, 155, 240
Latino Californians. See Mexican Californians
lawmen, 64–68
Leary, John, 32
Lee, Archie, 111
Lees, Isaiah, 65, 66
Leese, Maria Paula Rosalia, photo of, 106
legislature, accomplishments of later sessions, 145; committees established by, 143; meeting of first, 10, 79–81, 142, 143, 145; meeting of second, 143, 145; original structure of, 138
"Legislature of a Thousand Drinks". See legislature, meeting of first
Lester, Peter, 116
Leuchtenburg, William (historian), 3
Lies, Eugene, 201
Life and Adventures of Joaquin Murieta (book), 28–30
Life in California, by Alfred Robinson, 99
Lighthouse Board, 229
Linares, Pio, 70
Lincoln School (Sacramento), photo of, 115
Lincoln, Abraham, 118, 234–235, 238, 253, 257
Ling Sing v. Washburn (1862), 111
Little, John F., 204
lobbyists, 145, 146
local government, 199–223

Los Angeles, 45, 58, 109, 209, 210, 211; map of, 209; photo of plaza, 200; vigilantism in, 45
Los Angeles County, 11, 15, 199, 209, 210, 212
Los Angeles Policemen, photo of, 65
Lotchin, Roger W. (historian), 218
lotteries, 78
Louisiana, legal system of, 170, 171
Louisiana Mounted Volunteers, 44
Love, Harry, 32, 33, 34, 35, 128
Love, John, 53
Love, John Lord, 151
Low, Frederick F., 145, 147, 148, 149, 154, 155, 156, 157, 234
Lyman, Amasa M., 210
Lyman, Edward Leo, 23
Lyons, H. A., 81

Machin, T. N., 149
mail to California, 231, 243–246
Malakoff Diggins, photo of, 89
Mandeville, James W., 151
map of California counties, 22
Mare Island, 229; drawing of, 228
Marin County, 52
Mariposa County, 33
Mariposa grant, 238
Marlette, Samuel, 151
Married Women's Property Acts (MWPAs), 170, 171, 176, 189
Marryat, Frank, 4, 76; drawing by, 227
Marsh, John, 30
Marshall House Hotel, 206
Marshall, James W., 204
Marvin, John G., 152
Marysville, 160, 223
Mason, Bridget "Biddy", 109
Mason, Richard B., 226, 233, 241
McCall, John, 253
McCarver, M. M., 75, 77
McCauley, John F., 53, 54
McClatchy, James, 119
McCloud River, 257
McCollum, Ike, 64
McConnell, John R., 151

McCorkle, Joseph, 143
McCullough, John G., 151
McDonald, Tom, 68
McDougal, John, 137, 138, 143, 149; evaluation of as governor, 152
McDougall, James A., 79, 151
McDowell, Irvin, 251, 252, 253, 254
McGrath, Roger, 18
McKay, W. R. I., 248, 249
McKee, James, 204
McKee, Redick, 232
McLaughlin, Patrick, 42
McMeans, Selden A., 150
McQuaid, John, 60
Mead, Elwood, 226
mechanics' liens, 90, 92
Melone, Drury, 150
Meloney, Aaron, 150
Mendell, George H., 255, 256
Menken, Adah Isaacs (actress), 175
Merrifield, Arzo D., 215
Merrill, Karen R. (historian), 224
Merritt, Samuel, 143
Mexican Californians, 4, 9, 37, 97, 99, 129; and American citizenship, 103; gender discrimination against, 173; land titles of, 102, 173; political impact of, 12; relations with Anglos, 201; toppled by Americans, 100
Mexican Court of First Instance, 201
Mexican-American War, 99, 100, 102, 209
Middleton v. Franklin (1853), 90
Midway Island, 229
Military of San Francisco (lithograph), 131; see also *Plate 10*
Miller, John F., 257
Miner, Bill, 66
mining, 6, 233
Minis, William, 151
Mirror of the Times (newspaper), 117
Mission San Fernando, 129
Mission San Jose, 34
Mission San Luis Obispo, 99
Mission Santa Cruz, 99
missions, 97; secularization of, 99
Modoc War, 233

Mokelumne Hill, 37, 39, 83, 84
Monagan, Bob, 16
Mono County, 61
Monterey, 13, 45, 74, 103, 130, 227
Montgomery Block, 77
Moody v. McDonald (1854), 90
Moore, Shirley Ann Wilson, 18–19
Morehead, Joseph, 141
Mormon Battalion, 209
Mormons, 109, 208, 210, 211, 213, 248
Morse Detective Agency, 65
Morse, Harry, 63, 64, 65, 66, 68
Moulder, Andrew J., 152
Mt. Vernon, 211
Mullen, Kevin J. (historian), 47, 215
Mulligan, Billy, 43, 44, 49
Murieta, Joaquín, 18, 20, 27, 28, 30, 36, 128; assumes leadership of gang, 33; capture of, 34; portrait by Nahl, 29; raids by, 33; see also *Plate 2*
Murray, Hugh C., 81, 82

Nash, Gerald D. (historian), 12, 165
National Equal Rights Party, 182
National Woman Suffrage Association (NWSA), 177
Native Americans, 4, 7, 12, 20, 129, 130, 145, 152, 225, 254; and American citizenship, 103, 105; and federal Indian policy, 232, 233; and frontier violence, 68, 69; and Spanish/Mexican settlers, 97; and Treaty of Guadalupe Hildalgo, 102; compared to Chinese and Blacks, 114; decimation of, 98, 99; genocide against, 81
nativism, 105, 108, 147
Neagle, David, 50
Nevada County, 54, 204, 206, 208
New Almaden Quicksilver Mine, 234
New Mexico, 79
New Year's Day in San Francisco's Chinatown (painting), 133; see also *Plate 13*
New York Volunteers, 36
Newlands, Francis, 226
Nichols, H. L., 150
Niles Canyon, 34

Nixon, Alex, 68
Nome Lackee Indian Reservation, 232
Nordhoff, Charles, 132
Northern Pacific Railroad, 85
Northwest Ordinance of 1787, 235
Norton I, 232, 233
Nugent, John, 39, 40, 44, 51

O'Riley, Peter, 42
Olds, William, 158
Olivera, Augustin, 199
Olmsted, Frederick Law, photo of, 19
Ord, Pacificus, 79
Orsi, Richard J., 255
Oulton, George, 151
outlaws, 27
Overland Mail Company, 231
overland travel, 229

Pacheco, Romualdo, 138, 148, 149, 150, 157
Pacific Mail Company, 229
Pacific Railroad Act, 132
Pacific Wagon Road Office, 230
Paddison, Joshua, 20
Page, Samuel, 206
Parker, Samuel H., 245
Peachy, Archibald C., 84, 237
Pelton, John C., 217
People v. Hall (1854), 114
People v. Naglee (1850), 108
People's Party, 46, 51
Peralta family, 20, 129; photo of, 173; see also *Plate 4*
Perkins Bill (1863), 118
Perkins, C. S., 109
Perkins, Carter & Robert, 109
Perkins, Richard F., 118
Perkins, Robert F., 245
personal injury law, 89, 90
Phelan, James D., 119
Phillips, George (historian), 233
Pico, Andrés, 20, 129, 201
Pierce, Franklin, 228
Pierce, Winslow S., 150
Pioneer (newspaper), 177
Pisani, Donald J. (historian), 237

Pixley, Frank, 151
Placer County, 205
Placerville, 64, 206
Player-Frowd, J. G., 132
Pleasant, Mary Ellen, 116, 118
Political Code of 1872, 162, 163
Ponce, Narato, 65
Pond mining company, 43
population, during Gold Rush, 105; growth of, 1846–1849, 4, 6
Powers, Jack, 70
Price, Johnson, 150
prisons, 51, 75, 82, 113, 141, 155
Probate Confiscation, by Marietta Stow, 186
Progressive era, 13
property law, 170–173, 174–176, 184–189
prostitution, 28, 56
Purdy, Samuel, 149, 241

Quechnajuichom Indians, 97
Quinn, Isaac, 149

racism, 81, 96–125, 145, 249
railroads, 13, 118, 132, 157, 163, 225, 231, 236, 254, 255, 256. See also Central Pacific Railroad, Southern Pacific Railroad, Union Pacific Railroad
Ramsdell v. Fuller and Summers (1865), 87
Rankin, Ira P., 234
rape, 58
Rawls, James J., Bix
Real Del Monte mining company, 43
real estate transactions, 87
Reconstruction, 118, 225, 250
Redding, Benjamin B., 150
Reddy, Patrick, 60, 61
Reid, C. F., 55, 56
Republican Party, 118, 131, 147, 148, 155, 157, 225, 231, 239, 246, 248, 254
Rich Gulch, 27
Rich, Charles C., 210, 213
Richardson, William H., 46, 47
Ridge, John Rollin, 28
Riley, Gen. Bennet, 4, 5, 226; issues proclamation organizing government, 6, 103
Riley, William, 204

robbery, 53, 55, 56, 63, 75
Roberts, Sam, 37
Robin Hood of El Dorado, The (book), 30
Robinson, Alfred, 99
Rohrbough, Malcolm J. (historian), 102
Rolfs, William, 203
Roll of Attorneys (book), 84
Rolle, Andrew (historian), 16
Roman, Richard, 150
Romero, Thomas, 70
Roney, Frank, 119
Rosales, Vicente Pérez, 35, 36
Rough Creek, 60
Rowell, Isaac, 250
Rowland, John, 237
Royce, Josiah (historian), 51, 145
Rubery, Alfred, 249
Ruddle, Allen, 32
Ruggles, David W., 116
Ryan, Arabella, 47
Ryan, James T., 250

Sacramento, 4, 6, 10, 11, 13, 34, 43, 111, 118, 148, 160, 207, 244; becomes capital, 144, 154; vigilantism in, 45
Sacramento Company I, Second Regiment (1863), photo of, 17
Sacramento County; local government in, 219, 220, 221
Sacramento Railroad Station (painting), 132; see also *Plate 12*
Sacramento River, 133, 220; see also *Plate 15*
Saginaw (sidewheeler), 229
Salazar, Juan, 70
Salmon Falls, 204
Salmon v. Hoffman (1852), 87
Salmon, Francis, 88
Salmon, Mary Catherine, 88
Salt Lake City, 231
San Andreas, 33
San Bernardino, 109, 200, 209, 211
San Bernardino County, 201, 208, 210, 212, 213
San Diego, 209
San Francisco, 4, 28, 37, 65, 67, 68, 128, 134, 143, 160, 206, 207, 227; fires and fire companies in, 215; local government in, 213, 214, 217, 218, 219; vigilantism in, 45
San Francisco Bay with Alcatraz and Steamship Princess (painting), 130. See also *Plate 9*
San Francisco County, 44
San Francisco Customs House, 238
San Francisco firefighters, 134; see also *Plate 16*
San Francisco Police Department, 65, 66
San Francisco post office, 128; see also *Plate 3*
San Francisco Woman Suffrage Association (SFWSA), 176, 177
San Gabriel, 211
San Joaquin County, 66
San Jose, 34, 130, 244; as first capital, 137, 143, 144
San Luis Obispo, 70
San Mateo County, 44
San Quentin prison, 42, 51, 53, 54, 64, 142; photo of, 52
San Rafael, 52
San Salvadore, 208
Sanderson, Jeremiah B., 116
Sanderson, Silas, 85
Santa Barbara, 85, 200
Sargent, Aaron A., 255
Savage, James D., 232
Savings Union and Trust Company of San Francisco, 85
Sawyer, Lorenzo, 257
Scannell, David, 49
Schliemann, Heinrich, 126
Schuele, Donna C., 21, 22–23
Scollan, John, 38
Secor, Frances, 250
segregation, 116, 117; challenges to, 118; de facto and de jure, 120
Selby Smelting and Lead Company, 243
Semple, Robert, 7, 17
Seneca Falls Declaration of Sentiments (1848), 176
Senkewicz, Robert M. (historian), 47
Sequoia National Park, 257

Seward, William H., 231
Sharon, William, 50
Shasta County, 155, 257
Sherman, William T., 49
Sherwood, Winfield, 77
Shover, Michelle (historian), 233
Shuck, Oscar, 148
slavery, 9, 20, 103, 109, 246
Sloat, John D., 226
Smith, Caleb, 234
Smith, Persifor F., 229
Smith, Robert, 109
smuggling, 241
Snyder, A. J., 236
Snyder, J. R., 9
Sonoma, 244
Sonora, Calif., 44
Soto, Juan, 65
Southern Pacific Railroad, 225, 255, 257, 258; see also Central-Southern Pacific Railroad
Spiritualism, 176, 177, 179
Stanford, Jane Lathrop, photo of, 180
Stanford, Leland, 45, 118, 132, 149, 155, 156, 157, 179; photo of, 180
Staniford, Edward (historian), 3
Stanton, Caddie, 179
Stanton, Edwin M., 238
Starr, Kevin (historian), 12, 127
State Agricultural Society, 162
State Board of Equalization, 162
State Burial Grounds, 162
state hospitals, 160, 161, 206
State Reform School, 160
state seal, 130; see also *Plate 6*
Stevens, Emily Pitts, 177, 179
Stewart, George W., 257
Stewart, William M., 151, 235, 254
Stocking, Lucinda, 171
Stockton, 66, 160, 161, 206, 244
Stockton, Robert F., 226
Stone, Livingston, 257
Stovall, Charles, 111
Stow, Marietta, 182, 184, 186, 187
Straskel, Francis, 236
Stratton, W. C., 158

suffrage, 176, 183, 185, 194
Sullivan, James "Yankee", 44
Sumner, Edwin Vose, 246
Sutter, John, 148, 232
Swett, John, 152, 159
Swett, Leonard, 234
Swisher, Carl, 138
Sydney Ducks, 36

Tac, Pablo, 97
Tammany Hall, 44, 49
Tang, Fung, 114
Tanner, George, 75
Tator, Nettie, 184, 186, 192
taxes, 142, 234, 235. See also foreign miners' tax
Taylor, Bayard, 128
Taylor, Quintard (historian), 97
Taylor, William, 126, 127, 128
Taylor, Zachary, 10
Tejon Indian Reservation, 232
telegraph, 231
Telegraph Hill, 126
Temple, Jonathan, 94
Terry, David S., 40, 41, 42, 44, 49, 50
Tevis, Lloyd, 53, 54
Tewksbury v. Laffan (1850), 87
Thomas, Daniel M., 210
Thousand Oaks, 32
Tobin, Richard, 85
Tobin, Robert, 85
Todd, J. A. (photographer), 89
Townsend, Edward D., 232
transportation, 90, 229
Trask, John B., 163, 165
Treaty of Guadalupe Hidalgo, 4, 108, 199; and rights of Mexican Californians, 102, 236; redefines citizenship, 103
Trujillo, Julian, 208
Tuolumne County, 171, 208
Tuttle, A. A. H., 150
Twain, Mark. See Clemens, Samuel

Union Iron Works, 250
Union League, 225, 249, 250, 251
Union Pacific Railroad, 231, 255

University of California, 16, 191
Usher, John P., 234
Utah, 79

Valenzuela, Joaquin, 70
Vallejo, 130, 229
Vallejo, Mariano Guadalupe, 51, 106, 232; photo of, 101
Van Ness, James, 49
Van Voorhies, William, 144, 150, 244
Vance, Robert H. (daguerreotypist), 86
Vasquez, Tiburcio, 66
Vega, Plácido, 252
Ventura, 32
Vermeule, Thomas L., 77, 79
Vernon, 244
Vigilance Committee! (moving panorama), 48
vigilantism, 6, 18, 28, 31, 33, 37, 43, 56, 70, 84; Committee of 1851 (San Francisco), 68, 152, 214; Committee of 1856 (San Francisco), 44, 85, 154, 228; photo of sharpshooters of 1856, 83; supports the legal system, 82; survey of, 44–51
violence, 27–68; used to suppress the nonwhite population, 28, 31
Virginia City, Nev., 43
Vischer, Edward, 129
Von Schmidt, Alexis, 255

Waban (brig), 51
Waldo, Henry, 203
Walker, William, 39, 44, 227
Walkup, Joseph, 149
Wallace, William T., 151
Wallis, Sarah, 187
Wang, Sam, 60
Ward v. Flood, 116
Ward, A. J., 116
Warm Creek, 211
Warren, Gilbert R., 151
water, and the law, 91
Watkins, Carleton E., 230

Watt, Robert, 151
Weber, C. M., 160
Weeks, William, 150
Weller, Charles L., 251
Weller, John B., 149, 154, 230, 231
Wells, Fargo & Co., 62, 63, 64, 241, 244–245, 246, 257
Western Union Telegraph Company, 231
Whig Party, 10, 68, 79, 131, 147
Whig, The (newspaper), 10
White, Richard (historian), 224
Whiting, Charles, 151
Whitman, George, 150
Whitney, Franklin E. R., 216
Whitney, Josiah D., 21, 165
Williams, Thomas H., 151
Williamson, Robert S., 255
Wilson, Joseph S., 236
Woman Lawyer's Bill, 192
women, 21; and fight for occupational rights, 189–192; and suffrage, 13, 169; as target of crime, 28, 56, 58; Hart, Sallie, 190; in the formation and development of state government, 169–176; legal rights of, 7, 22, 85, 86, 87; press for equal rights, 176–194; property rights of, 169, 170, 174–176, 236
Woodruff v. North Bloomfield Gravel Mining Co., 89, 133
Wool, John E., 226, 227, 228, 252
Wores, Theodore, 133
Workingmen's Party, 13, 15, 17, 112, 113, 119, 133, 156
Wozencraft, Oliver M., 103, 232
Wright, George, 233, 234, 248, 249, 250

Yaqui Camp, 33
Yosemite, 19, 133, 257
Yosemite Valley from Glacier Point (painting), 133; see also *Plate 14*
Yuba River, 83
Yuma Indians, 100
Yung Wah tong, 59

DESIGNER:	Terry Bain
COMPOSITOR:	Integrated Composition Systems, Inc.
TEXT:	11/14 Adobe Caslon
DISPLAY:	Adobe Caslon Regular, Italic and Small Caps
PRINTING AND BINDING:	Malloy Lithographing, Inc.
INDEX:	Robert A. Clark

www.ingramcontent.com/pod-product-compliance
Lightning Source LLC
Chambersburg PA
CBHW040931240426
43672CB00022B/2996